SEX SIGNS

Judith Bennett

SEX SIGNS

Every Woman's Astrological and Psychological Guide to Love, Men, Sex, Anger, and Personal Power

Pan Original Pan Books
in association with Macmillan London

First published in Great Britain 1981 by Pan Books Ltd,
Cavaye Place, London SW10 9PG
in association with Macmillan London Ltd

ISBN 0 330 26500 8
Photoset by Parker Typesetting Service, Leicester
Printed and bound in Great Britain by
Hazell Watson & Viney Ltd, Aylesbury, Bucks

To Z
Without whose love, understanding, encouragement and support this book could not have been written.

And my patient children Anina and Nicky, who filled my life with joy, and from whom I have learned a great deal.

And my good friend Gerald Born, whose sage advice I cherish.

Contents

Introduction xi

ARIES WOMAN
Checklist of Aries Traits 1
Aries Personality 2
Aries Relationships 10
Aries Sexuality 18
Aries Anger 22
Aries Lifestyles 25
Summing Up Aries 29

TAURUS WOMAN
Checklist of Taurus Traits 31
Taurus Personality 32
Taurus Relationships 46
Taurus Sexuality 53
Taurus Anger 60
Taurus Lifestyles 63
Summing Up Taurus 67

GEMINI WOMAN
Checklist of Gemini Traits 69
Gemini Personality 70
Gemini Relationships 87
Gemini Sexuality 98
Gemini Anger 107
Gemini Lifestyles 112
Summing Up Gemini 116

CANCER WOMAN
Checklist of Cancer Traits 117
Cancer Personality 118
Cancer Relationships 131
Cancer Sexuality 140
Cancer Anger 148
Cancer Lifestyles 152
Summing Up Cancer 154

LEO WOMAN
Checklist of Leo Traits 156
Leo Personality 157
Leo Relationships 167
Leo Sexuality 176
Leo Anger 182
Leo Lifestyles 186
Summing Up Leo 188

VIRGO WOMAN
Checklist of Virgo Traits 189
Virgo Personality 190
Virgo Relationships 198
Virgo Sexuality 208
Virgo Anger 215
Virgo Lifestyles 220
Summing Up Virgo 224

LIBRA WOMAN
Checklist of Libra Traits 226
Libra Personality 227
Libra Relationships 235
Libra Sexuality 241
Libra Anger 245
Libra Lifestyles 248
Summing Up Libra 251

SCORPIO WOMAN
Checklist of Scorpio Traits 253
Scorpio Personality 254
Scorpio Relationships 266
Scorpio Sexuality 274
Scorpio Anger 280
Scorpio Lifestyles 284
Summing Up Scorpio 287

SAGITTARIUS WOMAN
Checklist of Sagittarius Traits 289
Sagittarius Personality 290
Sagittarius Relationships 304
Sagittarius Sexuality 312
Sagittarius Anger 319
Sagittarius Lifestyles 322
Summing Up Sagittarius 327

CAPRICORN WOMAN
Checklist of Capricorn Traits 329
Capricorn Personality 330
Capricorn Relationships 342
Capricorn Sexuality 356
Capricorn Anger 362
Capricorn Lifestyles 366
Summing Up Capricorn 369

AQUARIUS WOMAN
Checklist of Aquarius Traits 370
Aquarius Personality 371
Aquarius Relationships 384
Aquarius Sexuality 400
Aquarius Anger 406
Aquarius Lifestyles 412
Summing Up Aquarius 416

PISCES WOMAN
Checklist of Pisces Traits 417
Pisces Personality 418
Pisces Relationships 425
Pisces Sexuality 430
Pisces Anger 436
Pisces Lifestyles 440
Summing Up Pisces 443

THE COSMIC WOMAN
Checklist of Cosmic Traits 445
Cosmic Personality 446
Cosmic Relationships 464
Cosmic Sexuality 469
Cosmic Anger 474
Cosmic Lifestyles 478
Summing Up the Cosmic Woman 481

Introduction

I am a therapist who has spent a decade helping women in a variety of ways: as founder and president of the Life Crisis Counseling Clinic and of the Flexible Careers Counseling Center, both in Chicago, and both concerned with helping people in the areas of relationships, sexuality, and health; as a sexologist currently studying for a Ph.D. in human sexuality; and as a teacher who has taught people around the world about love and intimacy, self-esteem, assertiveness, awareness, sexuality, and how to use anger and power constructively. I am also a professional astrologer who has studied various astrological approaches, Jungian dream analysis, numerology, palmistry, handwriting analysis, and Tarot cards, all for the purpose of helping my clients and satisfying my own curiosity. I am senior editor of *Forum, the International Journal of Human Relations*. In this capacity, I receive over fifty thousand letters a year from readers who wish to share their personal lives. I was born in Hungary on April 13, 1944, and was educated abroad and in the United States. I'm a graduate of the University of Chicago, and the mother of two children, a girl and a boy.

Shortly after establishing the Life Crisis Counseling Clinic, I received a phone call from a psychiatrist. He wanted to refer a suicidal patient to me for a psycho-astrological consultation. I accepted the client, but with serious misgivings. After all, it was a grave responsibility, and I would only get one crack. I'll have to do better than my best, I told myself.

Usually I hold a dialogue with my clients, and each session takes an hour to an hour and a half. Each psycho-astrology client receives a tape of our session and is free to call back at any time. So far, I have never received a single call to tell me I had given the wrong advice, but I have had many telling me the session helped.

This woman came to the session pale, withdrawn, and depressed. Her session took just forty minutes because she was very quiet. To say she said little would be an understatement. I plunged ahead, speaking as clearly and positively as I could, trying to convince her of the conclusion I'd reached by studying her chart:

that her crisis period would come to an end within four months. I remember telling her that I felt it was a test of her strength and love of life. I remember describing my belief that crises are actually our greatest learning times, springboards to evolution and happiness if we cope well.

I repeated that I felt her crisis specifically tested her courage. She had somehow, with the help of her subconscious, set herself the task of living without a family or a man to lean on. Mentally, she believed she was independent, but her emotions were resisting. Fear of the future and self-pity were all she seemed to feel.

I remember cautioning her not to expect that the world would help her out, but I stressed that in just four months, if she persisted, there would probably be a great opportunity for a new job and a romance. I told her, too, that nothing was likely to happen if she hid in her room; though the coming opportunities were indicated in her chart, she had the free will to accept or deny them.

Very gently I tried to get her to accept the fact that we are really in charge of our own lives. If we accept the existence and importance of our subconscious, if we listen to our dreams and inner voices, we'll find a hidden purpose in just about everything that happens to us. There are no coincidences, in my opinion, and her fears and depressions had come to teach her something important; they would pass.

I could not tell if she really listened or if the taped reading would help her. Usually my clients leave me feeling high. The point of my readings has always been to shed new light and bring fresh awareness into a person's life—past, present, and future. Greater self-knowledge eventually produces greater harmony and better relationships.

I do not "predict the future." I predict probable patterns of human behavior. I predict the probable effects of current planetary cycles on a person's life, at the same time stressing free choice and individual responsibility. I engage my clients in a dialogue, reviewing the best possible choices open to them.

In my consultations, as in this book, my aim is to help the client sort out what is best for her. In the above instance staying home might have denied this woman her opportunity. It would have been unproductive behavior, and I pointed this out. I finished the consultation, as I always do, with a practical, tailor-made "how to cope" segment, which is always well received. When this particular client left, however, I was very concerned. For all I knew, she might kill herself the same day. Yet my intuition told me to remain optimistic; I would hear from her again.

About six months later, I began to receive requests for psycho-astrological consultations from a group of women who seemed to know one another. I finally figured out that the initial contact had come from my depressed lady. Apparently she was alive.

Almost a year later, she called me back. I have never forgotten the conversation, which went something like this: "Hi, do you remember me? I came to see you about a year ago. I was awfully depressed." I told her I not only remembered her but had thought of her often, hoping that the job and romance had come through and had given her the boost to start living again. She then continued:

> Everything you said on the tape has come true. When the time came, I forced myself to go out and be in places where I could meet people. I was very skeptical that what you told me would really happen, but when I got a new job offer out of the blue, I decided I might as well go all the way and try the romance department.
>
> Believe it or not, I met a man I am living with now. It's a good relationship, my job is fine, and I am a new person. I want to thank you, and I want you to know that I carry the tape of that session with me in my purse. I've also told many people about you.

I thanked her for letting me know, and I leaned back and closed my eyes. This was clear confirmation of my method. Psycho-astrology, combined with my knowledge of therapy and sexuality, has been helpful even in the hardest cases, even in just one session. Since then, there have been hundreds of instances where the technique has given more meaning and hope to people's lives.

Let me state my position succinctly. *Planets do not rule destiny. People rule their own destinies, and they do so most effectively when cognizant of a universal rhythm.*

Through years of experience, I learned to refine psycho-astrology into a unique tool for self-development. Its validity as I use it has been proven to me over and over again. The women in my sessions relaxed quickly when they heard that others with similar charts had also had problems and had overcome them. They learned some new things; they made important choices. They gained more faith in the order of things. They came away more prepared for their own roles, actions, and reactions, and for the events that might befall them. Many began to develop a belief system that relieved prolonged agonizing and helped them to gain detachment from the pettiness of their all-too-human egos.

In the course of our sessions, we concluded that life is not the meaningless, chaotic thing it may seem when one is confused, angry, or depressed. Anger and depression can be confronted, and what's more, there are ways to build on the knowledge gleaned from such episodes. Life can be seen as a constant challenge and a gift. And life may be one step on a ladder of reincarnation, each step with a purpose of its own, each containing a lesson in love and in relating, each accompanied by struggle. Albert Einstein once said, "God does not play with dice." It seems he had the same idea of the regularity, purpose, and order of the universe, and of our lives in it.

Perhaps the most important thing to come out of my consultations has been my clients' perception of the value of change. Most people who came to see me were suffering from aftershock or future shock: a bad love affair, illness, loss, fears of going out, getting a job, having a baby, moving to another city, getting married, getting divorced. Change was always the ogre, or so it seemed.

What underlies most fear of change is ignorance and lack of self-trust. Recognizing this, I shared with my clients some of my own fears and how I had overcome them. I suggested they make a "Risk List" to learn how often they had already taken risks—and succeeded. The Risk List became one of the most popular exercises (see "Taurus Relationships").

It is my belief that change is natural and, in the long run, probably beneficial. How we cope with change determines much of the quality of our lives. I asked those who came to see me to tell me what they feared the most, and it usually turned out to be something they could live with.

Self-esteem was another major stumbling block. I gave clients a reading list and suggestions on growth seminars (one of the best is Dr. Nathaniel Branden's seminar on self-esteem and love). I advised them how to improve their self-images and body language. I gave clients material and practice exercises on communications skills, including sexual communication. I bolstered their confidence by pointing out all the richness and good qualities inherent in their chart, reminding them of the wisdom they had already accumulated simply by living. I was able to help most of them to at least recognize, if not choose immediately, the road that would lead them to give up their most binding fears.

I did all this with the help of psycho-astrology. Just about everything I taught and everything I learned from my clients in a decade of therapy is in this book. Let me tell the reader about *Sex Signs*. It is a psycho-astrology guide to female potential, health, and happiness, and it explores areas beyond the scope of other astrology books. It deals specifically with women, delving into the hidden world of female psychology, sexuality, anger, fear, guilt, power struggles and changing needs. It teaches the reader how to find love. Love consists not in finding the right person but in becoming the right person. *Sex Signs* rejects predetermination or predestination as well as the strict use of sun signs.

Sex Signs is a breakthrough book, a dramatic, unique marriage of astrology, psychology, and female sexuality. It goes directly to the point most relevant to today's woman: how she can develop awareness of herself, become attuned to the universal planetary rhythms that affect her, and obtain a key to her own love and power. The only things not included in *Sex Signs* are individual forecasts. Each person has her or his own unique chart, but such analyses are not within the scope of this book.

Instead, I have devised a way to blend and compress that kind of personal information into *psycho-astrological female portraits*. You will find in this book thirteen different types of women, twelve corresponding to the signs of the Zodiac, plus one more, the Cosmic Woman—the lady who really has it all together. The reader can first read the chapter that describes her sun sign. Or she can read the checklist of thirty-five personality traits that appears at the beginning of each chapter and choose the one that best describes her, regardless of whether it matches her sign.

Almost every astrology book these days is based solely on sun signs. At parties, one often hears, "Hi, what sign are you? I'm a Leo." But over the years many women have come to me saying, "I've read the description of Leo, Virgo, Libra, etc., and it doesn't fit. *What's wrong with me*?" My response is an emphatic "Nothing." Sun sign descriptions seldom work. They are too simplistic and general to provide important information or real insight. They also offer no way out of the rut of a supposedly permanent character.

The main reason I have based *Sex Signs* on blended astrological portraits and not on sun signs (or moon signs or any other specific planetary influence) is that I feel a woman must be liberated from the view that her sun sign is her character cast in stone!

A Gemini reader may identify most with the description of the Aries Woman. Should she discard the information, scratch her head in confusion, or put herself down for being a "bad" Gemini? I say the *variable choice* of who she is and will be is hers. I want no woman to be bound by the inflexible, stereotypical thinking promulgated by sun sign enthusiasts.

The reader need not know astrology to learn from this book. Her role model may be the Aries Woman, the Gemini Woman, or the Pisces Woman, regardless of her sun sign, as she herself decides. And, as explained later in this chapter (see "Phases"), she may find that she is going through a phase accurately described by one chapter, whereas a few years back, she was quite a different woman. Her old self may be portrayed in another chapter.

What exactly is psycho-astrology?

Astrology is an ancient method of studying changing patterns and cycles. Its boundaries overlap a vast system of metaphysics. *Psycho*-astrology blends the ancient wisdom of astrology and the modern expertise of psychology, and I believe it is a dynamic, productive way to study and comprehend human nature. It is food for the curious mind, an aid to knowing oneself and understanding how one relates to others, a superb guide to cycles, to treasures buried within, and to coping with the network of energies that constantly surround and influence us.

I use psycho-astrology as a creative way to tune in and communicate with people. It helps me to channel my intuition, to structure and integrate what I have observed, experienced, learned, felt; and it translates astrological language into a modern idiom. Psycho-astrology has also been a personal bridge for me. It has allowed me to expand from humanistic, academic psychology into the psychic frontiers of a new type of astrology. It has forced me to use, to verify, and finally to trust my intuition as much as my logical mind.

In *Sex Signs*, I use psycho-astrology as a barometer of the flowing, flexible cycles of a woman's growth. With it, I try to promote her recognition of the responsibilities she bears for her own fulfilment, in relation both to herself and to others. In all, I hope to communicate to the reader my accumulated experience with the disciplines I use as a therapist and in my own life.

Who is psycho-astrology for?
Sex Signs is for the woman who wants to familiarize herself with her psycho-social-sexual self, to recognize her inhibitions and reduce or eliminate them, to give and receive love and pleasure. She will find here invaluable insights into her personality. She will receive advice, inspiration, information, leadership, encouragement, support, and a catalyst for growth.

If the key to life is love, the key to romance and marriage is sexual communication. Human sexuality is a critical component of romantic love. We express our sexuality in ways we were taught by our parents, our peers, and society. We think of it, for example, as primarily a genital interaction. In actuality, nearly every instance of social intercourse involves a sexual response.

Sexual energy is inherently a natural and healthy force. It is the joy of being alive, the drive to connect, to communicate with feeling and to live with meaning. All of us have the capacity to experience pleasure, to adapt to change, and to feel comfortable as we become intimate with others. If we are in total harmony with our free-flowing sexual energy, we are able to live with self-respect, love, freedom, and creativity. We can take the risks necessary to effect change, and we are capable of appreciating the responsibilities of deep intimacy as well as of worldly success.

But if we have trouble . . .
defining our needs,
giving and accepting love,
developing our sexual potential,
making relationships work,
using our anger constructively,
attaining goals,
. . . then this book will, I hope, be a valuable aid to fashioning a fulfiling lifestyle.

The thirteen sisters of sex signs
This book is based on thirteen psycho-astrological portraits of women. The different types are described, beginning with the Aries Woman, ending with the Cosmic Woman, and including every astrological sign in between.

There are twelve signs in the Zodiac, and I have used their symbolism. I've added one more, not because I think a planet beyond Pluto is about to be discovered and added to the Zodiac's planetary collection (though that too will happen), but because I believe women today are looking for role models. The thirteenth chapter describes the ultimate woman, the one who is so spiritually, sexually, mentally, and emotionally independent that she has become totally, securely interdependent. If that seems like a paradox, I refer you to chapter thirteen.

Each woman is a blend of different influences, including her genes, her background, and the input of parents, teachers, friends, lovers, children, society at large, and also the media. In addition, she has her own vision of herself, but it is seldom realized. Here, too, the thirteenth chapter might help.

An individual chart contains at least fifteen different factors an astrologer works with, such as sun sign, moon sign, ascendant, midheaven, elements, qualities, planetary aspects, Arabic points, and midpoints, to mention a few. But since this is not a technical book, there will be no discussion of which planets other than the ruling planet influence each female portrait. Here only the results count, and I leave the explanation of the process of arriving at them for a later date. I am very sure that each reader will find an accurate description of her innermost self in *Sex Signs*.

The woman who reads *Sex Signs* need know nothing about astrology to benefit a great deal. Nor does she have to know her own chart in order to understand and learn.

How to use this book

Each of the thirteen chapters is preceded by a Checklist of Traits. This list contains thirty-five characteristics that describe each type of woman. Since most women know their sun signs, I advise the reader to turn to the chapter on her sign and go over the checklist. If she has thirty or more of the traits listed, this chapter probably describes her accurately. She should read it first.

If the reader feels that the sun sign checklist does *not* describe her, she is advised to go through the other checklists. She will find one that does, and she should start at this point, regardless of her sign.

A woman should not be alarmed if she finds herself described at various points in other chapters. There are universal links, as well as universal problems, shared by many types of women. That's what sisterhood is all about. Finding herself in more than one chapter should only solidify her feeling that she is not alone. And if she can benefit from the advice in several different chapters, more power to her! To quote famous astrologer Alan Leo, "Each part of a whole reflects the whole within itself. Thus, each of the twelve signs of the Zodiac reflects the whole Zodiac within itself."

Phases

The woman who finds that one chapter describes her as she was five years ago and another fits her current self is on the right track. For the book is designed to show the developmental richness of a woman's life. It helps her to see where she is coming from and points the way ahead.

A woman reader in her twenties, for example, may have a Scorpio sun sign, but she may identify right now with the chapter on the Aries Woman. This need not confuse her. I believe it simply means that she is more an Aries than a Scorpio or that she is undergoing an Aries phase in her life. This phase may, in time, give way to another. By reading *Sex Signs,* this woman will gain valuable insight about herself now and about the direction she can take next.

Another example of a woman in flux is a reader in her forties with a Capricorn sun sign. The Capricorn chapter may describe her to a tee when in fact she is unhappy with her life and wants to change it. She will find in this book the insight and practical advice she needs to analyze not only herself but also the sister she may want to emulate. She may, for example, wish to be more like a fiery Leo. She need only read the chapter on the Leo Woman to see whether her fantasy is worth pursuing and how this might be done.

Still another reader may review her life and conclude that she has gone through many phases and is comfortably settled in her present lifestyle. In this case, *Sex Signs* will give her a big pat on the back.

Today's woman is a complex person living in a complex era. She is often confused about her needs. She is under great pressure to become a person in her own right but may find it difficult to break away from her early conditioning and her dependence on a man. Her perceptions and status are in flux, and society has done little to prepare her to live in the post-contraceptive, pre-equality world of future shock.

I believe that my phase-by-phase approach is extremely important, because the modern woman can no longer be described by old stereotypes, nor can she be taken for granted. She is wife, mother, partner, daughter, lover, friend, professional. She is also whore, saint, angel, devil, muse, Amazon. What has to be remembered is that women (and men) are in a constant process of change. Today's woman has more choices than ever. She is changing rapidly and experiencing more stress. This book takes that factor into consideration.

Why not sun signs?

In my view, a woman who says her sun sign description does not fit should have the option to consider herself another astrological *type* and be supported in her view. She should also feel free to break away from other potentially harmful stereotypes. As I have stated before, I feel a woman must be liberated from the sense that her sun sign is her character cast in stone.

There are other reasons why I am not basing *Sex Signs* on sun signs. A sun sign description, while a valuable way for the beginner to relate to astrology, is far too simplistic. It is convenient because most people know their sun sign, but it is only one of many factors that go into the making of a chart. The holistic astrologer casts and interprets a chart based on at least the following "symbols": ten planets (though we call them stars), the ascendant and mid-heaven axis, and the moon's nodes. Progressed charts and transits are also integrated with the natal chart to provide a complete understanding of the person at a given time.

I also find technical problems with sun sign astrology. First, people born on overlapping dates, called the "cusp," do not usually know which sign they are. For a woman who was born on the exact cusp of, say, Aquarius/Pisces to determine whether she is an Aquarius or a Pisces (sun sign), she must know her exact time of birth and have a chart cast for that time. The sun moves into a sign at different times each year, and sometimes even the cusp date might change by a day.

If she does not know her time of birth, the astrologer must use a complicated process called rectification to determine what the time must have been. Rectification is a technique of working backward in time, using dates of major importance to the client in order to arrive at the correct moment of birth. Unfortunately, there are many rectification methods, and two astrologers using different methods can easily arrive at different birth times, and this different charts, for the same person.

Another problem is historical. There is a group of astrologers called siderealists who use a Zodiac based on constellations. But the constellations we call Aries, Taurus, etc., are not where they were in ancient times. The sidereal Zodiac is different from the tropical one used in most astrology textbooks. The tropical Zodiac is based on the earth's seasons.

The tropical Zodiac takes the position of the sun at the vernal equinox (when day and night are of equal length in spring) as zero degrees of Aries, the first sign of the Zodiac. The signs are then assigned thirty degrees each, with the twelve signs composing the total of 360 degrees. The division of each sign into thirty degrees appears arbitrary, but most Eastern astrologers use the tropical Zodiac because the fact is that it works.

The horoscope is divided into twelve houses. Some astrologers use the equal house method, in which each house had exactly thirty degrees. The rising sign or ascendant of the person determines the "start" of the horoscope, on the left-hand side. The ascendant is determined by the time of birth; its sign (Aries through Pisces) corresponds to the constellation that rose on the eastern horizon at the person's time of birth. Other astrologers use varying house methods. Most Western horoscopes are now cast with the Koch or Placidus method, both of which divide the horoscope into unequal segments. Thus, one house might have fifty degrees while another has only twenty-five.

Psycho-astrology relies to a degree on classical astrology and some of its interpretations. However, it supports the modern astrological view that the total study of the person should be based on the total chart, on intuition, on a knowledge of psychology and human sexuality, and on growth cycles. It departs from classical astrology in holding that negativity is mostly in the mind of the person, not in outside forces. Though an event may occur, it is the person's *reaction* to and *interpretation and preception* of the event that will determine the outcome, not some cosmic overseer.

Summing up, I am against using sun sign astrology because it is all too often a confining influence that many women interpret as reflecting badly on them. I do not wish to burden any woman with a negative view of herself. Most women already suffer from low self-esteem and are much too susceptible to restrictive outside authorities as definitive of their own worth. I feel that psycho-astrology counteracts these tendencies and is a liberating, not a confining, influence.

Why I wrote *Sex Signs*

No woman need subscribe to my personal philosophy to get a great deal of help from *Sex Signs*. However, I think it is important for me to communicate what I believe, for it puts things in a clearer perspective. In this book, I rely on my training as a professional counselor, psycho-astrologer, teacher, and student of human nature and social and sexual behavior. I also draw on my experience as a mother, wife, daughter, lover, confidante, and professional working woman. I bring to bear my education, observation, experience, character, and intuition.

I believe we have not yet seen the tip of the human psychic iceberg. We harbor infinite spaces of unconscious knowledge, genetic memory, reincarnational knowledge.

I believe we operate on two primary levels: the level of the higher self, our beacon, and the level of the lower self, our personality. The higher self is wiser and less hung-up. The personality is earthbound and has the usual problems we all face. The higher self is the storehouse, synthesizer, and guiding light of our many lives and personalities. It decides, within certain universal laws we have not yet deciphered, what experiences it needs in its next lifetime on earth. Though the beacon's purpose is always to evolve into a more positive, loving, and complete being, the personality usually runs into conflicts.

I am an optimist and believe we are all on a path of evolution that we want to make positive. We don't always succeed, and as a result, we sometimes slide backward. It is nevertheless the central task of life to choose among our options and design the right kinds of experiences to accomplish our present tasks and evolve toward the Cosmic Woman.

The experiences we need, no matter how difficult, are those that will move us along our path. Sometimes we slip; sometimes we fly. Personally, I think it is the negative energy of guilt, fear, and repressed anger that keeps us from soaring. That's why it's important to be able to identify it and learn ways to eliminate it in ourselves.

Each person is a combination of many factors. We are in constant change and motion. I believe, as do many physicists, that once we understand the structure of the atom we will have the key that unlocks the secrets of the universe. I also believe that if we come to know and love ourselves and others, we will have the key to the purpose of life.

Love is the source of our power and creativity. Love is the basis of *Sex Signs*.

The chapters

In every chapter, there is an analysis of psychological character, the changing cycles of human need, self-esteem, sexual character and needs, ability to cope with anger, choices of mates for love and marriage (at times completely different), the need and capacity for personal growth, and alternative lifestyles. In the psychological analysis there is advice on recognizing strengths and weaknesses, with suggestions for adjusting the latter. There are answers to such questions as: How can Aries learn to disclose emotional vulnerability? How can Gemini take advantage of her constant need for variety and stimulation? How can Scorpio best channel her immense power needs? How can Capricorn balance professional goals with a good home life?

Each type is strongly individual in value structure, need for security, and dependence/autonomy demands. I map the evolutionary changes in these factors as a woman goes through the cycles of her life. For example, it is helpful for Aries to be aware of her slow emotional maturation, for Capricorn to know that her happiness will increase throughout her life, and for Pisces to anticipate a wandering eye later on. It helps women to know that they share certain problems and qualities with others.

Comments on self-esteem appear in each chapter, for this is the foundation of growth, intimacy, and love. Without loving oneself, one cannot love others. This book features advice on how to gauge one's self-esteem and how to increase it.

Just as each woman differs from the next in psychological makeup, each differs in sexual character. A woman who understands her own sexuality will be more comfortable with herself and her love partners. What are her sexual needs? How does she cope with guilt and experience pleasure? Sex is communication. It is one of our greatest pleasures. But for many of us the sexual experience is dulled because our culture educates us out of pleasurable sharing. We have learned to turn sex into the dumping ground in our relationships. Self-knowledge and new skills to build intimacy can help us turn that tendency around.

Anger and sex are closely aligned. The anger we cannot handle positively expresses itself in the damage it does to healthy sex. I discuss anger, its relationship to sexual behavior and communication for each type of woman, and I include individual ways to focus anger constructively. Uncontrolled anger can and does take many forms: power struggles with a partner, competitiveness, hostility, inability to reach orgasm, and lack of sexual desire, among other sexual problems. Each type of woman is advised how to express and release anger. The thirteenth chapter explains how to make anger work for her and harness it as an aid in her life partnerships.

For each type of woman there is a mate most suitable as marriage partner, father of her children, and, should she wish, provider. There are others who may be right for a pre-, post-, or extramarital relationship. I examine, for example, how Aries can meet her need for stability as well as for excitement, how Sagittarius can cope with wanderlust, how Aquarius may react to intimate friendships, how Pisces can overcome her tendency to clinging dependency.

Self-knowledge can illuminate options beyond the normal scope of romance, marriage, and divorce. Accordingly, I also discuss these options. The final segment of each chapter covers, for the first time in astrology, alternative lifestyles beyond monogamy. It discusses the needs of each human regarding personal growth and intimacy; it analyzes changing sexual needs and assesses the advisability of each lifestyle. For example, there are women committed to a lifetime of sexual and emotional exclusivity with another. I want also to acknowledge those women whose emotional and sexual needs are not met by traditional monogamy. Some need separate, different partners for romance and marriage. Others require experimentation, free from deadening guilt, with a number of romantic liaisons.

For women, *Sex Signs* contains valuable clues to self-knowledge, self-esteem, and the development of sexual and social potential. For men, *Sex Signs* offers insight into women and into their own femaleness. I hope and believe that all who wish to increase their capacity for love, sexual pleasure, health, and happiness will profit from this book.

Dates for sun signs

ARIES	March 20/21 to April 20
TAURUS	April 21 to May 21
GEMINI	May 22 to June 21/22
CANCER	June 22/23 to July 22/23

LEO	July 23/24 to August 23/24
VIRGO	August 24/25 to September 23
LIBRA	September 24 to October 23/24
SCORPIO	October 24/25 to November 22/23
SAGITTARIUS	November 23/24 to December 21/22
CAPRICORN	December 22/23 to January 20/21
AQUARIUS	January 21/22 to February 18/19
PISCES	February 19/20 to March 19/20

The above list of dates is used in traditional sun sign astrology to determine the sign under which one is born. Too often the image seems to be cast in stone and does not fit the evolving characteristics of a person at a particular time. There are many good reasons for this. Other factors besides the position of the sun may be exerting a strong influence upon a person's development. A strong ascendant, planetary aspects, cycle of the moon, or various combinations may overide the effect of the natal sun. A person may go into a phase that is more akin to another sun sign and proceed with that cycle until it reaches its natural conclusion. For example, a person born under Taurus may act like a Leo and assume many of the characteristics associated with that sign until the Leo phase is ended and the Taurus personality reemerges, modified to be sure by the lessons of Leo behavior. So it is with all of the signs; they are in a constant state of flux. It is very important to know just where one is in the process. To be aware is to know yourself. This is the aim of astrology and psychology—to increase awareness of the self.

The following chapters represent the thirteen composite archetypes that have been constructed of various elements—sun signs, moon signs, rising signs, planetary rulerships and aspects—to assist a person in locating the phase or combination of phases that they may be experiencing at a particular time. If thirty of the characteristics listed at the beginning of each of the chapters seem to fit your honest appraisal of yourself, chances are that some of your planets are touching the universal archetype of that constellation.

The Cosmic Woman represents a person that has mastered all of the lessons of the Zodiac and has experienced a complete evolution into a cosmic being. If she appears to be too good to be real, don't despair, for she does exist. Just keep an open mind and learn to flow with the changes that are constantly taking place in your life. Once you have attuned yourself to the stars, it is surprising how rapidly you evolve.

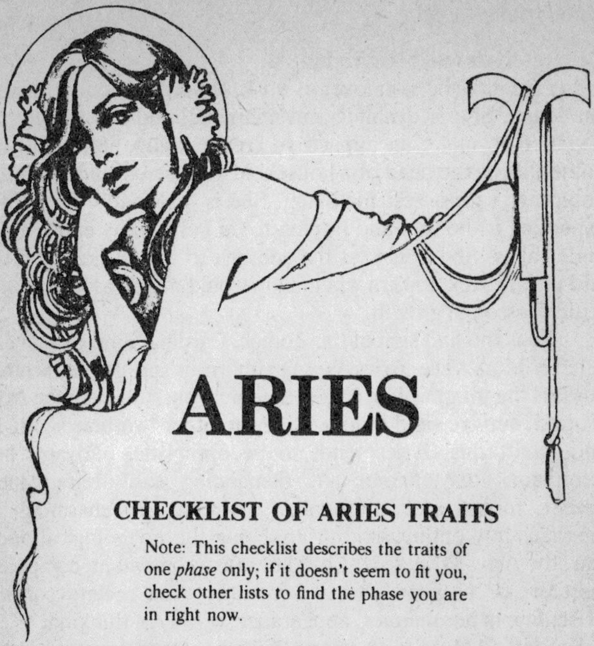

ARIES

CHECKLIST OF ARIES TRAITS

Note: This checklist describes the traits of one *phase* only; if it doesn't seem to fit you, check other lists to find the phase you are in right now.

1. Highly Motivated
2. Pioneering Leader
3. Needs Challenge
4. Strong Personality
5. Fortunate
6. Positive, Optimistic
7. A Winner
8. Rebellious
9. Insensitive
10. Risk Taker
11. Impatient
12. Impulsive
13. Competitive
14. Dominant
15. Responsible
16. Achieving
17. "Masculine" or Just Different
18. Androgynous
19. Extroverted
20. Easily Angered
21. High Self-esteem
22. Good Sense of Humor
23. Detached
24. Selfish
25. Proud
26. High Libido
27. Dislikes Details
28. Arrogant
29. Blunt
30. Easily Bored
31. Dynamic
32. Charismatic
33. Catalyst
34. Huntress
35. Idealist

Aries personality

General traits and background

In her relationships, in love, in work, the Aries Woman demands challenge. She is dynamic and energetic, and she usually feels impelled to make an impact, to create change. She like to be influential as the head of a household or business and tends to be outgoing, with a zest for living. She is frequently competitive, expecting to be first and hoping to be best in any endeavor she undertakes. She possesses the courage to tackle most situations and may be able to turn what many would regard as failure into a critical lesson in growth.

Aries is the first sign of the Zodiac, Cardinal Fire; its planetary ruler is Mars. The Aries Woman, born in springtime, seems to possess the tough will of a seed that must push through the frozen ground, survive, and bloom. Like the other two fires signs, Leo and Sagittarius, Aries tends to be optimistic, buoyant, fiery, dominant, gutsy, flamboyant, demanding, easily bored, inconsistent, foolish and irrational at times, usually charming, and inexhaustibly enthusiastic. Mars being the mythological god of war, the Aries Woman is also at home as a combatant, competitor, debater, or pioneer; she is frequently what society considers masculine in her manner, appearance, or way of thinking.

Scarlett O'Hara is an example of the Aries type—optimistic, passionate, and sometimes tough to get along with. A survivor though foolishly impulsive, proud to an extreme and fond of challenge, Scarlett glows and rages, fascinates and repulses us. One can dislike her, one can find her irresistible, but one cannot ignore her. She is her own worst enemy, but in the end she endures. She even manages to convince her audience that tragedy can be a way of life, that winning is a wholly subjective experience. To the Aries Woman, being a winner counts heavily indeed.

A woman is the Aries *type* if she is described by thirty or more of the adjectives on the Checklist of Aries Traits. She need not have been born an Aries (sun in Aries) in order to be an Aries-type woman.

A woman need have no planets in the sign of Aries to be going through an Aries *phase*. The Aries phase of a woman's growth is characterized by the following:

1 rash, impulsive decision making.
2 a completely new start in life, or multiple new starts (often involving a business enterprise).
3 headstrong and/or rebellious attitudes, especially if these are replacing formerly cooperative ones.
4 a highly motivated and stubborn search for independence utilizing avenues which are more likely to be "masculine" than traditionally feminine (for example, a woman who goes back to school in middle age to study law, or who switches careers though it is highly inconvenient to others).
5 the conscious setting of new challenges, usually in both personal and professional life.
6 a feeling of just batting one's head against the wall, accompanied by a resistance to giving up regardless of what anyone else says; stubborn, unyielding, rebellious, or autonomous thinking.
7 any medical problems or injuries which repeatedly occur on the head (this indicates an Aries influence but does not by itself mean an Aries phase).

The Aries Woman is usually an eternal optimist, facing many exhausting starts and stops with strength. Tomorrow is indeed another day for her, as it has ever been for *Gone With the Wind*'s Scarlett.

Highly motivated, pioneering leader, needs challenge

The Aries Woman is frequently capable of running more than five things at a time and often does so. She is typically born with an intense drive to succeed, an impatient compulsion to rise to the top. She usually has a need to prove herself, to have control over a situation, and together these traits enable her to find management positions quickly. Only Saturn-ruled, ultra-ambitious Capricorn joins the ranks of leaders as consistently, though perhaps not as fast, as the Aries Woman.

In order to function at optimum capacity, the Aries Woman needs to be mentally challenged. Her mind is usually her strongest point, though she may also be physically powerful and is often very attractive.

Aries is seldom lazy and often feels compelled to do, accomplish, produce. If she is merely sitting, she may feel unproductive and become frustrated or begin to brood. She must constantly exercise her mind and her options in the society at large. She needs to know she can externalize her impulse for leadership and action, sooner or later finding dynamic outlets for her ambition and frequently remarkable initiative.

In her private life, the Aries Woman needs to be challenged to grow. She must learn to release control from time to time and to be willing to show her weaknesses as well as her strengths.

Strong personality

One thing about Aries that no one will dispute is that she is likely to stand out because of her zany clothes, her confident stride, her dominating body language, or her loud, booming voice. Whatever the means, she attracts attention naturally. If she is the rare shy Aries, she will still find a way to seem odd enough to be noticed.

Her personal magnetism, coupled with vibrant energy and an indomitable spirit help her overcome and face change with courage. People sense this about her and often look to her for guidance or leadership, roles she is likely to accept.

Fortunate

The Aries Woman frequently makes her own luck, as well as her own misery. She seems to have a sort of cosmic protective mechanism that helps those who help themselves. In her case, as her luck would have it, she keeps the mechanism working by thorough preparation and by taking advantage of the opportunities that present themselves.

Positive, optimistic, a winner

Part of her good fortune, as well as part of her strength, comes from her inborn optimism. Lady Aries is frequently a winner in the stakes of life. She is bound to have set and met her own obstacle course. Deep down, she believes she can lick just about anything, and she often does. She manufactures her own sunshine and can usually lighten a tale of woe. Friends often count on her to cheer them up, and even confirmed pessimists tend to smile at the childlike optimism with which she greets life.

Rebellious, insensitive, risk taker

The Aries Woman is frequently short on compassion and sensitivity. Let others take care of themselves, she may say. She often finds it difficult to empathize with people's troubles, instead dismissing them with a wave of her hand as mere temporary setbacks. She may need to respect others' feelings more, to tone down her internal cacophony and hear their music.

Her need for stimulation may be so potent that it outweighs her need for security. This may enable her to take risks remarkably easily, but it may also make her harsh, insensitive to another person's concern with safety. She herself is apt to find such thoughts too constraining. She typically hates limitation, sometimes rebelling against conventions her parents and society consider necessary to the upbringing of a "good girl." She seldom wants to learn how to nurture people in the stereotypical feminine sense of the word; she may resent staying home to bake cookies, do the household chores, and quietly support her man. Details are not usually her forte, nor is self-effacing supportiveness.

Impatient, impulsive

The Aries Woman marches to her own beat and is often reluctant to assume discipleship as a prelude to leadership. Especially when young, she would rather pole-vault than climb.

For example, at an airline counter or a personnel office, she may be so impatient that she doesn't care who is in line or what their needs are.

These me-first moves may get her what she wants on a short-term basis: she may be first to purchase a ticket or land an interview. But it is likely that in the long run she alienates the very people who may be more important than that ticket. However, her personal, immediate needs often act on her with such speed and force that she forgets other considerations. The Aries Woman can block herself by acting impulsively on short-term needs, seeking their satisfaction alone and rejecting compromises.

A grave danger of her impatience is that it may make her skip through experiences too quickly, especially early in life. She has a tendency to stay on the surface and not dwell in the depths. At times it may be necessary for Aries to sift through her emotions and live through an experience more fully.

Competitive, dominant, responsible

The Aries Woman has a potent chemistry, a powerful impact, high-frequency vibrations, intelligence, and strong will power. Her mental horizons are generally broad, and she may get scattered. She tends to resist the limitations society has put on women, often preferring to run free, live untrammeled. She almost universally seeks to relate to men as equals and to achieve on the same level. She has an optimistic view of the world and may regard it as a setting in which to prove herself in many roles. She typically wants to compete and win without playing games of submission. She knows these are games and may consider them a waste of time. And if there are rules to the games, she would rather make them up herself.

The Aries Woman is willing to take total responsibility for running a home, a business, or a life. When she tries to run not only her own life but the lives of those around her, she can unknowingly create interpersonal problems. But this same tendency ensures her access to the business world and the world of high finance.

Achieving

Classical astrology teaches that Aries types are pioneers, and this is true. But today's Aries Woman must decide how to cope with this inborn trait and live with it happily in a male-dominated world.

It is very important to accept one's inherent qualities, negative as well as positive. In the case of the Aries Woman, it is important that she acknowledge her own impatience, her selfishness, her tendency to thrust herself headlong into an experience and then rush out of it. It is important that she accept these traits as part of her, peculiar to her self and her Aries heritage. Once accepted, they can be put to highly positive uses. As an enterpreneur or pioneer she may have conflicts about traditional female roles, but the Aries Woman also has tremendous potential for accomplishment and individual achievement.

"Masculine" or just different, androgynous

The Aries Woman is frequently subconsciously aware of feeling somehow different from other women. Sometimes she is comfortable with this awareness and uses it to her advantage. More often, she experiences it as a kind of emotional exile. Born in a female body, she very often has what we call a male consciousness.

The Aries Woman is born to a difficult task. If she wants it, hers is the challenge of creating the twentieth-century model of androgynous behavior. The word *androgynous* comes from the Greek words *andro* ("male") and *gyne* ("female"). To a certain degree we are all androgynous, but the Aries Woman has an exceptionally well-developed male side. She is thus capable very early in her development of uniting and synthesizing important aspects of the male and female in one body and personality.

Carl Jung, the great Swiss psychiatrist who studied with Freud before branching into astrology and metaphysics, believed that everyone has a contrasexual inner partner. His theory has had a major impact on our understanding of the human psyche.

Jung taught that inside every man is a woman. He called her the *anima*, or inner feminine partner who acts as a man's guiding spirit and puts him in touch with his deepest feminine instincts. As long as the anima is repressed (as it appears to be in most Western men), the man projects his femininity onto the woman with whom he is most closely involved emotionally. She then carries all the subconscious projections of his affective (feminine) needs and complexes.

Jung also believed that every woman has an *animus*, an inner male partner representing "masculine" needs such as action, achievement, and logic. Repressed, the animus is projected onto the man in her life, much as a spotlight projects colors on a screen. The most special man—father, lover, or husband—is the screen for the repressed needs of her animus.

In practical terms, this means that women, until they mature into self-knowledge, expect men to live out their own repressed needs for action, achievement, power, aggression, or independence. What distinguishes the Aries Woman is that she is closer than most to her own animus. She is frequently able to be active, powerful, achieving. On the other hand, she is frequently unable to be receptive, passive, and emotionally vulnerable. The task of integration is everyone's task. The challenge for Aries is to learn to be more "femine."

Extroverted, easily angered

The unconscious repression of anger, guilt, or fear can create illness. No one can truly enjoy life or sustain love and creative achievement without reducing and eliminating negative emotions.

Different women react in different ways to emotional stress and restrictive pressures. Pisces tends to daydream and overindulge in drink or drugs; Sagittarius may travel; Virgo may overwork; Taurus may collect; and Cancer may eat. Aries mostly reacts by fighting back. She is easily frustrated and angered, and she often flies off the handle.

The Aries Woman tends to be naturally extroverted and able to blow off steam, an advantage when it comes to releasing negative emotions. She is usually proud and self-righteous, often finding it easier to show anger than hurt. She is likely to override her guilt about hurting someone and vent her frustrations readily, resembling a child who expects to be excused on the basis of high spirits or inexperience.

High self-esteem, good sense of humor, detached

The Aries Woman is normally quite self-confident, often courageous, and goes after what she wants. Everyone has pangs of anxiety and suffers from fits of insecurity, and she is no exception; but her fears usually fuel, not block, her drive to prove herself. "Get on with it"—no matter what the cost or consequences—is frequently her motto. She consolidates her self-esteem through action and the exercise of leadership. If she opts for a career outside the home, she tends to do so out of a deep need—to earn full self-respect.

She tends to have a fine sense of humor. She likes to laugh and see the absurd side of life. Existential nightmares are not her cup of tea, and she is unlikely to feel sorry for any character patient enough to do nothing but wait for Godot. To Aries, involvement in life is essential, and it seems to her that one can hardly accomplish that without laughter. Her pride may be the only stumbling block that prevents her from laughing gaily at herself as well.

Her sense of humor may sometimes serve to keep her detached from details and from other people's troubles. Aries frequently feels more than a touch of arrogance and superiority, and she may use her humor to shield herself from the complications of the world at large.

Selfish, proud

The Aries Woman, like all fire types, is normally quite selfish. Her insensitivity and impatience may diminish as she matures. Intuitive, perceptive, and proud, she tends to overestimate her own talents. She may go through life with a thinly disguised god complex and a conveniently hazy memory for the frailties of human nature, above all her own.

Under her extroverted expressiveness lies a basic trait that may impede her growth—pride. On the positive side, it may help her to resist failure and defeat. On the negative side, she may manipulate feelings and people to make it appear that she never loses. She must remember that pride is double-edged and try to use it in an affirmative way.

High libido, dislikes details

Early in life, the typical Aries Woman feels unable or unwilling to shoulder heavy emotional involvements. She wants few responsibilities and is apt to cast off restrictions or obligations almost on principle. Rather than expose herself to pain, she may rush on, frustrated and impatient. She will almost surely bail out of those relationships that promise growth only after struggle and confrontation with her deeper self. This tends to change in her thirties, when she may be more tolerant.

She may search for the best, fastest, and most unique love and sex experiences around, but she seldom stops long enough to give people a second chance. She is a quick study and a quick judge but can make some bad mistakes. Though she is loyal once she settles on a commitment, if a Niagara of energy does not flow in her direction, she may just wander off on more adventurous pathways.

She has the passion and appetite for living that the French call *joie de vivre*. Her goal in life is not only to survive but to climb every mountain and test every peak.

Arrogant, blunt, easily bored

The Aries Woman may feel that she knows more and knows it better than most, that she should be first and be unquestionably accepted as best. By viewing herself in permanent competition with others, and by gauging herself in terms of an illusory perfection, she puts herself under a lot of pressure. She tends to be extremely hard on herself and demanding of others.

She is usually frank, blunt, and quick-spoken. She dislikes beating around the bush. If you don't really want an answer to a question you ask Aries, I advise you not to ask. She tends to answer the most embarrassing questions with often embarrassing answers, even on occasions when not asked. Putting her foot in her mouth is an Aries pastime, and discretion is rarely her preferred mode of communication. Aries also dislikes secrets, and devious Scorpio is a challenge to her and tends to drive her to distraction. When Aries feels that she is not "in the know," she can be insufferable with her relentless questions or satirical observations, all designed to ferret out the desired information.

The Aries Woman generally cannot stand being left out, nor can she tolerate boredom. She will sometimes go to extremes to shake up a scene that appears pleasantly tranquil to others but that she experiences as dangerously stifling. She seems constitutionally opposed to restrictions and considers boredom the biggest drain on her energies.

Dynamic, charismatic, catalyst

Some may find Aries difficult to live with, but she is usually the most exciting person around, and a very good friend. A flattering description of her is "dynamic," though others may call her pushy. In any case, the Aries Woman has that indefinable something we call charisma. Energetic and vital, she often attracts people who are bored or depressed, more resigned to routine than she is, and can turn them on to life again.

She is frequently a catalyst even before she knows what the word means. As a teacher, she may inspire her pupils to think in fresh ways. As a parent, she may raise her children to be independent and capable of originality. As a woman, she may choose a lifestyle, or more than one, that is not the norm. By defying social convention, she can show others the value of being a ram rather than an unquestioning sheep.

Huntress, idealist

The Aries Woman tends to like the chase as much or more than the conquest. She is not usually interested in possession, either, preferring the free-spirited, unhampered path of the trailblazer. She may idealistically believe that a new world is coming and that we do better to look ahead rather than backwards. No matter how harsh the present seems, Aries can usually pull herself out of the doldrums, resist the popular "it ain't worth it" philosophy, and go back to the barricades to fight for her cause. Aries usually pursues the positive path and is capable of bringing joy to many people.

Aries relationships

The Aries Woman usually makes a complex, demanding, passionate mate and partner. She has the potential to create a finely tuned, balanced, exciting, offbeat relationship. Like Don Quixote, she is forever searching for an ideal.

Where romance is concerned, Aries believes in giving but also wants the moon. She tends to become overinvolved with people and projects because she thinks this is giving. She may overdo to show her independence and separate identity, but her excesses may also be an avenue of escape from intimacy.

She may unconsciously desire a relationship where no one is labeled strong or weak, where each partner is a leader. "All chiefs and no Indians" appeals to her, and she may test a man mercilessly on his own leadership powers.

For the Aries Woman love is often a battleground. One can usually tell if she cares by the degree to which she argues. If she disagrees with her man over strategy, details, philosophy, love, life, and work, he can relax. This is her prelude to seduction. She more often than not gains energy from lovers' spats and the contest of wills. Watch out, however, for lack of interest or absent-mindedness, for they are signs that she is getting ready to move on.

Aries often dominates her early sexual relationships. In the first part of her life, she tends to be assertive, even masculine, and may be out of touch with her receptivity, vulnerability, and tender side. Her dependencies are usually deeply buried and may be projected onto men. While she needs proof of love from others, she can seldom ask for it or give it. She probably has not yet learned to nurture herself and others on the deepest feeling levels.

The Aries Woman, like other fire signs, tends to be loyal and sweepingly generous, but she needs partners as assertive as she is, partners who demand respect, sensitivity, and equal rights. She must be mentally sparked to be physically turned on. She usually needs lots of space, freedom to change and experiment, to set and meet new challenges. She will remain loyal to anyone or anything as long as the relationship remains exciting, as long as there is mutual respect, and as long as she feels the potential for more inner and outer territories to explore and conquer.

In love, friendship, and marriage, the Aries Woman ideally wants to be totally involved, both sexually and emotionally, but it may take her decades to find out how. Usually it is not until her thirties or later that she learns what she truly wants and needs in love and partnerships. And it generally takes her just as long to find out what she is willing to give. It will often take a wrenching effort for her to learn to replace her "me, myself, and I" mode of relating with a relationship characterized by mutuality.

Childhood

The Aries Woman often grows up identifying with male role models and is usually closer to her father than to her mother. She is often a tomboy and frequently resents being a girl. She may prefer climbing trees with the boys or reading in private to gabbing with her girl friends. All her life she may trust males more than females and feel she understands men better. When her breasts begin to develop and her femaleness becomes inescapably apparent, she may develop a complex about some part of her body. She may throw herself into her studies more than ever and become known as an "intellectual." Some Aries girls prefer being the class "brain" to being sexually attractive, though they may harbor a secret desire to be a sex symbol.

The Aries girl is often angry and frustrated throughout adolescence and may find it difficult to accept that she must grow into a woman, with all that means in our culture. She may be the originator of dutch dates. Conversely, she may decide to flaunt her sexuality and use men. Her hostilities may come out in attempts to dominate people or, more constructively, in various leadership positions at school.

Margaret is a case in point. She grew up an only child, the apple of her father's eye. He treated her more as a son than as a daughter. When Margaret came to see me she was twenty-four, married, mother of two children, and head of various volunteer organizations in her neighborhood. A vivacious, large brunette, she had an engaging laugh, frank and inquisitive eyes, and a nervous habit of twisting Kleenex during our sessions. It seemed to me she wanted to cry, and the wadding of tissues was as good a substitute as any teddy bear.

She had decided to seek counseling, she said, because she felt that her energies were scattered, that she was unclear about her goals, and that she was more hostile than her facade indicated.

I grew up being called by boys' names by my father. He loved me, but I had the feeling it was a conditional love. He wanted me to be outstanding in sports and in school, and the silent message was that being a girl was somehow a handicap. My mother didn't help me much either. She was busy trying to live her own life and thought I pretty much lived my own.

Well, I did have my own life, structured, defined, and fairly under control. In fact, it seems to me that my life has been *overcontrolled*. Even now, everything seems to be running so smoothly that I question it. I don't know whether I am bored, naive, or if I just don't recognize my own good fortune.

I have two lovely children, a good husband, and a stable marriage. I am respected by the family and people in our neighborhood. I think I am a good wife and mother. I don't think I have been a good daughter, however. I feel I let my father down because I am not "the best," a professional, achievement-oriented woman. I also think I let my mother down, for we have never been able to get mother/daughter close. She may have tried. I think I've always resented her for not giving me more mothering in my growing years.

I wasn't sure what was really bothering Margaret, so I asked for more information about her adolescence.

I was a model child until I turned about twelve. Then everything changed. My father pushed me more than ever to prove myself. I continued to get the best grades but became increasingly resentful, and I began to feel that I wasn't respected for just being me, that I constantly had to produce in order to earn his love. I rebelled by becoming very sexy. I started smoking, staying out late, and flaunting everything I had. The more unhappy my parents became, the more uncomfortable I got but I wouldn't admit it. Something was driving me to rebellion, and it seems to me I still haven't got it out of my system.

In the course of psycho-astrological therapy, Margaret focused on what it meant to her to be a woman. She had very mixed feelings about it. She could play the roles required of her, but inside she was still frustrated and angry. She also felt somewhat guilty about it, though she pretended to dismiss this aspect with cheery Aries indifference.

It seemed to me that Margaret had never resolved her own feelings about her sexuality and femininity. Her wild swings between being a bright student and Daddy's "son" and being a provocative, sexy high school girl had not been harmonized. She seemed to feel deep down that she had to "earn" people's love, that she had to be brainy. Though she had taken a traditional feminine route, in some way she found it unacceptable to be a woman. Daddy had taught her that to be a female meant being a second-class citizen; being playful, sexy, and sensual was rebellious behavior and carried little significance in the real world.

Margaret explored her sexual feelings with her husband. Unfortunately, he could not accept the fact that his "solid citizen" wife was suddenly questioning the validity of her way of life.

Eventually they were divorced. For a while Margaret saw only women and told me later that for the first time in her life, she was in touch with all the various shades and subtleties of being female. Her lifestyle in a gay commune was in complete contrast to her situation when we first met. Later still, she remarried and opened her own business.

How the Aries Woman relates: lovers and other intimates

The Aries Woman in general relates better to men than to women. Many a romance starts as a friendship and then becomes a working relationship. She usually needs to be mentally stimulated in order to be physically turned on more than once by the same man.

The Aries Woman is capable of stripping a male of his ego trappings and the protective symbols of his masculinity. The fact that she has a female body and a more or less male way of thinking gives her the edge in getting inside a man. At her worst, she may use what she knows to control and dominate him. At her best, she can build a rare camaraderie with him.

She needs a large arena to show her strength, and she would rather risk a loss than not try at all. She usually needs a partner or lover who is active and involved or she may have trouble respecting him; and she may also want a basis on which to test him other than his performance in bed.

The Aries Woman tends to be intensely competitive with those she likes or loves and to disdain losers. This combination puts her, as well as those she relates to, in a double bind. If she wins, she may lose respect for a friend or lover and end the relationship. If she loses, the same thing may happen for different reasons.

Like a spoiled child, she wants her way and wants it now. She is arrogant, frank, and inquisitive. She usually wants to be reassured by the man she has chosen that she is first and best, and she shuns a relationship in which she feels unappreciated or without control.

She respects power more than submissiveness, bluntness more than discretion. She demands a lot, gives some, and will always try to win. Until she finds true love, she often gets her greatest pleasure from hunting and being in control. She frequently enjoys putting the moves on and pursuing her quarry. She may think nothing of going after a man, and she gets a kick out of running everything, even the lovemaking. But much of this behavior may be bravado or acting, almost a challenge to herself—a self-focused training course in how to overcome and win.

A principal trouble spot for Aries is likely to be her partner's resentment at her attempts to run the relationship. She is almost always mystified and challenged by, yet fearful of, people who can see her vulnerabilities. She may secretly want a man who will discover, explore, and love her hidden self, one to whom she can surrender—but when she finds him, she will almost surely try to dominate him, outwit him, and fight him to the utmost!

The Aries Woman in love

At the beginning of a romance, the Aries Woman can intrigue and attract almost any man. She has unusual charm and magnetism, a penetrating mind, an appealing, fresh honesty, a strong will, and a powerful "aura."

She is usually perceptive, honest, disdainful of pretense. She deals directly and tends to confront men about hypocritical attitudes, sex roles that create inequality, and habits that result in boredom and the deadening of relationships.

The Aries Woman usually falls in love easily and is often more in love with the idea of movement and excitement than with the man himself. Sometimes he may be incidental to her needs, just a temporary partner in a sexual adventure currently labeled love.

She may find it difficult to discriminate between long-lasting love and infatuation. Since she tends to resist deeper self-knowledge, she is frequently victimized by her own misconceptions. I have met Aries women in their forties who admit that they know little about their underlying motives and still make choices as impulsively as ever. If she is lucky, the Aries Woman finds a man with whom she can settle for quite some time. If not, she is bound to experience a variety of upsets in her love life, though these seldom block her quixotic search.

When she is lastingly in love, the Aries Woman blooms like a rare flower. She glows with vitality, elan, and pride. Her energy doubles (if possible), and her happiness is infectious. For probably the first time in her life, she begins to know the pleasure of being receptive.

Aries in love is compelling, throwing herself totally into the experience. She may go through a very basic reevaluation of herself and her values as a result of love. She opens her senses and feelings more fully. She may become more patient, sensuous, and self-indulgent. She is also apt to indulge others more and become tolerant for the first time. Her perspective of time changes as she begins to understand why so many people enjoy luxuriating in the moment, how lovemaking can slow one down and be all-encompassing. She may try to live a more unscheduled life and enjoy the fact that there are no deadlines in love.

Aries in love learns how to give as well as how to receive. Love teaches her how to consider another's needs and feelings as important as her own. At the same time, she may learn to allow her individuality to bloom in the hothouse atmosphere of sharing. She is apt to have distrusted partnership previously, fearing it would bar her individual progress. Even when she is in love, the Aries Woman is unlikely to lose sight of her demands. She wants and needs a very particular type of man in order to make the relationship work in the long run.

What kind of lover she needs

A man who isn't completely sure of his masculinity and strength should probably not tangle with the Aries Woman. A man who is not willing or ready to confront issues and emotions should also avoid her. On the other hand, a man who is aware of his own humanity and above all wishes to be challenged in order to grow is invited to enter a relationship with Aries. A man who offers her emotional support, who helps her to admit and embrace her weaknesses, who truly wants a woman with the potential to be a whole, independent being—this is a man the Aries woman can love and who can keep her forever as a lover or friend.

Everyone needs lovers and friends who provide bridges to feelings that are waiting to be freed. The Aries Woman needs a partner who can tolerate psychic warfare, one who accepts the energy of anger and assertion as easily as the energy of love. She needs a lover who can see behind her mask of toughness to bring out the softness underneath, a man strong enough to be sensitive, a man who is threatened neither by his own dependence needs or by her projected ones.

To love the Aries Woman means to perform a constant balancing act between her demand to be first and the demands imposed by work and by other intimates. In return, however, she can raise a man's spirits sky-high. The lucky man who survives the initial testing will be made to feel he is the most special creature walking the earth. And in the heart of his Aries Woman, he surely is!

Patterns in the Aries Woman's sexual relationships

In her sexual relationships, the Aries Woman tends to display the following patterns (which, to some extent, apply to platonic ties as well).

She probably dabbles in early sexual experiments. She may be a tomboy or be "masculine" in her thinking and at times in her clothing, but she is always vital and magnetic. She is likely to be fascinated with sex and consider it as much a female as a male prerogative (this view may be ahead of the times).

She often marries early, impulsively, passionately, and to the wrong man. She is bound to give it a valiant try, however, and may stick it out because of a sense of responsibility. She may also feel she is teaching herself a lesson in patience (this is not necessarily the best means, in my opinion).

Often she finds that love and sex do not necessarily coincide in her life. If she is happy with her mate, she is bound to be monogamous. If not, she is bound to play around but less likely to experience guilt than many women.

The Aries Woman is likely to experience true love at least once in her life, often in a premarital or postmarital context. She may choose a husband who is not her romantic ideal but is a good provider.

She is usually able to find solutions to problems in her lifestyle. She may be involved in a fulfilling career and use it as an outlet for love problems. She may be able to change enough to make her marriage or relationship work.

If she divorces, generally she allows herself a good long time before trying the knot again. She tends to enjoy her freedom and likes to operate independently.

What Aries needs to learn

The Aries Woman needs to confront her own tendency to repress weakness and make others responsible. She must stop testing her men and begin to assume half the responsibility for failure or loss of direction in the relationship. She must avoid blaming the man she loves for not being "strong" enough. She needs to learn to listen more sensitively and to become more patient. Above all, she must be aware of and overcome her tendency to disclose only so much and to try to control much more.

To make relationships work, she must live and let live. She must learn to respect and accept another's rhythm, pace, melody. She must eventually learn that she can be receptive without feeling inferior, soft without succumbing to weakness, and undemanding without fearing lack of response. When she learns to flow, when she realizes that *letting* it happen is often better than *making* it happen, relationships will work.

To be truly autonomous, the Aries Woman must recognize and open up the repressed feminine side of her nature. To be truly strong, she must recognize and embrace her own vulnerability. Slowly she must look inside and see that what usually underlies her frantic pace and her demands is the fear of letting others in, the fear of letting go emotionally. When she feels safe in a relationship, she may be ready to initiate some changes. She may then give in to her need to be taken care of, to be stroked, to receive gifts of love and fantasy to weave into new patterns.

The Aries Woman must learn to ask for love and assistance when she needs it. She finds it easier to ask for practical help, though this too may be a minor blow to her pride. But asking for emotional support she may consider tantamount to admitting that there is something fundamentally wrong. Fire signs who have high energy patterns and live by constantly running, giving, controlling, and seldom receiving can burn out too early.

The Aries Woman who does confront her deep fears and who begins to share without resistance may be pleasantly surprised. She may find out that what she called love or friendship until then was only an imitation of the real thing.

Aries sexuality

The Aries Woman approaches sex as she does everything else in life: zestfully, impulsively, and with total commitment. She gives all she has and takes all she can get in return. She is open to anything—but don't ask about tomorrow—sexual exclusivity is not her bag. The challenge of the hunt excites her.

Aries is an exceptionally passionate, sensual, and sexual woman. Romantic, erotic, and vain, she needs monumental reassurance from a sexual partner. When she feels insecure, she is jealous and possessive. When she feels secure, she is as loyal as any fixed sign (Taurus, Scorpio, Leo, Aquarius) though still wildly unpredictable.

Aries' sex secret is that while she enjoys being and frequently is sexually dominant, she is secretly hoping for a partner who appreciates and flows with sexuality highlighted by extreme swings from dominance to passivity, an exceptionally live eroticism, and an equally strong need for mental stimulation to spark and parallel the physical turn-on.

Sexual energy can be positive or negative. The Aries Woman flows with dynamism, vibrancy, and power, but when blocked, she is horny, bitchy, impatient, angry, and finally ill. Repressed anger, fear, and guilt anesthetize the female capacity for pleasure.

Aries has an enormous appetite for pleasure. She will try anything once and appreciates a man who is openminded. She prefers varied sexual techniques, feathers and fur, velvet and candlelight, fantasy and music, vibrators and leather. Public sex is a secret fantasy, waiting to be fulfilled. The man who can help turn her fantasies into realities commands her affection and loyalty. She looks for a man she can trust enough to exchange fantasies with, and sometimes sexual roles.

The Aries Woman needs a partner who is highly sensitive and can bring out in her a receptivity and flow that are not much in evidence during the daily display of fireworks. She wants to be made love to slowly. She prefers partners who do not rush her to a speedy commitment or to the quick completion of intercourse. Lady Aries chases rainbows and makes the world revolve all day, so bed is often the only place where she can relax and go slowly.

Aries seeks total pleasure, and it is a testimony to her drive that her path is littered with the bodies of those who didn't fit the bill. Secret and adventurous places, exotic haunts, and dangerous territory all lure the Aries Woman. What she finds, she wants; what she wants, she wants to rule.

Like the Scorpio Woman, to whom sex means pure power, the experienced Aries Woman choreographs and executes the sex act for a definite purpose. With an eye to the door should the experience be dull or the man weak, she initiates sex and directs it in order to test the male. Will he match her in humor, in willingness to experiment, in ability to change roles? Can he take over? Can he also lie back and take a passive role?

However, Aries experiences plenty of internal conflict. On the one hand, she wants total pleasure and suspects that it ultimately comes through committed emotional bonding. On the other, she likes to keep her sexual options open. Mental curiosity, love of discovery, and the desire to test old rules and behavior in new territory never die. The problem of how to have her cake and eat it keeps the Aries Woman occupied.

Our culture teaches women especially to find love, sex, and commitment all in the same relationship. The Aries Woman tends to split love and sex. She may have many sexual relationships over the decades, but she will have had few deep emotional bonds. It is easier by far for her to engage herself sexually and intellectually than to involve her heart. For some time, she finds it easier to conquer and leave than to stay and explore mutual vulnerabilities. Though capable of loving deeply, she resists her own need to do so. The more the Aries Woman feels emotionally attracted to a man, the more cautiously she pursues the relationship.

In bed we are all vulnerable. We have to anticipate "letting it all hang out" sooner or later if we have a good partner. The Aries Woman picks partners slowly and carefully; she knows that from the start a sexual relationship can present more challenge than she bargained for. She may have many partners, but she will have only one true lover at a time.

She dislikes routines in anything, including sex. She tunes out and turns off if a partner is applying preconceived, automatic, self-conscious stimulation techniques. Other women may find this a turnoff too, but the Aries Woman is quicker to speak up and leave. Describing her connubial lovemaking, one Aries (who stayed with the relationship) said, 'I lay there undergoing my husband's ministrations as he meandered through his ritual that carried him to orgasm. . . . All the while, I was mentally ticking off what page of our well-thumbed marriage manual he was struggling with. I knew that when he got to page 16, he was nearing climax." This lady solved her problem by having other, much more imaginative and longer-lasting lovers.

There are two clear-cut possibilities for the Aries Woman to gain sexual freedom. One is in an anonymous situation, such as a sex party or a one-night stand. The second is when she is truly joined in loving union. Only these extremes really excite her. In the former, she has no investments, and her challenge is to give a great performance. In the latter, she is challenged to express herself totally and join her deepest self to another while maintaining a separate identity.

When Aries really lets go, she turns into a tigress. She doesn't allow fear or guilt to interfere with sexual exchange and gratification. She screams, thrashes, sobs, scratches, and finally exhausts herself in ecstasy. Sex becomes the ultimate trip, a cosmic experience.

To fully participate in lovemaking, one must utilize all the senses. The Aries Woman is comfortable with vocalizing during lovemaking. She seems to know that sounds enrich communication and conduct sexual pleasure through the whole body. She must make a conscious effort, however, to completely use her sense of touch. Though touch is a key to sensual pleasure for Aries, it isn't too well developed. She is too rushed to touch and feel textures around her. She needs to slow down, to caress the bright flowers she already appreciates visually, to rub velvet across her cheek or brush her partner's hair with her palm. She needs to remember to close her eyes and feel the cool texture of satin sheets, the fuzzy nubbiness of wool rugs, the wispy delicacy of lace.

Though the Aries Woman has to work to use her own sense of touch, she loves to *be* touched. She likes tender, light stroking and a feathery touch to help her relax and begin lovemaking. Once she gets turned on, she prefers harder stimulation. Many an Aries has told me she becomes frustrated if her partner continues to caress a breast softly when she would rather have it kneaded. Here, honest communication is the only answer.

The sexual cycles of the Aries Woman seem to be related to the fact that hers is the earliest sign of the Zodiac. She is most arousable and receptive in the early hours of the morning. We know from recent research that male sexual hormones reach a peak at that time. For Aries, it is the most natural time to couple.

The Aries Woman, like all women, likes a man who knows himself and accepts his sexuality. But she seems to prefer a man who finishes the sex act with hard thrusting. She also prefers a man who allows her freedom of movement while guiding her to receive the full impact of his penetration and his rhythm.

The Aries Woman likes aggressive fantasies that involve exhibitionism and power. She often visualizes herself wearing a black garter belt, stockings, and boots, carrying a whip, and acting out a scenario of sexual domination in front of a frenzied audience. Another favorite fantasy involves initiations. She loves to initiate women as well as men into sex and to imagine being introduced to a new sexual trip. Group sex and homosexual encounters are frequent fantasy themes.

Women who are relaxed about their own sexuality can please themselves with masturbation. Since the Aries Woman feels comfortable with her own body, she enjoys masturbation. She also likes to try new sex toys. Dildos, feathers, artificial penises, massagers, benwa balls, leather and bondage outfits—all are potential sexual accessories for Aries.

Aries anger

A major block to healthy sexual expression is anger, which is connected to low self-esteem and the feeling of being ineffectual. The struggle for self-esteem and a sense of importance as a person is a basic human concern. Sexuality in an angry relationship is not a source of pleasure, nor is it a basis on which a couple can share growth and build mutual respect. Repressed or improperly expressed anger is destructive to self-esteem and to relationships. Anger properly communicated and directed can be a powerful motivating force, an agent of change, and a personal resource.

For the Aries Woman, anger is a time-tested coping mechanism that comes more easily than tears. She uses anger to attack when she feels defensive, to cover inner doubts and fears, and to manipulate her way to personal power. What she loses is intimacy.

Repressed sexuality produces anger. Repressed anger produces inadequate sexual functioning. A woman who smiles when she feels like screaming, agrees when she really wants to disagree, or gets a headache whenever the subject of sex is brought up by her partner—may wind up anorgasmic. She often seeks many sex partners in a vain search for satisfaction. She psychologically castrates her male partners by never climaxing and sabotages herself by repeatedly putting herself in situations where she can't possibly get what she needs. Love is based not on self-denial but on the affirmation of self. One who is angry cannot be affirmative. Angry women hold back sexually. Improper or poor sexual stimulation is only a secondary cause for sensory, orgasmic impoverishment.

Obviously, ridding oneself of anger is the answer. However, wild fights that grow in volume and frequency are destructive and are not recommended. Controlled-release fights, the method described by Dr. George Bach in *The Intimate Enemy*, are constructive. In these, partners begin with honest, level-headed statements of their anger and needs and conclude by negotiating for space, change, or compromise. Blowing off steam by beating a mattress or some other inanimate object is also recommended unless done with the intent to punish or blame the partner.

The Aries Woman usually knows when she's angry, and this puts her in a minority. Most people have trouble identifying anger, which is often called depression, masochism, or frustration instead. It is essential that people recognize and admit when they are angry and learn ways to share their anger constructively.

The Aries Woman in her twenties thinks nothing of expressing anger explosively and manipulatively. She won't hesitate to leave the table in the midst of an argument, walk out, and slam the door—especially if she realizes she is losing the fight. In short, she gets in a rage and runs, attempting to show the party who dared to arouse her who the real boss is. What is missing is the realization that she *chose* to get angry and the commitment to work through the anger with the other person. At this stage, she is using anger as a power ploy. She is likely to leave many sexual partners dissatisfied until she stops running.

In her thirties, the Aries Woman simmers down a bit. She begins to disclose her inner workings to her partner. She learns to discuss what makes her angry, to reveal how this relates to childhood experiences, to acknowledge the fears and insecurities her anger covers. She now throws dishes and fights it out right away. She uses her anger as facilitator and intimacy maker, bulldozing psychic walls instead of raising them. At this point she needs a man who will listen, whose ego can take the periodic explosions, the exploratory conversations, and the heated sex.

In her forties, the Aries Woman definitely mellows out. In mid-life, she learns to balance, to get in touch with the opposite Libra qualities: harmonizing the "I" and the "We," cooperating, sharing. She has now accepted anger as a fact of life and has begun to figure out how best to use it as a catalyst. In mid-life the Aries Woman is more afraid of loneliness than women with other signs. She begins to hunger for a solid union. She has created a pattern of destructive and unforgettable exchanges, of stern independence, and she now sees the need to change in order to grow into the Libra nature which makes her complete. She no longer cherishes being in a position to slam the door on problems and arguments . . . particularly if she has no one to leave behind that door.

In her fifties, the Aries Woman has, to a degree, tamed her

anger and made it a tool for growth. She has finally learned to manage confrontations diplomatically without feeling an affront to her natural pride. She has learned that her ego is not enhanced by anger and that significant relationships will not advance to the sound of screeching cars and aggressive, nonproductive warfare.

The Aries Woman feels her anger is justifiable. She feels superior to the person who makes her angry, and in the heat of the moment it is she who expects an apology. Basically, this reaction stems from her pride. She has difficulty taking any step she believes will leave her in an inferior position.

In order to demilitarize her anger, she must recognize those situations where she *needs* to get angry: to gain energy to change an old situation, to shore up the courage to be honest, to be heard by someone who normally ignores what she has to say. Choosing to be angry is a pragmatic policy that builds self-respect through the awareness that a choice has been made. The Aries Woman must recognize that as long as she uses anger as a weapon she cannot expect to have a lasting and sexually potent intimate relationship. She herself must exemplify caring behavior, which never includes destructively used anger.

A man would have to be brought up very atypically and be exceptionally sensitive and bright to understand the complexities of the Aries Woman's anger. The burden is on the woman to recognize that in order to build intimacy she must do away with unproductive explosions.

I advocate a five-step system to settle differences with a partner while using anger productively.

1 Decide on a no-fault relationship. No one needs to be blamed or made to feel guilty.
2 Agree to acknowledge the anger you feel for your partner. Decide not to let anger last for more than a day. Decide not to discuss a major issue when either of you is hurried or under stress.
3 Accept unconditionally your right, as well as your partner's, to be angry.
4 Renounce the right to vent anger hurtfully just to get your way. Learn to say, "I am angry with you, but you know that I will not attack you." Hurt feelings can be aired without blame and attacks. Be specific, keep your tone even, and do not let one incident contaminate the whole relationship. If you feel unable

to keep a level tone, let your anger out first in another room by taking a bat, rubber hose, or pillow and beating on a convenient, unbreakable object.

5 Ask for your partner's help in dealing with your anger. No one likes being the sender or receiver of anger, but a coalition is unbeatable. You are enlisting a potential enemy as a friend.

To use this process, the Aries Woman must specifically renounce the idea that relationships are founded on competition and instead embrace the spirit of cooperation. She must learn to give up using anger to call the shots or punish a wrongdoer. Finally, she must recognize that inner harmony can be achieved and outer harmony maintained only when she has learned to respect another's rights as much as her own. When the Aries Woman learns to use anger constructively, as a prelude to change and a pragmatic way of keeping her relationship free of debris, she will be opting for free-flowing sexual energy and the potential to feel and share total pleasure.

Aries lifestyles

Monogamy and nonmonogamy

Monogamy is defined as sexual and emotional exclusivity. Strictly speaking, this makes most Americans, married or not, nonmonogamous, for few people today are emotionally monogamous. But here I will use monogamy in the loose sense, meaning only sexual exclusivity.

A woman may be looking for characteristics in a husband different from those she seeks in a lover. The Aries Woman is especially choosy when selecting a provider and father to her children. She knows herself to be capable of grand passions, but she also knows they need to be grounded. Thus, she may choose a husband who fulfills her needs for stability and respect in the eyes of the community, one who is an upholder of form and continuity (not an Aries forte).

As a mate, the Aries Woman is ardent, loyal, sentimental, and practical. If she is satisfied with the choice she has made, she may direct her need for excitement into sexual passion with her husband, but the Aries Woman often carries on several platonic friendships with men. Her need for people, stimulation, and challenge can be met in multiple relationships that celebrate her multiple selves.

The following represent typical situations that could influence the Aries Woman to become nonmonogamous.

1 Need for adventure. She is on a trip and is suddenly attracted to someone. She is likely to act on impulse and jump into the experience. She suffers no guilt since in her mind this is no reflection on her marriage.
2 Boredom with husband. Sooner or later, the Aries Woman may find that platonic friendships do not fill the vacuum created by the waning of marital passion or by lack of growth in the partner or relationship. Although she can be driven at times into melodramatic and risky affairs, she is far more likely to be revitalized than to be destroyed.
3 Low self-esteem, repressed anger. She may go off on sex hunts to prove herself. She may disclose her infidelity to her husband at a later date, ostensibly in the name of honest communication. Usually, her real aim is to spite him. This is a poor strategy in which sex and anger are simultaneously misused. In the best circumstances, these incidents can serve to open up feelings and to galvanize the partners to take necessary action.
4 Lack of respect for partner. The Aries Woman cannot love someone she does not respect. This situation is deadly and usually means the end of the partnership or marriage in any viable form. If the shell survives, sex will not be an important part of it. The Aries Woman who finds her husband emotionally dependent on her for his survival, much as he was as a small child with his mother, feels stifled and eventually rebels. She will probably be driven to multiple affairs and seek out a man who is more her match. She will not hesitate to bail out of the original relationship emotionally and legally.
5 Extreme jealousy by the partner. This can drive the Aries Woman to seek less restrictive relationships. She cannot stand to have her independent movement controlled or her freedom questioned.

Alternative lifestyles

Monogamous marriage appears headed for trouble, and many people are experimenting with different ways in which a couple can survive as a unit both emotionally and economically. The

Aries Woman is in the forefront of many social movements. In the area of expanded lifestyles, she may be interested in the following:

Intimate networks: The Aries Woman will willingly and wholeheartedly participate in this movement, which advocates friendship with both sexes, neither ruling out nor requiring occasional sex.

Communes: These are not a prime choice for the Aries Woman, for they provide much competition from other women in close quarters and entail many routine household chores, which Aries can't abide. In a commune, people may agree to share sex partners and rotate kitchen and cleaning duties. The Aries Woman, while open to anything, finds it difficult to have relationships where all are Indians and where leadership is episodic and dictated by communal decision making.

Group marriage or extended families: This type of situation is suited to the Aries Woman. While she may be uncomfortable with other females on her turf, the advantages may outweigh the difficulties if the friendships are solid and sex is shared comfortably by all. The forecast: she will probably be able to stick with this arrangement and use it as an opportunity to work through her fears of homosexuality, act out her bisexuality, and learn to be "we" -conscious as opposed to self-absorbed. She will eventually want to revert to a one-to-one situation that takes less energy to control, though she will miss the scope, both passionate and intellectual, of group marriage.

Ménage à trois: This is a good temporary arrangement in which couples may share their sex lives and lifestyles with a third person. The Aries Woman prefers, as many other women do, that the third partner be male. If jealousy does not rear its head and territorial imperative does not become more important than passion, this is a workable relationship.

Open marriage: Because of her frankness, the Aries Woman is better suited to this revolutionary arrangement than most other types. If determined, she can make a go of it. I suspect that she will be more involved on principle than from gut desire. Though she prefers to be honest and dreams of complete soul-baring with her mate, she will have to work to put it into practice.

Gay bisexual lifestyle: I have met an unusually large number of openly gay Aries women. Many have come out of traditional marriage and gone into gay partnerships. This lifestyle provides Aries with a forum for her avant-garde beliefs, her androgynous sexuality, and her anger at sexist socialization. Because she tends to live in extremes, she may swing back to heterosexual behavior again with equally strong convictions.

New age Lady Chatterley: This may be a prototypical situation for the married Aries Woman who is not fulfilled by her husband sexually. Because she is basically loyal, she remains married, but she will also search for outlets for her primitive sexuality. She will find many lovers and will rarely be compelled to destroy her marriage.

The common denominator of all this is change. People need change. In our twenties, our sexual and emotional needs are radically different from what they are in our fifties. Marriage partners may choose parallel paths and be content without ever reaching a real meeting of minds; or they may converge at different points and find a new level of union; or their paths may diverge totally. What varies from sign to sign is not the need to experiment and the reality of change, but the courage to take the risk involved in exploring alternatives.

The Aries Woman is outstanding in courage and risk-taking ability. Her personality qualifies her to be a leader in the area of alternate lifestyles. Though she is jealous and possessive, she is also committed to social change, adventure, revolution.

We have to recognize the inverse relationship between monogamy and sexual pleasure and the direct link between sexual pleasure and the reduction of aggression and violence. The Aries Woman can lead the way in the creation of a new society which will take us in this direction.

Summing up Aries

In general, all the Aries woman wants is everything! Her healthiest and most fundamental drive is to be totally in charge of herself and her own life.

As she goes through various cycles, she can be difficult, bitchy, or demanding. She may take out her frustrations on other people. She may blame outsiders for failures and weaknesses she fears are hers but resists "owning" or acknowledging.

It is fascinating to reflect that in order to grow and be fulfilled the Aries Woman must work on many of the qualities of her opposite, Libra. The Aries Woman needs to develop cooperative attitudes, more respect for others, patience, a dash of sensuous self-indulgence, and a better appreciation of her environment. She must learn that there are times when the needs of others take precedence over her impulses or desires, and times when it is in her own best long-term interest to give up some of her insistent clamoring for me-first, me-best independence.

John Donne said, "No man is an island." No woman need try to accomplish everything proudly on her own. Aries must realize that she can slow down, enjoy each step on her path and share her joy. In life one cannot always accomplish a journey directly from A to C without occasionally detouring to B. One must be prepared to savor and accept each experience as a learning phase. This may be especially difficult for Aries, who would probably rather "do her thing" or "stir up some action."

The Aries Woman may resent the fact that life and worldly success in a male-dominated society are in many ways more difficult for a woman. She may find it hard to appreciate some traditional feminine shelters. On the one hand she may feel trapped by her own masculinity, while on the other she may appreciate its potential to contribute to her happiness. She constantly wonders how to deal with her ambition and need for adventure and how to find love.

Aries must learn how to take her potentially negative traits and turn them to positive use. She must be ready to examine her own excesses. When she gets in a hurry, what is she missing? Which traditionally female roles has she assumed, and which has she rejected? What brings her joy and what upsets her? What has she done about traditionally male roles? Each day, she may have to rethink how to live her life, how to balance "mothering" with professional drive, activity with passivity. The Aries Woman must find ways to blend sexual love with competition, alliance with domination, dependence with independence, aggression with softness. For her, self-development comes as much from facing fear and sharing loneliness as from outer activity and triumphant change.

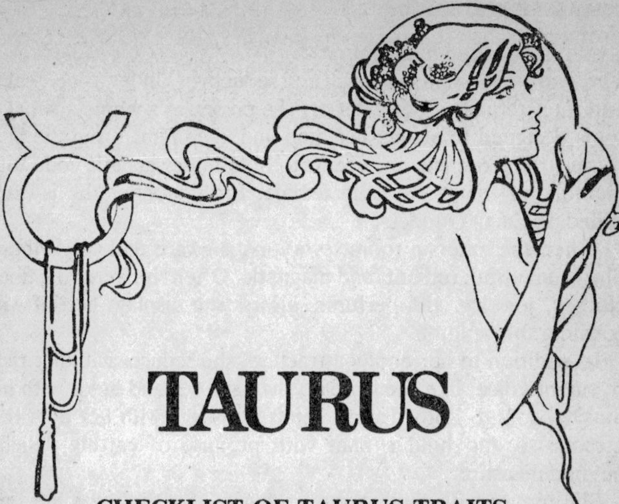

TAURUS

CHECKLIST OF TAURUS TRAITS

Note: This checklist describes the traits of one *phase* only; if it doesn't seem to fit you, check other lists to find the phase you are in right now.

1. Romantic
2. Artistic
3. Self-conscious
4. Habit-bound
5. Dogmatic
6. Organizational, Managerial
7. Gentle
8. Self-indulgent, Lazy
9. Possessive
10. Luxury- and Comfort-loving
11. Appreciative
12. Sensuous
13. Cautious
14. Stubborn
15. Persistent, Tenacious
16. Jealous
17. Placid
18. Shy
19. Conservative
20. Money-maker
21. Sentimental
22. Greedy
23. Affectionate
24. Self-righteous
25. Honest
26. Dependable
27. Pragmatic
28. Methodical
29. Builder
30. Kind
31. Productive
32. Patient
33. Tolerant
34. Humble, Self-deprecating
35. Nature-loving

Taurus personality

General traits and background

The Taurus Woman is sensual and seductive. Under a cool, calm, and intellectually aloof exterior, she possesses a whole arsenal of tools designed to attract her man and keep him. From the bedroom to the kitchen, she seems to hold in her genetic code total memory of things eternally female. Little wonder she is often called an Earth Goddess.

When she enters a room, everyone is aware that she is there. She is beautiful, radiant, and magnetic. Often she wears the finest clothes, jewelry, and perfume; always she displays herself with considerable aplomb.

In addition to her bodily attraction, she seduces with her rich, resonant voice; like the Lorelei, she captures and holds with her musical sound. Lady Taurus sends messages with her eyes that mesmerize and hold a man with promise of earthly delights beyond measure.

She moves with the grace of a dancer, for she loves her own body and cares for it well. Having control of herself, she is a master illusionist and will often create just the environment necessary to complete the fantasies of her loved ones.

Physical contact is important to the Taurus Woman. She needs to be needed, touched, and fondled. She expresses much of her caring through sex, but she is never in a hurry. She expects the very best in love and sex and settles for nothing less.

She fancies her own environment and likes to entertain at home. Since she is a gourmet cook, her parties usually feature the best food, the finest accessories, and the most exciting people she can find, all coddled in a relaxed and luxurious atmosphere.

Taurus is the second sign of the Zodiac, Fixed Earth. The fixed part gives her obstinacy, persistence, tenacity, dependability, and sometimes a rather pompous, self-righteous air; while the earth imparts a solid, conservative, materialistic quality that produces a salt-of-the-earth woman, sensual and slightly bawdy.

Each sign of the Zodiac is said to be "ruled" by a planet and its vibrations. Taurus is ruled by Venus, the goddess of love and beauty. Venus and all the qualities associated with her affect the life of the Taurus Woman. Luxury without guilt delights the Venusian nature.

The Taurus-*type* woman is one who has the sun or other important planets in Taurus, planets in the second house (the natural house of Taurus), a Taurus ascendant, a powerfully aspected Venus. Taurus types are also those who are temporarily going through a Taurus *phase*. In this case, the person need have *no planets* located in the sign of Taurus. The Taurus type is described by the checklist of traits at the beginning of this chapter. The Taurus phase has the following characteristics:

1 A desire to control the material resources of life in order to bring about security and leisure.
2 A need to possess and control, be it things or people.
3 Transformation through the release of material concerns; the regeneration of values.
4 Dogmatism based on selfish desires rather than rationality based on objective facts.
5 A deep love of nature that transcends the material and brings harmony with all living things (the meeting of Pan in *The Wind in the Willows* comes to mind).

The Taurus phase is also characterized by its duality. A dichotomy between the pursuit of material gain and the ideals of spiritual beauty often causes inner turmoil. Compulsive spending needs to be curbed lest the deeper spiritual values be sacrificed. A constant war between body and soul also exists, since the pleasures of sex and the good life often receive a disproportionate amount of energy. Balance and harmony between these two forces must exist for the Taurus Woman to be happy.

The Taurus Woman lives a simple yet complex life. However, unlike her Scorpio sister, who lives on many secret levels, the Taurus Woman is very up-front about her life and about who and what she enjoys. Simple pleasures appeal to her—good sex, good food, and good company, usually in that precise order.

Taurus is the constellation that governs money, Venus is the planet that rules love; and these two qualities may not be as unrelated as they first seem to be. Love is what we feel for the people and things we desire to have closest to us. Money enables the Taurus Woman to possess many of the things and travel to many of the places she holds dear. Love, however, can only be *freely* given, and this is sometimes a hard lesson for the Taurus Woman to learn.

Her concern for ownership colors the fabric of her life. Even the smallest item is catalogued and remembered. Woe to the person who discards one precious scrap of paper, an old letter, or an out-of-date magazine without first asking; the wrath of the bull will descend even when small possessions are threatened. One can imagine, then, the red fury when someone tries to take her man—her most precious possession.

A key word for her is *resourceful*. She has a knack for manipulating the world's resources for her own personal use. Her looks, her talents, and the things she owns are all resources that can assist her in achieving what she desires. The greatest challenge for the Taurus Woman is to get outside herself and beyond her possessions. The love of luxury and comfort begets selfish tendencies in her, and she then cannot understand the needs of others.

Romantic, sentimental

Much has been said about the practical and materialistic side of the Taurus Woman, but few people are aware of the deep romanticism that runs in her veins. Send her a rose (which she dearly loves), and she will love you forever. From that single rose her rich imagination will fill vases with the most perfect bouquets. The romance factor cannot be underestimated. Lady Taurus would feel right at home in King Arthur's court. The thought of a knight on a white horse is enough to make any red-blooded Taurian consider throwing over friends, family, and job to follow him wherever he beckons (which she has been known to do).

If you have ever wondered who in the audience was crying softly during the wedding ceremony, chances are it was Taurus. She is very sentimental, and anything that evokes past memories or that is strikingly beautiful will cause the tears to flow. A visit to her attic is like a trip back into her life. I know one Taurus lady who has kept every letter she ever received, all tied up in neat packages tucked away in a trunk. A word of advice to the Taurus Woman: excessive attachment to these sentimental memories is not in your best interests. One of your biggest challenges is to let go of many past memories and live completely in the present.

Self-conscious

Early in her life, the Taurus Woman may be painfully self-conscious. Her body may seem to be awkward; the parts may not seem to fit together too well. I have always thought Cinderella was probably a Taurus. Sensitive to the taunting of her sisters, and unaware of the great potential she had, the poor creature was not aware of the transformation that would soon take place.

As time passes, her innate sense of self becomes stronger, and the Taurus Woman learns how to use it to her best advantage. Although she does not always have a good feel for her relationships with others, she has no question about her place in the universe. Since she has such an idealized concept of beauty, the Taurus Woman needs to accept herself as she is and not as she thinks she should be. Once this happens, she will be well on her way to becoming what she really is, a beautiful and aware person.

Artistic

The Taurus Woman is never happier than when enhancing the beauty of life. Her home will be a harmonious blend of the traditional and the new. Since everything adds to the creation of the proper atmosphere for her love nest, she studies every detail.

She loves music and may play an instrument herself. Her rich, sensuous voice is one of her finest qualities, and she delights in using it. Drawing and painting also come easily to her. Her fine sense of proportion, keen powers of observation, and subtle use of color make her well suited to the act of putting paint on a canvas and to the life of the artist. Her enjoyment in touching and feeling objects makes her a fine sculptor as well. Molding clay enhances her sense of power, and for the same reason she may take up pottery, which allows her to reconnect with clay—a product of the earth from which she comes and to which she is drawn.

Her greatest artistic achievement, however, is the art of fine living. Each action in her life is carefully drawn, and each possession carefully arranged.

Habit-bound

The Taurus Woman is a creature of habit. Her breakfast menu, her morning rituals, even the route she takes to her job, seldom vary since they have proven to be effective and efficient. Being of the earth, the Taurus Woman is familiar with the cycles of life. She recognizes the ordered progression of the sun, the moon, and the planets as they form their patterns in the sky, and she relates this order to her own life. Cycles are measurements of change. Life does not progress without change, and change necessarily involves some crisis. The Greeks gave us the word *crisis*, which does not imply catastrophe but rather suggests a time to decide—a time for decision.

As aware as the Taurus Woman is of the necessity for change, she often digs in her heels and stubbornly refuses to acknowledge it. She procrastinates and waits until the time for decision is past and then allows familiar patterns and habits to dictate change for her. She must learn to make conscious decisions, or she will be at the mercy of the cycles she knows so well.

As an exercise in instituting change in her life, the Taurus Woman needs to break routine and try different things—a new route home, shopping at a different market, sleeping late and breakfasting in bed. She will find that breaks in routine bring welcome relief from the boredom of habit.

Self-righteous, dogmatic

The Taurus lady *knows* when she is right. Deep within her is a bell that seems to ring when she is. Imbued with a deep sense of order and the natural progression of events, she quickly translates this into the everyday fabric of life. You may question her about almost anything, and she will answer. But never question her source, for often even she does not know from whence her information came, and she seldom questions it.

Despite her shyness, her self-deprecation, and her poor self-image, she has a deep self-respect. Whatever the external realities, she is able to maintain the worth of her own self. There is a thin red line, however, between self-worth and self-righteousness. The line can become even thinner if the Taurus Woman becomes successful and secure. She is apt to forget her own hard-won battles to build a secure and bright future, and she may chastise those who have not won the same battles because they are not like her. But even though her advice is a little pompous and self-righteous, her many friends still seek her out for it.

She tends to convert her opinions into dogma, and she may hold on to an old idea, even though she knows intellectually that it is no longer valid, simply because she cannot change.

Her emotions are closely tied to her beliefs. She can be especially dogmatic with friends and relatives whom she loves deeply. Often, since she loves them so much and wants the best for them, she assumes she knows what the best for them *is*. One of her hardest lessons is to realize that she cannot work out other people's karmas; they must assume responsibility for themselves.

Organizational, managerial
Lady Taurus has some of the most well-organized cupboards, drawers, and closets in the Zodiac. She may not be as tidy, neat, and well dusted as her earth sister Virgo, but she must know where her possessions are. She even has filling cabinets for her bills, letters, and recipes.

Because of this never-ending need to set the world in order, she may be drawn to research, librarianship, city planning, writing. In fact, any activity where a great many diverse bits of information have to be organized into a workable and functioning system will appeal to the Taurus Woman.

She is also acutely aware of the passage of time. She has a time clock within her head that measures off the cycles of life and computes how much time should be allotted to different tasks. When she makes a commitment to be somewhere at a certain time, she is there. If she says she will have a task completed by a certain date, you can rely on her.

Her sense of time and love of organizational detail is often applied to the management of people as well. However, as soon as the human element enters the picture, the task becomes a little more difficult. People present too many variables to fit conveniently into the same slots as books, invoices, and recipes. Here she must bring into play her considerable political ability and her knowledge of people.

The Taurus Woman likes an ordered house and ordered life. Time, materials, and place are all important to her. She is never happier than when they all form a harmonious whole of which she is the center. But her strong will can bulldoze feelings out of the way in order to complete a task on time. She must be very careful not to overlook the feelings of friends and loved ones, and she should plan time and space for them as well.

Gentle, placid, shy
For the gentle touch, the gentle word, or the gentle action, the Taurus Woman cannot be surpassed. Like her symbol, the bull, she only rages when she is angry or is caught up in the passions of sex. By choice she is very placid. The two horns of her symbol represent the horns of a dilemma. She can either be completely at peace with the world, or she can express the violent rage that is within her when she is angered. There seems to be little, if any,

middle ground. Many Taurus Women choose to suppress anger, for they learn early on that if they are constantly in a state of turmoil their health suffers. They are especially sensitive in the throat and shoulders, areas which continual stress and anger can weaken.

In many ways, the Taurus Woman is unflappable. She may just have returned from a round of shopping and Little League practice when her husband announces his boss is coming home with him for dinner. Her calm and stoic acceptance of this predicament is next to unbelievable. She knows that what will be will be, and besides, she has probably planned for just such an emergency and has a banquet prepared and frozen, just waiting.

Most of her life she will be shy around new people. This usually is the result of a poor self-image during childhood and of the pain inflicted on her by her early peers. New surroundings and new faces make her uncomfortable, for they present unknown quantities that must be confronted. Confrontation politics is not the Taurian style, and she avoids it like the plague. Any situation that produces unpleasantness is hard on her nervous system. Only when driven or pushed into a corner will she take a stand and fight for her own rights. She could avoid much unhappiness if she would learn to confront problems as they arise.

Self-indulgent, lazy

Comfort and contentment are important to the Taurus Woman. Bathe her in perfumed water, wrap her in a soft fluffy blanket, give her a hot-fudge sundae and shower her with love and affection; she will be yours for life. And be assured that if you don't do it for her, she will do it for herself. There is no question in her mind that she deserves the very best.

In most instances she will be able to keep her self-indulgence in bounds, for when she cares to exercise it, few other signs possess the self-control that she has. Her biggest problem comes with food; here, the will that can literally move mountains, divide the seas, and stop thundering herds of horses dissolves into the ether. Most Taurians have a weight problem that they have to deal with their entire lives. The Taurus Woman's unwanted pounds and inches, appear in the hips, which are naturally generous anyhow.

Food also represents security to the Taurus Woman, and this, coupled with her tremendous appetite and zest for eating, can add up to trouble. The eating scene in the movie *Tom Jones* represents a typical Taurus phase. Here, the physical pleasure of eating was tied to the promise of sexual pleasure to come later. She truly believes that the way to a man's heart is through his stomach (since she knows her own so well). She is a superb artist in the kitchen. She never likes to see food wasted and your only disappointment at leaving her table will be your diminished will power.

By nature, the Taurus Woman takes her time. Never try to hurry her; she cannot be budged unless she wants to be. She sets her own priorities and takes her time executing them. She organizes her life so only she has the time to enjoy it. Leisure appeals to her, and she may feel just right frittering it away or stuffing it so full that it appears to be work. The choice is hers, however, and she delights in those kinds of choices. The closer she comes to her ideal of comfort and luxury, the lazier she becomes. She should continually seek new challenges in order to overcome this.

Possessive

The Taurus Woman not only wants to have the use of a "thing"; she must possess it. Once she has clutched something to her ample bosom, she will simply not let go. Ownership is everything. She is apt to have four sets of pots and pans, eight sets of dishes, fifteen lace tablecloths, and all of her deceased mother-in-law's furniture.

She is just as possessive with her family and lovers. She has chosen them, and for that reason they are as much her chattel as are her clothes, jewelry, and furs. If she practices this to excess, she can become a very dominant wife and mother, leaving little space for her loved one's growth. Many children rebel very early when they feel her clutching them too tightly. On the positive side, however, she attends to them with as much care and concern as she lavishes on the rest of her possessions.

Let no one try to steal her husband or lover. She sees red, and the raging anger so often associated with the bull is unleashed. She attacks frontally with no holds barred. All of the power and strength she can muster (and her power is considerable) will be brought directly to bear on her opponent. She can be a very angry lady.

Luxury- and comfort-loving

Ruled by the voluptuous Venus, the Taurus Woman loves luxury. Even though it costs a little more, she believes in going first-class.

It may be a strain on her pocketbook, but it is ever so much more satisfying.

The Taurus Woman seems to have an innate sense of value and quality. She would rather have an oriental rug than a serviceable carpet. Why order from Sears when both Bloomingdale's and Neiman-Marcus have catalogue departments? She knows intrinsic value, and what may appear extravagant to some will be a good investment for the Taurus Woman. Her antiques and furnishings will appreciate in value; she will be able to sell her art in a financial pinch; and the jewelry she has acquired over the years may well provide the down payment on a new business.

Appreciative

The Taurus Woman does not have great expectations. She knows the ways of the world and the shortcomings of people too well to expect more than she can see and hold in her hand. She does not dream the mystical dreams of her Pisces sister or build the fantastic air castles of Aquarius; rather she constructs her own reality of mortar and bricks. But when something nice happens that she doesn't expect, or when someone makes good on a promise, she is one of the most appreciative people around.

In fact, her appreciation is almost childlike. If someone gives her a gift, she will cherish it forever. If someone is kind to her during hard times, she will remember it as long as she lives. It seems to come to her as a total surprise that she can be on the receiving end of things. Possibly her weak self-image makes it hard for her to believe that people would truly *want* to be nice to her.

Being of the earth and of Venus, Taurus has great appreciation for the physical world. She is a good judge of horseflesh and responds to the fine form of any man who is muscular, strong, and well-proportioned. Being receptive, she experiences as much as she can and retains most of what she sees, hears, feels, tastes, and touches; she enjoys all things of the senses. Her capacity for appreciation comes from her vast store of memories, experiences, and feelings about the world and its peoples.

The difficulty inherent in all this is that the Taurus Woman cannot balance enjoying and appreciating with doing. I would advise her to jump into new projects, to translate her ideas and stored appreciation into some concrete action. She needs to take risks to balance her retentive nature.

Sensuous

The Taurus Woman is like a finely tuned pipe organ. Her senses are its keys, and every key causes the music to flow. Each note is distinctive, and each key activates yet another octave. Only when all the notes are sounding does she feel harmonious and complete.

The Taurus Woman's senses are highly cultivated. She is like a Rubens nude: robust, sensual, lusty, with an ample appetite for living. She likes to feel the air on her skin and the warmth of the sun. And I have yet to meet a Taurus who didn't delight in the sensuality of a rich dessert.

As with many of her other traits, Taurus masks her sensuality with a veneer of conventionality. Often she learns during childhood that in our society, one should not enjoy the body or the feelings the body has. Yet she never quite believes this hypocrisy, and she goes on experiencing as much as she feels she safely can. It is only when she really trusts that she pulls out all the stops and exposes the extent of her sensual nature. Happy the man she trusts!

Cautious, stubborn

The Taurus Woman is plagued by many fears. High on the list is the fear of making mistakes. She so wants to do the right thing that she sometimes falters in doing anything at all. I know one Taurus lady, a secretary, who read every letter she did not less than four times. Though she produced perfect letters, they were oftentimes late in reaching their destinations.

Taurus rarely bets on anything that is unsure or variable. Knowing the natural progression of things often enables her to foresee their outcome. She does not like to gamble, preferring the long-term, steady profit of secure stocks to windfalls that may or may not materialize.

Her reticence concerning change is based upon the possibility of loss or pain. She would rather take her chances with known quantities than risk losing everything she has worked so hard to gather and build. The negative result is that she becomes even more stubborn and possessive than she normally is. It is difficult for her to fly free with such attitudes. She must learn that not every situation can be controlled or predicted. She is one of the great stabilizers of the earth, but if she doesn't respond positively to change, then stagnation, immobility, and decay may set in. She must consciously begin to take risks if she wishes to keep in step with the times.

Lady Taurus feels that time is on her side. She likes to have her own way and uses delaying tactics to get it. She will refuse to do anything that she feels is not in her best interests. Also, if something offends her sense of decency, honesty, or propriety, she will become stubborn and refuse to budge an inch. This quality can be a vice or a virtue. If she thinks she is right based on her judgment and experiences, she will not bend. She must constantly strive to be more flexible and to respond, not in terms of her perceptions, but in terms of situational reality.

Persistent, tenacious

The pioneer woman exemplifies the persistence and doggedness of the Taurus Woman. The Taurus Woman finishes what she starts—even if it takes years. Be it business, a project, or a human relationship, she seldom tires of trying to make it work. She feels that if she works hard enough, lasts long enough, and does not give up, she will accomplish what she wants in the end.

She clings to a belief or an idea with the same fervor. Once she has made up her mind that her views are correct (and this may take some time as she tries to be fair and impartial in her deliberations), she holds on for dear life. Even if she later is proven wrong, she still has a conviction in the back of her mind that she was right, in some sense, all along.

Professionally, the Taurus Woman shows the same persistence, and she will work overtime without complaint in order to get the job done. She is reliable and generous with her time and will train the new recruit, get the coffee, plan the budget, and even organize the football or baseball pool. She knows that the small details are often as important as the overall concept.

She works hard to make friends, to win over in-laws, and to develop a camaraderie with co-workers. But everything changes, friendships as well, and not all are worthy of retention. Being stubborn, she will often refuse to give up on something that does not serve her own best interests. When she is able to see things as they are rather than as she wishes they were, she will learn to let go. She then only needs to release, as painful as it may be, and her life will change for the better.

Jealous
The Taurus Woman is as possessive of others' affections as she is of the goods she owns. She does not want anyone to get too near to the things she loves, including her friends and family, for fear they might steal them or harm them in some way.

Her strong Venus nature encases her loved ones in a protective crystal shell. Trying to understand the Taurus Woman is like trying to understand the many facets of love itself. She protects and holds, lavishes affection and nurtures; yet she feels that she is the only one capable of doing so. Woe to anyone who tries to supplant her or trespass on the territories of her love.

In her less developed state, the Taurus Woman focuses this feeling on material objects and covets things that others have. She can be jealous of the wealth, success, or beauty of her peers. As she progresses in her development, she will learn that this is a negative emotion and adds little to her self-esteem.

Conservative, money-maker, greedy
The Taurus Woman is a conservator from childhood. Recognizing that the earth's resources are precious, she wants to use them wisely. She will never throw something away if she feels there may be a use for it in the future.

She may involve herself in organizing a local recycling movement, a preserve for wildlife, or a stop-the-expansion-of-industry/clean-up-the-air program. In her personal garden, nothing will be cast away. Old leaves and plant stalks will become mulch for new growth; her sunflower seeds will be carefully processed for planting next year.

Her tastes in clothing and accessories will lean to the conservative. She abhors flashiness and has a keen eye for subtle quality. While she herself is virtually indomitable, she doesn't want to appear that way outwardly. This is another of the masks that prevent anyone from thinking she is too far-out or avant-garde. The respect and acceptance of the people she encounters is very important to her, and she will do little to jeopardize her position.

Saving money is second nature to the Taurus Woman. Her conservative nature requires a little nest egg hidden away for emergencies. Her moneymaking activities may including mining, manufacturing, growing food or flowers, and selling real estate, all of which reflect her knowledge of the earth's resources and what they can provide people.

Her talent for making money seems endless. She considers nothing too menial or "low-class" if the bottom line means profit for her. She sees possibilities when those around her see desperation. She may begin on a very small scale; canning jams and jellies at home can make her a rival of the Knotts Berry Farm if she is determined and if the profits are forthcoming.

When the impulsive Taurus need for security and self-respect goes unchecked, greed may be the result. Success becomes directly associated with material wealth in her mind, and without the balance of a developed spiritual nature, she runs out of control, grabbing at each penny she sees. Her natural, caring concern for people then takes a back seat, and she begins to enjoy life less.

She also feels that money gives her power over her own life, she derives from it a sense of release from responsibility and a feeling of freedom and mobility. At the same time, she can be quite generous, giving pieces of her hoarded treasure in order to secure love, attention, and loyalty from those close to her. The gifts are seldom without strings, however, and Taurus needs to cultivate a truer sense of giving until the act feels natural and expresses genuine love.

Affectionate

The need to be touched and loved is very strong in the Taurus Woman. She uses the sense of touch to convey her feelings to others. Deny her affection, and she becomes like a plant without water. As a child she vies for the affections of both parents and often feels siblings are getting more than their share. She can sustain herself for great lengths of time without sexual contact, but her natural glow fades if affection is withdrawn.

Honest, dependable

You can trust a Taurus Woman with your money, your secrets, your life, and generally even with your man. She truly believes that honesty is the best policy. In her evolved state, she is extremely honest about herself as well and will be the first to admit her faults (but don't *you* bring them up).

She dislikes contracts and written agreements but her word is sacred to her and she always fulfills her promises. No commitment is too small for her to remember, but she outwardly overlooks commitments made to her if confrontation is required to effect fulfilment.

The Taurus Woman is a godsend in an emergency, in times of tragedy, and during periods of deep stress. She can cooly make decisions for others, and her feeling for the cycles of life, for the natural occurrence of birth, growth, and death, make her invaluable to those less capable of seeing the broad picture. You know you can count on her, and better yet, she knows it too.

Pragmatic, methodical, builder

Will it work? This is the question the Taurus Woman most often asks. She is careful in her considerations and thus can be sure in her judgments. Once she has made plans, she carries them out methodically, almost to a fault. Like a master mason, she first lays the foundation well; then, brick by brick, she builds towards reality. However, she must guard against becoming enslaved by her methods, since this can cause delays in reaching her goals.

Taurus loves to conceptualize, pattern, seek materials carefully, and build slowly. Architecture, renovation, rehabbing, decorating, designing, and inventing appeal to her and can be lucrative career possibilities and her persistence and confidence in matters affecting her environment often have good results for all of us.

Kind, humble

The Taurus Woman embodies true humility. She takes action and does for others out of kindness. The spotlight does not appeal to her, but when she is remembered she graciously accepts. Although it is difficult for her to accept praise, she needs to concentrate on dealing with it when it does come her way. Too often she competes with herself to do the best possible job and then forgets to bolster her own self-esteem by seeking recognition. She rises in the business world not by openly competing with others but by her staying power and integrity.

She goes out of her way to insure that she will not trample on the feelings of others. She opens her arms to stray animals, and stray people. As she evolves, her "stringless" gift giving is legendary.

Productive, patient, tolerant

The "author" of the Puritan ethic could very well have been a Taurian. Taurus does not rest completely until she has acquired or produced something of worth. As one of the most energetic signs, she usually has a variety of projects going at the same time. Each receives equal, devoted care, although too often, her excess energies are used to begin yet another project when she could better apply them to finishing what she has begun.

Her patience is legendary, and few things can cause her to lose sight of it. She expends vast amounts of energy explaining procedure and theory over and over again. She makes a good teacher when she overcomes her sometimes moralistic nature.

She is tolerant of others' flaws, though not of her own. I have seen Taurus Women abide husbands addicted to alcohol and drugs without passing judgment. This high tolerance for people carries over into her philosophy too. Lifestyles, ideas, and politics that are unacceptable to many cause her little problem. She is open and is one of the best listeners you can find. Do not, however, misconstrue her understanding nature as a sign that she is ready to impulsively join in; her conservative streak is strongly rooted.

Nature-loving

The Taurus Woman relates to and loves nature, both as a broad concept and as a specific experience. She will try to learn the name of every plant and animal within her purview. She loves to involve herself physically with a natural habitat, and she will look everywhere for the perfect naturally woven basket to carry when she picks flowers in her garden, and true to her nature, she will hold on to it dearly.

Gardening is an avocation that most Taurus Women pursue in one way or another. If she lives in a concrete-and-glass high-rise with a tiny balcony, Taurus will endeavor to grow cherry tomatos and a herb garden on it. If she has a vast expanse of rich soil at her disposal, she will supply half her friends and all her relatives with the freshest, plumpest vegetables in the country. She plants, nurtures, and harvests according to her deep-seated sense of cycles.

Taurus relationships

Because the Taurus nature is so definite and deeply rooted, nearly all the traits delineated at the beginning of this chapter carry over into any relationship she endeavors to develop. Once she has made a commitment, she will put forth her best effort to make any of her many relationships work. She forms a wonderful half of any duo—mate, best friend, co-worker, commiserater. She needs these one-on-one encounters to fulfill her curious yet complex nature. At the same time, she is a perfectionist and expects her family, friends, and lovers to live up to exacting standards. She can become very critical very quickly when intimates do not meet her criteria.

Like her opposite, Scorpio, she may arrive at a position of power, not so much because she seeks it, but more often because she has proven she can handle it, distribute it, and enhance it.

Though often not intentionally, the Taurus Woman may use sex and intimacy to gain wealth, which she in turn translates into security, luxury, and beauty. She is attracted to people of wealth and learns appreciation for the things it can provide. Her natural good taste make her excellent company for those who are accustomed to the finer things in life. Although the law of polarity may cause her to marry beneath her station and thus suffer from a lack of material wealth, she can still function with those who have it.

Her *approach* to permanent relationships is healthy. She is loyal, steadfast, and oriented to the home. She enjoys comfort and likes sharing life's fineries with her friends and loved ones. She remains a faithful wife or friend until she is betrayed. Her temper boils when she discovers someone has deceived her, when her intelligence is insulted, or when she has proof that someone has taken advantage of her. She has one of the highest levels of tolerance in the Zodiac, but when her limit is reached, she reacts with lightning speed. It may take months or years for her to recover . . . if she ever does. When it's love, it's all or nothing. She demands the same loyalty she offers. In friendship she can give as well as receive but is insistent upon a fifty-fifty ratio.

She allows nobody to force her into doing anything against her will. (She can, however, be led if the proverbial carrot is affection.) Unless her friends and intimates recognize this early on, they may unexpectedly be confronted with her strong will, either as she exerts it directly or as she uses it as adhesive to keep herself from being swayed off her dead-center course.

Although one of her greatest needs is for affection, she may often not be affectionate towards others. Her mate may be confused by long periods of silence in which she seems to be in a world of her own. She is probably resting her karma, much as the earth rests between cycles of productivity and growth.

The Taurus Woman tends to trust men more than she trusts women. She will also come to the aid of another Taurus before any of the other sign types. She loves older men and will often be seen with one at her side. They seem to inspire her trust more quickly and serve to mirror her own stability to the outside world. On the other hand, she fears growing old and thus places great importance on youth and youthfulness. Because of her own youthful attitudes and freshness, many think of her as being younger than she really is.

As she becomes more evolved, the Taurus Woman drops some of the masks she has used to keep her fears hidden. She begins to show her sexual nature more and more. Where motherhood was once the only permanent route she could consider, she now wants to experiment with new freedoms that strong parenting (the only kind she understands) prohibits. She doesn't lose her love for children, and she still feels she must prepare them to assume the responsibility for her earth; but she begins to feel less bound to the duty of rearing her own.

She also begins to let it be known that she can manage money and function in the financial industry along with the best of them. She has an uncanny ability with real estate and banking. When she applies her strong will and naturally materialistic tendencies, she can direct the day-to-day operations of a profitable corporation as efficiently as any man.

For all her common sense about money and other practical concerns, she stubbornly refuses to give it proper respect in matters of the heart. She often seeks a relationship that provides excitement, thrills, mystery, and sensual sex. Perhaps she feels that her life is too methodical and boring, and she yearns for adventure. It is not uncommon for her to marry a man she has only just met.

She is possessive, habit-bound, and dogmatic in her love life. Her smothering love and failure to provide space, coupled with her rigid insistence on emotional superiority, can cause her relationships to become dull and boring. After the adventure wears off, she may regret her choice but will often stubbornly hang on. It is much too difficult for a Taurus Woman to admit she has made a mistake.

In love, the greatest challenge for the Taurus Woman is to

overcome her possessiveness. She is always tempted to play protective, jealous bitch. People cannot be private property; the beloved must have space to grow. She can only have by letting go.

Childhood

The Taurus child is often content to spend many hours playing by herself. Her parents may worry that she is too solitary. Her rebellious nature only surfaces when she is pushed too much; otherwise she is well mannered and usually stays out of trouble. Having a self-imposed inner control, she will often resist discipline that she considers unreasonable. However, affection works wonders; she may have stubbornly resisted your demands, but a hug will set everything right.

Her early years are likely to present one of two extremes: the child who has to assume a great deal of responsibility and never has a chance for a "normal" childhood; or the pampered child who is given everything and has virtually no responsibility. Silver spoon or stainless steel, she has a beautiful disposition.

The Taurus girl usually relates well to her peers and those around her. She may be very shy and timid, but given time, she emerges a diplomatic though reserved adult. At the same time, she looks only for the unvarnished truth and can take people aback with the depth of her perceptions.

She has a good relationship with both parents but usually favors her father. She is the apple of his eyes, and he will do a great deal for her. She tends to become very dependent upon her parents and looks to them in times of trouble instead of taking care of problems herself.

How the Taurus Woman relates:
Lovers and other intimates

The Taurus Woman is characteristically very giving in her relationships with intimates. This openness extends beyond her body into her mind and spirit. When she marries, she gives herself completely to her man. She is one of the more monogamous of the signs and seldom strays unless given good reason. Her initial impact is very exciting and magnetic. She has a sense of elan in the early stages of her relationship with a man.

If she does seek sexual partners outside marriage it is often because her one-dimensional mate cannot satisfy the myriad elements that comprise her total being. If she has married someone who is not her intellectual equal, she may seek that quality in a younger man. If the marriage fails to provide the financial security she must have, she will lose little time in rectifying *that* situation, too.

Her fears about security, both financial and emotional, can cause her to lose her *joie de vivre* and can cloud her otherwise brilliant insight. In turn, the excitement she injects into most of her romantic relationships may disappear. Many times she shies away from intimacy due to self-doubt. She is protective and nurturing by nature, and she also applies these qualities to herself. If she fears rejection or hurt, she can dredge up long-forgotten memories that reinforce her self-preservation mechanisms.

Taurus, you must learn to take risks in the course of developing or improving relationships. I have found the following "Risk List" to be an excellent tool:

1 Write about your biggest fear. List all the details. Expose yourself directly to fear.
2 Tell your closest friend something that has been bothering you in your relationship for a long time.
3 Do something fun that you've fantasized about but have been afraid to try (all the better if you do it with your lover/mate/husband).
4 Share with your lover the sexual fantasy you've been afraid to tell her/him. You may even want to venture so far as to admit to fantasizing it while having sex.
5 Get an empty chair, sit across from it, and pretend the person you are most jealous or envious of is sitting there. Tell the "person" why you feel as you do.
6 Take one step to acquire for yourself the quality you are jealous or envious of in this "person."
7 Choose one habit you are uncomfortable with and make a plan to eradicate it (try to pick a habit that affects *you* more strongly than it affects those around you).
8 Give a gift to a friend for no special reason, and don't expect anything in return. Again, so much the better if it's something you possess that the friend cherishes.
9 Sit down and talk with your boss about one thing you are uncomfortable about on the job. Don't get carried away... One thing will reinforce you enough to set about achieving total comfort on the job.

10 Make a list of all the fantasies you can remember from your childhood. Go do one of them.
11 Throw away two things that you have had for years and will never use.
12 End your involvement with a project you've been working on for a long time, one you know will probably never be beneficial.
13 Apologize to someone you self-righteously argued with when you knew you were wrong.
14 Go out and meet one new person on your own; talk with her/him for at least a half-hour.
15 Ask a friend to role-play your mother, and tell her something you have wanted to tell her for years. It doesn't have to be something you dislike; you can tell her how much you appreciated that blue dress in 1958!

When the Taurus Woman learns to consciously take risks and observe the results, she will find that all kinds of changes occur. After a few weeks of experiencing the exhilaration of risking, she will find she can do it without fear. The only constant in life is change; she must make herself more flexible and accept the processes of change in her life.

Until Taurus rises above her possessive, controlling, and fearful tendencies, her relationships resemble the process of bartering for the best price on a bale of cotton. She holds back her true emotions, exchanges them for those of others, and risks losing them only on a sure thing. Little wonder her intimates often tire of her games.

Fear is one of the greatest inhibitors of growth, and the Taurus Woman must actively eliminate it if she is to flow with the life energies she knows so well. The only self-interest she should keep in her life is that which she uses for self-improvement. When the Taurus Woman lets beauty and harmony be her guide, she knows instinctively what is right.

What kind of man she needs

The Taurus Woman has the internal stability, intelligence, and energy to live a productive life. What she often lacks is the fire and self-love necessary to bring these qualities to the surface.

She needs a man who will mirror her strength and emotional stability. Her idea of a real man includes tenderness, sensitivity, imagination, and concern about her future. Her man needs to possess common horse sense. She can be captivated by a witty, charming, and sensuous man as long as he bears her gifts.

Her stubborn nature largely dictates her relationships. When her man is attentive and even a bit adoring, she melts. He can then match her will and help her overcome her plodding deliberations. If he's a bit impulsive, he will lend balance to her sensual enjoyment of life.

Her man should use subtle prodding to drag her away from her cherished home and possessions. She wants her partner to share in her love of the earth, and if he can get around her natural cautiousness, she may even lift her feet off the ground occasionally.

Advice to the man in her life

1 Be prepared to fall in love quickly, totally, and permanently.
2 Coddle her, be gentle, be appreciative, but avoid patronizing her; she has a keen sense for deception.
3 Encourage her; challenge her; prod her, but subtly.
4 Remember her birthday, your anniversary, and any other important date in her life.
5 Give her gifts. Almost anything will do so long as it has beauty and sophistication.
6 Compliment her frequently. Help her learn to accept the praise and recognition she so often shuns.
7 Return her loyalty. Reassure her that you can and will provide for her as long *as it makes her happy*. Make her aware that she can change and you can learn to accept and love the evolved woman she can become.
8 Let her organize your life, but make it clear that you want the privilege of input.
9 Bite your tongue before you ever make a statement that will cause her jealousy to surface. Be considerate, and above all conscious, of her jealousy. You can help her overcome it by trying to understand it.

If you are the man she chooses for life, you can consider yourself lucky. The combination of Venus and earth can make her the most exciting sexual conquest you've ever experienced. Her need to nurture and care for those she loves will foster one of the deepest feelings of security you've ever had. Treat her as you would a delicate flower or a succulent mango; experience her depths, for she will certainly take you there. Her potential is great indeed, and you can share the joy of helping her evolve.

Taurus sexuality

Taurus the Earth Goddess is a very sexual being. She may seem very placid and composed on the exterior, but underneath the rhythms of the earth beat strongly. Her sensual nature takes over in the bedroom.

She makes an art of lovemaking. Scheherezade surely was a Taurus. Never undertake making love to a Taurus Woman unless a large block of time is available for her to express her repertoire. Just kissing her can bring some men to orgasm. Her touch, both gentle and tender, excites and caresses. Once she sheds her facade and inhibitions, she is capable of crying aloud. Fully aroused, she can go for hours at a time, days on end. When she is in the mood, she is insatiable. However, she wants mutual expression and will not be content just lying there.

Sexuality is an integral part of the Taurus Woman's life. She strives to maintain a certain decorum for the public but is very aware of her sexual drive and feels no shame over it. Often it is tied to her emotions, and it is hard indeed for her to have sex and not fall in love.

She is one of the most effective users of body language you will encounter. When she sways her ample hips, crosses her long legs, or bats her bedroom eyes, she is sending messages to men that she possesses a female's femaleness. Her low-cut dress reveals sufficient cleavage to raise the libido of any red-blooded male. She carries herself well and packages her body as she would a loving gift; it all adds up to stunning beauty.

The Taurus Woman is not looking for a power play in bed. Her sexual nature can be characterized as generally direct and uncomplicated. She is driven by healthy animal lust. She wants sex because it feels good and it is natural.

Although she may have deep-seated insecurities about her self-worth, she does not have any doubts about her sexuality. Her opposite sign is Scorpio, who may have a tendency to use sex for gaining power and money. For Taurus this is not the primary goal; it is a bonus.

There are three key words that help in understanding Taurus

sexuality. One is *passion*. The act of mating unleashes some intense and overpowering emotions in the Taurus Woman. She feels an ardent affection and love for her mate that surpasses the bounds of the merely physical. Her mind also reaches out, and her hopes and fantasies become bound to the beloved. The communication she expresses during the heights of passion is possibly some of the most important she has to offer. For the Taurus Woman, sex is multifaceted. There is something healing and soothing about its intensity. She never feels better, more alive and stimulated, than after some good hard sex.

The Taurus Woman is a creature of enormous *sensuality*. She is most happy when all her senses are being titillated at the same time. Conceivably she could have sex while eating a bonbon, listening to a Rachmaninoff concerto, having a foot massage, and sniffiing a lily of the valley. Body contact is important to the Taurus Woman, and she welcomes being touched. Signals of affection such as a kiss, a gentle squeeze of the buttocks, a brush of the hand over a breast, or a bite on the neck really turn her on. Her fantasy stimulation begins immediately, and it is then difficult for her to get her mind on anything else.

The Taurus Woman's sexuality has a strongly *procreative* dimension. She has a tremendous need and drive to bear children. Even with her somewhat ambivalent attitude towards motherhood, the sight of a baby's bottom will send hormones rushing through her bloodstream. Being of the earth, she has innate knowledge of the purpose of procreation and will not feel completely fulfilled as a person unless she brings forth a child to nurture, embrace, and teach. If, for some reason, she cannot bear children herself, she will not hesitate to adopt. She makes a wonderful foster parent, and few of her friends would give the slightest thought to leaving their children with anyone else. You can be sure that if she doesn't have children of her own, those of her friends and relatives will come to regard her as a second mother.

Once she is aroused, the Taurus Woman subtly demands satisfaction. She is most comfortable when having sex in long, lazy bouts, with time out for popcorn, soda, and a gooey dessert; then it's back into the sack. She is happiest when having sex in her own bed or in natural surroundings that are comfortable for her. Her bedchamber will be plush, executed in laid-back good taste, full of beautiful appointments, and subtly understated. She may use yards and yards of rose-colored fabric and lace to create a comfortable nest, or she may create a subtle artistic illusion; whatever the style, you can be sure it will provide a dramatic backdrop for her and her mate to settle in for a night of serious lovemaking.

With a canopy of stars over her head, she can be pleased under a grape arbor, in a grassy meadow, or on a bed of leaves. Dispelling the heat of her sex into the earth beneath her can make her soar to new heights, and she'll take her partner right along with her.

Early sex experiences

In matters of sex, the young Taurus girl tends to deal in extremes. She is either very conservative or very precocious.

At one extreme, perhaps due to the loss or incapacitation of her mother, she may assume a great deal of responsibility. When she shares the duty of rearing brothers and sisters, she develops such an adult posture that she has little time for childhood games and few opportunities for sexual experimentation. With the responsibilities of an adult thrust on her, she will assume corresponding habits and attitudes. She then grows up too fast and becomes too conservative. She is probably the last girl in her class to give up her virginity (after Virgo and Capricorn).

On the other hand, the Taurus girl who has all the security and comfort she requires will experiment much earlier. On a dare she will masturbate with a carrot and try other novel means of self-gratification. She will associate with older boys because of her tomboy nature, and since she recognizes that they have more experience, she will gladly be the patient in the game of "doctor." She likes the feel of such thrills, and she usually continues to experiment clandestinely until she has made the rounds of the boys who "know how." She is fond of bawdy stories and will be one of the first to stand on the corner with a friend and exchange them.

During this time, Taurus develops her uncanny ability to choose trustworthy people with whom to share personal experiences. Her fear of being unacceptable requires discretion, even at this early age. She can usually recover if someone slips up and gossips about her behavior, but that person will never again win her confidence. By this time, her legendary temper is full-grown.

Young Taurus girls radiate exuberance and charm. They love to have their own way and are fond of gifts of affection. They are curious about their bodies and things sexual. They are also easily seduced. Once they discover that sex feels good, they may let their sexual appetities run away with them.

By adolescence, the Taurus girl is usually well-adjusted and able to handle her own life quite well. There is an element of self-love and self-preservation in her makeup that keeps her self-esteem high. As the woman emerges, she comes to cherish her body and the pleasures it can bring to her. Although it may take her awhile to develop a self-image she finds acceptable, she constantly tries to improve on what nature gave. She will exercise and diet to keep her body in shape.

Her appearance is very female, and she learns to walk with the bearing of a princess. She is one of the few girls in her class who doesn't seem too upset when she develops breasts and the boys begin to notice. Her natural knowledge of things sexual endears her to fellow classmates, and by the time she is in high school, she had decided what she wants. Although she has a basic drive to procreation, she seldom has the traditional teenage infatuation with motherhood. She will embrace motherhood eventually, since it provides her with security, a stable place in society, and companionship for her "golden years."

Much of her philosophy of life is developed by the time she graduates from high school. Her attitudes are strong; she can take people as they are, and she usually has an odd assortment of friends. It is during this time that she cements her down-to-earth character and comes to grips with the power of her temper.

Love and sex

Because the Taurus Woman's nature is binary, she is constantly seeking to unite the two parts. Sex and love are no exception. She recognizes that there is a close relationship between the two, but her logic sometimes confuses her. It usually follows that if a man loves her, he wants to have sex with her. This does not necessarily mean that if a man wants to have sex with her, he loves her. Her need for love and affection is as strong as her need for sex. Without love she can feel as empty as a shell from which life has fled.

The Taurus Woman wants pleasure more than excitement. Her greatest block to receiving is that she lets her mind get in the way. She can be too analytical. Sex is the sharing of deep emotional pleasures; attaching too many other things to it will block fulfillment.

She does not seek to take charge of the sexual relationship and is willing to follow the lead of her mate. She wants to accommodate him and will probably even try anal sex to please him, although she may complain that it hurts. She has little tolerance for pain but often embraces mild discomfort if it enhances the totality of sexual passion. Although she appreciates lusty sex, the warmth and affection that follow are what she really craves.

The Taurus Woman can go to extremes in everything. She is constantly torn between a need for sex and a longing for security. Because her sexual need is so great, she may turn to nymphomania or prostitution for gratification, but she is usually very conventional and wants a home life, complete with children.

She can assume the role of an active or passive partner, both in heterosexual and homosexual relationships. Once the Taurus Woman has taken the step into lesbianism, she does so with all the passion of her sign. She retains her feminine character and puts on an effective mask that the outside world will not be able to penetrate. She usually chooses a young partner and makes her career an important part of her life.

The Taurus Woman's sexual response pattern in intercourse seems to be the following:

1 Total fascination with the object of her desire—and she will have well-laid plans for getting him into bed.
2 Slow, seductive arousal in an atmosphere heavy with romance, in which her inhibitions are peeled away layer by layer as her temperature slowly rises.
3 Total involvement of the emotions and the mind, building to a slow, natural orgasm or peak.
4 Orgasm in which the body shakes and continues periodic spasms for a long time. She need only feel the touch of her lover at this time to send her into complete and ecstatic oblivion.
5 Complete feeling of release with a soothing and analgesic effect on the entire body. Some of her innermost desires and feelings can rise to the surface at this time, and an attentive lover will do well to listen and communicate. It can only enhance the next sexual union (which is sometimes only minutes away).

What kind of lover she needs

Like Venus, Taurus shines with reflected light. She reflects true beauty, not only in the things she gathers around her, but also in the men she chooses. To really appeal to the Taurus Woman, a man must be beautiful. Younger men often capture her heart, for they have not lost the beauty of youth. If they are well muscled and powerful, so much the better.

There is a wide spectrum of types that appeal to her. In general, her man should be well proportioned, handsome, and muscular. She likes a man with a strong interest in sex and a high sex drive who knows what he's doing. She will be satisfied with diminished anounts of both if he gives her a lot of love and respect.

She likes to be dominated by a man who is all man. Being eternally feminine, she looks for the best the male species has to offer. Her fantasies are types more than specific bodies. Cowboys with rugged faces and tough beards—the typical Marlboro ad—fill much of the bill. She has a penchant for nature types, such as a California surfer or a deep-sea sponge diver, and for men from exotic places.

A man who holds her, fondles her, spends time getting her in the proper mood, possesses her, and takes her for all he is worth while nipping her, kneading her, and shouting his love—such a man is her idea of good sex. It helps if he also has repetitive powers, for once is never enough for the Goddess of Love.

Her throat is one of her most sensitive parts, and she has an unusual enthusiasm for oral sex. Linda Lovelace in *Deep Throat* was undoubtedly a Taurus. She also likes to have oral sex performed on her, and *soixante-neuf* (69) is one of her favorite sexual appetizers.

In extreme cases, the Taurus Woman can be a devotee of coprophilia, an attraction to filth and excrement. In these encounters she becomes sexually aroused by rubbing her body with it, and some urinate on their partners as part of foreplay.

She is generally not turned on by kinky sex aids. She dislikes the smell of amyl nitrate, and prickly condoms prevent her from feeling the penis in its natural state. She may consent to the use of a well-placed dildo but will want it supplanted by the real thing before the sex session is complete.

If she does not have control of her perpetual self-doubt, if she continually berates herself, or if she was abused physically or emotionally as a child, she may become a masochist. Whipping and strangulation are routes she then chooses. Again, illusion is of the utmost importance; she may put the man in the role of a masked burglar who has come to steal her possessions and in the process makes her submit to all kinds of sexual acts. Strange as it may seem, the post-sex warmth, communication, and feeling of fulfilment are as intense at this time as during her more conventional sexual phases.

Her normally down-to-earth idea of sex/love coupling can be forgotten temporarily if she is far away from home. If she is reasonably sure her actions will not be recorded, a taxi driver in London, a bellboy in Hong Kong, or a seat-mate on a plane to Atlanta may be the recipient of her sexual favors.

The Taurus Woman applauds the New Age of sexual freedom. The lessening of some of the hypocrisy of our society fosters an integration of all phases of her life and allows her self-image to match her inner reality; her sensual and sexual being can emerge. Interestingly enough, she can bring this fantastic melding about without social approval if and when she learns to enhance herself from within. She has a knack for making things that are normally less than acceptable quite normal for her.

What she needs to learn

Taurus must learn that the needs of the body do not always mesh with her inner concepts of beauty and reality. Her remembrance of a remote ideal past when inner realities matched outward manifestations of love and sex often causes dissatisfaction with the way things are. The flesh must be given its due, but her idealistic need for romance and beauty must also be met.

The Taurus Woman will not find love by controlling the people around her, her environment, or the many beautiful things she owns. If she really loves herself, she will attract what she needs. If she really trust in others, she will find that they shower her with the affection and love that she really desires.

She must not invest her emotions in people who are not truly worthy of them. She is the eternal optimist, believing that if she loves people enough, they will return that love. So seldom is this the case that she often turns these failures inward and blames herself. This is a clear example of her tenacity and stubbornness getting in the way of an honest appraisal of people.

There is a time to remain silent and a time to speak out. The Taurus Woman needs to let her mate know what she wants, otherwise frustration and repressed anger will follow. Her nurturing qualities often cause her to overlook one of her other principles: give-and-take. She makes sure she gets hers in bed; she can make sure she gets hers in life too.

Another healthy revelation for her is that sex and love do not necessarily have to be coupled all the time. The casual affair is often as satisfying for her and not nearly as draining. It's a good opportunity to release some of her excessively romantic energies. It follows, therefore, that she must learn *when* to experiment. Love and sex will not come knocking on her door. She must move out and try different patterns when she feels the urge.

When Taurus feels that her body is out of balance, she needs to look for the force that is at work, for the source of the energy that is overtaking her. Perhaps she needs to practice moderation in her sexual appetities; or maybe envy and jealousy are at the root of her problem. She may be experiencing the effects of repressed or misinterpreted anger or she may be subconsciously denying herself some pleasure because of her intense sense of duty.

She will find her greatest happiness when she uses her talents, possessions, and natural energies in the most productive and positive manner. When the Taurus Woman realizes that each action results from choice, that she can be responsible for her own experiences, she will be on the Yellow Brick Road that leads directly into the New Age.

Taurus Anger

In the feeling of anger, the excitation charges the muscular system along the back of the body, mobilizing the powerful movements of attack. The main organs of assault are located in the upper and front-end of the body. . . . Anger is experienced, therefore, as a surge of feeling upward along the back of the body and into the head and arms. This surge of feeling is associated with a strong flow of blood to these parts. . . . If inhibitions and tensions exist which block this surge of feeling, they eventually produce illness.
Alexander Lowen, M.D.
Pleasure

Like many others, the Taurus Woman does not recognize anger as an emotion that is as common as love, depression, joy, or happiness. Few have ever seen the Taurus Woman truly angry. Behind the calm, patient exterior, she has buried the bruises, slights, and hurts that a less tolerant, more self-aware woman would never harbor. This anger eventually overloads her circuits. She will explode in blind rage months or years after the events causing the original pain. The incident that triggers her explosion may be so minor that it has little relation to the scope of her anger.

Women have to walk a delicate tightrope in expressing emotion. They are conditioned to deny negative feelings other than jealousy. The Taurus Woman knows her place and respects authority. These attitudes reinforce the denial of her deep, sensitive nature. She fails to recognize when someone has taken advantage of her, and she is often unaware of her legitimate right to a healthy expression of anger. And most Taurus women have problems understanding *when* it is appropriate to release frustration and anger.

The following are examples of how the Taurus Woman can mask her true emotions and repress anger.

In her thirties, Taurus develops a caustic, controlled style for dealing with life's displeasures. She uses icy rhetoric to deliver nonstop lectures when her ire is even slightly aroused. This defense mechanism keeps her feelings at a safe distance.

She may become expert at baiting others into angry confrontations. She maintains a smug look, smiles superficially, and merrily waltzes away. It's as if the expression of their anger helps to relieve the pressure of her own. She also uses this tactic to reinforce her feelings of control. She can become preoccupied with this type of game playing rather than confront the unhappiness or resentment she feels within.

Her life is full of *shoulds*. She loves to *should* everyone else into her way of thinking. Her judgment of them can be harsh and unforgiving. (It is only used to keep her feelings of self-hate at bay. She projects her repressed anger and unhappiness onto others.)

She often avoids anger by overwork, especially if she is avoiding domestic unpleasantness. She is too tired from discharging all her responsibilities to truly interact with her mate. If she doesn't get down to the source of the problem, then she doesn't have to get angry. The result of this tactic is too often deterioration of her sex life. It can become the perfunctory "Wednesday night after the children have gone to sleep but before it gets too late."

The Taurus Woman's innate fear of helpless surrender to the forces of nature both motivates and detracts from her internal balance. Only when she feels dislodged from her stable center will she move to regain equanimity. Her complex reactions to events around her are usually well hidden.

The Taurus Woman is often uncomfortable with emotional expression that connotes lack of control. In this case, tears are the ultimate sign of weakness. She fears others will think she is not really adequate. She remains intensely private about her inner desires, fears, and anger. The same characteristics that give the Taurus Woman the strength and stamina to conquer misfortune render her helpless in expressing hurt, fear, frustration, and anger in a constructive, self-caring manner.

The roots of her anger often lie in her feelings of inferiority and insecurity. She is not given to self-analysis, nor to seeking advice, except from a few close confidants. She has few intimates because of her fear of losing control and being too vulnerable to the winds of love and lust. She rarely permits honest, useful feedback.

She feels her anger is unwarranted. Her greatest problem in this area is that her buried anger often gets translated into depression, self-hatred, and despair. She is once again caught on the horns of dilemma. She often idolizes her mother and remembers that she was always instructed to be a good little girl. Like her Virgo sister, she is preoccupied with doing the right thing. She still must cope with the illusions that are forced on women from childhood on: good little girls do not talk back.

Her body, however, has always been aware of her feelings. The physical toll of repressed anger is indeed great. She may gain weight or experience severe neck and shoulder pain, migraine headaches, even repeated sore throats from tightening her throat muscles in response to displeasure. She blocks her emotions so skillfully that a severe strain is placed on the heart, which can eventually result in heart attack.

Unlike the delicate Cancer or the more ethereal, watery Pisces, Taurus has a strong body and can endure years of this kind of self-abuse. She may become withdrawn and quiet, but the effects of her suppressed rage will eventually surface.

Changing patterns

Self-awareness is essential for change. The Taurus Woman may not want to confront herself or her behavior, but she will have to if she wants to change her reactions. Rage is not just anger expressing itself; it *is* the self, searching and puzzled.

In dealing with her anger, the Taurus Woman needs to:

1 Accept conflict as inevitable.
2 Realize anger is manageable if expressed at the time it is initially felt.
3 Remember that she can always learn from another's counsel.

4 Accept that group encounters teach us the value of sharing equally with others.
5 Allow others the right to make their own mistakes.
6 Allow others to grow in a free and unabandoned manner.
7 Respect others' private spaces and abilities.
8 Define her own needs and boundaries.
9 Learn where her needs and desires begin and others' end.
10 Remember that the expression of anger will not automatically change another person's behavior.
11 Remember that she can never possess another person.

(For communication skills, see "Libra Anger." For more advice on how to identify anger, see "Scorpio Anger." For exercises in greater self-awareness, see "Capricorn Relationships.")

As she evolves, the Taurus Woman will see that expressing all her emotions is natural for her. Her concern about how expressing her anger will affect others' opinions of her will dissipate when it becomes clear that she can do it with the same admirable flair she uses to express her joy. Like the earth she is so much a part of, she must display all her qualities at one time or another.

Taurus lifestyles

Monogamy and nonmonogamy

The Taurus Woman enjoys—even requires—monogamy in marriage. She works hard to provide comfort for her mate and her children. She'll even leave her precious home (though not the care of it) and take a job to insure the financial security so necessary to her existence and to insure that the protective bubble over her loved ones does not develop cracks.

Her innate cyclic nature cannot ignore the changes in our society. Couple that with some concrete proof that an emerging lifestyle can help meet new demands, and Taurus will adapt to it. Once she sees the value and the blossoming of a New Age concept, her nurturing, methodical nature will see to it that it grows. Especially helpful in winning her over will be evidence that new concepts are good for her children.

Normally, she will only risk upsetting the routine of her family life under the direst of circumstances. Once she has given up (or, God forbid, been left) she will begin instantly the search for someone to help her stabilize her life. Her dogged determination and "I did it once, I can do it again" attitude will make her shape up her body, select a stunning new wardrobe, and literally propel herself into the mate marketplace. Typical situations that might push her to infidelity are:

1 Lack of complete respect for her mate. She wouldn't have settled down with him if she didn't respect him, and when she loses this necessary marital component, she will begin to look for it elsewhere.
2 Years of neglect and disregard for her needs. She's stubborn for sure, even when it comes to her own fulfillment. It takes a long time and repeated failures to recover his initial infatuation before she decides it's time to get what she needs from someone else.
3 Complete failure of her mate as a lover. She is the embodiment of love. She *must* have intimacy, touching, caressing, stroking, or she wilts like an orchid planted in the Sahara. She will tolerate many other deprivations for much longer than she will put up with the denial of give-and-take sex.
4 Lack of total financial security. If she doesn't feel, see, and sense security, watch out! Few things mean more to her, and she is capable of making great sacrifices for it; if it demands total reorganization of her well-constructed life, so be it.
5 Constant loneliness. Again, her need for intimacy, for being needed and appreciated, causes her to spring into action. She knows the difference between being alone and being lonely, and though she delights in the former, she has little tolerance for the latter.

If she is far from home in a romantic setting and can be sure that her security, position in the community, and reputation for being down-to-earth are safe, she may well falter. An older Taurus Woman can find a lusty young man irresistible. If she reasons that nothing and nobody can be hurt by the experience, she will be rejuvenated by the freshness of a brief and erotic tumble.

Children are a necessary element in any lifestyle the Taurus Woman may find herself involved with. A true heir of the Taurian-type pioneer spirit and determination of the past century, she believes in the lessons life can teach us all. She loves the earth, appreciates the struggle for life on it, and understands the importance of willing it to the children of the future.

If the choice is hers, she will probably elect to live her life in the country. There she can quietly gather possessions, establish a comfortable home, and exercise the maximum influence on the populace around her. If she winds up in an urban environment, she tends to create a closely knit community that she can trust, help to build and nurture, and above all feel secure in. She finds outlets for all her earthly energies in the city, and if she opens up to it, she can learn from the vastness and density that exists there.

Alternative lifestyles

Single woman: Her tenacity, persistence, and patience can enable Taurus to embrace this lifestyle. Although she delights in companionship and sexual fulfillment, she will remain single until she has found her Crown Prince. Her need for the highest quality in everything, including her men, makes her very selective. Once she has found her "ideal man," she will probably firm the relationship up and make a strong commitment within months. And should she somehow slip up and make a wrong choice (which is very, very seldom) you can count on her to be the last to outwardly recognize it and admit to it.

Intimate networks: This social movement advocates friendships with both sexes, neither rejecting nor embracing sexual involvement.

The Taurus Woman prefers males to females in friendship. Her possessiveness may get in the way of her natural flow with people, but she will exercise her patience and tolerance to overcome this if she feels the end result will be worth it. She is close to expert at endearing herself to others, and when she gets a good handle on the worth of exchanging experiences with friends, she makes good choices. If she is stable in her primary relationship with a man, the sexual variations of this lifestyle will become acceptable, even interesting, to her.

Open marriage: This arrangement almost never works for Taurus! Her innate possessiveness and jealousy generally preclude even slight consideration of this alternative. The mere thought of giving another woman permission to enjoy *her* man can cause her thinly veiled self-doubt to emerge and devastate her for days.

The Taurus Woman can be very understanding and sensitive to others, and she is loath to infringe on anyone's right to seek happiness and fulfillment where they choose. She will probably even listen to the close friend who has entered into an open marriage tell of the joys, the peaks of enlightenment, and the satisfaction such a relationship has given her. Listening with interest and performing are two vastly different things, however, and Taurus is relatively unshakeable in this case.

Ménage à trois: Again, her jealousy and possessiveness do not lend themselves to this kind of sharing. Taurus is more apt to try it during that rare trip to visit an old college roommate—but only if she is sure it will remain her secret, and if she has a deep-seated trust in the people she joins.

This situation could be ideal for Taurus; it could help her bolster her inner security, eradicate her deep attachment to possessions (her man being the primary one), and even enhance her self-esteem. The possibilities are endless: her husband could reassure her of her own place of divine prominence in his life by allowing her the experience of even more sexual fulfillment; after a night of romping, touching, and feeling, she would still be the one waking up in his arms and padding off to tend his breakfast. She could then see the folly of considering her man as another of her possessions as she witnessed him temporarily "belonging" to another. Alas, unless Taurus has evolved dramatically she is destined to stick to her routines, which *never* include sharing her man.

Group marriage: If Taurus has gotten past monogamy for monogamy's sake, this situation can provide her with even more security and emotional richness. The opportunity to enlarge the colony of people who rely on her stability and dependability is definitely there.

Again, it would take a fairly high level of growth for the Taurus Woman to consider this as an alternative to the proven one-on-one marriage. Something for her to consider: experimenting with this type of arrangement can be good for her. If it doesn't work out, she shouldn't feel like a failure. Experiments aren't always judged by total success or failure. The side effects can enrich her relationships, make her grow, and enhance her already heady sensuality.

Communal living: Taurus is an excellent candidate for a commune, especially if she is entering as a single woman. She loves to care for people and help them make good decisions for themselves (though often she tries to determine exactly what is or isn't a good decision). The gardens and larders of this commune would be the envy of the county, for she loves few things more than working the soil and tending the kitchen. Her practicality and productivity can be infectious and can serve to solidify the diverse attitudes of the residents. Her love of teaching and her tremendous money-management talents could prove invaluable.

The problems would arise when her possessiveness and jealousy took over. She could easily assume "ownership" of each and every member and then be crushed if anyone tried to contribute equally. It would become *her* commune, and although she would generously provide for everyone, the spirit of the concept would ultimately be lost.

Gay/bisexual lifestyle: If she opens up to another woman in intimate circumstances, the Taurus Woman often finds she prefers the gentle interchange. Her sexual needs are great, indeed, but she prefers lengthy, sensual, and erotic sessions in bed. Another woman can often identify with the attention to detail and the give-and-take attitude that typify the Taurus Woman's sexuality. Taurus's strong masculine side can be attractive to feminine women. And if this lady of the earth overcomes some of her deep-seated conservatism, she can often grow to accept the love she gives to and gets from another woman.

Insofar as bisexuality is concerned, if it requires sharing her man with another woman in a ménage à trois situation, she will probably reject it. If in a dating situation, she finds herself equally attracted to men and women, she will indeed have a dilemma on her hands. She can't get what she needs totally from either in this case, and she is prone to settling down with one person for life. This could be another ideal situation for her to grow into. Learning to share her possessions opens up all kinds of new options for her developing adaptability.

Summing up Taurus

Much of the Taurus Woman's energy is used in gaining control. She feels that material wealth will provide her with security and happiness in turn. More than any other sign, Taurus carries unhealthy tendencies towards gross materialism. She also tries to exercise too much control over those around her, not so much for the power this brings, but more for the sake of their best interests. She must learn that everyone has to develop a sense of their own best interests and learn to fulfill them unaided.

Her strict self-control can make her quite introspective. Her deep-seated feeling of inadequacy drives her to seek approval from those around her. When it pays off, she should accept it and enjoy it. The evolved Taurus Woman will seek a balance between giving and receiving.

The Taurus Woman is sharply focused on life's basics. She believes a comfortable home and a family are as important as a career. As she develops, she will learn that combining the two successfully can enhance her feelings of security. However, her many virtues and positive attitudes can be sublimated if she becomes too greedy for the material things she loves. Being too possessive can antagonize those she works so hard to comfort. Her natural giving nature is to be admired, and she should develop a sense of pride about it.

The Taurus Woman's determination to live without making mistakes often sets her up for failure, which in turn reinforces her fears of inadequacy. She is tolerant of others but judges herself too severely. She needs to release herself from the false encumbrances of self-doubt and regenerate her values. Her great love of nature and knowledge of the cosmos will aid her. As she grows, her expansive view of life and of the order of things will teach her that there is more to living than possessing.

Freed from the burden of too many possessions and the responsibility they bring. Taurus will be able to flow with the changes she encounters. Her innermost being will soar, and her generous nature will emerge to succor coming generations. The Earth Goddess will be reborn.

GEMINI

CHECKLIST OF GEMINI TRAITS

Note: This checklist describes the traits of one *phase* only; if it doesn't seem to fit you, check other lists to find the phase you are in right now.

1. Mercurial
2. Quick
3. Scattered
4. Capricious
5. High-strung Nervous
6. Entertaining
7. Stimulating
8. Talkative, Communicative
9. Clever
10. Witty
11. Charming
12. Inconsistent
13. Unpredictable
14. Versatile
15. Outgoing, Adventuresome
16. Freedom-loving
17. Inventive
18. Broad-minded
19. Cerebral
20. Of Two Minds
21. Inquisitive
22. Footloose
23. Impractical
24. Youthful
25. Dramatic
26. Multifaceted
27. Game Player
28. Neurotic Sex Drive
29. Short Attention Span
30. Changeable
31. Noncommittal
32. Opportunist
33. Devoted
34. Ambidextrous
35. Spendthrift

Gemini personality

General traits and background

The Gemini Woman enlivens existence on this otherwise dull and predictable planet. Her fantastic imagination, graced with a lively wit and exhilarating charm, permeates her life, her speech, her attitudes, and her writings. Forever young, she can transmit this feeling to those around her. There is something highly refreshing about her personality.

She takes pride in her ability to entertain and excite men. She so enjoys the chase that she has somewhat of a reputation as a tease, for she doesn't expect to have sex with every man she excites. As volatile as air itself, she catalyzes the environment and the people around her. She is aware and sure of herself. Her antennae are constantly scanning the room for any change of mood, any subtle nuance, or any stray male who may have entered. She wastes little time in finding her target, and if her fixed gaze does not capture him, she literally talks him into a corner.

Gemini is the third sign of the Zodiac and is Mutable Air. The mutable part makes her changeable. Being always on the verge of changing into something else, the Gemini personality is hard to pin down. She is an ever-changing kaleidoscope of moods, roles, and even people. You can never really say you *know* a Gemini Woman; more often, the real question is which one of her many selves she is at the moment.

Air does not like to be bottled up; it seeks to escape. It is hard to confine, it wishes to be free. The air acts as a vehicle for sound. It connects people, thoughts, and places as it blows its verbal message back and forth. Thus, the Gemini Woman is a communicator and deals with messages of the intellect.

Each astrological sign is said to be "ruled" by a planet and its vibrations. Gemini is ruled by Mercury, messenger to the gods. Fleet-footed Mercury facilitates all communication. Learning, letter writing, reporting, newscasting, traveling, and gossiping all fall under the aegis of Mercury.

The Gemini-*type* woman is one who has the sun or other important planets in Gemini, planets in the third house (the natural house of Gemini), a Gemini ascendant, or a powerfully aspected Mercury. Gemini types are also those who are temporarily going through a Gemini *phase*. In this case, a woman need have no planets in the sign of Gemini. The Gemini type is described by the checklist of traits at the beginning of this chapter. The Gemini phase has the following characteristics:

1 Intense mental activity; inability to turn off the mind.
2 Finding very little pleasure in sex; using it to attract, excite, and release nervous tension.
3 Total immersion in people, projects, and experiences, followed by boredom and disinterest.
4 A compulsion to communicate everything that is seen, heard, or felt.
5 Feelings of fragmentation; self-scattered emotions; multiple personalities seeking to find a wholeness.
6 Wanting to escape the responsibilities of the world and of relationships.

The Gemini Woman seldom chooses violent ways to express her innermost frustrations. She is more apt to escape into the world of fantasy, where she can release her pent-up nervous energy. Soap operas, film magazines, true romances, and movies offer her a perfect outlet. She may be entranced with the idea of sex but will not actively pursue physical/sexual unions. She would rather experience sex vicariously on the silver screen, go home to her tidy house, and forget it.

The Gemini Woman has a twofold aspect, symbolized by Castor and Pollux, the twins. The sign is an enigma, with each twin aware of the other, each seeking to please the other, each loving the other, but both trying to escape from their own mirror image. Complex relationships, a complex love life, and a complex personality are traits of the Gemini Woman. Most everyone is aware that the surface image of the Gemini Woman is in constant change; but few understand her innermost feelings.

The Gemini Woman is often tall and slender. She carries herself with assurance. It is obvious that she is going where the action is. She can often be found sunning herself; she delights in the sun's rays and energy. She has very good proportions and keeps her shape well into middle age. She projects a youthful air.

She dresses well, for she realizes the importance of a good appearance. She is rather flashy and fond of show. Alert and alive to the moment, she does not reflect on her past actions—even an hour ago is almost an eternity away. She lives very much in the present, and usually for the present.

The Gemini Woman, all too aware of the complexities of her

dual nature, seeks wholeness. She often seeks her other half in someone else. She needs to learn that the contrasting energies she carries within must be balanced before she can find true happiness outside herself.

Her mind can sometimes be her worst enemy. It is so hyperactive and powerful that if she does not have movement and response around her, she often tries to create it. To relieve boredom she incites those around her to fight. She then sits back and watches the fireworks. When her manipulations are discovered, she keeps very few friends.

A key word for her is *involvement.* The Gemini Woman is curious about everything. There is nothing she will not try. No dare or challenge goes past her. She would become involved at Land's End, if by nothing more than talking to the goats. She is not happy unless burning the candle at both ends. If she has a space where nothing is happening, verbal exchange is absent, or activities cease, she feels that her life is a failure.

Mercurial, quick, scattered

Mercury, her ruling planet, is symbolized by quicksilver. She is just as shiny, alive, and agitated. And like the element mercury, should you drop her, she breaks into a thousand tiny fragments.

Her movements are quick and fluid. So is her mind. It can jump from one topic to another with the speed of lightning. She is one of the most intelligent of the Zodiacal signs, and there is nothing under the sun that will not attract her quick and energetic mind. However, she often lacks reason and judgment, not to be confused with intellect. In her quest for knowing, she often overlooks the obvious and doesn't have the common sense to put her findings to practical use.

Most people are no match for her quickness and for the range of things she has encountered on her many mental flights. These qualities, coupled with a ready wit and the ability to put down any opponent who is not quick enough on the draw, make her a formidable debater. She seldom loses an argument.

Just as mercury scatters if it is dropped, the Gemini Woman has a tendency to scatter her energies. Too many interests, too many romances, too many wasted intellectual pursuits, leave her depleted, separated into little pieces. Her greatest task is to keep from becoming fragmented. She needs the will power of her Taurus sister and the concentration of Pisces to keep her energies in one place long enough to accomplish what she desires.

She also needs to learn to slow down and enjoy life a little more. She is always in a hurry. She searches for the quickest way to do things. Drip-dry clothes, microwave ovens, and fast foods appeal to her sense of "let's get it over with so we'll have more time for important things." She sacrifices much in order to find a shortcut and save time. However, because she squanders time on unfulfilling pursuits, she seldom enjoys the fruits of her labors.

Capricious

The Gemini Woman will follow a whim wherever it may lead. Her sudden and unreasonable changes will drive those about her wild. However, she seems to know what she's doing, and if you follow her, at least your life will never be dull. So whimsical that she could be a character out of *Alice in Wonderland*, the Gemini Woman follows a voice deep within her that compels her to act. She always regrets not paying heed to her inner messages and directions. The Gemini Woman resembles the Capricorn Woman as she jumps from one project to another, from one career to another, and from one relationship to another. However, Capricorn knows why she is jumping from mountaintop to mountaintop and has calculated the exact result of her moves. The Gemini Woman, on the other hand, takes a leap in blind faith that it is the correct thing to do, no matter what the outcome.

Routine drives the Gemini Woman crazy. Anything that can be predicted or reduced to a formula in anathema to her. She would rather work for a circus than a dry-goods store. She goes out of her way to introduce new challenges into her life. And she appears as erratic as the motion of the planet Mercury. Don't try to figure out why she is doing something; just accept it and jump on the merry-go-round with her, and you'll have fun.

The Gemini Woman has a great sense of humor, her wit and charm are legendary, and she is game for anything, the more on the spur of the moment the better. Her voice has a lilt to it, almost a melody. She enjoys laughing (although she may laugh at the wrong time) and can keep up her banter for hours.

The Gemini Woman is a quick-change artist. She can switch roles as quickly as a chameleon changes colors. From party girl to housewife to career woman to serious political analyst, she moves across the spectrum with a quick flutter of her long lashes. Titania could not be more magical in her ability to project completely different personalities.

Never expect to be able to predict the moods of a Gemini Woman. They shift from moment to moment, like the patterns in a kaleidoscope. One harsh word is enough to cause a complete shift in her emotions, which are as volatile as warmed morning air rising off the floor of the desert.

The Gemini Woman is very hard to pin down. She changes her mind rapidly. She may say yes one day, and no the very next. You seldom have to wait long for a response; she speaks off the top of her head, often without taking time to think.

High-strung, nervous

The Gemini Woman is as high-strung and nervous as a racehorse. Ever poised for the next occurrence, she has the air of a battle-ready warrior. She never knows when she must flee, but she is constantly ready for flight. By being constantly poised and expectant, she insures that very little gets past her. On the positive side, this tenseness gives her a great deal of optimism and that feeling of anticipation so important to anyone wishing to try new ventures. When she is in this mood, no negativity can daunt her.

The Gemini Woman will not make a decision without first polling all those involved. She does not like to be blamed for anything. She feels shattered when someone yells at her and will dissolve into the floor when harshly criticized.

Her lungs and nervous system are her weak points. She is prone to accidents involving the hands and arms. Often she trips and falls because she is racing ahead without looking where her feet are going. She needs to strive for self-control, calmness, and an awareness of her path.

Above all, she needs to channel her excess nervous energy into areas that will bring her happiness, which often eludes her. If she learns to direct and balance energy, she will be able to control her own experiences rather than so often becoming a victim of circumstances.

Entertaining, stimulating

The Gemini Woman loves to entertain. Unlike her Taurus and Cancer sisters, whose affairs feature abundant food as the center of attraction, she herself is the main course. She is in her element at a party. She can be charming, she can be witty, she can exercise her word power. She will tease, excite, and be the life of the party.

When her guests leave, she is totally exhilarated and feels no responsibility for the lives of those she has touched.

She has a backlog of interesting things to talk about and is never at a loss for words. She will dredge up some long-forgotten bit of information about the cholera plague of 1850, the sex life of the fruit fly, or the social significance of Philip Johnson's glass house in Connecticut and build an interesting evening's conversation around it. She never tires of telling stories and remembering the funny things that have happened in her nonstop, no-turning-back life.

She may even treat you to a song or a piano rendition. Her voice is apt to have a poetic quality to it and be filled with expression. This ability to get the most out of a word and imbue it with emotional content is very much a Gemini characteristic. Her musical tastes run the gamut, but it is almost a prerequisite that the music be dramatic, moving, and full of character.

Whatever the method, the Gemini Woman will stimulate thinking in those around her. She delights in stretching minds. The expectant air she exudes, the gyrations of her mind as it skips from image to image, subject to subject, almost demand that you jump on the roller coaster and be taken along for the ride. She makes an excellent teacher because of this very ability.

Just as she cannot stand to see a mind at ease, a lazy body also causes her to spring into action. She will invent some project, devise some plan, or simply push the body into an activity. She isn't too concerned about the outcome, believing that some good is bound to come from action per se. I have one Gemini friend who is constantly pushing, prodding, and nagging her Libra husband into action; although much against his will, he is usually delighted once he gets involved.

Talkative, communicative

The Gemini Woman is the Zodiac's natural communicator. She loves movies, television, stereo, computers, libraries—anything that facilitates a constant exchange of information. When news is happening, she wants to be as close to it as possible. If she took time to check her facts, she could be an excellent reporter.

The telephone is like an extension of the Gemini Woman's personality. She will have an extension in each room, with one in the garage and basement for good measure. She is ambidextrous and may be performing several tasks in the kitchen while talking to a friend. Because of her quick, perceptive mind and her desire to get to the next point, she often interrupts the person to whom she is speaking.

The Gemini Woman invented free association and blank verse. Her free-flowing conversation drives Taurus, Libra, and Capricorn wild. She often doesn't even finish one sentence before taking off on another thought. When she soars into the wild blue yonder, she will not remember where she started or where she has been—but wasn't the trip fun? She never looks back, always ahead. Had Lot's wife been a Gemini, she would never have been turned into a pillar of salt.

She makes an excellent audience, but don't be fooled. She listens carefully only so she can interrupt and get her four cents' worth into the conversation. She is a compulsive talker and has an opinion on everything; she rubs the Blarney stone daily just in case the truth needs a little elaboration to make it interesting.

The Gemini Woman is very selective about the information she divulges. Her computerlike mind analyzes and screens all data, releasing just enough to give a story the particular slant she wants. She makes a good propagandist; part of the truth is all she cares to handle. Her ability to deal in half-truths and truths that are slightly stretched gives her a reputation for being somewhat tricky. If she is questioned directly and pointedly, she will tell the truth. Thus, you must be very direct when dealing with Lady Gemini.

Words are her chief medium; she has an outstanding talent for self-expression. She also has an artistic flair and can express herself in interior decoration, by painting, and with the voice.

Clever, witty, charming

A Gemini Woman lives by her wits. Though the situation may look impossible, she will discover a clever, workable solution. She constantly hones her intellectual abilities and is ready to turn any twist of fate to her advantage.

Her ready wit has saved many a dull dinner party. Her insights are keen and to the point; she has a way with words. She see humor in places where many are too insensitive to notice. The spice of her wit creates its own welcome. She is just as much at home in a tavern as she is in the banquet hall of Windsor Castle. Pity the prince or drunkard who tries to match wits with her. She never loses.

As verbally caustic as she can sometimes be, she seldom offends. Her secret is the charm with which she delivers a rather unvarnished truth, the clever package she puts it in. I have seen Gemini tell a man that he is a complete pig and have him laugh and agree that he probably is. She can be so direct, so forceful, and so sweet that the combination is irresistible.

She can turn this combination of traits into a fantastic bonus in any situation where great diplomacy is required. She works well in the diplomatic corps if she has learned to control her natural urge to reveal everything she knows and can temper her hair-trigger responses. She would do much better if she thought before speaking rather than vice versa.

Inconsistent, unpredictable

The Gemini Woman is nearly totally unpredictable. She is a jump ahead of everyone, including herself. The only constant to be expected from her is the unexpected. The fact is that she herself doesn't know, and doesn't want to know, what she will do next. Life is much more exciting if the future is unknown. Never expect a Gemini Woman to be on an even keel; she is a living variable.

The Gemini Woman's attention to the things at hand varies too. An "out of sight, out of mind" approach often signals loss of friends, business troubles, and lack of personal growth. She has driven many bosses wild by improving and rearranging filing systems that have been in effective use for years. The truth is that she is very unorthodox. She delights in finding a different way of doing things. She will gladly exchange traditional ways for her way, but even that won't remain constant. She just as easily changes her own way as someone else's.

Versatile

The Gemini Woman can try just about anything and excel. Somewhere deep in her being, there seems to be a plan for just about any venture under the sun, and she alone has the ability to draw upon that knowledge. Her versatility allows her to learn things quickly and to obtain the necessary skills in a very short time. As long as something is new, it is exciting. She will drop an old project that does not interest her and just as quickly take up a new one. Because she has a very short attention quotient, when something is no longer new, it becomes boring. She would rather be dead than bored.

The Gemini Woman is so afraid she's going to miss something that she will try to be in two places at the same time. She can handle two jobs simultaneously. She may give both a lick and a promise, but she does enough to insure passable results. She usually has her fingers in more pies than Jack Horner and cannot possibly handle all the work she undertakes. She is never happy unless she has more than one project going at once. Only when demands are made on her time does she feel important and needed. Blank spaces horrify her.

"Jack of all trades, master of none" sums up the Gemini Woman. Her interest in a variety of things and her ability to undertake so many of them at once give her great dexterity in learning new skills, though she seldom masters them either. She needs to learn how to persevere and follow things through to completion. It is not enough to figure out the principle; she must also be willing to do the work.

Outgoing, adventuresome

Ruled by Mercury, Mutable Air, Gemini likes to run around. As a child, she excelled in races, bicycling, and exploring. As an adult, she is a seasoned traveler, as much at home in a foreign port as she is in her well-appointed apartment. Often she is much happier in the city than in the country; the hum of traffic, the bustle of shopping, the museums and the art galleries—all offer an excitement that the serene countryside does not afford.

She has an active nature and is eager for adventure. She is often found rushing helter-skelter in search of the new and the different. Wherever there is something new, exotic, and exciting you can be sure to find her. She is sure about where she is going, and surprisingly enough, she always knows how to get there.

The Gemini Woman is a good sport and will try anything once. Need a friend to go elephant riding in Jodhpur? Want to pan for gold in the Yukon? Yearn to hunt antelope on the Serengeti Plain? The Gemini Woman will be right at your side, spurring the elephant to move a little faster.

She is just as outgoing in her personal relationships. She enjoys meeting all sorts of new people and is eager to learn as much from them as she can. She has the ability to pick the brain of friend and foe alike and can learn from one as easily as from the other. She is the first to grasp that all life is a school and that learning comes from experience as well as from books.

Freedom-loving
The most important possession a Gemini Woman has is her freedom. She is definitely a no-strings-attached, independent lady. If someone tries to possess her time or her body, she immediately pulls away. Both commodities are hers to do with as she pleases. She may choose to squander either on useless pursuits, but the choice must remain hers. Air knows no boundaries, and the Gemini Woman wants very few. She desires to be as free as the wind, and just as mobile.

She seeks the same quality in her relationships. She does not want to be bound by the restraints of responsibility and duty. Although she will assume a great deal of both, again the choice must be hers. She does not want to feel that they have been imposed on her.

The Gemini Woman often turns to avenues of pure escapism. Alcohol, drugs, nicotine, movies, love stories, soap operas, and compulsive work habits offer escape valves that help her let off excess energy. Whatever the opiate, however, none is effective unless she learns to operate within human boundaries. It is difficult for her to live with this basic limitation.

Inventive
The Gemini Woman loves gadgets. Walk into her kitchen, and you feel that you have entered the next century. She will spend a great deal of time figuring out how to create labor-saving methods and devices. She has just the fertile mind to do it.

She is just as inventive when it comes to making situations workable. New challenges are just what she needs. Difficult tasks on the job, impossible complications at home, complex problems that stump the experts—all spur her on to her most creative levels. She knows that every riddle has an answer and every puzzle can be solved, and her active mind is the right tool for the job. She is constantly designing procedures, solutions, and systems that will simplify the complicated.

Broad-minded
Every story has two sides, or so the Gemini Woman believes. Therefore, she will seek to hear both before she makes up her mind. For all her flighty tendencies, she will be very fair in her judgments. She takes very few things personally; rather she views most action as taking place on a stage that is removed from her immediate influence.

Being somewhat unorthodox, she does not cast stones at the far-out ideas and ideals of others. That something has never been tried before is ample reason for the Gemini Woman to try it. Who knows, it may work and be more fun than the old way.

Cerebral, of two minds, inquisitive

The Gemini Woman has a mind that races ahead of her body. Thus, she finds it difficult for her pen to keep up with her thoughts. In fact, it is hard for her to still her mind once it has been set in motion. The wheels keep turning no matter how she tries to stop them. Insomnia, confusion, error, and nervous exhaustion are often the result of not being able to control the mind.

Her curious mind asks the question "Why?" She probes, studies, analyzes, until she is satisfied that she knows the answers. At times she is so full of questions that she feels she doesn't know anything at all.

Her restless mental state often leads to insecurity, for she doubts that anything can be known for certain. There are so many variables and possibilities that can color what is so. The Gemini Woman constantly seeks self-improvement. She will sign up for night classes, start working on her real-estate licence, or buy a set of self-help cassettes; in short, she is open to anything she thinks will improve her lot, sharpen her intellect, or bring in more money (a constant problem). She is an intellectual creature and is fascinated by puzzles, word games, anything written by Dorothy Parker. If she must sit still mentally, she is likely to explode emotionally.

Her personality is a wonder to behold. Her dual nature allows her to think one way and act another. This causes her no immediate problem, but it may cause her mate or friends to scratch their heads and wonder if they understand what she is saying. This duality manifests itself in many little ways. She may start off for her destination and go in exactly the opposite direction. She may be having lunch with you and repeatedly use someone else's name when addressing you. Her body sometimes seems to be in the room while her mind is somewhere else.

Being of two minds, she seldom accepts the reality in front of her. She seeks to read between the lines and is very good at doing so. However, she can easily read in something that is not there, and that's when she makes some of her most dreadful mistakes. There seems to be very little middle ground for the Gemini

Woman; for her, it is all or nothing. One of her minds is fascinated with things as they are. She is almost encyclopedic in noting details that escape others. She has an uncanny ability to understand why things work. The other mind, however, is fascinated with things unseen. Stories of ghosts, seances, and Tarot readings will send goose bumps up and down her arms.

She enjoys the good things in life but realizes that few things last forever. Rather than storing up, she uses. When things are gone she'll buy more. She subscribes to the philosophy "Eat, drink, and make merry, for tomorrow you die." Even here, however, she is of two minds. One part of her is concerned with the idea of security, while the other is more cognizant of the ephemeral nature of existence. The former concern usually wins out the Gemini Woman, however.

She is rather like the Grand Inquisitor; there is no hiding from her. She will ferret out the facts even if it takes all her time to do so. Once she sets her mind on something, she leaves no stone unturned. Having such an inquisitive mind, she makes a good student and researcher. She instinctively knows where to look for information.

Footloose, impractical

The Gemini Woman spends a great deal of time trying to break the shackles others have placed on her. Much of love and marriage has built-in conditions, strings the Gemini Woman cannot tolerate. She is happy when she is loving, but don't try to use that love to tie her down to routine, obligation, or permanence. She must be able to exit a relationship as easily as she entered.

She does not like the permanence of possessions, either, and she will give away or throw away material goods that are not being used. If she hasn't touched it in three months, she thinks she'll never need it—and out it goes! She wants to be ready to move at a moment's notice, and the fewer things she has, the easier it is. She often lacks "gathering" energy (she uses it so carelessly), and she doesn't want to bother with a lot of clutter.

The Gemini Woman often appears impractical to her friends. She seeks stability in her life yet will throw it away if she becomes impatient. She wants to be loved but does not want to accept any responsibility for her beloved. She wants to learn but often blocks the attempts of those who would teach her.

She dreams very grandiose dreams but often lacks the translation ability to make them reality. She lacks the patience to follow through on many of her schemes. Her low threshold for boredom generates a lack of determination and persistence in seeing projects through.

Too often, she hitches her wagon to stars rather than to fence posts. Her dreams are built on desires and need to be grounded. She needs to ask herself if the dreams are possible, considering situational reality. She sees things in an almost ideal state. She needs to view them in light of hard reality and work towards modifying what *is* to match what *might be*.

Her dreamworld is often the basis of her rather skittish life. Her reality is so tenuous that it is always in danger of cracking or breaking from the weight of the demands she places on herself. There is a delicate balance between the two worlds. She must strive to maintain the ideal, melding her own realities with those life pushes towards her.

Youthful

The Gemini Woman doesn't seem to age and keeps her childlike innocence intact. As part of her character, her ability to love seems boundless; this in itself helps keep her young. In fact, there are very few times in her life when she isn't in love.

The Gemini Woman also works at staying young. She likes her slim figure and watches what she eats. She has very good skin and takes care of it. She even dresses younger than her years. Above all, she keeps a youthful attitude. Her innate joy in discovery, in learning, and her involvement in things around her give her an air of expectancy. She is nearly childlike as she finds that there is a whole world out there to explore.

Dramatic, multifaceted

The Gemini Woman seeks the drama in life. There must be action, dialogue, conflict. She seems to learn more quickly when life offers difficulties to be overcome, when there is a clear story and a plot that leads somewhere. She can also be dramatic in her self-expression, especially her writing. Reading one of her letters makes you feel you are right there with her. Her decorating also shows a flair for the dramatic, perhaps in the use of a bold color (she likes them all and has no favorites) or in the proper placement of an old Chinese chair and screen. Whatever the device, she achieves a striking scenario like few others.

You can never say you *really* know a Gemini Woman. Just when you think you have her down to a science, she reveals a facet you never expected. She may casually mention that she taught school in Alaska, once went scuba diving off the coast of Australia, or whatever, and that she hadn't thought you'd be interested. She has kept these "secrets" carefully concealed for the right moment. She knows how to make an impact.

Whatever the task at hand, one of her many selves will generally rise to the occasion. She may never have given first aid, but in an accident she is the one who has the presence of mind to apply a tourniquet. She is good in any emergency. If the books need to be balanced and cleaned up before the auditors come, she is the one you'll find working late.

Neurotic sex drive, game player

The Gemini Woman can be just as sexy as any woman of the Zodiac; she merely loses interest quickly. She is intellectually interested in the idea of sex but often less concerned about the physical reality. In some ways she would rather watch than participate although she knows that sex is an important part of life.

The Gemini Woman often uses sex to validate her ego. As long as she can attract and lure men, she feels young and romantic. When she gets a man to chase her, she feels she still has what it takes to make it. However, once the excitement wears off, she becomes distracted and cools rather quickly. An interesting note: she often thinks more highly of an old flame than of her current conquest. She has a tendency to idealize the man and later often recalls her idealized image rather than the reality of the person she experienced.

Sex, for all its lore, is not what attracts the Gemini Woman. She is much more interested in what a man can provide for her. Unlike her Taurus sister, she will seek the man with power and position rather than getting carried away and lusting after the gardener or delivery boy. Sex does not drive her; it is more a means to an end. The end is her own security and position.

Explosive sex is a mainstay of one of the many games she plays. She pictures herself as a light to which all the moths are drawn. To prove her cleverness, she will turn on and off. She will lead a man down a path of difficult return and artfully dodge his advances. If you want to please her, chase her but never catch her.

She cannot tolerate boredom. She wreaks havoc on many

families by stirring up feuds and resentments. This is another of her favorite games. If she can get her brothers and sisters fighting with each other, and everyone fighting with the in-laws, it makes a jolly good time for her. It also keeps in check their demands for consistency and responsibility from her.

She's big on self-directed games too. She will exaggerate her own accomplishments and then not measure up to her self-imposed demands. She will convince herself that she is almost invincible and will find to her dismay that she is not. She will tell a lie often enough to believe it herself and will be unable to face the truth when it comes to haunt her. This is probably her most dangerous game, and unless she is careful, it will lead to her downfall.

Short attention span, changeable, noncommittal

If you made a date with a Gemini Woman a week ago, be sure to call her that morning. It may have slipped her mind. She no doubt has it written on her calendar, but in all probablity, she will have forgotten to look at it when she got up.

All the work she has to do will be piled on her desk. She feels that if she tucks it away, she will forget it. She drops letters, books, and newspapers right where she stops reading them so she can be sure to find them again when she is in the mood. I have known some Gemini women who forget what they are saying in mid-sentence. Most, however, have a slightly longer attention span.

Chances are that she will change careers as often as she changes her favorite sexy sling-back shoes. The quickness with which she learns often results in career shifts into completely different lines of work. I know one Gemini woman who progressed from secretary to fashion model to jewelry sales to owning her own rare antiques business in a matter of four years. (By the way, she makes a great salesperson. She is so glib and persuasive that she can talk people into buying things they often have little, if any, use for.)

One has to be very shrewd to get a commitment from the Gemini Woman. She is quick to venture into unknown territory but will not stay long. She's never sure what the future holds and doesn't want to commit herself to something that could hamper her. Thus, she seldom gives a straight answer. If she can hedge or sidestep or say, "Well, maybe," she will. Even with such basic things as appointments, she will avoid being pinned down to an exact time. She has been known to simply not show up. Sometimes she forgets, other time she wants to avoid the person or issue at hand.

Opportunist

The Gemini Woman is a creature of the moment. She is so aware of change and its critical nature that she will grab an opportunity the instant it appears. She always sees at least two different ways to go and delights in making the proper choice—that is, the choice she feels is in her best interest.

She operates more by circumstance than by fixed principle. She has little regard for consistency or consequences. She is more interested in how a particular situation affects her and how she can turn it to her own advantage. Her view of the world is highly relative; she's the center around which it revolves. She does not question the ethics or morality of an event too closely lest it not to be her benefit.

If need be, she is apt to be dishonest to obtain her ends. For her, little white lies and minor infractions of the law are necessary adjustments to a rigid and unbending world. She has rationalizations to fit every peccadillo. She can fool herself and everyone around her. Her fall often occurs when she is not quite as clever as she thinks she is and meets people who can see through her games.

On the positive side, she has an uncanny ability to predict public fads and infatuations and can often capitalize on the opportunities she perceives. She has a shrewd eye for what the general consumer wants and knows how to package it. When opportunity knocks, she feels compelled to answer with action.

Devoted

In light of all her quixotic traits, her devotion seems unusual. She can be totally consecrated to a person, an idea, or a project. This trait brings out the very best in the Gemini Woman.

Once an ideal is etched on her mind, she will carry it to the grave. She may completely idolize a former love and measure all her other lovers against his memory. She becomes "hopelessly devoted." Her intellect tells her such a position is unreasonable, but it is a deep emotional response that she has little control over.

Ambidextrous

The Gemini Woman is able to use both hands equally well. There may be little significance in the fact that a person can write with both her right and her left hand, but it does help to identify Gemini traits. Besides having the ability to use both hands, the Gemini Woman is very dextrous. She can take things apart and put them back together easily.

Spendthrift

The Gemini Woman acquires knowledge readily and wants to put it to immediate and profitable use. She makes money easily and spends it with abandon. Her bank account is usually a mess. Both money and possessions slip through her fingers like running water. She will spend her last dollar for the sheer joy of spending. Being penniless seems to stimulate the Gemini Woman into new activity.

Her motto is often "Easy come, easy go." She feels there will always be ways to make more money, and her incredible mind will always provide a reservoir on which she can draw. She believes in having what she wants when she wants it, and she will spend her last dollar to get it.

She is a born gambler. She wants windfall profits, not long-term projects of the Taurus variety, not patient collecting of rents; she wants her profits yesterday. She wants the fastest results with the least expenditure of energy. She is attracted to racetracks, gambling casinos, and oil speculation. No lottery or raffle escapes her attention. If she loses, she does not lament; instead, she forges ahead with another scheme plucked from her mental trove. She thinks that if she tries often enough she is bound to make it big eventually; often she does. And if she doesn't, she can always try again.

Nothing appeals more to the Gemini Woman than a fresh start. I have a Gemini friend who has sold all her furniture no fewer than three times because she gets such a thrill from starting all over again. She moved through modern, country French, and Mediterranean with the ease of changing her dress. A new job, a new lover, a new car, all give her a healthy glow.

The only thing the Gemini Woman does not know how to spend is her emotions. She often lacks true compassion. Don't expect chicken soup from her if you've been sick—often not so much as a kind word will come your way. It is difficult for the Gemini Woman to empathize, even with those close to her. And on a broader scale, she has little tolerance for the problems of social classes or institutions that don't have a direct bearing on her life.

Gemini relationships

O! swear not by the moon, the inconstant moon,
That monthly changes in her circled orb,
Lest that thy love prove likewise variable.
William Shakespeare
Romeo and Juliet

Get ready to start jogging when you get involved in a relationship with a Gemini Woman. I don't mean just a mile a day—we're talking about the Marathon! She's one of the fastest thinkers in the Zodiac. Her motto is "Here today, gone tomorrow," so you'd better be able to keep up with her.

She makes friends easily and is seldom without new ones. Her wit, talkativeness, cleverness, and outgoing nature always guarantee that a crowd will be around her. She's also so outwardly broad-minded that almost anyone can feel "acceptable" in her presence. She will talk to anyone about anything almost anytime. She's as likely to make a new friend at the laundromat as she is at the ballet. The more eccentric or creative people are, the more likely they are to acquire a Gemini Woman as a friend. She appreciates individuality, openness, and glamor.

She seems to have a sixth sense for knowing when there's an emergency in the household or life of a friend. She arrives first, not so much because of her Good Samaritan nature, but more often because there may be something new to learn, a way to display her multifaceted knowledge and wisdom or to impress someone with her ability to think and act fast.

If you want to insure a lively time at your party, invite a Gemini Woman. She's a guaranteed mixer and fits in well at an Archie Bunker–type patriotic celebration or a fund raiser for the legal defense fund of the NAACP. A well-rounded personality is her specialty, and parties offer her a perfect forum for the game playing she so enjoys.

She has many friends and acquaintances whom she can locate in a few minutes' time; the reverse is seldom true. She moves much too quickly for most to keep up with her; she may be spending a weekend with a young college type during the summer hiatus between weeks with her mother and her steady boyfriend in Aspen. One thing is certain, however: she'll always have her mental address book with her in case she needs to verify a fact, elaborate upon something that has happened to a mutual friend, or gloat about a new conquest to a sorority sister.

Her fickleness is legendary. She can have three gentlemen fetching for her at a lawn party and dazzle a fourth with her charm, wit, and slender body. She can't abide boring situations or boring people, and because of her quick perceptions, she is apt to see through both and depart quickly, with little more than a backward glance.

She either likes or loathes people at first sight. Her snap judgments are seldom wrong. She is both skeptical and suspicious of others' motivations; thus, she doesn't have the proverbial wool pulled over her eyes very often. She sees very clearly and trusts her insights totally.

For the Gemini Woman, the most important thing in a relationship is comfort. She will not waste her time and energies with someone who makes her feel uncomfortable. Unless she is reasonably self-assured with people, she cannot dazzle, and her free-flowing wit seems to merely seep through a blocked audio system.

She has a way of knowing much about the people she is involved with, though she seldom allows herself such luxuries of vulnerability. The easiest way to gain information about her is to listen to her attentively. Her many travels in search of her soulmate, her other half, have taken her places and given her experiences that few others ever have. She is indeed a fascinating lady and commands the attention of everyone around her.

Gossip is often her stock-in-trade. She doesn't listen well, and she has a penchant for repeating things in an embroidered form. The telephone is nearly an appendage for her, and when she forgets to pay the bill and it's temporarily disconnected, she could just die.

She doesn't have a good understanding of her own emotions, and she tends to be quite private about them. On a rare day, with a close, trusted friend, she may pour her heart out about her emotional instability. But don't try to continue the conversation the following morning; she'll have forgotten all about it.

Like the air her sign represents, she wants things to be light and moving. She'll panic if the atmosphere becomes too calm and restful. If a relationship settles around her and her friends finally get comfortable with her, she is likely to stay away for awhile so as to gather more knowledge and wit to dazzle and confuse them. Although she inwardly craves intimacy, the thought of it often stifles and suffocates her. She'll play at it, but don't expect "heaviness" from her.

She can be absent from her circle of close friends for years and upon her return pick up right where she left off. She loves renewing old friendships; it provides her the opportunity to dazzle once more. The same holds true for old flames, and when she comes back, you can be sure she'll have mastered a new technique or rearranged her sexual priorities—it'll seem like you're experiencing someone new whom you already know.

She goes to her high school class reunion hoping that everyone will be the same, only older. She ages very slowly, retains a youthful air, and develops the most attractive worldliness of any woman you're likely to know. She secretly delights in showing off her good maintenance program, and she'll flirt with old high school beaux even if they've grown portly and are balding.

She is skilled at conducting several different relationships with several different people at the same time. Often they don't know each other and are from diverse ethnic and cultural backgrounds. She craves variety and has no great need to assemble her passel of pals.

The same is true of the love affairs in her life. She often finds herself facing the dilemma of having to say no to one so she can say yes to another. This can be the best solution to her never-ending search for the "right one." Her commitment to this ideal is very real and strong; she seldom feels guilty when she discards yet another man who doesn't measure up.

She tends to deal in quantity rather than quality when she gets involved in new relationships. Often people are eager to know her because of her talent for making light of things and adding excitement to otherwise dull lives. Hers is to learn about many, not to understand a few.

Childhood

Gemini children are usually very bright and quick to learn. They are like magicians—now you see them, now you don't. They are also known explorers. I once had a Gemini woman tell me how frustrated her mother had been with her as a child. She would throw tantrums and scream at the top of her lungs until her mother released her from the prison of the playpen. When the child could wander and roam about the house, she was in her true domain: It was boredom, even at such an early age, that motivated this

Gemini woman to experience life as it came at her.

Gemini girls develop mobility skills earlier than most because without them they cannot explore and search. When such activities meet with maternal disapproval, battles rage. Mothers often assume that children fear the unknown, and when Gemini girls are willing to confront anything, their bravery often baffles their mothers.

Gemini girls often have many friends who come and go. For variety, they will have an equal number of male and female playmates. It isn't necessarily that they have "boyfriends" earlier than other girls; generally they begin romantic relationships at about the same time. Theirs, however, often have a depth and intensity that others' lack. Little-girl crushes are a waste of time for the Gemini girl. She learns how to court and beguile little boys early; it seems she is in training for the "real thing."

The best parents for a Gemini girl are those who trust her and let her freely explore. Freedom is often the key to her heart, and her behavior will be exemplary if the reward is some new form of freedom. She will pull away from parents who attempt to get too close, just as she later pulls away from men and other intimates for the same reason.

Although she often shies away from being "Daddy's little girl," she does develop the idealizing or idolizing nature that colors her later years. She tends to be closer to her father than to her mother. This is especially so if her father has a glamorous, exciting career and her mother stays close to the home fires.

She'll be the first in her group of friends to suggest playing doctor or some other "intimate" childhood game. She'll also probably be the first to exclaim, "Is that all there is?" Her "what I want to be when I grow up" fantasies will include doctor, lawyer, scientist, ballet dancer, socialite with great connections, and even politician if she's exposed to that possibility early enough. She doesn't mind playing house with her friends as long as her "husband" is in the Foreign Service and the setting is an island somewhere in the Mediterranean.

Her follow-up failures begin early in childhood too. Ask a Gemini girl to clean up her room, and it's like asking her to unbuild the Great Wall of China. Procrastination and a short attention span are qualities she is usually born with. She'll start by going into the room, but her mood will entirely dictate her progress. If she can find something to interest her or something to fantasize about amidst the rubble, you can forget the cleaning. On the other hand, you may find her washing her father's favorite pipe in the dishwasher because she thinks it's exciting to do something she isn't supposed to be old enough to do.

Gemini girls are graceful, due in large part to their ambidextrous nature. They excel at dancing and gymnastics; this gives them an opportunity to learn something and master feats that other children often have trouble with.

To successfully raise a Gemini girl, parents must be first aware of her innate charm. Lying is not beyond her, and she can be frighteningly believable. Her knack for embellishing the events surrounding a social function she attends and for making herself appear more attractive is something she carries with her most of her life.

She'll have plenty of boyfriends as she grows up and will be going steady with one (if not two or three) each week. She'll probably go to extremes in sexual experimentation too. She'll either say yes to all of them or withhold her sexual secrets until marriage. If she finds a boy or young man who offers her a glimpse of her other half, her elusive soulmate, she'll probably fall for him head over heels. She'll also discard him just as quickly when she discovers he isn't the "right one."

To make her adult life perhaps a little more stable, parents should take care to instill a sense of situational reality in the Gemini girl. She must learn at some point in her life that her other half can only emerge from within her. She must also learn that people aren't nearly as boring as they seem to her; she need only stop and listen to them to find that they are of much denser fabric than she imagines. You really can't tie her down, pen her up, lock her in; you can, however, give her a home base from which she can launch her many exciting trips and to which she can return for rejuvenation. That home base is often her own self-assurance, self-respect, and self-esteem, when they are all developed to their full potential.

How the Gemini woman relates: lovers and other intimates

Often the Gemini Woman's rather unrealistic approach to relationships isn't designed so much to fool those with whom she comes in contact as to serve as her own defense mechanism. She fears intimacy and reality and spends much of her energy in flight or fancy.

She is often surrounded by many people, which hides her deep-seated feelings of loneliness not only from others but from herself. In her frantic quest to gain omniscience about people and circumstances, she often fails to use others as a mirror to truly understand her actions. Her "out of sight, out of mind" attitude spills over into her relationships quite naturally. She concentrates on the things at hand and throws herself into the moment with seemingly complete abandon. The dishes can pile up in the sink, the laundry can form mountains on the floor of the bedroom; if there's something new and exciting at her disposal, little else matters.

She also has a tendency to idealize people, to inflate them completely beyond their normal proportions. When they fail to live up to her fantasies, she is disappointed. She must learn to be much more realistic about her relationships in this respect.

Her ego is fed when you tell her how much you enjoy her entertaining ways. She can go on for hours about her past experiences and travels, peppering it all with humor. She needs this sort of communication and spends a great deal of time polishing her personal style.

She'll also be over to help you paint the living room and lay the new carpeting. It helps if it's a small room, since her threshold for boredom is so low. She may get the ceiling and two walls done and discover she has to run off to ready herself for a party.

She loves people who can finish her sentences in their minds. Too many words bog her down; she hasn't a lot of patience when it comes to explaining the significance of some gossip. New experiences, new knowledge, and new gossip don't threaten her. If she stumbles across a foreign word she can't pronounce or understand, you can be sure she'll gloss it over with her personal interpretation. The next time, however, she'll know the traditional meanings, pronunciations, and origins.

Her denial of reality carries over into relationships as well. She can be furious with a friend one day, and the next totally deny that anything was ever amiss between them. She doesn't like to recall unpleasantness and will go to great lengths to avoid having someone tell her about her often unsavory behaviour.

Bigamy is more acceptable to a Gemini Woman than divorce. She needs stimulation from many different directions at once, and she is often in a love relationship with a one-dimensional man. If he doesn't provide physical stimulation, she can survive; if he doesn't provide mental stimulation, forget it! She likes to make

her men jealous to reinforce her feelings of being loved and wanted.
She will drive an earth-sign type of man crazy with her flitting, flirting, and changeable moods. She wants her man to follow her but can be terribly annoyed if he stays too close. She likes her freedom and at the same time finds it a personal challenge when a man tries to take any of it away from her. She is a bundle of contradictions, and this can work magic on a man who likes freshness, lightness, and change. It can be a bad dream for a man who is overly protective of his woman, who is jealous by nature, and who likes plenty of attention himself. Gemini will know what her lovers like and will spend half her time trying to please them, the other half tormenting them.

The Gemini Woman generally has the lazy-mother approach to child-rearing. She likes children and wants to have them around. Unlike many women, she isn't at all dismayed to learn that she is pregnant; after all, it's really another adventure, another experience that will certainly enrich her life in one way or another. I sense that succeeding pregnancies won't be as thrilling for her, for giving birth does require a certain amount of staying still and establishing roots.

She won't be as overprotective of her children as her Taurus and Cancer sisters. She will generally allow them all the freedom they require, and her constant movement will often stimulate them to explore and grow. She does expect her children to excel at something as soon as they master mobility.

During her thirties and forties, the Gemini Woman may become more honest with herself and begin to form a close circle of good and permanent friends. She may also acquire a career that teaches her some discipline and provides her with a goal towards which to work. Once she sets her mind to it, she has great potential for career success.

The Gemini Woman in love

The words of Victoria Woodhull rather aptly characterize the Gemini Woman in love: "I am a free lover. I have an inalienable constitution and natural right to love whom I may, to love as long or as short a period as I can, to change that love every day if I please." Gemini needs a lot of patient understanding. She really needs and wants love; what turns her off is the responsibility that comes with it.

So long as she is the center of attraction for her man, she will move mountains for him. If he has a day off, she'll call in sick so she'll be available for his pleasure. She'll prepare special meals for him (since she isn't enamored of the kitchen, this is quite a feat). She can often second-guess his needs and seem to read his mind when he needs a special favor; when he wants to go to the fights with the boys on Saturday, she tells him it's fine since she has already made plans to see her Aunt Pearl from Toledo. He'll never know she doesn't *have* an Aunt Pearl from Toledo; he'll think she's priceless for having arranged her schedule to fit so well with his.

If she feels slighted or taken advantage of, she'll either blow her stack and walk out, leaving him scratching his head, or she'll stay and have difficulty putting her finger on what is boring hell out of her these days. Nothing is immune from her escapist tactics when she chooses to employ them.

If her lover showers her with gifts when she needs them, predicts her moods and changes, and gently prods her to tell him what she needs and wants, he will be successful. He needs the wisdom to recognize her duality; she may seem very much in love with him today, and tomorrow act as though living with him is a tremendous bother.

When she is in love, she looks as though she is on cloud nine. She moves faster than ever, due partly to her fear of losing her freedom. She may employ her great talent for writing and pen poems to her lover daily. While she's singing him a love song in bed, her mind is plotting ways to insure his permanence at her side. She is very vulnerable when she truly falls in love, and this can be a blessing or a curse, depending on how secure she has become within herself.

Patterns in the Gemini Woman's sexual relationships

The concept of the primary relationship was tailored for the Gemini Woman. She doesn't make commitments easily because of her dual nature, her need for ever-changing scenarios, and her fear of being tied down. She won't directly confront this aspect of her personality; instead she will bend over backwards to continue in a sexual relationship with one man while adding others to her stable. She sincerely believes in the Primary Commitment; her involvement with other men is simply for variety!

She's not particularly attracted to married men if they are in residence with their wives. She doesn't like sharing the spotlight; God knows, the beacon is often not bright enough for her alone, much less for a space crowded with others. She's not too fond of triangles either—unless, of course, they involve two people devoting all their attention to her. She fears being left out, which is a natural spin-off of her loneliness.

After she ends a relationship, she often idealizes the man she has left. She will build elaborate fantasies around him and obviously expect her next man to live up to them. The Gemini Woman is very vulnerable in love situations. Since the excitement of the chase is often a greater reality for her than the happiness that comes later, she may end up teasing a man and then running away before he can catch her. This ultimately causes a great deal of stress, and her nervous system can suffer.

She often marries more than once. She can be so unsettled and bored when she first falls in love that sustaining a relationship with her is difficult. Middle age often modifies her wandering ways, and she is more apt to accept the responsibility of conventional life-styles. She is still susceptible to boredom and must work hard to find excitement within the structures she builds.

What kind of lover she wants

Every Gemini Woman has a secret list of qualifications for lovers. She needs a man who:

1. Likes getting two for the price of one.
2. Will stay up all night gossiping with her.
3. Can think of the words to "Shine On, Harvest Moon" more quickly than she can.
4. Will leave work early to see the dress rehearsal for the community theater musical she is starring in.
5. Will take her to a double-feature old-time movie show.
6. Will praise her for her sexiness even when she has been up all night doing crosswords puzzles with him.
7. Will buy her a sumptuous box of chocolates with the lunch money he's allocated himself for the week (she's his forever!).
8. Looks nice but doesn't spend hours creating an effect.
9. Is as multifaceted as she is, only less so!
10. Can function well in the good old American tradition of sexual "quickies."

11 Loves all her changes and can keep up with her while remaining relatively stable himself.

What she needs to learn

Boredom is the ultimate downfall of many Gemini Women. The following is a list of ten activities she may undertake to use her boredom constructively:

1. Confess out loud to yourself in a mirror when you're bored. Ask yourself: a. When did I become bored today? b. Why? c. Where did the boredom originate? d. What is this boredom? e. Who am I bored with?
2. Talk to the very next person who bores you. Ask why she/he thinks you may be bored. Ask if she/he ever becomes bored in that particular fashion.
3. The next time a project or chore has you bored to tears, finish it!
4. Talk to your boss about one of the more boring aspects of your job. See if there's something you can trade it for to maintain a higher level of interest and ultimately a higher level of productivity.
5. The next time you are bored while having sex or preparing to have sex with your mate, share a fantasy with him that he isn't aware of. Ask him to co-star with you.
6. Call attention to the low (read: boring) spots in your relationship with your lover. See if he's bored at the same places and times. Work them out, and share your boredom with him.
7. Make a list of six things you both find boring in your relationship. Make it a priority to work these out in order.
8. When you see a boring project looming on the horizon, try to insure that it is preceded and followed by something really exciting.
9. Ask a friend if she/he has a boring task to complete. Help finish it; it'll only take half the time and require half the boredom. This will help you achieve some discipline, share a rather unorthodox intimacy, and learn to ask for help with *your* boring chores.
10. Look in the mirror and thank yourself for boredom. Without it, you probably wouldn't be the energetic, fun-loving, and creative person you are.

A Gemini Woman often feels she just isn't where she'd like to be (wherever that might be). It may help her to prepare a sort of screenplay that delineates where she is now and where she'd like to be in Act II. When she compares the two, it'll be easier for her to see what direction she must take to bring reality closer to her desires.

She needs to develop a stronger sense of compassion. She can begin by practicing on herself, and she will probably find that her skills will flow over into the lives of others in a natural progression. Gemini Women often have a near overdose of "me," and the following exercises can serve as an antidote.

1 The next time you feel insensitive or angry with yourself, sit on the floor with one of your favorite fantasy selves opposite you. Talk to it as if it were you. Address your positive qualities.
2 When you feel indifferent about a friend, tell her/him why. Then say you want to learn to reach out; ask your friend to be patient with you, and then reach out as best you can. Ask if your reaching-out technique is effective. Ask for help in perfecting it.
3 Confess to a close friend, or even better, to your lover/husband/mate, the next time you feel really vulnerable. Explain why; ask them if she/he feels this way sometimes too.
4 Tell your lover/husband/mate what parts of your relationship evoke a feeling of vulnerability in you. Ask him where he feels vulnerable too. Work on overcoming these vulnerabilities *together*.
5 Ask a friend to do something special for you the next time you find yourself feeling vulnerable in a social situation—a back rub, a hug, a walk in the park, anything close and personal.
6 *Love yourself*. Your many positive qualities—helpfulness, cleverness, broad-mindedness, wittiness, sexiness—make you a very special person, a person who lights up the lives of many others. You *are* what you *are*—it isn't an act or a facade. Enjoy yourself as others enjoy you.

When the Gemini Woman learns to be accepting of her own nature, tolerant of those not as bright and witty as she, when she becomes secure in a love relationship with a man who can provide most of what she needs, she can finally relax. The energy she spends building her house of many gables and wings will not be wasted if at some point in her life she learns to live in it.

Gemini sexuality

To understand the sexuality of the Gemini Woman, one must first understand the workings of her mind. This is no small task; it is as labyrinthine as the circuitry of a computer. It is so tied to her complex inner nature that it seems inseparable from the total fabric of her life. She is indeed very sexual, uniquely and mysteriously so.

There are various levels of understanding the complexity of the Gemini Woman. There are also infinite manifestations of the sign. There is probably more variety among Gemini Women than among any of the other signs.

The Gemini Woman carries with her the search for her other half, the twin part of her. In this search, she flits from lover to lover, husband to husband, in hopes of finding her elusive "perfect mate," the "someone" who can satisfy her strong inner needs for identity and wholeness.

For Gemini, sexual fulfillment comes only with mental satisfaction. The Gemini Woman is more interested in IQ than in genitals. She must be able to respect the intellect, or satisfaction is not possible for her.

She may have many, many affairs and never find her true love. Although her body may be brutalized and her sensitivities trampled underfoot, she retains a semblance of having never been touched. When, in desperation, she feels her search is almost hopeless, she looks in the most unlikely places, seeking men who even vaguely match the mental model. During this phase she may become quite promiscuous.

The Gemini Woman tends to be nervous, restless, and tuned to a very high pitch. The close bond between her sexuality and her intellect creates an almost neurotic sex drive. Her search for a lover also becomes a search for an intellectual companion, the lost half of herself. Little wonder that many men find it impossible to understand the Gemini Woman; she often misunderstands herself.

In spite of her constant chatter, the many people she draws to her, and her frequent, tragic love affairs, she spends most of her life feeling lonely. She seeks the one perfect mate, an intellectual and emotional counterpart to rescue her from her loneliness. She is trying to achieve the emotional release of her whole being, not just the stimulation of her sexual anatomy.

Gemini's search gives her an opportunity to develop numerous close friendships and have many acquaintances. It can take her on journeys for which she may lack the fortitude, but along the way she picks up much of the vast knowledge she keeps stored in her head. When and if she decides the search is indeed fruitless, she can relax and enjoy seeing new places, meeting new people, facing new adventures.

She is prone to withdraw into very private spaces that few other humans can enter. It is here that she contemplates separation from and loss of her cosmic lover. During such reveries she feels completely alone and unloved. She spends most of her life looking for what she has lost—a search that is doomed from the start. When she inevitably gives up the search, she seeks a replacement that can take the form of oblivion. She may attempt to destroy the sensitivities and longings that fill her soul, to become polished at self-destruction, for she yearns to return to the cosmos, where her lover waits.

In terms of sexual encounters, the Gemini Woman craves variety. She delights in being taken by surprise when she least expects it. Steal her away from a wedding reception and take her to the boathouse. She'll love it. She also likes to be waylaid on the run—on an airplane, in the back seat of a car, in the darkness of the tunnel of love. She takes pleasure where she finds it.

She is sensory as well as sensual. She likes to see what is going on (a well-placed mirror or two). She likes to hear the sounds of love, but don't be too explicit, for she is somewhat a prude at heart. She likes to have the lights left on because she doesn't want to miss anything. Her bedroom, often as sumptuous as that of her Taurus sister, will be erotic. Soft lights, romantic music, rich liqueurs—all help to set the stage for her tempestuous tumbles.

True to the duality of her nature, she is a mixture of opposites. She is open about her love life, and a constant amazement to her friends as she reveals the innermost details concerning her body and mind. She enjoys shocking, but at the same time, she craves respectability. Deep within her soul is an iconoclast who delights in knocking over idols and killing sacred cows. Often her exploits are verbally exaggerated, far surpassing reality.

She has a freedom-loving spirit, but her sex life is often inhibited. She hesitates to try some forms of sex because she thinks they are distasteful. The physical side of life often is hidden away, every though she enjoys "dirty" talk.

She has an intellectualized concept of sex. After she has snared her male prey, she will often tire of him or, even worse, be bored. She is not really enthusiastic about an abundance of sex or child-bearing. Her interest in the erotic is largely verbal.

Fantasy is a very big part of sex for the Gemini Woman. The scenario she constructs in her imagination includes graphic details of the meeting, the chase, the seduction, and the dirty talk during sex. She is a master at this game, which is just as important to her as the real physical thing.

The idea of sex often motivates her more than the physical act itself; thus, she may appear to chase every man she meets. She isn't oversexed; she just feels compelled to sample as much variety as she can in her search for the perfect mate. In fact, it is a variety of sensations and experiences more often than deep feelings and permanent attachments that drives her to seek so many contacts.

The Gemini Woman is youth-oriented. She often has her most important love affair while she is still very young. This early imprint colors her future attitudes toward sex and love. Maturity and immaturity go hand in hand. All her life the Gemini Woman retains a youthful quality that can be truly beautiful. She simply refuses to give in to the traditional idea of old age. She has an eternal air of the little girl lost. This makes her very appealing—what man doesn't want to rescue a little girl lost in the forest of life?

She often uses her vast knowledge to eliminate unwanted competition, bringing it to bear on a rival. She maintains a healthy "one jump ahead" attitude. Often the competition feels the impact of a hit but has literally no idea whence it came. The Gemini Woman can have an unintentional and unconscious cruel streak. If her search for a soulmate is frustrated and other factors contribute to her boredom, she can appear to have little if any affection, ethics, or morals. Her attitude towards sex can become selfish, cool, calculated.

She demands attention to feed her ego. She is not concerned with things that do not directly effect or touch her. She often has a need to be the center of everything, and her level of interest in a man is high only if he seems to revolve around her.

Sex with her can explosive. However, unless it is attractively and effectively packaged and satisfies her seemingly neurotic needs, it will evaporate into the air like a warm breath on a winter day.

Two key words provide a better understanding of Gemini

sexuality. One is *excitement*. Her ever-roving mind, constantly in motion, demands excitement and stimulation. If it is bored, she is bored. The straight missionary position for sex will bore her to tears; she craves the new and different.

The other key word is *integration*. Gemini unites sex with a number of her other strong needs, and if deeper, emotional needs are not being satisfied, she is often sexually unfulfilled. If she can find inward reassurance that the man she is with will at least satisfy *some* of her emotional needs, then sex with him will be good, even terrific.

Many a Gemini Woman simply will not have sex with a man unless she feels that her sexual interest is tied to another interest, a deeper, more lasting, emotional one. Contrary to what many people assume, she is not into sex for its own sake. Pure physical joy, so important to her Taurus sister, is not important to the Gemini Woman. She wants more. When she puts her hand in his pocket, she wants more than to feel his genitals; she wants attention, security, companionship.

A Gemini acquaintance of mine has one of the most virile, attractive husbands in town. When her friends comment on his good looks and appealing aura, she is the first to admit that he's attractive; she also is the first to point out that there is more to him than his beautiful surface. She has even been known to wonder aloud why other women, and men, only seem to see the perfection of his body and face.

Early sex experiences

Curiosity marks Gemini as a child and young adult. She wants to know what is happening behind her parents' closed bedroom door and is likely to peek at one time or another. She is curious about the anatomy of her playmates and may explore that realm during childhood games.

A precocious child has sexual experiences early in life. She also tends to fall in love very early on. Her crushes often blossom into full-fledged love affairs, on her part at least. She ties much of her emotional life into this first relationship, and the imprint is lifelong.

If she is overly criticized or chastised for her mad crushes, either by a parent or an older brother or sister, this too can have a lasting detrimental effect on her life. If she suffers disapproval at an early age in her search for a soulmate, the disapproval can manifest itself over the years and become guilt when, as an adult, she continues and enlarges her quest.

She tends to be a highly emotional child and will run the emotional gamut more quickly than most. She has difficulty sticking with a single feeling. Fantasy plays an important part in her early development. She may have imaginary playmates with whom she engages in some pretty wild and far-out sexual activities. She has an ability to construct long, complex stories of the perfect love and act them out in the safety and privacy of her own room. Her fear of putting these fantasies into action often has a bearing on her sexual actualization later on in life.

Usually by her twentieth year, the Gemini Woman has received the imprint for her sexual development and will seldom deviate from it. True to the rest of her development, however, she can be as varied in her tastes for sex as she is in her personality.

Whatever her sexual orientation, she still pursues the ever-elusive lost part of herself. She seeks a mirror image from which to learn. She would be happiest if she could clone herself into an identical twin so that she could observe her actions more closely and accurately.

Love and sex

After a youthful period in which she generally falls completely, head-over-heels in love, the Gemini Woman refines her ardor and begins to learn how to use love. She can then fall for an ideal or idea, but often not with the man who shares her bed. It sometimes seems that she rejects love because it is too painful and hurtful for her sensitive nature. She prefers to use it. Sex becomes mechanized and offers little more than a nervous release.

Sex and love are almost synonymous for the Gemini Woman. They both become means to an end. In her cool and calculating way, the Gemini Woman learns to invest little emotion in the act of loving. She will often give her body but not her heart.

To separate sex from love, she needs to analyze more carefully her motivations for getting involved with a man. If she can learn that there is nothing inherently wrong in sharing sex to actualize a fantasy, acknowledging the experience as such, she can also learn to recognize the difference between fantasy sex and love sex.

The Gemini Woman's mind is her principal erogenous zone. She can be sexually turned on by talk and completely turned off by silent sex. The zipless fuck in *Fear of Flying* was invented for a

Gemini Woman. Besides erotic talk, her sexual desire can be heightened by word games in her palm, kisses on her rib cage, tracing the lines of her pelvic structure, and a gentle kneading of her breasts.

She is not often patient in her sexual advances. She can become the aggressor and let her sexual needs be known. She is expert at doing two things at once—performing fellatio while giving one of the most complete buttocks massages he's ever had, for example.

Her restless mind and her endless curiosity are always seeking more satisfaction from sex. She is open to experimentation and is interested in kinky sex toys and assorted vibrators and stimulators. Her "variety is the spice of life" attitudes are very apparent in her sexual nature.

Her sexual response pattern in intercourse seems to be the following:

1 Teasing, exciting, and raising the atmosphere to a fever pitch; delaying and talking or smoking to further the sexual anticipation.
2 When the moment is right for her, quick and complete involvement, no holds barred.
3 Explosive, verbal orgasm.
4 Quick cooling of passion; little affection, small talk well into the night; giggling, running to the kitchen for something to drink, great need for affection. For Gemini, once is enough in terms of intercourse.

What kind of lover she needs

The Gemini Woman needs a man who can give her his undivided attention, who will talk until the wee hours about every subject under the sun, who will express himself gutturally, have a quick sexual encounter, and then forget about it. Of course, he should also be knowledgeable, informative, intellectual, entertaining, companionable, a true friend, and comfortably wealthy.

The Gemini Woman likes variety in sex. If she can't find it in one man, she will probably look for it wherever it can be found. Therefore, her man must be versatile if he wants exclusivity. He should like mutual oral sex, shouldn't be averse to mutual anal sex (she can be real mean with a dildo) and should be ready for any other variation and fertile Gemini mind can imagine. If she wants to nibble on his nipples or massage his pectorals, he should be receptive. She knows how to stimulate a man, and he may never have experienced such a master. If he's open to experimentation with her, he must also be open to her experimentation with him.

She also needs a man with whom she feels comfortable and can relax. If the man is as high-strung and nervous as she, chances for meaningful sex are almost nil. Both will have a tendency to fly over the moon before getting down to the nitty-gritty. Gemini's man must know when to direct the playing into definitive sexual intercourse. She enjoys continued stimulation in all the same places during intercourse; it helps if he is octopuslike and extremely agile.

Her man must develop a high tolerance for attempts to make him jealous. She will often form platonic friendships with other men for the sole purpose of testing her mate/lover. The more jealous he becomes, the more she thinks he loves her. He needs to wean her from this tactic by providing adequate proof in other ways. To avoid frustration, he should only allow his jealousy to surface occasionally. However, if he totally ignores her and doesn't provide feedback, she is apt to leave because she feels bored. She likes some fireworks in her relationships on the sexual level. Her man can take her aside at a party and say, "Your flirting with other men is getting me so aroused that I'm having difficulty concentrating on polite conversation." This will often send her sexual anticipation soaring, and she'll probably begin moving towards the door.

There is really no one stereotype to which Gemini's man must conform. She can tease, coax, and excite the best sexual performance out of any male, from the macho type to the very effeminate. This is her specialty, and she seldom fails to arouse even the most impassive of men. In fact, she sometimes enjoys a man she can dominate physically and emotionally; this seems to feed her sadistic streak.

The only criterion she steadfastly applies is that the man be her intellectual equal. She constantly tests his intellect, for she believes that no one is really on the same level as she is. She enjoys worthy competition and would probably be more interested in sex if she thought it a real challenge. She is firm in her knowledge that if she loses an argument in the living room, she'll win it back in the bedroom. It takes shrewdness and understanding on the part of her man to even half way control her antics.

Once the Gemini Woman has turned off her emotions, she shows little sympathy for the weaknesses of others. She can easily assume the dominatrix role. Her seemingly natural cruelty and feeling of intellectual superiority make it easy for her to assume the role of the S-and-M mistress. If a man wants to be dominated and have his emotions walked on, the Gemini Woman can fill the bill.

Gemini's basic fantasy casts her in the role of star performer before a large audience. She holds everyone spellbound by her speaking ability, acting, and talented performances of life. Just as she has the audience firmly in the palm of her hand, she picks out those she wants to experience as sexual partners. Then, as the television cameras record it all for posterity, she undresses her favorites and chooses the very best to have sex with right then and there. Of course, true to her nature, the performance is followed by thunderous and never-ending applause (rather a female Tom Jones, captured on videotape forever!).

She needs a man who can help her actualize the practical parts of her fantasies, since she often has trouble acting on the stage she sets in her mind. She really *wants* some of these fantasies to become realities, and she needs a man with the patience to help her work through them. He won't have to purchase expensive perfumes, designer clothes, or exotic floral extravaganzas; she actually prefers simple permanent press and clean-smelling essences of lemon and pine. He does, however, need to respect the images of her mind as it ceaselessly creates new and different scenes for their mutual discovery and enjoyment.

Above all, Gemini needs a man who can dispel the abject loneliness she often feels. By the time she is in her mid-twenties, she has experienced more than most people feel in a lifetime, and she can join Peggy Lee in saying, "Is that all there is?"

Gemini is often left with a tremendous void that all the variations of sex, all the intellectual games, and all the wanderings of her travel-weary imagination cannot possibly fill. The man who provides this fulfillment must first be fully aware of himself, confident about his own nature and his life pattern; then he must be willing to spend the necessary time to help her find the lost part of herself.

The soulmate she seems forever seeking is often standing within her, patiently awaiting her final discovery—that what one often wants the most, craves the most, and spends the most time looking for is within oneself. Her man can help her focus her attention inward to see what she has thus far missed. He needs to be her friend and her sex partner, all rolled into one.

What she needs to learn

It is the rare Gemini Woman who finds the perfect mate, and she must be aware of the near impossibility of her search. Until she understands herself, she will be victimized by her own dreams. She will end up a lonely and bitter person as she flits from romance to romance (in her searching state of mind, "toad to toad" may be more like it) in search of her Prince Charming. She must learn to accept the men in her life as they are, not as she would like them to be.

This is not to say that she should give up her search, but only that she must learn quickly to recognize the man she really wants. She must gain the patience to look for him and wait for him constructively. She should not allow societal scorn to daunt her. She has to develop a thick skin in dealing with those people who would force her into a Cancerian mold—the place most women are put by traditional society.

Being a Gemini Woman requires a lot of strength, for she consumes prodigious energy while pursuing her many adventures and following her impulses to their natural conclusions. The stakes are high and the risks great, but the prize is a pot of gold at the end of her personal rainbow; if it pays off, the reward is well worth the risk.

The Gemini Woman often gives herself too quickly. She needs to slow down and discover whether her current attraction is really worth the emotional investment. She needs to hold back until she falls in love. Often, since her judgments are so swift, she would do better to postpone a decision until she has given a man the chance to reveal his inner nature. She intuitively knows what she is looking for, and the man she is currently pursuing may himself be looking for the perfect mate while hiding behind the dominant Leo image that seems to be in vogue at this time.

She needs to learn respect for the intelligence of others. Often her acid wit will be remembered long after she has forgotten how she used it on someone. Minds work differently. Gemini, ruled by Mercury, moves as swiftly as quicksilver. By contrast, the Taurus mind moves with the force of an earthquake. She needs to see the effectiveness of both approaches and understand that the intellect of any developed person is capable of great thought. She will notice a sharp rise in her own stock as she begins treating others as intellectual equals.

She has a tendency to pick losers in love affairs. She must begin to ask herself objectively a dual question: What can this man give me, and what can I give him in return? Only if there is mutual need and mutual benefit can any relationship work. Too often, the Gemini Woman takes what is available and tries to wring, squeeze, tease, hint, beg, steal, or force what she wants from it—and this is especially true of sexual/romantic affairs. At the same time, she rarely gives much of herself or expects him to, either. This can retard her personal growth and lead to complete disaster both in business and in love.

Her nervous sexual energy can be channeled into a creative outlet, be it a new interior for her home or a business where she can utilize her many-faceted personality. Frustration and anger get in her way too often. She needs to learn to release and express these emotions *constructively*. Since she can verbalize so well, she should perhaps join groups where she can learn about the sources of anger and frustration and see how others, perhaps her astrological sisters, cope with their problems.

Above all she must learn self-control. If she allows her natural tendencies free rein, she is courting disaster. She must put distance between herself and the way she sees herself. This will enable her to perceive what her life is *really* like and how she can change it. She must put brakes on her mind, or it will run away, aimless, careening off various stimuli it encounters along the way, never attaching itself to anything. Once she has tamed that wild stallion, she will be in a better position to understand her true nature and do something about it. How she deals with her inner self will determine a great deal about how she deals with sex and relationships.

Gemini anger

On the surface, the Gemini Woman appears to have a very good understanding of her anger. She is often verbally expressive and direct with it. She is vocal about most of life's irritations, even to the point of being a chronic complainer. She may even wear her anger with pride. She is capable of deriding her closest friends and condemning her strongest supporters if they do not conform to her expectations. She has a streak of cruelty that is virtually unparalleled in other signs—and she has the words to express it, too. She is often viewed with awe because of her ability to "put people in their places." She is, however, totally unenlightened about the origin and appropriateness of her anger, and also about the impact it has on her and others.

The Gemini Woman's greatest difficulty is in compassionately understanding life. She rarely empathizes with another person's plight. She can be at once the most intellectual, the most creative, and the most unfeeling of women.

Where does this lead her? She will insist on rational, logical explanations for all her emotional reactions. She may get so out of touch with her feelings that she becomes a habitual complainer: her husband is *completely* inattentive; her office machines are *always* broken down; her daughter *never* does what she tells her to do. She is rarely satisfied with her lot in life and will tell everyone about her dissatisfaction. If she isn't careful, she can become the stereotypical whiner.

We often equate the verbal expression of anger with an understanding of it. Verbalizing, however, can be an intellectual response to a very important emotion. Often people harangue others because they do not wish to confront themselves. They want to avoid the root causes of their anger. They are afraid to change, to risk the vulnerability of feedback about their own behavior and attitudes. As a result, they become habitual nags or fighters and always project their rage. This rage is really self-hate. Eventually, if the situation becomes chronic, they are no longer able to feel any emotion. In this case, the constant verbal barrage serves only to deaden their emotional being. It is an unhealthy, unproductive method of coping with life's challenges. Accepting feedback, even angry feedback, is one of the most important challenges for a Gemini Woman.

Gemini can be intensely jealous. Her friends' successful relationships, their beautiful homes, their money in the bank, can all drive her into an internal frenzy. She will bury her jealousy under seething frustration and cover it with sweet words that totally deny its existence. She will then manipulate her interactions with others so she never has to expose this facet of her personality.

Even with her jealousy carefully masked, her anger will build until she can no longer deny it. It is usually then that she drops her guard and allows others to see her true feelings. Since Gemini tends to forget emotional exchanges, she totally forgets what she says during her tirades. She is incapable of owning up to any of her negative feelings.

She must deal with the issues of control and manipulation most of her life. No matter how good a job she or a co-worker has done, she will complain about imperfections or even invent them if need be. She becomes increasingly difficult to satisfy as she grows older. She will harbor resentment towards those who stand in her way. She covers her true feelings with light, caustic bantering, and they can then only emerge in the form of outbursts. She can be set off by an insignificant slight or provoked into a rampage by a mere look. She usually keeps her cool through the most trying emergencies. Later, after the crisis has passed, all those involved will be torn apart for their failures. You can never predict what will touch off her anger.

The Gemini Woman avoids having anger directed *at her*. She plays all kinds of mind games to avoid confrontations. She fears that her anger can give someone else power over her, and she needs to feel that she is always in control. If someone gets angry with her, she will insist that she is right in spite of logic, facts, or eyewitness reports. She never feels she deserves such harsh treatment.

Her anger takes many forms. Unlike the Aries Woman, who can enjoy a good fight with someone, the Gemini Woman wants to be the one to do *all* the fighting. She expects you to sit by and take her verbal haranguing. How dare you talk back to her! She can recall a time three years ago when you were blantantly wrong, and she'll even use that as ammunition. Her style may vary from direct to elusive, but the basic ingredients are detached coldness and cruel, self-righteous monologues. She does not want to hear what others have to say—they're wrong anyhow!

Since she can be so blind to the feelings and motivations of others, she may think she has just put you in your place when in fact nothing she said has the remotest connection to you or to the issue at hand. At other times, her perceptions may be so acute that she'll shred your self-esteem. She will then walk away and let someone else repair the damage. Later, confronted with her insensitivity, she will forget all about the disagreement and deny it ever happened. You're either mistaken or exaggerating. Consciously or not, Gemini can be amazingly deceitful. She is aware of what she has done in every instance; she simply refuses to take responsibility for her actions. All is "forgotten" until the next time you cross her—when she will lay the same trip on you all over again.

One Gemini Woman with whom I am acquainted shares a business with her husband. When a disagreement crops up, it generally becomes a full-fledged battle. She often says, "Go ahead and do it your way—all I know is, the way I want it done has worked before, and if you want to be a jerk about it, go ahead." Now, logic like that is hard to understand, but it prevails in most of her arguments. She can be an incredibly cold-blooded woman in her moments of anger, calling attention to all her husband's shortfalls in this particular business; and always, without fail, she brings his forgetfulness into the picture and derides him for it. Later, it is impossible to tell that an argument or a battle has occurred. Her demeanor suddenly becomes sweet, light, and thoughtful, and her pleasant banter with customers again shines with wit and cleverness.

Paradoxically, the Gemini Woman views emotion as a messy and unnecessary complication in most people's lives. She prides herself on her control. She also forgets within hours any loss of control that may occur. She rarely has an accurate picture of herself; her self-image is very blurred. One of the greatest mistakes you can make is to criticize or attempt to control her actions. She feels she has the intelligence to call all the shots. You may be bright, but you can't hold a candle to her.

She often exaggerates her self-confidence and is not nearly as sure of herself as she seems. She masks her vulnerability because she equates it with a flaw in character or with weakness. She can cry easily, but the circumstances must be right; she will only do so when the nervous tension is too great for her to contain herself any longer. She will also cry when she knows she has lost something of real value to her—her job, for example. She always wants to be the one to end things. If you try to usurp her self-ordained prerogative, she will be devastating in her campaign to correct your obvious error in judgment.

She can be exceedingly cold and withdrawn. If she does not like or respect you, she can be totally uncooperative. This is especially harmful if she is in business or is self-employed. The thing that makes her most angry is incompetence. She has a very low level of tolerance for most things. Failure to carry your share of the load is another sore point with her. She will often overload subordinates with work to test them, and if they dare slip up or drop the ball, she will lose faith in their abilities quite quickly.

Gemini uses her anger to control, to cover up, to manipulate.

Of all the signs of the Zodiac, she is most aware of and concerned about her anger. She can easily become hysterical. She and her mate may very well fight daily. She abhors physical violence but is not averse to using it if she is pressed. She sometimes retreats into "I'm just a lost little girl" when her husband's rage threatens her. Ten minutes later, she'll attack from yet another angle.

Thus the Gemini Woman needs to consciously stand back and observe her own actions. She must learn to apply the rule. "Do unto others as you would have them do unto you" until it becomes habit.

Gemini, you should be aware of the constructive side of anger:

1 It can catalyze stagnant situations.
2 It can motivate others to think.
3 It indicates feeling and depth of feeling.
4 It can be a very up-front, direct approach to letting someone know you are displeased.
5 It can clear the air among people.
6 It can indicate a need for more sharing and dialogue.

Anger is a real energy and has to be expelled from the solar plexus, from the diaphragm, before rational discussion of problems can happen. If it stays trapped within the physical body, it creates illness, disease, and even death, over the long term. The Gemini Woman is particularly susceptible to stress and nervous-system problems; thus, she shouldn't bottle up emotions at all. Her emotional body needs to be synchronized with her physical body. It needs expression through the physical body in healthy, loving ways. The following are positive ways of displaying anger and transforming it into a gesture of love:

1 Do not expect another to change with its expression.
2 Do not blame or put the onus of change on another.
3 Share responsibility for the expression of frustration and anger.
4 Do not use anger to hurt or punish others.
5 Admit that anger is self-directed and that its expression creates positive change.

The key to the loving expression of anger is compassion—compassion for ourselves and all others involved.

The Gemini Woman, more than any other, understands the need for freedom, for making her own decisions. When she overcomes her need to manipulate and control situations, she will also be a shining example for others to follow.

Gemini, here are some hints that will help you deal with anger as a true emotion:

1. Be compassionate with yourself and with others.
2. Laugh. Humor provides detachment and release.
3. Cry when you need to; don't let it get to the point where your tears are like a raging, rain-swollen river sweeping along a path of self-destruction.
4. Develop a sense of human detachment to better understand your own feelings and motivations.
5. When discussing problems, stick to the specifics. Don't bring things into such exchanges that don't belong there.
6. Do not let others' expression of anger threaten you.
7. Do not assume responsibility for the actions of others so readily.
8. Find a healthy physical activity to release tension and small amounts of anger.
9. Accept your own anger; share it without blaming anyone for it.
10. Polish your ability to hear your partner nonjudgmentally.
11. Do not assume confrontation.
12. Let your intimates know your habitual reactions. If they are in the dark about how you react, they won't know how to avoid causing negative responses.
13. Use anger to connect with other people. Don't retreat and wait until it subsides before interacting with those who cause it. Share your good feelings after expressing anger positively.
14. Be rational, and respect the individuality of others.
15. Make *feeling* statements, not *intellectual* statements, about your anger. If you can express your joy at a beautiful sunset, you can express your anger at an insensitive boss, mate, child, parent, in-law, friend.

Gemini lifestyles

The free spirit and dual nature of the Gemini Woman largely determine the varied aspects of her lifestyle. She can be the stereotypical nagging wife, the corporate vice-president, the dutiful wife and mother, or the seasoned jetsetter. Then again, she can be, or try to be, all of the above at once.

Things are changing in our culture, and the Gemini Woman likes nothing better than change. She is often the vanguard of liberation on her block, and her powerful verbal support for any movement can often enlarge various subcultures—for she can make things seem so glamorous that others can't wait to get involved and have fun too.

She often has a deep-seated loneliness that propels her from place to place, person to person, experience to experience. Her seemingly unending search for her other half requires that she embrace many different people from many different walks of life. After all, she can't be sure where she'll find what she's looking for.

Her cleverness and wit draw people to her, and she often becomes a sort of unofficial "cult" leader for her large circle of friends. Her lack of intimacy, however, dictates that many of the relationships she enters are doomed to a short, if exciting, life.

She often shares interests with many different people. Her extroverted nature and outward self-confidence, coupled with her vast knowledge and worldliness, often inspire people she comes in contact with. They may think that if she can learn about communes, open marriage, and other alternatives, so can they. By sharing their knowledge, many Gemini Women have spurred enlightened friends to try new and different techniques with their mates and intimates. For example, she'll probably be the one to suggest injecting sexual toys into an otherwise fairly dull sex life. Her happy-go-lucky attitude may even cause her women friends to consider an affair if their marriages are dull and lack growth.

Her attitude is often somewhat devil-may-care, and if her teenage daughter or son comes to her asking for advice about getting involved with an intimate network of other young people, she'll be excited for them (just as she would be for herself). She'll usually be very proud of any of her children who choose to fly in the face of traditional society to find happiness. She knows that her search has been long and often difficult, and she'll be apt to give them advice and "lessons learned" stories to help them avoid the pitfalls she has encountered.

The Gemini Woman sometimes embraces so many different lifestyles and habits that she perfects none. It would behoove her to spend a little more time in each different environment she enters; perhaps she could then enhance the lives of those she encounters there.

We are beginning a new decade with some new values and ideals; we are now moving away from remote government leadership, from nuclear, close-knit, small families, from the depersonalization that has occurred at an alarming rate for the past twenty years. The turmoil of the 1960s was a terrific inspiration to the Gemini Woman. It almost seems that it was tailored to her windy mind. The 1970s should have been a time to reflect on the changes begun in the previous decade, but she, like so many, wanted it to be just as exciting.

The beginning of a new decade is like wiping the slate clean, and this fresh start appeals to the Gemini Woman. She needs to reflect on her "personal past decades," to see patterns and shortcomings. This is a time for her to grow and settle down in her mind. It provides her a perfect opportunity to realize, and to admit to herself, that the other half of her isn't likely to be found in someone else. She should reevaluate her methodology and look to herself for more appropriate solutions to her aloneness.

Alternative lifestyles

Single woman: Gemini often marries young, choosing as a husband someone she idealizes or idolizes. She often marries more than once since it takes superior talent to keep her from boredom. Being single may outwardly appeal to her as a lifestyle offering freedom from routine, with "nobody to answer to." Inwardly, however, her sense of loneliness or aloneness is magnified when she's single. This may propel her into yet another marriage for many of the same wrong reasons that motivated her previously. She must learn to create excitement in her life, to constructively bring out the childlike wonder in her lovers and mates. In everything there is a built-in possibility of boredom, and when she learns this, she'll also learn to relax and take a more in-depth look at life.

Intimate networks: This lifestyle advocates friendship with both sexes and neither encourages nor discourages sexual intimacy. The Gemini Woman often has intimate networks in her life, though they are seldom equally as intense for her as for those she is involved with. She maintains a certain air of detachment, at the same time encouraging people to draw near so she can dazzle and impress them. More often than not, her friendships with men probably involve at least some sexual intimacy. She may form fairly deep friendships with many of the men she first encounters in sexual situations. When she learns to appreciate people for what they are and not for what she thinks she can make them be, her intimate networks will be considerably more intimate and can provide her with the security and companionship she so rarely has.

Open marriage: The arrangement is possibly the best solution to her need for excitement and change. She doesn't handle jealousy very well, which can cause problems with this lifestyle, but her commitment to a primary relationship can actually enhance the philosophy of open marriage. In an aboveboard, honest marriage, trust is an absolute necessity. If she is realistic in her expectations, she can be trusting enough to allow her mate the freedom this lifestyle offers. So long as she doesn't think that each man she encounters in this arrangement is Mr. Right, she'll do fine. It may even be a place for her to learn that getting to know someone often eliminates the superficial boredom that plagues her.

Ménage à trois: The Gemini Woman commands, and often demands, center stage. She adores being adored. If she enters into a ménage à trois, it better be with two people who have the same goal in mind: exciting, pleasing, and satisfying her. She can be very alluring and stimulating and will have no problem dazzling two people at once, but the nature of this concept dictates three people *sharing* each other and a common sexual experience. She's long on having experiences but needs to work on her compassion—both for herself and for others.

Group marriage: This provides another good opportunity for her to have stimulation from many different directions and people, though the management of such a lifestyle could possibly be too tedious for her. It requires quite high levels of tolerance as well, and the Gemini Woman usually moves too fast and in too many directions to become highly tolerant. In fact, her intolerance for the needs of others is often one of her greatest character flaws. She needs to become actively interested in what others have to say, how they perceive life, and what they need in order to function in such a sophisticated marital arrangement.

Communes: The communal experience can be an exciting and fulfilling one for the Gemini Woman. First of all, however, the commune must encompass many, many people. She has a tendency to go through groups like a twister cuts across Kansas. She can provide much stimulation, excitement, and pioneering spirit for communes; she can elicit wit and cleverness from almost anyone. She has a definite knack for making people try harder. Before she can be truly successful in this living arrangement, she must learn to relax and develop consistency in her habits. The Gemini Woman tends to drop the ball regularly out of boredom or in favor of something a little more exciting and glamorous. Dependability, however, is a manistay of group living experiences, and each person must carry her/his load. Gemini must also learn to control her manipulative powers, since they are often at the root of disharmony among her friends.

Gay/bisexual lifestyle: For a number of reasons, this particular lifestyle appeals to the Gemini Woman. It remains one of the more controversial of all the alternative lifestyles, and this fact alone is enough to pique her curiosity. Often underground, this lifestyle requires considerable communication between people to gather and spread trends. She loves talking and communicating with people she doesn't know, and the close-knit nature of homosexual communities furnishes an excellent arena for her performances. The difficulty she often has with other women can be a problem here, and she will have to develop a much higher level of self-respect and compassion to survive.

Summing up Gemini

The Gemini Woman is indeed one of the most exciting women in the world. She has many, many positive traits that are often overshadowed by her insecurity and by the search for her elusive soulmate, her other half. She contains all the essential elements of a happy and evolved woman. Too often these parts are scattered and strewn about, much like the windblown seeds of the cottonwood tree.

"Getting it together"; "Self-improvement", "Working it out"—all are concepts the Gemini Woman naturally rejects because they *sound* tedious and boring. She needs to find joy in the mundane, to learn that the repetition of patterns provides the consistency necessary for growth.

When the Gemini Woman clears her life of illusion and stops living in the darkness of fantasy, she emerges with the brillliance, speed, and grace of a shooting star.

CANCER

CHECKLIST OF CANCER TRAITS

Note: This checklist describes the traits of one *phase* only; if it doesn't seem to fit you, check other lists to find the phase you are in right now.

1. Subjective
2. Intuitive
3. Introspective
4. Moody
5. Emotional
6. Imaginative
7. Dreamy
8. Patient
9. Retentive
10. Fearful
11. Overprotective
12. Fretful
13. Security-conscious
14. Domestic
15. Materialistic
16. Subtle
17. Manipulative
18. Thin-skinned
19. Petty
20. Vengeful
21. High Sex Drive
22. Sensitive
23. Nostalgic
24. Crabby
25. Sentimental
26. Magnetic
27. Tenacious
28. Sensitive Ego
29. Mediocre Self-esteem
30. Possessive
31. Self-centered
32. Selfish
33. Great Sense of Humor
34. Dramatic
35. Cancer's Feminine Mystique

Cancer personality

The lunatic, the lover, and the poet
Are of imagination all compact . . .
William Shakespeare
A Midsummer Night's Dream

General traits and background

The Cancer Woman is a fascinating, changeable, guarded female, a nymph, muse, mother, poet. She is part doer, part dreamer, and seldom the twain do meet.

Cancer is especially associated with the moon. That is why Cancer-type people are sometimes called "moon children." Perhaps the label "child" is consistently attached to Cancer because of her intense emotionalism. Physically, Cancer-type people normally have rounded faces that resemble the full moon.

The Bible likens the moon to the tree of life. The Cancer Woman is the tree of life and nourisher of others on the physical plane. She is invested in the basics: food, shelter, reproduction. Her emotional life tends to be stronger than either her physical or her mental and logical impulses. If *eros* and *logos* are interpreted as respectively feminine and masculine, the Cancer Woman is definitely richly supplied with the first and undervalues the latter.

Her lifelong challenge is to bring her own ceaseless changeability, akin to the ebb and flow of tides caused by the moon, into balance with her equally deep-rooted resistance to change. She must learn to live without trying to control life, to accept it as a dynamic process full of unpredictable factors, and to transcend her protective-mother role and become a full-fledged human being.

Cancer is the fourth sign of the Zodiac, Cardinal Water. The other two water signs are Scorpio and Pisces. The cardinality of her sign pushes the Cancer Woman to action and self-expression. It anchors her to the present, though much of her would prefer to live in the past. Because she is cardinal, she harbors a desire to expand her world beyond the home. Because she is water, she is often reluctant to do so. She is emotional, impressionable, absorptive, imaginative, psychic, subjective, dramatic, indulgent, and self-indulgent.

She readily absorbs and retains every type of energy, from psychic impressions to fast food, but she finds it difficult to release. She tends to store things for a rainy day and thus condemns herself to accumulate a vast collection of unnecessary emotions and fat cells. Typically, she must fight fat and bulk all her life.

Lady Cancer stuffs her house with collectors' items as relentlessly as she stuffs the stomachs of those she invites to a never-ending round of meals. She tends to have the most gorgeous and gourmet-fed children on the block, to be an expert gardener and household advisor as well as muse of sensuality to her mate and mother to the world.

She is apt to be passive yet to make her mark. Though she is moody and introverted, her keen emotional insights border on clairvoyance. Though she is dramatic, she often shies away from self-knowledge and genuine, deep self-revelation. Do not sell her short, however, and never write her off as a mothering wallflower. She frequently assumes important public responsibilities and becomes a popular personality. She is potentially an excellent public speaker, storyteller, and humorist.

The Cancer-*type* woman is one who has the sun or other important planets in Cancer, or the ascendant in Cancer; many planets in the fourth house, the natural house of Cancer; or a powerfully aspected moon. The Cancer type is described by the checklist of traits at the beginning of this chapter.

Cancer types are also those who are temporarily going through a Cancer *phase*. The Cancer phase has the following characteristics:

1 Giving birth and nurturing; motherhood, biological or symbolic. The woman in this phase can be a full-time mother to her children, or she can mother the office, neighborhood, and everyone she is in contact with. Portnoy's mother, as described in Phillip Roth's book, typifies this aspect of Cancer.
2 Nesting; setting up a protective, nourishing, oasislike environment free from the cares of the world. Cancer often has a green thumb and gardens outdoors or fills her home with plants that look as healthy as if they came from an arboretum.
3 Feeling a sudden urge to study gourmet cooking, collecting, home decorating, or floristry, or to start a home-care business.
4 Seriously pursuing psychic hobbies, especially mediumship and seances. She may have visions, clairyoyance, telepathy, and recognition in this phase.
5 Overindulging in food and worry. These are Cancer fetishes. Worrying about anyone dear to her or about various aspects of house and home is a sure sign of the Cancer phase.

6 Being moody or intensely concerned with the basics, with survival; having problems with her mother or with mother figures.
7 Experiencing an urge to return to the place of birth.
8 Having problems with the stomach, alimentary canal, breasts or chest cavity, uterus, mucous membranes, or elbows.

In the best sense, the Cancer phase offers a woman overall protection and enables her to enjoy a sense of cosmic motherhood without possessiveness and energy drains.

The Cancer Woman can choose to express her emotional energy positively or negatively. Because it is the staff of life to her, it is essential that she learn to channel it positively. On the positive side Cancer is unconditionally loving, flexible, strong, intuitive, magnetic, nurturing, yielding, emotional, creative, visionary, energetic, giving, caretaker, persistent, discriminating, feeling, and patient. On the negative side Cancer is smotheringly loving, moody, inconsistent, stuck, a negative medium, using, controlling, manipulative, possessive, helpless, irrational, dreamy instead of active, fearful, imitative, clannish, materialistic, clinging, defensive, overindulgent, and passive.

Typical Cancer professions are: agriculture, animal breeding, baking, biochemistry, boating; work with canals, ponds, fountains, oceans, rivers, brooks, baths; work with the disease of cancer; caretaking, catering, collecting; commerce and banking; cooking and domestic affairs, either in one's home or politically; psychodrama, water therapy, and other work with emotions—in general, counseling with methods that do not rely exclusively on words; parapsychology; fishing, floristry, food preparation or storage, gardening, glasswork, homemaking, hotel work, work with kitchens or kitchenware, work with land (growing things, selling and buying land, etc.), merchandising, meteorology, work in the milk industry, nursing, nutrition, obstetrics; managing, selling and buying, constructing places near or on the water, plumbing, municipal politics, real estate; work with restaurants, silver, swimming pools, or taverns; social service, storekeeping; and occupation connected with women in general.

Subjective, intuitive

The Cancer Woman tends to operate as if she were the center of the universe, her own ultimate guideline for evaluating all she feels and sees. Whereas a primarily logical person looks for criteria that are objective and outside herself, the subjective Cancer lady looks to her own sixth sense first and last. She does not believe in judging a book by its cover, so she will judge it by its "aura." She trusts her own intuition best and consistently processes her impressions through this psychic filter. She has no great need for scientific confirmation since she tends to consider her impressions as facts.

To the Cancer Woman, feelings are quite definitely facts. She is not averse to using logic—it's just that she rarely needs it. Though everyone in town may plant bulbs in March, she knows it is foolish to plant until the first full moon in May. And her garden invariably supports her conviction.

The Cancer Woman tends to be subjective. She sees things from her particular, individual perspective, heavily biased by her emotional background. She uses her intuition to bid in bridge, to draw up her budget, to predict next year's elections and her daughter's grades, to choose her wardrobe, plant her roses, and second-guess her husband. She can be an outstanding psychotherapist, for she sees into people and "psyches out" things others are often unaware of. She is especially perceptive in family matters and highly intuitive about how people have been influenced by their origins and their mothers.

Introspective, moody

The Cancer Woman wishes to avoid overt conflict at all cost. Her usual policy is to evade the heat of action. Let Leo roar and Aries ram people head on; Cancer will stand by and watch for the first opening she can slip through without causing waves. She does not like to rock the boat; she would rather row it gently but surely to its destination.

She is sentimental and introspective. She derives so much pleasure and information from diving into her own unfathomable depths that she simply turns tail and zigzags away when something displeases her. Retreat does not faze her, for she knows she can usually get her own way if she waits long enough.

The moon is her mistress, but she must learn to master the moods that the quarter-moon seems to inflict on her four times a month. Clams normally live for 150 years, and they open and close regularly with the coming and going of the moon. Cancer may not live quite as long, but she too reflects the solar and lunar phases and the changes in the weather. Many a Cancer Woman swells up with the full moon and feels nervous two weeks later at the new moon.

The Cancer Woman's challenge is to channel her psychic sensitivity in the most productive and enjoyable direction. To fear her moods and the prescience that underlies them is the worst thing she can do. She should attempt to treat her sensitivity as a gift and use it in the service of people and causes close to her.

Emotional

The Cancer Woman normally lives in a state of internal anxiety of gigantic proportions. She is highly sensitive to people and ambience, and she reacts emotionally to everything from yesterday's newspaper headlines to her bank's change of hours. She often hides her emotions, however, and to those who don't know her well, she seems as placid as a sailboat in calm waters. But she is less the Rock of Gibraltar than an unpredictable sea.

Idle fancies or passing statements can throw her into a tizzy. Upsets make her stomach tighten, and she is a professional worrier. She adores music and is apt to fall into a romantic reverie at the sound of her favorite song or sonata. Flowers, scents, and pictures awaken old memories and strong feelings. Without intense reactions, the Cancer Woman feels only half-alive.

Imaginative, dreamy

The Cancer Woman is apt to be born with a storybook in her head and an internal landscape that would challenge a Rubens or a Bosch to do it justice. As she appears to be contentedly gazing into the distance or into her partner's eyes, she may be picturing Arcadian shepherds cavorting at a picnic or a pair of passionate lovers engaged in Felliniesque foreplay.

She has a pornographic, erotic imagination and tends to daydream of heroic macho men, elegant S-and-M orgies, luxurious homes sporting Roman baths and pleasure rooms. She often acquires a refined taste for erotic art and may collect it. If asked to differentiate between an erotic art collection and a pornographic one, she would probably answer that though the former is expensive and valuable, the latter is a better deal and more fun.

She is impressionable, more a dreamer than a doer except in emergencies. When necessary, she can rise to the occasion in majestic style. She may behave like an absentminded queen lording it over her subjects, but when her children or other close ones are in trouble, she acts with the speed of a hare. She may prefer her daydreams and inner world to the outer one, but she can function very well indeed when she chooses.

Patient, retentive

The Cancer Woman is a paragon of patience. She can outwait anyone, and she uses this stragegy to gain credibility, affection, or power. Hers is the eternal potency of water, which carves riverbeds out of gigantic mountains through the slow process of erosion.

She can't quite fathom the rat race or understand people who are always in a hurry. She has no intention of getting ulcers or having a heart attack over little things, thank you. Her fire sisters who elbow people aside indiscriminately won't catch her in such a frenzy. She feels out situations slowly and subtly, expecting the world to come to her before she must go to it.

Her entire outlook is retentive. Politically, she tends to be conservative, wishing to preserve old values and lifestyles. Economically, she is usually thrifty and wants to hold on to her funds. Socially, she tends to have long friendships. She likes the ritual of Christmas and birthday cards and keeps in touch over the years. In love, she will probably cling to her mate and her home base. Physically, she tends to retain water and to blow up quickly with extra calories.

Her memory is unusually good. She can probably recall her earliest years without effort and does not need hypnosis to recite what she learned about the birds and the bees in third grade. She tends to favor the fashions of yesteryear and often dresses with pretty, feminine charm that seems vaguely but deliciously out of date. She likes Peter Pan collars with embroidery, or traditional tailored pieces that never go out of style, and to her Mary Janes are shoes rather than drugs.

Fearful, overprotective, fretful

The Cancer Woman typically slays more dragons in her imagination than Queen Isabella persecuted heretics under the Inquisition. That is because Cancer lives with more dragons than anyone else, except perhaps her Pisces sister when she succumbs to the doldrums.

The moon lady is a worrywart. She complains, nags, whines, cajoles, and seduces, all with the intention of safeguarding her loved ones so as to spare herself further worry. Worrying probably makes her feel a participant in the activities of others.

Fear has a way of eroding her self-confidence. She may develop phobias about snakes, spiders, or heights. Fear can block her personal and professional growth by destroying her already weak initiative. Fear makes her cling to the safe route and the known path. It is responsible for her almost legendary overprotection of her children and general smothering of people. If she has a genuine desire to make people comfortable, she usually has an equally real fear for their safety and happiness.

The mother hovering breathlessly over her teenager with admonishments to be sure to fetch the milk, say hello to the policeman on the corner, call Dad at lunch break, avoid draughts, and come home on time is the Cancer Woman. If you have met a mother who warms her child's pajamas in the oven on cold winter days and bakes three desserts when Grandma comes to dinner, whose house the Tooth Fairy, the Easter Bunny, and Santa Claus never, ever miss, you have just met the Cancer Woman.

Security-conscious, domestic, materialistic

Only Taurus can equal Cancer in her energetic concern for security, the material aspects of survival. Cancer tends to focus on the basics: the quest for food, shelter, and the guarantee of comfortable, if not luxurious, living absorbs her. Sex is basic too, but the Cancer Woman tends to use it as her security blanket.

The Cancer Woman understands why progressive zoos create homelike habitats for their animals. As far as she is concerned, people who lack a home that resembles their childhood-conditioned ideal are almost always rootless, unhappy strangers on this earth. She believes that a good meal and nice family could fix just about everyone.

The Cancer Woman plans ahead, and her plans tend to revolve around material security. She wouldn't be caught dead impulse-buying, and fly-by-night fads leave her cold. She is more interested in steady accumulation: money that generates more money; a house that rises in value; clothes, jewelry, and furniture that have enough intrinsic worth not to depreciate.

She could not be convinced to throw caution to the wind and trust fate to protect her. She is determined to protect herself and usually feels that difficult days are just around the corner. In fact, she is somewhat of a pessimist, or perhaps a realist, depending on one's point of view. Liquid assets or actual cash are the real signs of security to her, and she may have an account with more than one local bank.

The Cancer Woman can become obsessed with existential uncertainty. She can become a miser who hoards resources for tomorrow and neglects to live today. When she clings to things too much, she usually become more anxious and may put on weight and enjoy life less.

Subtle, manipulative

The Cancer Woman spins her web subtly but dramatically. Nothing is too mundane to spark her imagination, and nobody is too insignificant to attract her notice. She is not the sort who turns around to stare at people, but she appraises them thoroughly out of the corner of her eye.

She is knowledgeable about the art of living because she herself is an artist. She tends to be a participant, rarely an outside observer. She is not usually the flamboyant center of attention, but she may be the only one who knows what is happening behind the scenes. She reads subtle clues with her intuitive eyes and sends them out herself.

Because she is a water sign, the Cancer Woman is almost never a direct, head-on announcer of anything. She is more comfortable acting indirectly, happier seeding minds through the power of suggestion than brashly hitting people over the head with her brilliance. If she wants something from an intimate, she will probably find it difficult to express her needs directly. She often has trouble asking for what she wants, and she may procrastinate so long that she misses the boat. She is often guilty, too, of the glass-head syndrome, believing that anyone who loves her should automatically know what she desires.

The Cancer Woman often falls in the trap of manipulating people, sometimes without consciously meaning to do so. She simply finds it temperamentally difficult to speak directly about topics that make her uncomfortable. She is uneasy with disagreement and overt conflict, with expressions of disappointment and hurt, with aggression and intimidation. She fears ridicule, and like a crab, she tends to withdraw into her shell in order to avoid it. Because she has a guarded, partially hidden nature, it is almost impossible for others to know what she is feeling. She can make people who love her feel like innocent but unwanted and ignorant bystanders. The clues she telegraphs are subtle, and she probably prefers it that way. She adores mystery, and she uses it to keep the upper hand. Loud, boisterous behavior and overt aggression are not her style. She feels she will always achieve more by being her naturally introverted self.

She may operate successfully by subtly manipulating those around her. However, in her primary relationship, she is likely to pay a heavy price in the long run. Mates who are consistently outmaneuvered or manipulated tend to end up resenting the invisible strings that Cancer so skillfully fingers. No partner likes to be set up to take the responsibility or blame for situations that are encountered by them as a couple, yet that is precisely what Cancer tends to do to her mate.

Thin-skinned, petty, vengeful

The Cancer Woman is vulnerable to sniping, criticism, and aggression, and she is uncomfortable with people who lack social conscience or personal sensitivity. She has very thin skin and is often hurt by an unintended slight. Since she has a long memory, this can create unfortunate situations. She is apt to file for future reference a careless remark Ms. Joan tosses off. Ten years later, when Ms. Joan comes to visit, she is likely to find Ms. Cancer cool and bitchy; and Ms. Joan will never know why.

The Cancer Woman is often petty about insults, real or imagined. Since she is so subjective, she tends to take almost everything personally. She can understand a busy doctor not remembering her first name, but she will never forgive him for not asking about her family. If she feels that she or her home and family have been betrayed, the Cancer Woman frequently retaliates. She can be extremely vengeful, for example, if she suspects her partner of infidelity. There is cruelty in her nature, and she is bound to make him pay for it; endless, merciless sulks, spending sprees, and accusations are not uncommon.

High sex drive, sensitive

The Cancer Woman is full of delightful surprises. She is shy, but she is highly sexual. She is intuitive, but she is also strongly physical. These combinations are difficult for members of the opposite sex to resist. She is a desirable woman who may promise little verbally but still convey the feeling that she delivers a great deal. She may faithfully guard the home gates or climb the ladder of worldly success, but she is rarely, if ever, out of touch with a deep, almost primitive sensuality. Purple and indigo are often her favorite colors. Her sexual nature throbs with the full-blooded blue-red lust of desire.

She seems to burst with the promise of wondrous enfoldment and tortuous inner paths. She is sensuous in the most basic sense. Just watch Cancer go through a store full of clothes and accessories, and you will see her touch nearly everything as she walks by. She will touch silk, suede, and fur twice, not with the tips of her fingers, but with the full, open palm of her hand.

She is likely to seek sensation, and the visual is not enough. She is not as gifted with words as some others, for the physical seems to her more real, somehow more important. Sex, to the Cancer Woman, is something she lives and breathes. She telegraphs sex in the way she walks, smells, cooks, smiles; in the way she creates mysteries with her body and moods; in the way she dazzles company with her superlative hostessing and intuitive attentions. She can please any man in bed, as long as he is accessible to her, as long as he is sensitive, and . . . as long as she finds him useful.

Nostalgic, crabby, sentimental

The Cancer Woman has a strong psychic link with the past, often through her mother or grandmother. She may miss the grandeur of the past, ignore the challenge of the present, and fear the possible decadence of the future. She probably wishes she had lived in an era when antiques were new, when collecting things was not as expensive, when the universe seemed more orderly and predictable. She is nostalgic for a time gone by, a wistful era of dance cards and crinolines, the smell of magnolias and roses, garden parties, and politicians who did not vie for equal time on television but kissed the baby instead.

Thus, it is small wonder that she gets crabby sometimes. After all, when she sees what could have been and compares today's reality to her visions, the present seldom measures up. Declare a moratorium on the past, turn her on to the wonders of the twenty-first century, and she may forget her memories—but only for the moment. *War and Peace, Gone with the Wind,* or *Anna Karenina* will bring it all back, and there she will be, wiping away the tears and softly sobbing, wishing people would leave her alone. The wonders of space-age travel may never excite Cancer as much as the thought of living in the lap of Southern luxury or consorting with the Russian aristocracy. And if anyone pushes her or insists she is wrong, she may just get crabby.

Magnetic, tenacious

The Cancer Woman has the gift of drawing people to herself while appearing to stand stock-still. She is active while appearing reactive, a combination many people find hard to understand. She is like an actress who knows her lines but sends them out wordlessly. Those who pick up the message are drawn to her by an almost telepathic cord.

She is exceedingly tenacious, persistent, patient, and stubbornly unyielding. What she wants, she will get, if not today, then next week—and she is not likely to part with it, either. One hopes that what she holds onto is what she needs, and that she learns to release negative feelings and influences as she matures.

Sensitive ego, mediocre self-esteem

In ancient Egypt, Cancer's sign was represented not by the crab but by the scarab, or dung beetle. Both creatures are protected by a shell, and the Cancer Woman, too, seems to need a layer of defenses to cover her soft, tender, vulnerable side. The crab, like the scarab, has the function of devouring the transitory and thereby effecting regeneration. The Cancer Woman, by absorbing the negative emotions around her and replacing them with her healing balm, can bring about spiritual transformation.

The Cancer Woman is often self-doubting and cantankerous. Above all, she fears rejection and humiliation; for example, she may see venom in the petty rejection of an angry salesclerk. Her biggest problem is that she personalizes everything and often feels as if the world might victimize her if she fails at all times to protect herself.

She is sometimes devious and often deceptive, retiring and yet an opportunist. Because she is attuned to people and can almost predict events, she can be extremely successful. She is a born politician, being interested in gossip and the efficient use of people's weaknesses. An excellent way for her to raise her self-esteem is to combine her domestic involvement with outside work. Whether she focuses on charity, therapy, the professions, volunteer work, or local politics, the Cancer Woman needs to find ways to avoid smothering her close ones, ways to spark her own self-confidence outside the nest.

Advice to friends: the Cancer Woman needs her ego built up. Do not push her, never demand! Instead, *ask* her gently and supportively, guide her to take initiative, and teach her to take risks. Be a model of action, not a complainer; be a doer she can admire but not fear.

Possessive, self-centered, selfish

The Cancer Woman is apt to be so invested in her man that she becomes exceedingly possessive. She may try to turn anyone she loves into one of her children. She frequently fashions relationships in which she is the mother or authority figure on whom others become dependent. This position gives her a great deal of control, and though she is loath to admit it, it is often control she wants.

She is insecure enough to be envious and jealous of people who appear in some way superior to her or who may seem to lay a strong claim to her man's affections. She is sometimes competitive with other mothers if they are well liked by her own children. She likes to rule the roost, and she must be Number One in the heart of her family . . . and Numbers Two and Three as well.

The Cancer Woman seems to want things on her own terms. She is clever at setting people up to fulfill her soft-voiced commands or even her unspoken needs. She tends to activate a nurturing instinct in friends and lovers, who often go out of their way to do as she bids them. She tenaciously holds to her view of how things should be done (try to cook in her kitchen or use her office or laundry room, and see for yourself).

The Cancer Woman is very selfish. She wants all of the good things for herself. She will go to great lengths to make sure that her wants are satisfied. She will not share her treasures with others. They are hers and hers alone.

Cancer Woman, you must learn to release your double standard and let go of people. You yourself do not wish to be owned; why try to own others? Your tenacity, if misdirected, can create dissent or disaster.

Great sense of humor, dramatic

If you are in a restaurant and you hear a throaty chuckle or an irresistible aria of giggles, you are probably listening to the Cancer Woman. She is a deliciously humor-filled person with a comic gift.

The Cancer Woman tends to dramatize life, though generally not flamboyantly. She is effective when she drops a tear or two, or when she gurgles her deep, sexy, quicksilver laugh. She can find humor in every story.

Cancer's feminine mystique

The Cancer Woman's special, astrologically delineated task is the generation, birth, and nurture of other creatures. She is the natural cosmic mother and teacher, caretaker not only of her children but of the whole suffering world.

The moon means change, growth, and decline—constant cycles of regeneration. The moon measures and determines terrestrial phases, exerting a mysterious influence on women's biological clocks, on vegetation, sea creatures, and bodies of water. The Cancer Woman's ruling planet has an essentially passive character, however, for it receives its light from the sun. Its most significant impact on our consciousness has been its archetypically feminine night side. The moon is seen in this role as maternal, enveloping, unconscious, and ambivalent in that it is both protective and dangerous. The devouring female, Jung's Terrible Mother, is the other side of the virginal, saintlike Mary, flawlessly captured in Michelangelo's marble *Pietà*.

The summer solstice launches the Cancer Woman, symbolically endowing her with a perfect potential balance between the night side, represented by her ruling planet, the moon, and her day side, symbolized in astrology by the sun. She is born with the destiny and the potential to be a woman energetic enough to provide a masculine counterweight to the dark, cyclic forces of her own feminine nature.

The Cancer Woman is maternal in the most universal sense: she is designated as caretaker of the physical and emotional realms. Carl Jung noted that the mother is in touch with the collective unconscious, the nocturnal side of life, and is the source of the Water of Life. Cancer's empathetic, sympathetic nature is maternal, and she is primarily energized by emotional urges and practical ideas centering around people she loves. The Cancer Woman embodies the anima role, in which she first bears the feminine image that every man projects upon women. She is, in fact, the collector of projections and in this sense the Eternal Woman.

Her qualities of solicitude, nourishing, care, prescience, and patience, her emotional/intuitive approach, need for roots, and ability to provide roots and protection in her turn, her feeling-dominated nature—all are quintessentially feminine. She gets people to take care of her, but in fact she can take care of herself. She may appear to absorb the life and light from others, but in truth she provides them with endlessly regenerated images and energy from the depths of her own soul. In this, too, she is highly feminine.

She is apt to be moody, insecure, charming, introverted, ceaselessly changeable yet resistant to change; a good teacher, even a preacher; touchy, bitter, proud, resentful; conservative, dramatic, guarded by perceptive; practical, protective, inspired, and inspirational; fond of her home, ambitious, sensual, slightly melancholic, with a tendency to hysteria; possessive, envious, sometimes greedy; powerful but often subtly so; indulgent, self-protective, spoiled; vengeful, closed, fretful, begrudging; nostalgic. She is strong yet vulnerable, sexy yet maternal. In short, she is utterly, totally, one hundred percent mysteriously female.

Cancer relationships

Cancer must learn how to love without trying to own the people she loves; she needs also to be more fully aware of when and how to end bad relationships. Breaking up may be hard to do, but for the Cancer Woman, it is pure hell. She seldom lets go, frequently clinging to losers or victimizers. She is often mistreated by men.

The Cancer Woman senses the real balance of power in human relationships, but unfortunately she often sees them as win-or-lose propositions. She always gets what she wants, but she frequently wants what deep down she does not truly need. Thus, she is a winner who in a hidden sense may be a loser. Her manipulative tendencies and introversion often shut out the very people she needs most; lack of communication, blocked emotions, self-pity, and moodiness are frequent Cancer problems.

She is apt to attract many friends and potential lovers, for people seem to bask in her need to give and do for them. She is often a substitute mother, amateur therapist, or spiritual midwife. Just as plants thrive in her greenhouse atmosphere, so do people trek to her door, anxious to receive her ministrations.

She fluffs pillows behind pained backs and concocts magical potions for sleeplessness, headaches, or stomach pain; she reads poetry to soothe frazzled nerves and always casts a protective net.

Sometimes her net is deceptively restrictive. People often become highly dependent on her and fall victim to her potent charm. As long as she uses her power to heal and help, no harm is done, but she must keep the Negative Mother from taking the reins.

When Cancer is frustrated, she tends to withdraw from the battle of daily life. Friends suddenly find her changed and frequently unreachable as she closes off and sulks. She can turn into a psychic drain, for she saps others' energy with her repressed hostilities. It is easy for those who love her to feel abandoned, fearful, or guilty, and since she seldom offers direct explanations, they are left to fend off worry and mounting resentment by themselves. This pattern may repeat itself cyclically, and it can leave a chain of unhappy relationships in its wake.

Childhood

The Cancer Woman frequently has an extremely strong link with her mother. It can be nurturing or destructive, helpful or hurtful. In most cases, its very potency is threatening, and many a Cancer feels the need to turn her back on her mother in order to establish her own identity. Years later, she may find herself imitating Mama, and one can only hope the tie has been cleansed of its destructive aspects.

The Cancer girl often has an outrageously domineering mother who skillfully combines the archetype of the destructive, omnipotent female Kali with that of the Virgin Mary, or saintly mother. She may be a very strong woman who uses her femaleness manipulatively to force others both to cater to her and to obey her. Her daughter often grows up ambivalent, conflicted about the power of the feminine, uncertain what motherhood is really about. Above all, the Cancer daughter grows up not really knowing herself.

The other pattern typical of the Cancer girl is an overprotected childhood. She may be ill or be a weakling or be the baby of the family who is coddled too long for her own good. She may live behind walls long after she should go out to experience life. She may be a homebody, happy tied to Mother's apron strings eating her homemade cookies. Later, fearful of being on her own, isolated, unsure of her resources and talents, she may resemble Laura, the heroine of *The Glass Menagerie*. In Laura's life, collecting—a Cancer hobby—has taken the place of relating.

Many Cancer women have dreams about their mothers, dead or

alive, expecially at turning points in their lives. Interestingly, four Cancer ladies told me approximately the same story. Each had been awakened the night after her mother's funeral by the mother's ghost tapping her on the shoulder and reassuring her daughter that she was at peace.

The more truly giving and accepting the Cancer Woman is, the more likely she is to be happy in her relationships. Unfortunately, she is normally conditioned to give with strings attached, to hold back watchfully until she is sure she can trust—which may be never. This insecurity stems in part from her especially strong mother influence and subsequent identity problem.

The Cancer girl tends to learn the importance of money very early, and money often continues to be an important concern. She is typically a product either of a family chronically short of money or of a family that spoiled her. She respects money a little too much and is usually avid for the luxury and status it can bring her.

The Cancer girl tends to be impressionable and easily influenced. On the other hand, she can fool people easily and often does so. She needs to make sure she does not fool herself in the process. What she is taught to value in childhood may not be what she needs to value later in life if she is to be happy; this is especially true where her materialism is concerned.

How the Cancer Woman relates: lovers and other intimates

The Cancer Woman can charm and magnetize people by offering to take care of them. She has a maternal yet seductive quality, a softened, persistent willfulness. She may resemble a spoiled child who promises to impart the unique gifts she has collected if only she is sufficiently loved.

The Cancer Woman tends to have many, mostly female acquaintances but few close friends. She can keep friends for a lifetime, for she is usually connected to those she loves by an intuitive link strong enough to counteract physical separations. She is also a good correspondent and loves to select and send cards for every occasion.

Her romantic life is a different and more complex story. She can find and keep a man; what is more difficult for her is to get rid of a man who is wrong for her or, alternatively, to maintain a sexual relationship after years of mothering.

The Cancer Woman is a prime candidate for early marriage

because her sleepy tumble out of the nest often prompts her to seek instant shelter. If she marries without emotional maturity and sexual experience, she will have problems. She and her mate are bound to grow at a different pace and in different directions over the years. She often marries the wrong man early and finds this out too late; just as often, she clings tenaciously to her mistake, hoping against hope to avert defeat or, even worse, ridicule.

The Cancer Woman tends to be proud, stubborn, and emotionally self-protective. Paradoxically, she, who is so giving, is also very withholding. Her secret fears, doubts, and jealousy barely ruffle the surface, yet these hidden emotions color her relationships. She easily feels abandoned or hurt, and she tests intimates to verify their loyalty to her. Her natural self-protectiveness may in time become a shield that prevents access and outflow. To the rest of the world, the Cancer Woman usually manages to look like an Academy Award winner, but over the years she may dig herself into a fearful rut that only she and her mate suspect.

Cancer, I advise you to evaluate the following as honestly as you can: (1) Your true desires in your primary relationship. Do your needs and desires mesh? Is your life fulfilling? (2) Your level of confidence and security, your possessiveness. How honest are you in your relationships? You must recognize your Achilles heel if you are to be happy. Your tendency to possessiveness and passive manipulation arises mostly out of usually monumental feelings of anxiety, fear, and distrust. In a word, the source of your problems is insecurity.

Insecurity in the Cancer Woman

The Cancer Woman's insecurity is classic in that it probably started with self-rejection generated from babyhood impressions. However, the most compelling and universal reason for self-rejection is rejection by someone else. Deep down, Cancer may fear that self-knowledge and revelation would uncover not a narcissus but an ugly frog. She is self-protective all her life, partially because of this belief.

Cancer, I advise you to make an inventory of all your assets. Concentrate especially on those you have ignored or taken for granted. If you are insecure, unaware of your assets, you will be unable to make the best use of them or to develop them further.

Make a list of all the risks you've ever taken, from the tiniest to the biggest. Next to each, write the outcome. You will see that you've succeeded far more than you've failed. Keep the "Risk List" with you and refer to it when you feel anxious and unsure about your next decision. Another exercise is to imagine the worst thing that could happen as a result of a risk you have decided to take. You will see that this worst outcome is most often not as bad as something you've already experienced and overcome.

A frequent result of Cancer's insecurity is excessive caution. The Cancer Woman tends to be as super-cautious as a newlywed giving a large party for the first time. But though the nervousness of an inexperienced hostess is understandable, Cancer tends to retain a generalized wariness for decades.

There is a world of difference between voluntary logical caution and involuntary obsessive caution. A young colt who has just learned to walk is naturally nervous and watchful. His movements are measured, slightly off balance, but rapidly improving. He has controlled grace, harmony, self-protective insight. However, the obsessively cautious person lacks these qualities, instead adopting a stiff, slow, tense, clumsy body language. The Cancer Woman's incessant caution is ultimately self-defeating; it is not a realistic response to situations that are no longer characterized by newness, that no longer challenge her survival.

Another frequent manifestation of insecurity is secrecy and manipulativeness. If Lady Cancer does not wish to let on what she thinks and wants, she is likely to try to get results indirectly. She may try to subtly control others in such a way that she achieves her goal without overt communication (i.e., without taking risks).

The Cancer Woman is so rich in sensation and subjective intuition that she is quite vulnerable. A hint of displeasure, a word, a nuance, a silence, a gesture, or a sound can hurt her. If she does not protect herself, she suffers. If she protects herself, she may go too far and encase herself in impenetrable armor or turn to possessiveness and exploitation. She must learn to walk the fine line between just enough caution and too much self-protection.

Cancer, you must learn to eliminate needless caution and to refrain from secretive, self-protective, self-rejecting acts. Throwing caution to the wind *at the right time* is utterly exhilarating, and you may be forced to try it. You will have to cope with new patterns of relating, new adventures, new experiences, for life will inevitably bring them. Holding back as a result of insecurity is as fruitless as wanting guarantees where there are none.

Coping with insecurity

The Cancer Woman in love

The Cancer Woman falls in love as she does everything else: slowly and cautiously. Impulsive action makes her uncomfortable, and she considers falling in love a serious commitment.

Cancer wants from her man material security first, exclusivity second, and social status third. She is unlikely to fall in love with a man who does not offer at least two of these. The only thing that can propel her into an uncharacteristic rash choice is the occasionally unbeatable urge to leave home. Once she has made up her mind to fall in love, she takes any dilemma by the horns and prepares to resolve it. She is bound to throw all her weight into one relationship, to try to make mutual dreams come true.

The Cancer Woman in love is a peerless partner for the man who wants to be babied, pampered, catered to, taken care of, slowly seduced; if he wants security, solid roots, traditional domesticity, and passionate sensuality that is more reactive than generative, he will find it with her.

The Cancer Woman is a superb player of romantic chess. She seems to know exactly how to make her man fall desperately in love with her. She is imaginative, perceptive, and persistent, a combination which most often makes her Number One in the competition for man. She understands strategy in the psychic warfare between the sexes without ever having consciously learned the rules. And she knows how to draw the lines in her favor.

In love, she is delightfully yielding, accommodating, and often quite domestic. She can manage both outside work and home, and nothing can stop her from creating the perfect domestic ambience. She is more than likely a good cook and fine hostess, and she will always cater to her man's tastes and desires.

Cancer in love is also exceptionally magnetic. She draws men to her as surely as the queen bee attracts devoted workers. She manages to be just helpless enough to inspire a man to take care of her, yet she is sensitive and self-reliant enough to put a great deal of effort into serving him. Submissiveness becomes her, for she yields with a sparkle and a wise look in her eyes.

The storybook in her head has extra appeal when she is in love, so that despite her caution and materialism, she is often starry-eyed and blind to potential problems. The Cancer Woman in love blooms with the sensuality of a fragrant rose, the delicacy of lily of the valley, and the exoticism of a hothouse orchid. At the same time, she is tougher than she seems.

In love, she considers no one and nothing more important than her lover. She is convinced she has the world by the tail, and it would take an earthquake or repeated infidelity to make her change her mind. She is bound to combine the erotic imagination of Anaîs Nin with the earthy sexuality of Lily Marlene. Love helps her to overcome some of her shy pragmatism. It makes her relax her guard and teaches her self-disclosure. The man who hurts her at such a moment will never regain her trust.

The Cancer Woman in love stands on the verge of a momentous decision, for to her love almost always means marriage. If love leads her to the altar, she must be careful that she continues to grow sexually. Too often, the Cancer Woman marries, becomes a domestic expert and mother figure, and takes the road to overweight and asexuality.

Patterns in the Cancer Woman's sexual relationships

The Cancer Woman tends to display the following patterns in her sexual relationships (to some extent these apply to platonic ties as well):

1 Her hormones awaken early, though her conditioning may deter her from acting. She tends to have a secret love affair with her sexual self and may be more open to physical experiments than to the risky ups and downs of emotional engagements. Masturbation may be a very frequent activity.

2 She tends to marry early, either to escape a difficult home situation or to gain security, hopefully with status.

3 She is apt to want a family and may have many children. She is unusually pleased by domesticity as long as she can run the house as she chooses. She must be allowed to control the budget as well, for managing money makes her feel secure. She needs to belong to a unit.

4 She usually forms relationships cautiously, even with her children. She rarely loves with abandon and may in fact apportion her affection deliberately, as if with measuring spoons. Her relationships tend to build slowly, to peak intensely, and to last with various degrees of closeness for a long time.

5 She needs to feel she is the center of some group and likes to be in control of her marriage or main relationship. She may not acknowledge her need openly.

6 She often has a troubled marriage. Though she seldom likes to cope with change or crisis, she can do it well. Few Cancer Women live as tranquilly as they would like, and many inch painfully toward separation or divorce.
7 She finds it extremely difficult to live and let live, and almost impossible to let go of anyone she loves. She may hang onto a disastrous relationship much longer than logic would dictate.
8 If she divorces, she is bound to take it hard. Guilt and depression are common, but with time, she heals well. A hint to the Cancer Woman: you can have several sequential marriages within the same marriage, and you would probably prefer it that way.
9 Though she is often a paragon of virtue and a good mother, she can also secretly pursue extramarital sex. She is gifted at illusion, and often the Cancer Woman who is named Mother of the Year in her hometown is the same one who enjoys passionate afternoons with a lover totally unlike her husband.
10 She is a good friend and wife as long as she does not feel betrayed. Her friends and her husband must be extremely careful not to hurt her, humiliate her, or make her feel isolated or abandoned. In these instances, she is likely to retaliate with a vengeance.

Lovers and husbands

Above all, the Cancer Woman needs a man who accepts her strange moods without demanding explanations. She probably couldn't give them if she tried, and it is far better for him to accept her as she is and cuddle her than to push her.

She needs a man who can build a cocoon around her, eventually enveloping the two of them and their offspring. She wants to feel protected from the ugliness and neediness of the world, and she dreads poverty. Therefore, her man should make enough money and have enough financial acumen to keep the funds flowing. She needs a mate who is solidly respected in the community, for she wants his respectability to cast a benevolent light on her. She needs a man with a deep sensuous streak, one who enjoys luxury and caters to her own need for it.

She needs a man stubborn enough to match her own tenaciousness and unwilling to be devoured by her. She will undoubtedly try to run the household, to own him in subtle or dramatic ways. Her man should be secure enough not to fight her at every step of the way, but if he does not draw the line and stand his ground, she will lose respect (all cardinal signs seem to have this in common).

Though she hates being pushed, she will probably test and prod her man on child raising, finances, home building, gardening and decorating, and community involvement. She needs a man who has his own absorbing ideas, pursues interests independent of hers, and stakes out a turf he can retreat to.

Cancer's man must appreciate her deeply feminine, receptive, nurturing side, but he must also perceive her ambition and insecurity. He needs to help her balance dreaming with doing and action with reaction, to replace passive aggression with honest dealings.

She needs a man who adores her but demands honesty, who won't get permanently lost in the maze of her subconscious, who will warn her, make her aware when she unknowingly follows her mother's dangerous footsteps. Her man will have to understand, too, that Lady Cancer is capable of running a home and an office at the same time and in many cases needs a professional outlet for her energies. He must learn to be objective enough to evaluate her as a friend would, for she herself is intensely subjective and emotional.

My advice to her man is as follows:

1 Avoid making her insecure, for this will bring out the worst in her. Find out what makes her feel emotionally and financially secure, and discuss what steps must be taken to accomplish this together.
2 Remember that she is often unaware of her insecurity, especially when she is under twenty-seven years of age. She is often engaged in some type of power struggle with her mother, and this must be resolved to her satisfaction before she becomes completely available to you.
3 Accept her moods as best you can. She is amazingly sensitive and intuitive, and she constantly picks up and reacts to vibrations.
4 Help her to accept and develop her intuition and psychic faculties in a positive vein.
5 Work with her to overcome her fears and the withholding that results from them. Don't let her overeat as an escape.
6 Insist on developing a budget for money, for time together, for good communication. The more practical your approach, the better she will understand and support you.

7 Give her lovely gifts, from flowers to jewelry. If you can afford it, give her a place of residence she can decorate to her heart's desire. And never forget her birthday!
8 Do not interfere with her friendships with women. She may be very close to some women friends and may at times talk to them more than to you. If you are jealous, remember that only more self-confidence and more open communication will help.
9 Do not try to own her, but do not let her own you either. Possessiveness is likely to be a big issue. Work toward resolving it.

Cancer sexuality

The Cancer Woman's most intriguing sexual secret is that she is much more dominant than she appears. Her modest facade disguises a tigress with a solid, repetitive repertoire. She won't be rushed, loves to be fussed over, prized, snuggled and wooed, but when she takes the reins, her man is the one to surrender.

The Cancer Woman tends to keep her intense sexuality under wraps. She does not flaunt it; she sends it subtly over the airwaves. The perceptive observer warms to the steady sexual glow telegraphed by her mincing, swaying gait and her teasing, laughing eyes. She seems to invite caressing, and the man who gets close enough to nestle on her ample breasts will find she wants more than a hug.

Our three primary cultural taboos are sex, money, and death. The Cancer Woman specializes in sex with love and prefers solid money as the foundation of love's edifice. She usually leaves speculations about the metaphysical aspects of life and death to others, especially to Scorpio and Pisces. Cancer is most invested in the quality of her life today and in assuring it for tomorrow.

She is reputed to dislike male roughness and to be a shy, sensitive maiden. In fact, she is a shrewd, maternally inclined conservative who probably tried sex very early and found it disappointing. A roll in the hay or a one-night stand is not her style. The Cancer Woman's kind of intense sensuality needs to be awakened, fed and fertilized by tenderness, then brought to bloom by passion. It may take a series of men to rouse her, and they must understand that the timid, delicate maiden needs to be gradually introduced to her potent libido.

She seems to be the type of woman who likes to be made love to and dislikes being the aggressor. In the early years, especially when she is playing roles and playing for keeps, this may be true. However, her old-fashioned sentimental femininity often covers a dominant Circe, poised on the edge of release. What makes her fly is a man who understands her need to dominate, accepts it, and from time to time is able to exchange roles with her.

Cancer's opposite sign is Capricorn. Her subconscious nature reflects the deep insecurity and consequent need for worldly possessions of that sign. The Cancer Woman's tendency to couple sex with love may well be a mythology sold to her in childhood, a convenient spice added to her natural fears. In reality, she is quite able to enjoy what used to be called free love. Her flights of imagination cover every aspect of it, and there is enough obligation and duty in her life that she may find voluntary, easy sex a welcome respite. Sex, and nothing but, often becomes her preference in later years.

The key word in understanding Cancer's sexuality is *conflict*. She frequently experiences conflict between her security-seeking domestic side, which is supported by society and by her upbringing, and her freewheeling, libidinous, voluptuous sensuality and sexuality. She often dams this up, with much assistance from society. On the one hand, the Cancer Woman is a stickler for etiquette, including the sexual proprieties; on the other, she needs to surrender to sex and cannot do so while bound by social role playing (the mother image we hold is almost wholly asexual, for example).

The Cancer Woman is caught on the horns of the modern woman's dilemma. She has tremendous sexual power and is very attractive to men. She is drawn to men and to the idea of marriage and family, but her attraction is frequently colored by fear and resentment.

For the Cancer Woman, sexual surrender that leads to mutual ecstasy must originate in her love of herself, of her own body and feminine nature. She must trust her own femaleness and invite the male's full-fledged maleness. This kind of sexual surrender is not an invitation to brutalization. It is a woman's greatest gift to a man, in which she opens and offers all of herself and is able, in turn, to help him open up.

Early sex experiences

The Cancer Woman generally seems extremely virginal and modest—so much so that one often has the impression that she goes to her bridal suite without an ounce of sexual knowledge or experience. But appearances often deceive, and though there are some who wait to be "deflowered" on their wedding nights, most Cancer girls are early risers and early sexual bloomers.

The mother or principal mother figure looms large in Cancer's upbringing. Sex may be shrouded in such secrecy that she receives no sex education at all. She may be so ignorant that upon getting her first menstrual period she thinks she sat on a tomato or in some red paint. She is seldom prepared by her mother for the reality of sexual relations, especially since Cancer daughters appear to be old-fashionedly modest, shy, and guarded.

Her sex education often consists of overheard snatches of conversation, pats on the head by an older sister, and stolen words over the fence or on the radio. She is sentimental and impressionable, and by watching films and television, she may form decidedly strange notions about what really happens once the lights are out. Her powerful imagination hypes taboos, and she may decide to try sex in secret and see for herself if the taboos are warranted.

The Cancer girl is apt to be practical, and she dislikes being ignored or fooled. She also has an insatiable need to be touched and admired. Often, sex in high school is the best way to meet these needs. She is not likely to assert herself at dances or to call a boy and ask him out for a date. If she is not pursued, she is content to take a back seat to more aggressive girls and wait patiently. Thus she learns how to send subtle messages of come-hither, and sooner or later she is ardently wooed by a variety of young men. She seems to have a chemical attraction to older men from the beginning, though later she may decide that it would not be practical to marry one.

The Cancer girl has strongly conservative and self-protective instincts. Therefore, she is unlikely to spill the beans about her sexual experiments. She is typically very secretive about her real activities, and neither her hairdresser not her best friend knows for sure.

More than a dozen Cancer teenagers have told me of losing their virginity as a result of careful contemplation of the pros and cons. Each chose her first lover cautiously and picked a place where she would be safe and unhurried. The Cancer girl is not likely to jump in the back of the car for a quickie. She protects her reputation, and she is normally uninterested in Erica Jong's zipless fuck. The overprotected Cancer girl may be forced to remain a virgin until marriage, but this same girl will often contract an early union in response.

Cancer sometimes has a crush on her father or another older male, perhaps to counterbalance her mother's overwhelming impact. She seeks her teachers' approval and is likely to be a good student thanks to her elephant's memory. She may be a copycat if she encounters a sufficiently admirable model of sexy femininity.

The Cancer girl has early tendencies to be turned on by other women, though she does not necessarily admit this. Bisexuality may appeal to her. Sex accompanied by a great deal of tenderness and feeling is important to her, and in the course of her life she may encounter many men but fewer women who are unable to give it to her.

Love and sex

In Cancer's opinion, love and sex are tailor-made for each other, much as in the famous song: "love and marriage, love and marriage/Go together like a horse and carriage." To Lady Cancer, nothing is more beautiful than a pair of shining, adoring male eyes spotlighting her to the accompaniment of the heavenly grunts and groans of an approaching orgasm.

The Cancer Woman typically prefers her love with security, admiration, lots of physical contact, and gentleness that ebbs and flows into an ocean of desire. Her imagination is so fertile that she usually constructs elaborate scenarios to stimulate her. She also needs permission to fantasize and was probably vastly relieved when the sexual climate relaxed enough to permit the publication of books like Friday's or like Alex Comfort's runaway best-seller *The Joy of Sex*.

She is sometimes more active in her fantasies than in her man's bed. She seems to have a built-in initial reluctance to engage in sex, and inexplicable holding back at the moment of starting and again when she is on the verge of orgasm. She does not take the initiative easily or speedily, probably due to her inherent insecurity. Starting sex means continuing, then going all the way, and orgasm means losing control, all of which may create restraints for Lady Cancer.

Being in love, even if it's an illusion, opens her sexually. It is as if love removes most of her inhibitions, so that sex with love becomes her best way to "come out."

She is not particularly experimental, but she is easily influenced. A highly sophisticated lover can teach her all kinds of exotic love games and find her a pliant, receptive student. Later in life, when she is more experienced, she easily assumes the role of the sex teacher and usually takes a much more aggressive stance.

Her fantasies are apt to revolve around romantic interludes—making love in water, walking on the beach under a full moon; satin sheets, big bed, candlelight, soft music, an ambience of sensual splendor; a Prince Charming who repeatedly helps her to vault over her guarded walls and introduces her to the most exquisite, forbidden joys of sexual union. The rape fantasy is a common one for Cancer; she likes to think about being subjugated. Her most secret fantasy is to eventually dominate the man who believes her totally submissive.

Her sexual response pattern in intercourse seems to be the following:

1 Initial reluctance, as if she had to climb over a wall and case the other side.
2 Slow arousal. She usually needs a great deal of dermatological stimulation; she is also apt to find a foot or thigh massage, or prolonged caressing of the head, shoulder, and breast, highly erotic. She tends to dislike quick penetration, preferring slow foreplay as preface.
3 Straightforward approach. The Cancer Woman usually does not need elaborate sexual techniques. She tends to stick with her favorite positions while her mental imagery supplies the variety that reality may lack. Lovers should not be surprised to find out that their modest Cancer partner runs hot sex scenes in her head, often starring a man other than the one she is in bed with (he has probably done the same just as often). Her favorite positions are missionary, on her side with penetration from the back, and woman superior. She likes a lot of lubrication and may want to add artificial lubrication. She does not mind sweat either and is in fact often stimulated by it.
4 Intense orgasms. She is capable of intense orgasms, especially after heavy foreplay and fantasies. She usually builds, and needs to build, tremendous body tension; she often has a rash on her chest, sweat on her back, thighs, or stomach, and a highly

flushed face. No woman can have an orgasm without building body tension, especially below the waist, and Cancer seems to know this instinctively.

The Cancer Woman who has never fully surrendered and clings to fears caused by sex-negative conditioning may need to do specific work with her body and body image. If she has never had an orgasm, I recommend Lonnie Barbach's *For Yourself*. If she has orgasms but for any reason feels dissatisfied, I recommend a series of awareness-, and confidence-building exercises, preferably with a counselor or therapist. The Institute for the Advanced Study of Human Sexuality, 1523 Franklin Street, San Francisco, California, is an excellent national referral center.

What kind of lover she needs

A man who is willing to go slow, to pamper her with words of endearment and devotion, is bound to get to first base with the Cancer Woman. She needs and wants an exclusive relationship, and the man who is right for her will want it too.

She needs a man who is able to provide a great deal of overall security, emotional as well as material. The man who can't fulfill this need—who never knows what time he will be home, does not wish to leave his telephone number when he travels, is never jealous or possessive, and could care less what she does when he's away for the weekend—is wrong for her. She may pay lip service to the idea of disliking possessive men, but she prefers a man who constantly looks after her to make sure she is happy, taken care of, and wooed by him alone.

She usually likes a man who is a steady, reliable lover but is also capable of flights of imagination and willing to share them. If he is smart, he will make sure she is always the star in these fantasies, for playing second fiddle to other women is not Cancer's cup of tea. Though she may play around from time to time, she won't want to know if her man does, even in fantasy.

Her man should be a gentle lover who, at the same time, is uninhibited enough to help her throw off her own restraints. The man who is catalyst for her sexual liberation is apt to hold her for a lifetime. An intuitive man, one who can feel her moods and flow with them without demanding verbal explanations, is good for her.

She tends to like oral and perhaps anal sex. Her lover should be open to these alternatives (at least one of which now appears to have become the norm). She needs a man who has a high sex drive but has learned good control. She is a slow builder, and a premature ejaculator would be totally frustrating to her. On the other hand, she can be extremely patient and good for a man who experiences periodic impotence.

She can be a selfish lover bent on her own pleasure, but her selfishness can also take pressure off the man who is secure in his own sexuality. If she is willing and able to take care of herself, he will be free of the typical male worry about "giving her orgasms."

The Cancer Woman usually likes some hard thrusting after the initial rounds of fondling and pleasuring. She likes a lot of stimulation on her breasts and buttocks. She is content with a man who has mastered this combination and probably won't miss fancy techniques, taiwan baskets, or vaginal vibrators. A further hint: sex in the shower may be one of her very favorites. Sex and water combined, whether on the beach or in the bath, sauna, or pool, is one of Cancer's greatest sexual/sensual pleasures.

The Cancer Woman prefers a man who plans ahead. If he is smart, he will arrange for music, chilled champagne, silk robes, and a beautiful bath equipped with a variety of scented soaps and oils. If they are married, he must be sure that her level of sensuality doesn't fall off, or he may find his Cancer wife retreating. Here, experimentation, private weekends in sensuous resorts, and other special efforts will become important.

She needs a man who brings out both the little girl and the passionate tigress in her. Her man should never typecast her or force her into a mold. One of the great sexual pitfalls in the life of the Cancer Woman is precisely her potential to adhere to predigested roles. She tends to lose her sexual vitality as she grows into the roles of wife and mother. Thus, she needs a man who will help her keep the spark alive, even allow her to expand sexually as she approaches her (and every woman's) sexual prime in her forties. Masturbation may be an aid; several Cancer Women have told me they like it to supplement, not substitute for, intercourse. Mutual masturbation is a good form of intercourse for Cancer.

The Cancer Woman may be a subtle dominator. Though she may claim to dislike S-and-M, she often plays the mistress role in her fantasies. Her man should be imaginative, self-confident, and aware of her fantasies, specifically in this area. Once Cancer finds an accepting partner, she may graduate to a whole new level of sexuality; meeting her own sexual aggression head-on, probably for the first time, she will elevate her relationship to new sexual heights.

The feel of satin, rubber, leather, suede, fine Swiss cotton, velvet, or any combination of the new "touchy-feely" fabrics will probably drive her wild. She may dream of a $95,000 chinchilla bedspread she saw featured in *Vogue*, but making love on a sensuous substitute will do. Skin stimulants are essential to turn her on; caressing her body with one's hair will arouse her, as will feathers, brushes, and silk pajamas. A partner who combs and brushes her hair, gives her a long massage, then takes her out to eat, is creating the right ambience for surrender.

Strongly perfumed creams and lubricants, flowery fragrances, massage oils with a fruit or flower odor, and musk are Cancer favorites. She tends to prefer strong scents or heavily laced perfumes, though she likes light alcoholic drinks that are pretty and ladylike. The color of the decor should also be right, for she is sensitive to all the vibrations that surround her.

Finally, the man Cancer needs will have to face the possibility that she will keep things from him. The Cancer Woman is complex and therefore not easy to satisfy. He must insist on keeping the communication between them open, for she probably will not. He must be intuitive himself and may have to learn the clues of retreat that she telegraphs from time to time. He must learn to differentiate between withdrawal in order to have privacy and withdrawal precipitated by anger or misery. It is likely that, given an initially successful period, their sexual relationship will be a strong bond and will carry them over many bumps. The Cancer Woman who accepts sex and likes it will keep it as a permanent, rich, always available oasis for herself and her partner.

What she needs to learn

The Cancer Woman needs to be totally honest with herself, first and last. Others don't fool her in the long run, but she can fool herself. She is deeply sensuous but apt to be inhibited initially. She prefers to have sex with a man she loves, but there will be times in her life when, for no reason she knows, she feels the urge to seek new horizons, to try sex pure and simple, sex for the sake of sex. She should be prepared for this.

She needs to learn to surrender completely. Though she is utterly feminine and receptive, she has a hidden need to grasp and control, and it often prevents her from genuinely opening up.

Once she recognizes this, she is on the road to true sexual give-and-take.

The Cancer Woman needs to learn to assert herself openly and directly, both in sex and in the relationship as a whole. She tends to be a passive manipulator and may not know what she really wants. She must overcome her natural tendency toward secretiveness and instead learn the value of exchange. She must tell her partners what she likes done, how, when; and she must listen to his sexual needs as well.

She needs to be aware of her insecurities, fears, doubts, and resultant need for guarantees that do not exist. She needs to have faith that tomorrow is another day. Often she is convinced that tomorrow will bring rain, never sun, and she spends excessive energy trying to protect herself.

The Cancer Woman needs to grow more comfortable with change. Sexual energy is life energy. The expression of sexuality is highly individualized and changeable. Neither love nor sex can be made to stand still, and neither force should be used to manipulate, own, or hold a person back. Life is a dynamic proposition, and so is sex a flowing process. The Cancer Woman must make herself accessible to learning, growing, sharing, moving, flowing. Water is her element, and water is never static.

The fact that she is frequently mistreated by men signals a need to be more realistic. She is practical but also easy to sway, impress, and dominate at the start of a relationship. By the time she recovers her wits, she often finds herself bonded to the wrong man. Thus, Cancer's biggest lesson in sex and relationships is to learn to let go. Timing and action are two valuable tools, and she must use them to her best advantage.

The Cancer Woman needs to know exactly what she wants, for she can have it. The problems in her sex life—and her life as a whole—arise from erroneous decisions. Thus, self-knowledge and sexual awareness are crucial ingredients in Cancer's good life.

Cancer Anger

The Cancer Woman is often called crabby, and for good reason. She tends to have a simmering temper that typically explodes in theatrical displays. She also cries a lot, and it is difficult to tell how often she dissolves into tears from joy, and how often from anger.

She tends to hold a grudge and to avoid discussion and confrontation.

I interviewed several Cancer women, and here are some typical responses:

1 "I love a great cry!"
2 "When I get angry, I must *do* something. I have to punch or throw or stomp out of the room. In essence, I throw a temper tantrum, which makes me feel better. However, it can create problems with my spouse."
3 "I don't get angry too often, but when I do, it's almost always my husband's fault. If he didn't treat me this way, I'd have no cause for anger."
4 "When things go wrong and I get angry, I actually get physically sick. I take to bed with a migraine headache or stomach cramps."
5 "When I get angry, I make up fantastic stories of revenge. I mete out cruel punishment; I am totally powerful and amoral. I replay my anger and my raging scenes over and over, and it allows me to say and do things I would never duplicate in real life."

The first woman may or may not know when she's angry, but she has found an automatic release. She just "turns on the faucet," in her words. She added that crying has been effective in relieving her tensions and that it produces results. Crying, for this Cancer woman, is a good way to cope with anger, as it diminishes neither her self-confidence nor her stature with others. Of course, if she resorted to this tactic in a work situation, it could be extremely destructive, crying from anger can paint a picture of helplessness and irrationality.

The second woman dramatizes her anger. She gains a feeling of accomplishment from actively expressing it. Physical release of anger is often what the Cancer Woman needs. She may bang on the table, break pencils, tear up papers, throw a wastebasket across the kitchen, box a pillow. One Cancer lady told me she tore her mattress in half after a series of arguments with her husband. It took considerable energy and ingenuity—and also led to separate bedrooms, which she had wanted for years.

The third lady sounds like a blamer. She assigns the responsibility for her anger to others, in this case her husband. I asked her if she had also made other people responsible for her love. She shook her head, visibly confused. When I explained the meaning of emotional responsibility—that our feelings are facts determined by ourselves—she replied that expressing her anger as blame kept her distanced from her husband. She told me honestly that that was exactly what she wanted. Thus, it appears that she was using her anger manipulatively.

The fourth woman is someone whose body is finely attuned to her emotions. Her brain signals her anger, and her body never rejects the signal and its consequences. In a typically Cancerian maneuver, she uses her anger to provide her with an excuse to retreat. Whenever she gets angry, she isolates herself. She pulls down her bedroom shades, turns off her phone, refuses to talk to her family, and lives in her shell. I asked her if the price of pain was worth it, and she said that she was used to it, that it didn't bother her. The Cancer Woman often prefers to stick with an old habit rather than try a new avenue, even if the latter could be considerably more useful and healthier.

The fifth woman seems to have found a good outlet for her anger in daydreaming. Most of us fantasize, and fantasy is a clever way to deal with anger as long as it does not end in total escape. I asked this woman how her angry daydreams affect her sexually. She told me that her omnipotent fantasies, which allow her to get rid of tremendous amounts of anger, add fuel to her sex life. She is not married but has a boyfriend who knows about her internal infernal adventures. She said she often calls him, asks him to come over and listen to her latest fantasy series. The boyfriend sounds like a patient listener, and she reassured me that sex was fine.

Typically, the Cancer Woman was trained to store up anger and express it dramatically. She may do so irrationally or as a planned maneuver. Sometimes she just bursts out with anger; sometimes she uses anger to achieve her goals (like the lady who finally got separate bedrooms).

The Cancer Woman has a strong tendency to filter anger through her body. She often suffers from it physically, for the equilibrium of her nervous system is extremely delicate. Her body is very susceptible to negative emotions; repressed anger can cause ailments ranging from repeated headaches to ulcers.

A very unfortunate result of the Cancer Woman's tenacious nature is that she clings to anger. The longer the negative state lasts, the more likely it is to make her sick; specifically, her stomach will take most of the stress. Cancer must learn to express her anger constructively and also to let it go.

Coping with anger

An important principle for Cancer to remember is this: *Anger is a reaction. When we feel angry, it is because something in our background or personal value system has been challenged. That something tells us we* ought *to react by being angry. But anger, like love, is a choice, a choice we make on the basis of our subconscious values and attitudes. Thus, we can choose to change it by changing the values that lead us to feel it.*

One of the things that makes the Cancer Woman angriest is to be ignored. She may be moody or retiring, but she needs large doses of recognition. She gets angry when it is not forthcoming. *The Cancer Woman must learn to ask for what she needs.* It is the surest way for her to get what she needs, and an excellent way to avoid situations that predictably make her angry.

Another thing that makes her angry is when someone she has loved, protected, and perhaps smothered decides to become independent. This often strikes terror into the Cancer heart. The Cancer Woman likes to be not only needed but indispensable— that is to say, to be in control. She must learn to overcome the insecurity that creates this grasping, to let go. (For hints on dealing with insecurity, see "Cancer Relationships." For letting go, see the Color Meditation technique in "Capricorn Relationships.")

The Cancer Woman is often angered by justice to young ones. Basically compassionate, she hates cruelty in any form. She can express her anger constructively on a personal level by helping to change those who take their anger out on children. On a societal level, she can work for legislation that protects children (for example, child-abuse laws) or help to establish halfway or crisis homes for needy children. She can also be an excellent educator and may feel useful in a teaching or guidance position.

She is angered by being pushed, exploited, or taken for granted, but she seldom comes right out and says it. She needs to be more straightforward and honest about her anger. Much of her anger would be dissipated if she were to break her patterns by open communication. Often, people simply don't know what makes her angry and when.

Cancer, the following practical tips may help you to cope constructively with anger.

1 Identify your anger. There are many signs you can watch for: body language linked to your inner feeling state; feelings of stress; your verbal expressions, tantrums, and other clear clues (you may have a favorite phrase that will alert you); a common-sense evaluation of your life right now; mirroring—others' reactions will tell you a lot about how you are feeling. They read the subtle clues you telegraph.
2 Identify the type of anger. Anger has different roots and may be: relating to a specific situation such as a job; related to your family; caused by past hurts that have nothing to do with the present; free-floating; irrational, impossible to pin down—consult a counselor if this is the case.
3 Decide what you can do to cope. Remember that you are not helpless and can: learn a mode of communication that avoids putting you and others on the defensive; work it out through physical channels; discuss it with a therapist; work with alternative or metaphysical methods to realign energy.
4 Take positive steps to defuse anger. Remember to: remain aware of the values by which you judge situations, and be ready to change those that cause unnecessary anger; have a sense of humor; practice detachment; practice a positive outlook; ask for what you need; cry, relax, get things out of your system without self-destructiveness; resolve to remove as many irritants or angry-making items from your life as possible; decide how.

Remember this: there is always a possibility that you want to hang on to your anger. If this is true, know it. Accept it for now, but give yourself latitude to change it later. (For specific communications skills, see "Scorpio Anger" and "Libra Anger." For more help on value systems, see the chapter on Virgo Woman.)

Cancer lifestyles

Monogamy and nonmonogamy

The Cancer Woman is apt to be highly family-oriented, to want and need family love in her life. At the same time, she is able to use sex simply as a source of pleasure, and she leads an alternative or secret life more often than appearances might suggest. She has some hedonistic tendencies, and they conflict with, but are not always checked by, her self-image as a good mother and wife. Still, the Cancer Woman is apt to be inherently loyal above all to her brood. She may not be sexually faithful to her husband, but if there is such a thing as monogamy with a family (nothing is more important to her), then we can say she is almost always monogamous.

She is apt to wish to remain monogamous all her life, for monogamy appeals to her value system. She was probably raised traditionally and has come to regard monogamous marriage as *the* way of life. But the maturing Cancer Woman often discovers sexual urges she never dreamed of, a lush sensuality and a need for excitement. As life goes on, she may continue to want stability, but she may also want excitement. She may feel guilty about extramarital sexual fantasies, but she frequently fashions a secret life for herself—in her head or in reality.

The following represent typical situations which could influence the Cancer Woman to become nonmonogamous:

1 Sensual, sexual, or emotional desiccation. She needs her waters of sensitivity, caring, and sexuality refreshed regularly.
2 Thirst for excitement and variety, either due to lack of experience and an early marriage or to the nonspecific feeling of being left out of the mainstream.
3 Moodiness or capriciousness.
4 Revenge (the "I'll get back at Harry" game).
5 Disappointment in her mate, either as a lover or as a father/provider. She may seek a new father for her children by this route.
6 Falling in love with a different man.
7 Falling under the spell of a fantasy or of a group that holds extramarital sex as the norm. She is impressionable.
8 Separation or pre-divorce blues.

Alternative lifestyles

Single woman: The Cancer Woman very rarely adopts this as a permanent lifestyle. She likes to be surrounded by her loved ones. If, in old age, she lives alone, she is sure to have a collection of things, animals, or plants to give her the feeling of not being alone.

Intimate networks: This movement advocates friendship with both sexes and is neither for nor against sexual involvements. The Cancer Woman may enjoy this a great deal. The only roadblock is her possessiveness.

Open marriage: The Cancer Woman is completely opposed to this idea, finding it nothing short of sublimely ridiculous. She probably won't judge those who like it, but she wouldn't want to try it for herself.

Ménage à trois: For Cancer it is a possibly fascinating experiment that can provide her with sexual stimulation and sensual enrichment; it can also be a vehicle for trying bisexuality or acting out a favorite fantasy, that of being with two men.

Group marriage: She is too possessive to try this, even though it may bring her added security. However, the concept probably intrigues her, and Cancer may be one of the steadiest readers of novels by such authors as Robert Rimmer. She imagines it, but she doesn't want to live it.

Communes: She may enjoy communal living very much. I've met many who do. The Cancer Woman is apt to do a great deal of work in the communal kitchen to mother the members and to be the fourth leg on the table in almost any communal endeavor. She is practical and wise, and if she feels appreciated, she may stick with this lifestyle (which is found only in certain coastal communities and in a few scattered spots in the rest of the nation).

Gay/bisexual lifestyle: The Cancer Woman is not irrevocably heterosexual. I have met many gay Cancers, and even more who claim to be bisexual. Of course, the majority are strictly heterosexual but are at least conceptually tolerant of this lifestyle. Cancer's gay tendency may be partly an extension of her intimate familiarity with feminine matters, her attraction to females, and her finely developed sensitivity.

Summing up Cancer

The Cancer Woman seeks the good life in all ways. She has a special gift for finding the best-quality basics that make the good life possible. Her interest in the material aspects of living can be dangerously strong, however. She is a fine caretaker, a sensitive, compassionate artist of living. She can set a perfect table, create a harmonious ambience, and provide comforts to her loved ones. Yet she must be careful to balance these outstanding and necessary qualities with spiritual/emotional love that operates without strings.

The Cancer Woman is an excellent teacher, but she must be sure to teach her children, pupils, or intimates values that will create a healthy society in the long run. A society that considers cars and television sets more important than children is an essentially sick society. In my opinion, one of the great tasks of the Cancer Woman is to understand her own materialism and set its limits, and then to pass on to others the urgent need to evaluate theirs and to put it in correct balance.

The following lines from Muriel Rukeyser's "Wreath of Women" point to yet another important aspect of the Cancer personality:

Women in drudgery know
They must be one of four:
Whores, artists, saints, and wives.

The Cancer Woman may not mind the routines of housework and childcare; she may indeed thrive on them. She has a tremendous amount to give. She is complex, absorbs information quickly, assimilates it well, and plays any of the above roles dramatically. She is like a tough plant that yet needs regular spring showers to keep it green, to guard the leaves from browning and falling to the ground.

Love may be a problem for her until she learns to love herself. Love may be difficult until she learns to give and get without keeping score. But love is the answer to all her dilemmas, and as she grows and matures, she will more and more find the kind of appreciation, recognition, admiration—and, yes, love—that will give true quality to her life.

LEO

CHECKLIST OF LEO TRAITS

Note: This checklist describes the traits of one *phase* only; if it doesn't seem to fit you, check other lists to find the phase you are in right now.

1. Amorous, Fiery
2. Romantic
3. Stylish, Regal
4. Formal
5. Warm
6. Social, Gossipy
7. Political
8. Has High Self-esteem, with a Flaw
9. Creative, Often Gifted
10. Self-promoting
11. Demanding
12. Magnanimous
13. Amateur Therapist
14. Inspiring
15. Good Executive
16. Hates Details, Shirks Routine
17. Big Spender
18. Authoritative
19. Opinionated
20. Brash
21. Proud
22. Complacent
23. Self-indulgent
24. Lax
25. Childlike, Fun
26. Gullible
27. Trusting
28. Vain
29. Anxious
30. Strong
31. Dramatic, Showy Actress
32. Self-conscious
33. Immature
34. Insensitive
35. Needs a Fan Club, a Following

Leo personality

General traits and background

There is a version of the story of Eve and Adam in which Eve takes a bite of the apple to become godlike. Subsequently, goes the tale, Eve and Adam are chased out of the Garden of Eden by an inferior class of gods envious of her luscious sensuality and open ambition to deputize herself a divinity.

Eve, the Eternal Female, had pronounced Leo traits and was probably experiencing the urges characteristic of the Leo phase of growth. In her ingestion of the forbidden fruit, her dynamic creativity and naive selfishness combined with typically colossal Leo nerve. Leo feels that the world will take care of her no matter what, and like a cat, she fully expects to live nine lives as paradisically as possible.

The Leo Woman is likely to be extremely proud of herself and to make no bones about it. Although quite capable of taking care of herself, she may prefer to be pampered, courted, and protected. She usually wants the most of the best and may well feel she has a divine right to it.

With her natural acting talent and propensity to dominate a scene, she may play at life. When things go wrong, her need to dramatize may turn to pomposity, boasting, or petty lies designed to bolster a sagging ego.

She is usually generous, gifted, and gay; vital, hearty, romantic; popular, outgoing, and frequently the recipient of many gifts, both verbal and material. Yet she may also have a talent for emotional discord. She is often petty, full of gossip, and complacement, and she may turn vindictive.

Typical Leo professions are: acting, entertainment, theater work; moneylending, brokerage, investment; cartooning, jobs involving humor and creativity; work in a club, amusement park, or park in the capacity of social director or coordinator; gambling, games, sports; cardiology, music; ornamentation, gold work, jewelry design; government service, management. Visits to circuses and card playing make good hobbies with a potential to be paid jobs.

Leo is the fifth sign of the Zodiac, the sign of love. It is Fixed Fire. Since the ruling planet that casts its rays over Leo is the sun, the heart of our solar system, Leo is naturally associated with matters of the heart. In the body, Leo rules the heart, circulation system, and lower back. Love energy that is blocked or misused will tend to affect the Leo-ruled regions of the body first.

The Leo type is described by the checklist of traits at the beginning of this chapter. The Leo phase has the following characteristics:

1 The birth of a strong involvement with oneself; an "I" phase such as characterizes the teenage years.
2 Intense romantic yearnings; mental and physical adventures.
3 The need to dominate in some aspect of one's life.
4 Possible sexual overdoing with the intent to find the ideal partner (this may be a very scattered energy phase).
5 Dynamic creative urges that demand expression. Children of the body as well as children of the mind must be allowed to be born. Women may feel a sudden panic regarding the issue of having babies.
6 A heightened sense of fun and humor.
7 Increased involvement in the field of acting or entertainment.

On the highest level, the Leo phase represents an opportunity to open one's heart to humanity and to love with one's whole being.

The Leo Woman is usually romantic, self-adoring, self-adorning, self-promoting. She may be a fashion plate. She will want the best in life and rarely assumes it is free. She is willing to sacrifice for it if necessary, and with her flair, charisma, and fire, she usually gets what she wants.

The Leo Woman usually has an unerring eye for the aesthetically effective and seldom forgets to use it in her own best interest. If she feels neglected or ignored, she may create a stirring drama in the bedroom, in the courtroom, or right on the sidewalk. For all her magnificence, Leo is perfectly willing and able to regress and become a pouting little girl. Though she is a most entertaining woman, she often manages to draw unhappiness to herself. Many times her romances end in disappointment, and her marriage may be built on the San Andreas fault.

Her greatest problem may be that she expects too much and does not give enough. She has an idealized view of mating behavior. She usually expects high romance, glamour, and flawless courting from her mate, though she herself may make a less sweeping effort. Her exalted self-image may be such that she deems it unnecessary to keep on trying. She is frequently raised to believe that marriage is a colorful ending, a *fait accompli*. She is just as often astonished to learn that her marriage is but the start of a long mating dance that may or may not end with her dancing solo.

At her best, the Leo Woman is the crown jewel of womanhood, high priestess of romance and love. She has only to break the chains of her own ego and vanity to be the most beautiful creature on earth, a modern Aphrodite ever rising anew from the ancient sea.

Amorous, fiery

The Leo Woman may be the greatest sex symbol of the Zodiac. Many actresses have a strong Leo influence in their charts, giving them an expansive, extroverted, dominant air, in most cases backed by vital magnetism.

All fire signs intensify the emotions and Leo intensifies the love nature. The Leo Woman's preeminent challenge is to develop her personal awareness of the power of love and her capacity to feel love. Because love's many ups and downs provide the thread that makes the fabric of her life hang together, the Leo woman tends to be almost driven to understand the nature and meaning of love. She senses very early that the heart is one dynamo of creativity, and sexuality another.

Her sex drive may be like a furnace that rarely goes out but constantly needs careful stoking. She tends to be optimistic and opinionated in her passions. She usually has many sexual partners during periods when she is not loyally devoted to one mate. She is bound to be high-spirited and can gold-plate a dowdy affair, scattering stardust in the mustiest corners of a romance. Her personal vitality provides the sunshine that often makes her unforgettable; at least in part, she derives her energy from magical dips into her sexuality.

She is often a medium for all the nuances of the human capacity to love, ranging from the affectionate, amorous, ardent, inflammatory, and tender to the autocratic, choleric, commanding, eruptive, fierce, fiery, and impulsive. She can generate an animalistic passion and be a savage lover. She is a good performer, but it is when her heart is genuinely involved that she truly makes sex what it is meant to be—the channel for love.

Romantic
The Leo Woman is a thorough romantic. With each encounter, she weaves her tapestry of romance and unfurls the pageantry of her fantasies. Guilt, self-pity, and masochism usually turn her off. She wants to live fully, with her heart in control, but if her ego leads the way, she may have pageantry and romantic trappings without warmth. Physical passion may take second place to flights of fantasy.

Music and old-fashioned romance may activate in the Leo Woman the hidden space that is the seat of her femininity. Fiery and thrusting, she may need to resort to such devices in order to refresh her feminine, receptive side. Romantic rituals and tranquility may provide her with the time and inclination to relax the control she normally would exert.

Stylish, regal
Even if she is a housewife all her life, the Leo Woman has an extra "something" about her that makes people take notice. She is normally chic in the extreme. She can be observed standing tall no matter what her actual height, surveying the territory with ease bordering on arrogance, and snapping real or imaginary fingers to attract attention and first-rate service.

She usually radiates self-assurance, drama, and dignity. She typically prefers red and orange, but should she wear earth tones, even brown, beige, and blue will glow on her as if with an electric charge. She likes tried and true favorites of the best quality and is happiest wearing natural fabrics adorned with original, oversized jewelry. She may design her own clothes and ornaments. She sometimes haunts junk shops and finds hidden gems. She can trust her taste, which is normally exquisite enough for her to make a profit if she resells her purchases.

Formal, warm
Leo may be the queen of society or an unknown, but she often has a queen's reserved demeanor. At a first meeting, she tends to be reserved. She prefers to be formally introduced to people, and she likes to have time to size them up.

She tends to warm up after the initial once-over, and her restraint then gives way to a natural warmth. She can be extremely comfortable to be with, a toucher and hugger, a matchmaker. As a hostess, she usually has a knack for putting people at ease. She seldom has all the tedious details of a cocktail party coordinated, but she will routinely create a glowing, charged ambience.

Social, gossipy, political

The Leo Woman tends to be a social person, acutely aware of the nuances of human behavior, intuitively perceptive about the politics of relationships. She may be a borderline extrovert who can measure words and honesty to the occasion.

She usually adores gossip. Her ears are long and open, her eyes see nearly everything; she is a sponge who often becomes an encyclopedia of local gossip, the alpha and omega of social information. Intrigued by people and their motives, she applies what she learns with varying degrees of wisdom, sometimes putting a foot in her mouth, other times knowing just the right piece of information to land a powerful protector.

High self-esteem, with a flaw

The Leo Woman may think she can tackle about any job on earth. She is usually a good administrator and a responsible chief; she also likes to counsel and advise people.

The Leo Woman's vocational self-esteem, especially in early adulthood, may be more solid than her self-reliance in personal affairs. Despite all she usually has going for her, she tends to suffer from insecurity of the sort common among women whose identity is strongly dependent on their status as a professional beauty or sex symbol.

As long as she feels loved, beautiful, or much sought-after, the young Leo Woman may feel fairly secure. If and when the attention fades and love disappoints, she may suffer an identity crisis—and this more than once. As she matures and understands that self-esteem comes more from a feeling of inner beauty than from adulation, she can change. She has the basic strength and stability to learn, survive, and love again.

The Leo Woman aims to manage. She is normally aware, deep down, that come what may she can charm, outwit, seduce, or slay any dragon barring her way. Leo, you must remember this: a woman who has a strong sense of herself, and likes herself, need not borrow her identity from any outsider, including her man.

Creative, often gifted, self-promoting

Promotion and sales work are naturals for Leo and usually interest her. Nobody can do a more reliable and showy job than the Leo lady who puts her mind to selling, publicity, or promotion.

The Leo Woman is her own greatest asset. She puts her stamp of unmistakable originality on any product or service she touches. If she designs a new hairdo, it will be bold, sweepingly different from last year's styles. If she is an artist, she will tend to use striking color combinations that demand attention. If a chef, she is bound to decorate her dishes with inventive flair. If a secretary, she will probably want to use colored paper from time to time and may furnish the office with glamorous accessories, right down to the paper cups.

Her creativity can be put to use everywhere. She can fire up her mothering, sex life, or career with it. She may plant friendships with her wit, teach, design stage sets, or excel at travel advice and scheduling. Her presence vibrates in her words, her looks, her furniture—anything she touches. It is a sad thing if Leo neutralizes herself in order to blend with the Smiths next door, for in denying her style, she is restricting her self-expression.

Leo, do not fear your Pandora's box of creative genius or limit its application by convention. Your role is to uplift with your own brand of inspiration.

Demanding, magnanimous

Though Leo is not the most complicated woman you are likely to meet, she has her idiosyncrasies. For example, she may be both extremely demanding of people and excessively generous to them. She seldom gives without expecting a great deal in return. Moreover, she may want it all on her terms. Though she may not be conscious of it, she often wants others to express affection and friendship in the same way she does.

She tends to set very high goals, even for herself. She dislikes looking less than her best; she rarely surrounds herself with people and objects that lack class. In her relationships, she will probably want a steady link. She may keep tabs on the whereabouts and emotional state of her friends, and she will not hesitate to call India if that's where they happen to be.

With her lovers, she is the soul of generosity, provided they remember to treat her in the way she expects. She wants extra attention most of the time, and more when she is under stress. She may seldom accept that others have priorities different from her own. In short, she may be a benevolent dictator.

The best way to cope with her demands is to be unfailingly demonstrative and tolerant. She probably doesn't mean to make others neglect their needs in favor of hers, but she is likely to be filled with a flamboyant sense of self-importance. If it finds no outlet, she will turn into a nasty, not benevolent, dictator.

Amateur therapist

The Leo Woman is known to say exactly what she means, except where she must be politic. She dislikes beating around the bush and finds hypocrisy a great effort. She has no respect for sycophants, though she often collects a group of yes-men (and women) around her. She greatly enjoys counseling and advising people, for it gives her importance and a large slice of authority. Usually she means well, and she may be very helpful, especially after she has dealt with some of her own conflicts.

Leo, try to demote your ego a bit. Give advice only when asked, and you will be doubly appreicated. Remember that most people dislike being told how to run their lives.

Inspiring

Leo is almost always a leader. She may be quieter than her Aries and Sagittarius sisters, but she attracts followers and has a track record of high performance.

Her main concern is likely to be reconciling her management talent and dominance needs with the personal style that enriches her love life. What works in one arena may not work in the other. She must calibrate the gauges carefully herself.

Good executive, hates details and shirks routine, big spender

The Leo Woman likes to manage people and projects and is good at it; she dislikes taking care of the details. She is usually clever at finding people to whom she can delegate details, and she works best when she has a staff trained to take care of minutiae.

In intimate relations, her tendency to delegate may be a problem. As a woman, she is still largely expected to be responsible for the maintenance of the household, with all its attendant drudgery. She may not mind planning a gala dinner, shopping for clothes for the family, or tending the home fires, but she is likely to resent having to budget leftovers and economize in general; and she may forget to order the wood for her heavenly fireplace.

She usually spends money easily, almost as if she expected it to replace itself. Some mates resent her attitude, often accusing her of thinking that money grows on trees. Her best bet is to make money herself and hire a maid. Another option is to live with or marry a man who will share household or family duties ungrudgingly.

Leo, a word of advice: never marry a stingy man. Even if you have no children, you are still apt to benefit from having a mate who is well organized in minor caretaking details, does not mind balancing the checkbook or dusting off the bookshelves, and does not get stomach cramps from your diet of riches.

Authoritative, opnionated, brash, proud

Problems may arise in Leo's career and private life as a result of her attitudes, but her biggest bugaboo is the *style* she tends to adopt whenever she asks for help. She is likely to walk into any situation with a chip on her shoulder and assume she knows best. She may refuse to listen at first and will often hand down her opinion unabashedly. She is stubborn and will not easily change her mind. But her biggest problem may be that she tends to *tell* people what to do rather than *ask* them to do it. This especially applies to situations where she is the one in need of assistance.

Humility is not a Leo trait. She would rather run the store than be a humble cashier; she is likely to tell the president of the company how to run his business; she is often the one who meddles in others' affairs to the detriment of her own. As she matures, she may learn how to ask and explain without offending. Her natural authority may glow instead of antagonizing, and her pride may become a source of confidence and strength. It may compel her to win.

Complacent, self-indulgent, lax

Cats need to sleep and stretch; the Leo cat must also take care of herself. On the other hand, if she rests on her laurels too long, the Leo Woman may become lazy. Temporary feelings of failure may also result in her sinking into complacency. She has a natural biological clock that seems to demand periodic rest periods. She must learn to indulge it without going overboard.

In her time-off phases, she may expect the world to come to her, and she thus faces the dangers of self-indulgence. If she feels too sorry for herself, or if her ego has been recently bruised, she may overeat, overdrink, or grow lax. What she needs is to get up, participate again, and institute a good program of self-discipline.

Childlike, fun

One reason for Leo's popularity is that she never completely outgrows the charming child inside. She may still believe in imaginary playmates, in a spirit world. She is the lady who nods her head with a smile as her child recounts his adventures with a talking frog. Partly because Leo finds the world of symbols fascinating, she is frequently carefree with money. Money to her is bound to be a mere symbol used to express her fancy.

The Leo Woman can be utterly charming, for she is childishly exuberant, impulsively generous, and naively trusting. She is still a child in her belief in spirits, cosmic overseers, and the importance of play and fun. She is the unusual adult who can play on the floor with children and feel right at home. She may dismiss stiff protocol anywhere; at parties she may take off her shoes or wade barefoot in the evening grass. Her child nature can also serve as catalyst for risks she must take as an adult. Leo's ability to capture and keep some of the spirit of childhood is one of her healthiest and nicest traits.

Gullible, trusting

As a result of her childlike nature, she tends to trust easily and be gullible. She may not listen to such admonitions as "Don't take candy from strangers" and "Never flaunt your assets." She seldom wants to bother with efforts to double-check people and procedures. Her combined naiveté and laziness may lead to some uncomfortable losses.

Vain, anxious

The vanity of the Leo Woman is notorious. Flattery will generally get you everywhere with her, and those who discover this may take advantage of her.

She may also suffer from perpetual anxiety. The Leo Woman often makes such grandiose claims about her role and her authority that she can seldom help but be secretly worried about living up to them. She is out to prove something and may pay for it with flutters in the stomach, twinges in the back, and heart palpitations. The liver may also be affected.

Strong
As a fire sign, Leo is bound to gamble in life, but she is an even-keeled risk taker who seldom mistakes imaginary flights for reality. If she wants to, however, she can *will* the world of imagination to become real. She has innate stability, especially in times of rapidly changing values.

Dramatic, showy actress
The Leo Woman has a tendency to dramatize. She can see the potential drama in every gesture or incident and easily blow it out of proportion. If she fights with her man, she may temporarily feel the world has ended. More precisely, she will tell her friends that the fight she has just weathered should earn her an Olympic medal.

She does a lot for show. If she has a sliver in her toe, she may start limping. A cough may mean she has pneumonia. A role she lands in the chorus line may be represented to her admirers as her big chance. Nothing is too small to become grand. She needs to project a certain image, and unusual character or lifestyle. She may bend the truth at times, but "show biz" is in her blood.

Self-conscious
Because she is such an actress, Leo is more conscious than the average person of her gestures, facial expressions, body talk. She often practices in front of the mirror to learn how to raise an eyebrow or flash a smile for the effect she wants. She may be the class clown, the trickster, the poet, the intellectual. Any role is all right as long as it makes her stand out.

She consciously seeks out people she can imitate and learns by watching them in life and on the screen. She can become a highly perceptive observer of people and use this ability successfully in her profession. She is likely to be able to compute people's reactions to her rather quickly.

Immature, insensitive
The Leo Woman has a tendency to retain a child's vision of the world, which can be quite charming. It can also prevent her from growing up.

She often goes on believing in ghosts, gremlins, and magically fulfilled wishes long after she starts voting. She may refuse to believe that the world requires her to grow up, to become more realistic and industrious than she was as a child. She may reject the kinds of responsibility her peers carry.

Her desires are so strong that she may be able to impose them on others or she may be so successful that she fails to develop sensitivity to divergent tastes and needs. When her mind is made up, it is normally difficult for her to alter it, and she may convince herself, as a good actress, that her view is always correct.

Needs a fan club, following

The Leo Woman is capable of starring in any play, but whatever role she takes, she has a great need to be liked, admired, followed. She seems to have a constitutional inability to compromise on this, and she usually does not try. She needs to shine, to be the center of attention, to be praised.

There is sunshine in her nature. When she is happy, she radiates warmth and light that naturally draw people to her. However, she also goes through cycles. When she is ill disposed, she drives people away by being petty or overly demanding.

Leo relationships

I believe myself that romantic love is the source of the most intense delights that life has to offer.
Bertrand Russell
Marriage and Morals

There are three consistent threads than run through the Leo Woman's love life: her tendency to be player and spectator in romantic lovemaking, her exaggerated expectations, and her egocentric romanticism. She has these traits naturally, and our culture raises women in such a way as to intensify them.

The Leo Woman's greatest challenge in relationships is to overcome her selfishness and allow herself to be genuinely involved. She is bound at first to approach love as a game or as a test of her managerial skills. She is quite likely to conceptualize love as a masterpiece akin to Michelangelo's *David*, a solid thing created slowly by passion, permanently erected in the spotlight, left by itself to reign supreme. In Leo's view, love is often an unchallenged and unchanging entity, made to serve her needs.

The Leo Woman wants what she wants and may go through countless miseries trying to get it. She is sometimes too fixated on the ideal for her own good; she may not be willing to change when change becomes necessary. She is strong-willed and proud; she may be outspoken, dictatorial, vulgar, boisterous, and condescending—all the while aching with loneliness. She is a good actress, but this can hurt her when she covers up vulnerability with bossiness.

The Leo Woman often attempts to dominate life and to bolster herself with pretense. Perhaps, for awhile, this technique works. She has the talent to inject sunshine into the midnight sky and convince others that it's daylight. But can she convince herself?

In her romantic fog, the Leo Woman usually harbors the expectation that she will sooner or later find the perfect relationship. She may think that it will be effortless to maintain, that it will automatically filter out what she does not like about life. But a relationship cannot give Leo, or any of us, a loving life. Only the development and utilization of her own love potential can.

The Leo Woman may spend half her life trying to transform frogs, believing they are princes; and the other half trying to reconcile her great expectations with the realities of life, of love and marriage, of her own and her partner's changing needs.

Childhood

The Leo Woman, on the surface, may have quite an ordinary childhood. She may be a good little girl who nevertheless usually displays enough strength of character and vision to let her parents know she is a survivor. She tends to be closer to her mother than to her father.

Since her nature is romantic and her talent for acting and fantasy is usually a great resource, she can construct her own world into which to escape. As she grows up, she may carry on a parallel make-believe childhood in her head; she may act it out in games or in school plays. She is likely to be a ringleader, a clown, or an organizer of some sort. She tends to like amusements, free spaces, and life on a large and interesting scale. The play may indeed be the thing, and life, though outwardly normal, may be full of internal sound and fury.

Leo often dreams of celebrities and may imitate their walk, dress, or vocabulary. She may silently swear to become famous herself. In the old days, she may have thought it necessary to "make it" with the help of men. Now, she may be spreading her wings more independently, fantasizing about fame and success, and about achieving it by herself.

She is so proud as to be hypersensitive, and she usually cannot take criticism. She can only cope with it by retreating temporarily into herself and designing a competitive game plan to prove she is "better than that." The Leo girl may harbor visions of such grandeur that she feels insulted by any implication that she is "average."

She is frequently physically striking and nearly always prettier than the norm. She may wear her beauty as a mark of distinction, and she has a knack for flaunting it and getting away with it. She is not likely to be outdone in the boy-girl department. Even the shy Leo girl usually develops a specialty—perhaps her large eyes, saucy walk, or glossy mane—which she then devotedly nurtures to perfection.

In all, the Leo girl is usually a handful, but she gives her parents a lot to be proud of. She frequently has a huge ego and must find constructive ways to feed and express it. If she does not receive help in this department, she may become tough and defiant, in which case the development of her femininity and her adjustment to being a female will be difficult.

How Leo relates: lovers and other intimates

The Leo Woman has a bent toward egocentric rulership. Endowed with good looks and desiring attention, she often dominates her man. She must learn to keep a tight rein on her ruling instinct and channel it into safe and constructive areas.

She may be a femme fatale, a glamorous queen who turns every man's head. She may have an irreducible, charismatic quality that reflects her intutition of her own great potential. She may project a sexiness that most men find alluring and irresistible, and that a few find quite frightening.

The Leo Woman has a nearly inexhaustible craving and ability to play the lead role. Until she overcomes her unconscious tendency to use men and relationships to feed her ego, she may be harsh and even militaristic. In the early years, she is seldom aware of this a problem. She may not be soft, pliable, and yielding because she has not yet learned to trust and enjoy her femaleness.

She is, nevertheless, bound to be a good friend, a giver; she seldom minds sharing the good life. She is unlikely to be petty or possessive of her goods, and if she harbors fears, they don't usually faze her much. She tends to have many friends of both sexes, many of them superficial. She is generous but keeps the best of her winning strategies to herself.

She is socially at ease and usually a free spender, this quality tending to endear her to some who might otherwise ignore her. She may have hangers-on and must make sure she sorts the wheat from the chaff. She may have many mousy friends, some of whom envy her. Others, the true ones, do not resent her need to be in the limelight and appreciate her full capacity for affection and fun.

Her romantic adventures take her through the gentle land of smiles, dotted with long shadows. She is apt to meander from arm to arm, from plush setting to plusher. She can graduate from shack to castle or survive in modest surroundings if she must. She takes most things in stride, but she tends to nag or whine a great deal if she feels discontented. She usually dislikes reforming her man, expecting him to be ready-made and ready to act.

She is a perennial optimist, and this is one of her charms. She may, for example, be stuck in a bad marriage. She copes with it somehow, finding a way to create sunshine and give herself an out—having a baby, taking a trip, or opening a new business. This is healthy, but it can also result in problems later. When a fixed sign, such as Leo, gets stuck in a relationship that does not meet her needs, she can usually build a good escape route and use it successfully. Often, however, she is reluctant to confront underlying problems, and she can find herself, years later, faced with the same problems that drove her to escape in the first place.

Barbara is a twenty-nine-year-old Leo. She has the charm and outward assurance of the Leo cat, and also her natural humor, warmth, and egocentricity. She came to see me after several of her romances broke up in a two-year period. Feeling blue, she was wondering why the pattern was self-repeating. It came out in the course of therapy that she had tried to use men to fulfill her own needs, with little regard for theirs. She appeared to have a poor understanding of men, seeing them strictly from the vantage point of her own elevated hilltop.

Barbara had been unable to believe a man could love her as a whole person. She saw herself as a sex symbol, and she had succeeded in attracting an impressive number of men. She could also hold them, but she somehow felt empty and restless. Though she seemed self-confident, she did not like herself enough. Knowing little about her deeper self, she was caught in her own projections and tended to blame the men.

As a Leo-type woman, Barbara was gifted but needed to be constantly indulged and shown she was well loved. She had an unrealistic view of relationships and expected that each new man would fill all her needs without being asked, without explanation. She expected total romance and minimum maintenance. Her wishful views and her self-image did nothing to create a sense of fulfillment.

The Leo Woman's need for independence is not so great that she does not also enjoy depending on her man—if he does not neglect her pride, vanity, and affection. She is often remarkably well balanced. She will go wrong only if she puts all her eggs in one basket, with the culturally approved label "His."

The Leo Woman must have varied ways of confirming herself, preferably directly. Running the home may do it, but unless her home is an impressive one and a challenge, it probably will lose its allure after a brief interlude. If she could afford it, buying her own baseball team would be more like it. I know a Leo who is running a sex therapy clinic, another who owns a gallery, one who runs her own needlepoint business, and three who conduct a catering and party service from their homes. All are happily paired.

Great expectations

The Leo Woman's major trouble spot is her unrealistic set of expectations about sexual love and relationships.

Lady Leo has a more or less secret agenda in her head. Whenever a new man appears to be a serious candidate, she runs him through a series of exercises designed to test whether he truly cares. Her expectation is that if he loves her, he will do many or all of the following:

1 He will love her regardless of her behavior.
2 He will *tell* her she is the best, finest, most gorgeous female he has ever encountered, without knowing how great her need is to hear this regularly.
3 He will *tell* her he will love her forever.
4 He will *tell* her she is the only one he will ever desire.
5 He will *tell* her she is brilliant.
6 Most of all, he will always *tell her whatever she needs to hear without her telling him what this is* at any given moment of the day.

But even Santa needs to have a letter spelling out Christmas wishes. How can a mere mortal man accede to Leo's *silent* demands?

A happy marriage, observed French author André Maurois, is an edifice that must be rebuilt daily. The Leo Woman is willing to rebuild the parts of the edifice that show, but she is not so willing to rebuild his foundation as well as repairing her own. She may feel that if he loves her, he will be brilliant enough to read her mind and know how to deal with her needs and the needs of the relationship.

The "glass-head syndrome," where each partner assumes the other to be a mind reader, is a widespread problem in intimate relations. Each expects the other to know what he or she feels, thinks, and desires. Each is bound to be disappointed frequently. Eventually anger builds, and then one partner is backed against the wall sputtering. "What have I said? What have I done?" as the other rages.

Leo, my advice to you is this: you must be fully aware of what you want out of your relationships. Write it down. Writing things down is a good way to become sharply aware and a fine way to keep up with the inevitable changes in you. Try to trace your expectations to their source. If you find them unrealistic or too high, they probably come from fairy tales, from the media, or from your parents' hopes for their little girl, which often carried unfulfilled wishes for their own lives.

Discuss your feelings periodically with your man, and also with your friends. Keep the lines of communication open. You might try painting a poster of your own intimate vision of Nirvana. Look at it; it will give you insight. Then evaluate how close your present relationships are to your ideal. Try to bridge the gap, but never expect people to be perfect or to know automatically what you want.

The Leo Woman in love

The Leo Woman in love invests her man with the most gorgeous kingly trappings. She can usually make him feel like a king and convince him that he is the luckiest man alive to have found his queen.

She is at her most considerate and highly motivated when she is in love. She will get out of bed on a cold morning to bring him breakfast. If he is transferred, she may quit her job without a word of complaint to move with him to a new city. She may do his laundry flawlessly. She comes the closest she will ever come to the traditional idea of the feminine woman.

This ultra-feminine phase of the Leo Woman in love is not to be mistaken for a lifelong pattern. She is not likely to give up some of her basic tendencies. She still likes to eat chocolates by herself, read in private, be free of household duties and detail, and she would dearly love to be served in bed herself. But when she is in love, she consistently acts to overcome her resistance to going out of her way for others—that is, for awhile. The proof of her being in love with a man lies in how attentive she is. Though she may be acting a part, she convinces herself, too. But don't be too sure she does not plan to be the matriarch eventually.

If she eliminates the problems that arise from her grand expectations and needs for excessive attention, Leo makes a fabulous partner. She can make her man blush with pride, agonize from excitement, break out in anticipation, squirm from longing. She may have him on a leash, but he will adore being led around. And when the tables are turned, nothing is more fun to watch than a lioness prancing in a diamond choker.

Like the Cowardly Lion in *The Wizard Of Oz*, she is a softie deep down. She has heart. When she is in love, she pours out her offerings. She can heal, adore, praise, worship, serve, support, and paint a golden forever for her man. The Leo in love softens. She purrs. She glows with hope. She is convinced the world is a beautiful place, notwithstanding Dante's vision and the atomic bomb. Very little can threaten her.

My advice to her man: beware of offending her, of being unaware of her desires, of not paying her court. You must be able to bring out in her, and help her sustain, her own love of self.

Lovers and husbands

The Leo Woman above all needs a man who can flow with her desire to be center stage and does not sabotage her attempts to express her creative energies. She needs a man who recognizes the natural actress in her and appreciates her. But he must also be able to help her separate the act from the person, for from time to time she almost becomes the character she is playing.

She needs a man who understands his own expectations from the relationship so he can guide her to become aware of hers. Her man should be discerning. He need not be an extrovert; she will make up for that. He need not be too sociable, for she will probably prefer to carry that ball too. But if he is a wallflower, she may start to curb her own needs to shine and later blame him for restricting her.

Since the Leo Woman can be mentally lazy, she is bound to appreciate a man who is intellectually alert and disciplined. She will probably cede the floor when he discourses on Plato or world economics. Her attention is never captured so effectively as when she watches a crowd gather around her man to listen to his pearls of wisdom. She also needs a man who is physically more disciplined that she is. In her youth she may not appreciate how important it is for her to learn self-discipline. Later she may resent it in her man too. She usually realizes its importance only after much experience.

She appreciates a man who is creative in any way he chooses. She has an eye for other people's talent and is not normally so insecure that she must become competitive. From time to time she may get a few digs in, but this is expressive of her need to sit on the throne too for awhile, rather than of her permanent antagonism.

She may think she wants a mate who allows her to be the star, and she is right. However, he must be able to hold his own. She needs to have some tension in her romantic relationship, a *yin* to her *yang*.

She may be attracted to a man who is more sensitive than she. She can be quite obtuse and needs to learn to be more thoughtful. Unfortunately, she is not usually a star pupil; the world of small emotions and gestures barely interests her. With perseverance, though, her man can teach her its importance in human relations.

Patterns in the Leo Woman's sexual relationships

The Leo Woman's sexual relationships tend to display the following patterns, which to some extent apply to platonic ties as well.

She is usually fascinated very early with movie stars, blond bombshells, and glamour that radiates sexuality. She tends to develop early and to play-act at being older. She is apt to try to pass for sixteen as early as thirteen, and she may steal older girls' boyfriends with her act. Still, it is mostly an act, and inside she is very much a little girl acting out a new fantasy.

She likes to do things *on principle*. She may just decide to lose her virginity on the principle that she has waited long enough. Emotionally, the first years of sex may fail to touch her deeply.

Playing and games are fun, but when it comes to intercourse, she may not want it or enjoy it until well into her twenties. But this won't stop her from being very active sexually, keeping the low-to-medium level of pleasure she derives from intercourse a secret. A tip to men: Leo likes lots of foreplay and may often prefer it as the main course.

She is unlikely to have many deep affairs before her marriage. She does not give her heart easily or quickly, and she is apt to be immature at the time she marries. Emotionally green, she is also sexually unfulfilled.

There seems to be a small but growing number of Leo women who experiment extensively before marriage. Those who get heavily into drugs and consciousness expansion may feel less pressure than their sisters do to follow social convention.

She may marry at eighteen or at twenty-three; she is unlikely to wait unusually long, for she would then feel left out. She is very much a social animal, and if marriage is the name of the game, she is likely to play it.

When the Leo Woman marries, she usually believes that her marriage was made in heaven, and on earth it shall survive. She is a romantic and usually wants marriage for life.

If the castle of her dreams crumbles more quickly than she imagined, she must examine her expectations and her own willingness to be a mature adult. Is she giving enough? Has she grown up? Is she still playing games that obstruct self-knowledge and sharing?

Hers is one of the luckiest signs in the Zodiac in that she has a good chance of keeping her marriage together—provided she learns to curb her impetuous tendency to consider herself the most important one in the partnership. She is almost always able to attract her man; she can even dominate him for a time, or perhaps permanently. If she ever becomes the head of her household, she may be hooked on that role forever.

She is likely to try to bandage and heal a bruised marriage, and she often succeeds. Her Achilles' heel is her great need to shine and live with fantasy expectations, but if she finds her own stage, the marriage may work well.

If Leo separates or divorces, she is bound to face an especially difficult period. However, it can be a period of growth, and she should understand that it is necessary. The Leo Woman is almost always divorced as a result of failed expectations or of an incomplete awareness of her own behavior and needs. A separation or divorce can teach her most of what she needs to know in order to build another, happier relationship.

Playing around normally runs against Leo's grain. She would

prefer being monogamous, totally involved with her man. Extra-marital sex is almost always a sure sign that something in the relationship is in decline and that she herself has become aware of it. However, it can also be a sign of immaturity and of ego needs so excessive that she seeks a source of adulation other than her partner.

What the Leo Woman needs to learn

The Leo Woman needs to learn how to love. Her astrological ruler is the sun, the heart and furnace of our solar system; her specific Zodiacal task is to open her heart.

Leo, you must:

1. Overcome your selfishness and resultant insensitivity.
2. Develop a better awareness of your inner self.
3. Lower your expectations.
4. Avoid being stuck in an emotional rut out of habit or on principle.
5. Find constructive outlets for your prodigious creativity.

If you take some of this advice, you will be a happier partner and friend.

Leo sexuality

The Leo Woman has a legend to live up to, the legend of the fabulous sex symbol. John Donne may have been writing about the Leo Woman's love nature in the following:

Come live with me, and be my love,
And we will some new pleasures prove
Of golden sands, and crystal brooks,
With silken lines, and silver hooks.

She is bound to be an early enchantress, a Lolita with far more sexual power than she herself can handle. Men respond to her before she herself can respond sexually without guilt or confusion.

Her sexuality almost never blooms fully until she is well into her twenties. She may function well sexually but not feel deeply. She may play to a full house and give a lively performance while remaining a semi-virgin at heart. She likes to be involved, but she may like to be admired, craved, and flattered even more.

She is usually kind but selfish, impressive but lazy. She is contradictory; she may dislike vulgarity yet find herself attracted to men who force her to drop her inhibitions.

She tends to make a cult of beauty—her own. She may wear jewelry to bed and perfume her sheets. On her first sexual encounter, she may behave decorously, insisting on a night light *and* a nightgown. Keep in mind that in reality she may be impatient to overcome the limitations of civilized behavior and may want her man to take the lead (and the consequences). Though she has a healthy sex drive, she seldom wants to expend too much energy attracting men. She is born with a kind of inner arrogance; making the most of her looks, she is usually content to lie back in splendor, awaiting her next Prince Charming. The Leo Woman is at home with sex and wants it combined with the resources money can provide. Rarely does she consider making love in a shack as exciting as shacking up at the Ritz.

Leo tends to fall in love often and love rarely. She may prefer the drama of courtship to the predictability of any permanent nesting arrangement. When she decides to love, her decision is usually rational and willed. Once she has made her choice, however, she tends to be loyal and stubborn about it.

There are three important keys to Leo's sexuality:

1 Remember to pay her undivided attention, and talk to her about her desirability. She would be happiest if she could outdo Marilyn Monroe, your ex-wife, and all your lovers, imaginary playmates, and childhood fairies in her capacity to capture and hold your loving devotion.
2 Be prepared to give more than you expect to receive. She may feel that the world owes her something special and that she is not required to pay it back.
3 Back your attention and your talk with telling vibes. Where her own interest is concerned, she has the finest antennae you'll ever see, with which she can pick up the subtlest sexual signals. Your desire is what really turns her on. If you enable her to be your queen in company and your whore in your princely bed, she may station herself with you for life.

Early sex experiences

The Leo girl seems to be fairly aware of the power of sex. She is bound to be a movie fan. As a teenager, she may spend long hours in front of her mirror practicing how to walk and behave like a celebrity. Even if she is shy. Leo will learn to attract notice; she may just be more subtle about it.

As a teenager, she tends to be outwardly confident and inwardly immature. She may be too proud to reveal a normal sense of fear or inadequacy, and she often covers up with charming bravado. She may grow up as a tomboy, wishing she had the status of a male in the eyes of elders.

She may develop intense crushes on movie stars and have special friendships with older people who can familiarize her with a world outside her own. She is usually quite social and may be a cheerleader, club leader, neighborhood sex expert, or everyone's advisor on boy/girl etiquette. She is receptive to peer pressure and must be careful about fads, including drugs. She may find it difficult to say no and may therefore become sexually involved before she really feels the urge.

She is not likely to be introspective. As a result, her self-awareness may be superficial, and her relationships may lack depth. Because she is strong-willed, she is usually able to make a good decision or to make a comeback after a bad one.

If her mother is an old-fashioned female devoted solely to domestic duties, the Leo girl will probably not wish to imitate her. Her mother's lifestyle may seem like a dead end to her, a stage too small and drab to allow her to unfold. Still, a mother is a strong role model for her daughter, and the Leo girl may internalize a feeling of uncertainty about what expression to seek for the feminine side of her nature.

If she grows up in a restrictive environment or an overly permissive one, she almost always goes through an intense identity crisis around age 18, when she attains adulthood, and 28, which corresponds to a major planetary cycle. These are times when she must decide how to be feminine, how to fulfill her sexual needs, how to acknowledge the feeling that it may be her birthright—or her cross—to have men cater to her.

By eighteen, she is bound to have some young man wrapped around her finger. She is finding out what it means to be a woman with the power that comes from having a strong will and the status of burgeoning femme fatale. How she copes with her personal potential, how she uses her power, will determine much of what happens in the next stage of her life.

Love and sex

A recently published sex encyclopedia defines sexual intercourse as "any interaction that involves a sexual response." By this definition, the Leo Woman has sexual intercourse a great deal. She usually fantasizes a lot and has many opportunities to act on her daydreams.

She is born to enjoy life and is likely to embark on a path filled with willing admirers, fiancés, many friendships, and probably a marriage or two. Frequently, her goal is to find the most convenient and pleasurable combination of love, affection, adulation, friendship, and fun—the very best of the easy life.

It is difficult to know how much of her experience consists of action and how much is just words. Leo talks a good game but does not always follow through. Nor do her facts necessarily reflect other people's viewpoints. She tends to dramatize everything and to be impulsive. One day, she may view the man she is in love with as perfect. The next, she may sour on him just as completely, seeing him in a new light fostered by disappointed romantic expectations.

Theoretically, she is interested in variety in love and sex, but she tends to have a hard time instituting behavior that facilitates it. She often expects her partner to be the catalyst, but he may have to be able to read her mind and body language in order to please her.

She tends to be possessive, though this does not always stop her from maintaining a subtle double standard with an escape hatch for herself. She demands complete loyalty and is loyal herself as long as she is content. It seems that her man is usually the vulnerable party, for many a Leo lady has not learned to open herself up to the risks of loving. In early adulthood, she may be used by men who are more calculating than she, those who have learned all the right moves and have choked off feelings.

The Leo Woman prefers sex and love to mesh, but they do not always go together in her life. In her fantasies, love is as perfect and eternal as the Taj Mahal. In her real life, love may fall far short of the ideal, and she usually takes this as license to play around. However, when she is in love, her power and will to comfort, to build her lover's ego, and to arouse him totally are hard to match. She seems to know how to make him feel like a king, how to remind him of his luck at having found his queen.

The Leo Woman tends to like heavy foreplay, so much so that she may consider the word itself an insult. She often wishes simply to play, touch, hug, lick, and experience their two bodies intertwining, and she may consider such "preliminaries" just as exciting as penetration itself.

Once the first sexual moves are done and she feels secure, she has the potential to be mind-blowingly passionate. She may surprise herself at the intensity of her sexual expression. Until now she may have suspected that she promises more than she delivers, but when she is really aroused and can finally dig deeply into her feelings, she finds otherwise. Where she used to purr, she may now scream. She may kick, bite, and scratch with abandon. It is as if a new door has opened, revealing her ability to go far beyond earlier imagemaking games and mere coquettish arousal.

She may become sexually dominant. She may like the woman-on-top position and milk it for every ounce of mutual desire. Suddenly, it seems, she has tapped into an ancient knowledge of sexuality and discovered the best tantric positions and breathing techniques. Sexual passion can make her shed her passivity. Every trace of her reluctance may vanish as she increasingly gets lost in her own world, in the explosion of a new sensual sharing. She can be the leader, shaking her hips, closing her eyes, tossing her famous mane—a wild dervish doing an exotic ritual mating dance.

If she experiments with sadomasochism, she will probably prefer the dominant role. She might discover that she enjoys wearing garters to bed, or various Frederick of Hollywood outfits. She usually likes oral sex very much; once she lets go, she tends to be a grand exhibitionist. She may like to watch herself make love or engage in group scenes.

If her normally conservative instincts keep her within the conventional boundaries of sexual behavior, her fantasy life is likely to be extra potent. Her fantasies may revolve around themes of exhibitionism, sexual variations she may consider "abnormal," adultery in various forms, bisexuality, sexual scenes with celebrities, and romance set in other historical eras, featuring Leo herself in titillating costumes. She may also enjoy pornographic films. I have met many Leo women who have experimented with bestiality and incest.

Leo's sexual pattern generally takes the following form:

1 She is constantly aware of her impact on men; she is often on a tense but pleasurable edge of anticipation.

2 She is likely to set up a situation in which she can flirt and play, and in which a man has many chances to build her ego and turn her on. She tends to control the sexual interaction. She may calculate, often semiconsciously, every glance or hip movement. She may turn her man on more quickly than she herself becomes aroused.
3 She tends to be slow to arouse and needs a steady buildup. A leisurely sexual meal is her cup of tea. If she has quickies, they are likely to be with men who mean nothing to her.
4 She is proud performer and usually a pleasure to make love with. She is sensuous, delectable.
5 She often has a tendency to become a spectator on the scene of her own lovemaking. This reduces her emotional involvement and intensity. For sex to be wholly satisfying, mind, body, and spirit must all be engaged, here and now.
6 She may focus on the atmosphere or on her lover's technique so much that she does not concentrate on her own feelings. She may be orgasmic but remain untouched on deep emotional levels.

The Leo Woman who overcomes excessive self-involvement or detachment becomes a lover in the deepest sense.

What kind of lover she needs

Ideally, the Leo Woman needs a lover who is generous, provides her with luxury, and flatters her enough to be her number one fan. It should be clear from the preceding description what her needs are. What follows is *WHAT A MAN SHOULD NOT DO* if he wants to remain her number one. These are sure ways to turn off your Leo lady: being poor and without ambition or prospects; talking to her exclusively of yourself; taking her to cheap places; disliking jewelry, art, interior design; being blind to how she decorates herself and her place; lacking manners; forgetting important dates, like her birthday; talking about other important women in your life; criticizing or nagging; making unflattering comparisons of her to others; refusing to cater to her; taking care of your own sexual satisfactions and ignoring hers; publicly ridiculing her; being stingy.

What she needs to learn

Leo must learn to *feel*. She is usually so involved with her image and with living up to it that she may forget to nourish her inner self.

She must make an effort to really know herself. She may nag her mate about his inadequacies without examining her own.

She may not like being feminine in the traditional sense, for she often would prefer to be catered to rather than cater to a man. She may dislike taking care of the routine aspects of her relationships. She must learn to define what about being a female is important to her individually. She must also be open to her man, who may have important things to teach her about equality in the relationship.

She needs to overcome her proud reluctance to admit failure. Acting is fun and fine, but not as a way to consistently discount feeling. She would also be wise to examine, and in many cases to reduce, her idealized expectations.

She may need to learn to love herself in a new way. Yes, she is probably proud of her looks, gifts of creativity, and power. But is she truly content? Is she sensitive to the subtle feelings that color the spectrum of love and self-love? Only she can answer this, and only if she knows herself well.

Leo anger

The Leo Woman is no stranger to anger. She has plenty of natural aggression and tends to go through cycles of accepting and rejecting it. Her fiery temperament can help to express her anger, though at times she may explode with it instead. Suppressing anger is dangerous for her, expecially since she often has a nervous, irritable disposition to begin with. Circulatory problems and heart ailments are common to the Leo whose natural spunk and animosity find no outlet.

I interviewed a number of women who are Leo types, or who were going through a Leo phase, on the subject of anger. Here are some of their comments, which are probably typical of the Leo attitude toward anger:

1 "I get most angry when someone treats me in a way I resent. If I walk into a restaurant, I expect instant attention and a good table. If I call a person or a public service on the phone and some clerk puts me on hold as if I were just another dumb caller, I get angry."
2 "I tend to use anger to show my strength. I find I get a lot of mileage out of a cool, controlled anger, especially in professional situations. I rarely blow my top or feel outraged,

because I get enough anger out of my system by the other method, and it seems to produce results."

3 "I get angry when I feel people are intruding on my space and time. For example, I get angry about the widespread assumption, which includes my children, that I can be bothered at any time with petty demands. It seems to me women are victimized by the myth that we are supposed to be always available. I think that underlying that is the common attitude that woman's work is never done, and that it is never as important as a man's. My husband rarely is bothered in the way I am; repairmen tend to tiptoe around him so as not to bother him. What really angers me is that I have trained our children to do the same—for him!"

4 "I am not aware of being angry. Sometimes I get a sharp pain in my back or I get queasy when I am upset. But I have not thought of my upsets as connected in any way with anger."

The first woman represents a reaction that is particularly Leonine. When Leo's pride has been hurt, she tends to get angry. The Leo Woman expects to receive first-class treatment all the way. When it is not accorded her, and when her self-esteem is shaky, she is bound to resent it.

Anger is most often a direct reaction to the feeling that a basic, dearly held value has been violated. When someone treads on the toes of our cherished, often subconscious "shoulds," anger can result.

The second interviewee represents another commonly held Leo belief, namely, that anger may be necessary to show dominance. She says this is constructive for her in that it allows her to express her anger in a controlled manner and frequently prevents it from accumulating. She has apparently mastered the skill of timing her anger, controlling it, and making it work for her. However, her comments also indicate a possible confusion about the meaning of strength.

Strength is a frequent issue in therapy among women. What is strength, and what is weakness? Many women ask. We are getting rid of some old stereotypes, such as the macho male and the submissive female. As we become more flexible about sex roles, we are allowing more latitude in the definition of strength and weakness. Women and men are showing and perceiving strength, weakness, and emotions in new ways. Each woman must find her own level of comfort within boundaries acceptable to her, her mate and intimates, and her culture.

The third woman may have been speaking for womankind when she shared her rage at being taken for granted. She told me the following story. She was head of production in a paper mill. It was a very responsible, high-pressure job. She had to respond to different demands all day and every day, was often the liaison between members of the union and management, and worked in a noisy, polluted environment.

The factory recently had been cited for minor safety violations, and it somehow fell on her shoulders to deal with the repairmen. She said that at first she accepted the task without a second thought. However, when it became obvious that the remodeling involved a thousand petty details that ate up big chunks of her time and patience, she realized that she had been given this "housecleaning" job because she was the only woman on the supervisory level in production.

Workmen came and went, interrupted her phone conversations, questioned her about trivia. She suddenly felt exactly as she had felt as a young mother raising babies—perpetually available, never allowed to say no. People, it seemed, once again expected her to put up with what she came to call "the rape of my space." She decided to get angry, coolly took up the situation with her boss, and got action. The workmen were told not to bother her with trivial details, and while the work was in progress, she moved to a soundproof executive suite. In this case, anger was a calculated tool, carefully wielded to produce change.

The fourth woman may be the rare, saintly human being who never gets angry. It is more likely, however, that she is ignorant of her own anger. The Leo Woman is often unable or unwilling to identify her own deeper feelings. She tends to live fast and on the surface, rarely delving into murky depths. She may be suffering from an awareness gap or from inhibitions about anger.

At age twenty-seven, the fourth woman had probably never had an orgasm. She said she was not sure that an orgasm felt like or whether what she had experienced sexually was as good as it would ever get. She seemed to me a perfect illustration of how generally repressed feelings, including anger, often bring about the deadening of the whole personality.

Coping with anger

The four basic steps in coping with anger are:

1 Identify your anger.
2 Acknowledge it to yourself.
3 Decide if you want to discuss it with anyone else. This decision largely depends on whether, and in what way, your anger influences your relationships.
4 Work toward accepting your anger as a natural emotion. Feelings are facts. Being angry does not make you a bad person. It clues you in on something you should know about yourself.

Leo, you must examine your self-image carefully. In what way does it influence the natural flow of communication with people? What effect does anger have on your feelings about yourself? You may feel that you are a frivolous gadabout who need not worry about such "heavy things" or that you are too queenly to have to account for your feelings to others—but what about to yourself? (For specific communication skills, see "Libra Anger." For further advice on how to identify anger, see "Scorpio Anger.")

It is important for you to be aware of your own values. People's attitudes are largely a result of their values, which in turn are largely formed in childhood. If, for example, you suffer from a feeling of being mistreated, you may be reacting to a princesslike upbringing or to a childhood of deprivation which forced you to escape into magnified fantasies.

In terms of anger, Leo, you must:

1 Accept conflict as inevitable, human, and real.
2 Accept your own need to be dominant in many situations; express and use it as a strength rather than a fault.
3 Reevaluate the definitions of strength and dominance, of weakness and vulnerability. You may find that you need terminology that is not based on inappropriate leftovers from men's lives, problems, conditions.
4 Be aware that anger is usually caused by your particular belief system ("He owes me this" or "I should not be treated this way!"). You can change some of your values, but only if you understand what they are.
5 Know that feelings of exclusion, jealousy, vanity, arrogance, fear, injustice, and powerlessness all trigger anger in a variety of people. You are not alone.

Many constructive uses of anger have been identified by women in my groups. Here are the most relevant, practical, and affirmative ways you can use your anger: to release tension, overcome fear, or create conflict so as to produce change; to gain power, mobilize assertiveness, or help you separate from your parents and create an independent identity; as an energizer, catalyst, relief for boredom, signal for needed change, or way to eliminate your "shoulds."

Leo lifestyles

Monogamy and nonmonogamy

The Leo Woman generally does not fit the old-fashioned mold. Her appetite tends to be too large to be satisfied by a man or a marriage all her life. She is apt to have extramarital affairs, and she may marry more than once. She may be a model wife and yet entertain lively sexual fantasies about movie stars or other celebrities. Fantasies, after all, are not dangerous and need not be fulfilled through action.

Leo may want to add an exciting line of work to her marital role, and this may enable her to sublimate growing pains. She is also capable of swallowing disappointment, anger, or failed expectations and keeping her marriage in reasonably sound state, perhaps forever. She has the will power to do just about anything. Perhaps the only universal and irrevocable truth is that she changes many times in the course of her life, and so also do her needs.

The following are typical situations which could influence the Leo Woman to become nonmonogamous:

1 Disappointed expectations.
2 Sensual starvation.
3 Ego starvation.
4 Increase of anxiety or stress. She tends to cope by becoming frantically social and/or sexual.
5 Feelings of exclusion. She hates to be left out. Thus, if the "in" thing is sexual experimentation, she may try it.
6 Needs for sexual dominance.
7 Fear of abandonment. Despite her flamboyance, the Leo Woman has a vulnerable ego that often harbors a fear of being left. She may habitually do the leaving instead.

8 Desire to act out fantasies.
9 Lack of fun and lightness in her marriage. If her man lacks a sense of humor and cannot enjoy life, she is almost sure to compensate, to seek sensual pleasure elsewhere.

Alternative lifestyles

Single woman: The Leo Woman may enjoy the single life from time to time. She often finds that freedom has its advantages, such as not having to account for how she spends her time or money. But she is above all a social animal, rarely an introvert with a strong need for privacy. Thus, single living is not recommended as a permanent way of life.

Intimate networks: This movement advocates friendship with both sexes and neither rules out nor requires sexual involvements. For the Leo Woman, this is probably a boon. She can be quite happy as long as she keeps her jealousy and tendency to pettiness to a minimum.

Open marriage: The Leo Woman is fairly conservative. She is rarely a pioneer, being more often interested in maintaining the pleasurable aspects of the status quo. Thus, open marriage is not likely to be her bag.

Ménage à trois: Leo may try it. The extra fun, pleasure, and affection, perhaps also the chance for exhibitionism, may thrill her . . . for a time.

Group marriage: Leo usually does not wish to share her mate in any formalized way. In fact, if the truth be known, she probably doesn't wish to share him at all. This is not for Leo, who is too self-focused; it is a possibility for her opposite, Aquarius, who is more group-conscious.

Communes: As with group marriage, she may have problems, except that here she is not under ritual obligation to participate in mate sharing. If she can find a comfortable niche and a position in which she is well recognized, she may enjoy this lifestyle. Some Leos become administrators of communes, while others run a smaller portion, such as the kitchen.

Gay/bisexual lifestyle: The Leo Woman has a strongly developed male side and often needs to be in better touch with her femininity. This is true of heterosexual, bisexual, and gay Leos. She is not averse to trying bisexuality, and there seems to be a fair number of gay Leo Women. *Chacun à son goût,* she feels, and one rarely sees a Leo reproach someone about her or his sexual preference. On the contrary, she may admire wide experimentation, though she does not necessarily engage in it herself.

Summing up Leo

The Leo Woman is most often a scintillating creature with enough *joie de vivre* and determination to make her appealing to many. She needs people's approval and tends to bend over backwards to get it. She is apt to be misguided by false friends and by her own love of the limelight.

She is usually strong, stubborn, self-conscious, and a good actress with a charismatic style. She has a tendency to be superficial and egocentric, pompous and glamour-struck. What she does with her considerable talent and personality is individually variable and a lifelong concern.

On the positive side, the Leo Woman can teach us the nature of pleasure. Pursuing leisure and romance, enriching her senses and love life, indulging her creative bent—these are her specialities. Our country, born and raised in the sensory impoverishment of the Puritan tradition, needs her. Our stress-filled citizens, of whom women and the young are the most starkly affected, need to learn how to relax, how to play, and how to "make" love ("be" love is a more appropriate expression). The 1960s, which saw the burgeoning of the human potential movement and enabled Americans to graduate from cold showers to hot tubs, was a Leo phase.

Leo is the sign of love. The Leo Woman is preoccupied with the nature and practice of pleasure and the art of love. She may start by being manipulative, possessive, selfish. She may end by making many people happy. At her best, she teaches by *being* a loving woman herself.

VIRGO

CHECKLIST OF VIRGO TRAITS

Note: This checklist describes the traits of one *phase* only; if it doesn't seem to fit you, check other lists to find the phase you are in right now.

1. Altruistic
2. Selective
3. Low Self-esteem
4. Hard Worker
5. Demanding
6. Perfectionist
7. Self-righteous
8. Persuasive
9. Incisive
10. Encyclopedic
11. Honest
12. Practical
13. Modest
14. Undemonstrative
15. Self-effacing
16. Repressed
17. Compulsive
18. Tidy
19. Dedicated
20. Monogamous
21. Variable Sex Drive
22. Curious
23. Mobile
24. Hyperenergetic
25. Nervous
26. Health-conscious
27. Organized
28. Healer
29. Worrier
30. Humane
31. Responsible
32. Good Teacher
33. Critical
34. Efficient
35. Has Character

Virgo personality

General traits and background

The Virgo Woman has had bad press. Her critical abilities are often resented, her modesty and caution scoffed at, her wit feared, her preciseness usually mistaken for lack of vision. Her sexual loyalty is frequently called prudish or interpreted as the latest sin—uptightness. It seems she can't do right by us. Virgo mirrors our own negativities, illuminates our faults, reflects our own narrowmindedness and faultfinding. In sum, she does us all a great favor!

The Virgo Woman is often strikingly, hauntingly lovely. Her intelligence and cool, sultry beauty are ageless. She tends to be wise, practical, articulate, witty, devoted to good deeds, independent, trustworthy; she is insistently curious, perceptive, honest, and sensitive. She is frequently a workaholic, suffers from lack of self-esteem, and is restless, compulsive, hypochondriacal, anxious, and usually impossible to please.

The Virgo Woman seems born for responsibility, often of the mundane variety. She may tend her garden carefully, following the rules Voltaire suggested in *Candide*, and find that someone else harvests the profits. She may spend much of her life feeling maligned and unhappy, yet she rarely loses sight of her goals. Productive service work is one; total, perfect health is another.

Our word *hygiene* derives from the Greek. In Greek mythology, the health goddess was called Hygeia and was often depicted as the Maiden. Virgo is astrologically shown as the Maiden carrying a sheaf of corn in her arms. She is also called the Virgin, signifying her lifelong concern with purity and perfection in human affairs. Our modern symbol for medicine is the caduceus, the magic staff of Mercury. Mercury is the astrological ruler of Virgo and signifies the mind.

The connection between the mind and the body was well known to the ancients. Virgo is meant to perceive and grasp this link, to help others understand and apply it in their lives. The Virgo challenge is to learn to bring matter under the control of mind, and to do so in a positive way. The Virgo Woman can be earth magician, keeping alive the rituals of cleanliness of mind and body.

Virgo is the sixth sign of the Zodiac, Mutable Earth. Mutability gives the Virgo Woman a restless, nervous, searching, and adaptive disposition. She wants to "do good" and often does. She is hard to please, hard to keep up with, and harder still to know.

More often than she is a leader, she is a taskmaster, teacher, or reliable follower responsible for crucial details. Earth makes Virgo natives utilitarian, down-to-earth, concerned with the material aspects of living, self-effacing, industrious, conservative, accumulative, thrifty.

All earth signs, Taurus and Capricorn included, are concerned with form and are therefore astrologically associated with matters of the body. Fire signs are astrologically linked with the domain of the spirit, air signs with the domain of the mind, and water signs with the soul.

The general health and care of the body, the diet, and the assimilation of food are all primarily Virgo matters. Virgo in medical astrology refers to, or rules, the diaphragm, intestines, bowels, solar plexus, and sympathetic nervous system. Thus, Virgo types tend to be affected by emotional stress in these areas first and foremost.

The Virgo phase of growth is characterized by the following:

1 Insistent concern with the maintenance of one's body and general health; possible hypochondria; faddishness; obsession-compulsion with cleanliness or perfection in general.
2 Circumstances that confine one to disagreeable duties; life or work loaded with detail (property or real estate contracts and court claims may be especially involved); sometimes, a cycle full of petty details and tying up loose ends.
3 Liability to chronic sickness, specifically abdominal and intestinal troubles or illness related to one's place of work.
4 Intense concern with self-care, diet, mode of dress, and educating others about these subjects.
5 A job in the field of criticism (literature, movies, etc.), research, editing, work with small animals, civil service. Many people in a Virgo phase work in health institutions (see Virgo careers, below).
6 Domesticity. The English "mistress of the manor," for example, is a Virgo role; so are such pursuits as growing plants with a green thumb, enjoying cooking, and administering a household.
7 Numerous small trips for utilitarian, educational, or professional purposes.
8 Feelings of being duty-bound, perhaps depressed, inadequate,

underqualified, underutilized, constricted (a negative Virgo phase).

Typical Virgo professions are: accounting; administration; work with animals, especially small animals or pets; the armed forces; domestic service; service work of any type; professions associated with the health and care of the body; chemistry; civil service; clerking; crafts, particularly where precision work is involved; criticism; dental work; data processing; diet and nutrition; doctoring or nursing; editing; management consultation, with an emphasis on efficiency; personnel; farming; food industry; gardening; child care; herbalism; healing in general; hygiene; technical illustration; interpreting; labor and labor relations; library work; mathematics; municipal service and politics; treatment of nervous disorders; nurseries; pattern making; physical culture; police work; public health; relief work; work in restaurants or sanatoriums; scientific work; sewing; needlepoint; shopkeeping; statistics; stenography; tailoring; teaching; textile work.

The Virgo Woman is often quietly attractive. She tends to underplay her looks and her charms; she is subtle but strong. She can be hypercritical. She may alienate people with her incessant flow of barbed witticisms and uncannily accurate observations, which she frequently does not know how to stop. One can ignore her if one is surrounded by a bevy of chattering, glamorous beauties vying for attention—but only until Virgo decides to go into action. She has a variety of tricks up her sleeve, not the least of which is her compelling mental power.

The Virgo Woman has the wherewithal to achieve a great deal. She is a stickler for detail, a perfectionist, an independent woman who abhors clinging vines. She is usually extremely demanding and industrious; she tends to be tense, tidy, efficient, practical, incisive, modest. She is often emotionally repressed, compulsive, and judgmental. She is anxious to find and serve causes she believes in, to be available for friends and raise excellent children. In general, she is most concerned with society's approval and can easily slip into the role of Miss Goody Two-Shoes, the girl next door, or the sultry sophisticate, as required.

The Virgo Woman often has two selves: the one she presents for people to see, and a secret self that may be permanently veiled. It is this double aspect that continues to intrigue and challenge people who might otherwise let her go.

Altruistic, selective

One of Virgo's great gifts is her ability to give. She will probably feed chicken soup to the sick and stray, rescue dogs from the municipal pound, fight for children in Biafra, try to develop a new vaccine, or undertake the reorganization of the local library system.

Though she tends to give freely of her energies, she has resilience and accurate judgment. She knows what is worthwhile and what will turn out to be a waste of her time. Virgo Sophia Loren said in a recent interview that her life revolves around her family and her career. She sees very few people and prefers to have almost no social life. The Virgo Woman can say no and mean it.

Low self-esteem, hard worker

Virgo is usually such a hardworking, intelligent person that she is worth her weight in gold. She stands as a beacon of trustworthy industry in a society that has lately been questioning the value of hard work, evidently in reaction to the ultra-puritanical work ethic of our ancestors.

She tends to work hard and play little. As a result, she may go through periods when she feels left out and prematurely aged. She may rebel at long last and perhaps experience a selfish Aries or Leo phase or a playful Sagittarius phase. She needs the buoyancy of the fire types and their inherent leaning toward self-confidence.

The Virgo Woman seems to have been born with the shakiest self-esteem of all. She seems destined for a life of labor, for years of doing more than her share and being appreciated less. She husbands her resources carefully, is adaptive, and at all costs wishes to avoid dependence in old age. She tends to overprepare. She has to work very hard to allow her need for pleasure and love to unfold into fulfillment.

She often lives as if she had to squeeze everything she wants to experience and prove (to whom, I don't know) into the first half of her life. She seems to have a fear of time running out. In fact, it may be that she trusts nobody and nothing to provide the flow of necessary resources, least of all herself.

One symptom of low self-esteem is self-denial. The Virgo Woman many times overextends herself and then refuses to accept her due; seldom does she take as much as she gives. She typically is more active than receptive, more the upholder of duty than the recipent of pleasure.

She may be the mother who registers her children in the best schools, takes them herself, and shops in the bargain basement for her cocktail dresses. She seems to trust her intellect and logic far more than her emotions, perhaps in the belief that life is apt to disappoint her. Setting up negative thought patterns, she colors her life in grays when it could be, instead, a brilliant combination of the colors of the rainbow.

Demanding, perfectionist, self-righteous, persuasive

Virgo demands top performance from herself in every task she undertakes. She seems to view the world as a rational place in which everything and everyone has a role and a purpose. She is bent on finding her own and fulfilling them to a tee. And she will accept no less from others.

She may believe that everyone who doesn't follow rules, especially the rules by which she lives, is probably quite crazy. Such a simplistic view may be comforting to her, but it also creates constant disappointment. This, in turn, may confirm her basic view of the world as a tough place to "get satisfaction." Her demands are often justified, though her tone is frequently so harsh as to be intolerable to people with weaker egos or principles. She seems to see a purity of form and perfection of detail that escape other eyes.

Things matter to her intensely, mostly on the basis of the utilitarian principle. It is difficult to refute her when she marshals her well-thought-out and logically presented arguments about tax reform, health care, political corruption, school redistricting, or labor relations. Virgo is usually convinced that what she believes and what she does are essential, and she cannot understand how anyone could—or indeed, why anyone should—disagree.

Incisive, encyclopedic, honest, practical

The Virgo Woman has penetrating, trenchant mental powers, and she relies on them heavily. She dislikes artificiality and dishonesty. She can smell a sham a mile away and is the last person to be taken in by a con. She may dedicate herself to stamping out deception and dirt. She is, for example, an outstanding investigative reporter. She can solve Scorpio's enigmas, clarify the unconscious mysteries of Pisces, and order the muddled priorities of Libra, all for a real and pragmatic end. Because she knows where the bodies are buried, she is a dangerous foe.

Modest, undemonstrative, self-effacing, repressed

Middle-of-the-road in appearance, Virgo seldom wants a huge audience. She is more often the busy bee who gets things done behind the scenes than a shining cynosure. If she becomes famous, it is because she has done her homework thoroughly. She has probably learned all the basic details of her craft and analyzed all the ramifications of the network of power.

She is often very shy and uncomfortable in public. She may want to cover up her assets. In the course of her life, she is often challenged to develop more openness, spontaneity, self-trust, and freedom of expression. Snow White's modesty and self-effacing fulfillment of duty prior to being "discovered" suggest a Virgo phase.

The Virgo Woman may be the wife who shows her affection by patting her husband furtively on the arm instead of kissing him. She is apt to shake hands with her sons rather than hug them once they pass the first bloom of babyhood. She may envy people who consider touching intimates a natural part of social intercourse.

It is seldom in Virgo's nature to be effervescent. She must learn to praise and accept praise. She is generally restrained in the expression of her emotions, as though she feared that they would take hold and relegate her to a hell of lost souls if she relaxed.

The Virgo Woman is resilient and tends to bounce back in times of crisis. She is close to nature and often feels more at home on a solitary walk than at a party.

Compulsive, tidy, dedicated

The Virgo Woman is apt to feel that she must engage in perfect service, in love that is pure, self-sacrificing, conscientious. Her standards are very high, and she is on a determined lifelong quest for perfection. She may resemble the compulsive, driven half of the Odd Couple.

Virgo is bound to have a medicine chest filled with all varieties of drugs, herbs, and medical aids for any health emergency; to have lists on prominent display throughout the house and in her handbag so as never to forget any detail of her responsibilities (and others'); to feel compelled to read a three-week post-vacation accumulation of newspapers prior to throwing them out. On the other hand, the Virgo Woman can also be impossibly sloppy. She can periodically swing from germ-free cleanliness to overflowing ashtrays, dying plants, and dirty dishes—and do so just as compulsively.

The Virgo Woman does not give her love easily. This is part of her discriminating nature. She studies her man carefully and sizes up every aspect of his being. As a defense against being hurt, she seldom wears her heart on her sleeve, but once she loves, she loves completely. Virgo does not play with anyone's affections, and strict monogamy is her preference. She is particularly vulnerable to her mate's straying from the straight and narrow, for she tends to base her choices and expectations on absolutes.

Monogamous, variable sex drive

The Virgo Woman almost never throws herself at a man or puts herself in a situation where she must defend her turf. When she makes her move, she does it with the maximum likelihood of success, and once she stakes her claim, she is unlikely to tolerate uncertainty or competition.

She needs a total relationship with her man. Nothing else reassures her, and nothing else really interests her. To turn on sexually, she usually needs a compatible, trustworthy ally, an individual who holds her securely in his arms while he makes passionate love. She quickly senses any dwindling of interest.

If sexual success depends on a woman's ability to let go fully and excite a man, the Virgo Woman is apt to run into difficulties. She does not easily express her need for sex or achieve full-blown excitement, and she is probably better off with a man whose sexual barometer is not too closely tied to hers. She tends to be emotionally and therefore sexually restricted; she needs to be aroused and taught to release her passions herself.

She may prefer to play the role of asexual conjugal partner or matron. But I have also met a few Virgos who needed a variety of partners, indiscriminately chosen, in order to get in touch with their passion potential—after which they happily settled into a heated exclusive relationship.

Basically, the Virgo Woman depends on her partner to teach her to savor the full pleasures of sexuality. If she finds him, she can turn over a new leaf with astonishing rapidity and surprise herself with the vigor of her sex drive and the technical range of her sexual knowledge.

Curious, mobile, hyperenergetic, nervous

The Virgo Woman has an insatiable curiosity, so much so that it is not rare for her to read three books at once. She is usually in constant movement, both mental and physical. She may be a chain smoker or fidgeter. She needs to see things, to get around, to get the story. She wants to put things in perspective, to dig for the facts. She almost always likes to travel, see new lands, compare, analyze, dissect. She also likes to plan her adventures.

She usually has an abundance of nervous energy, and it may take her decades to learn to channel it properly. She tends to scatter it, to periodically wind herself up and run nearly maniacally on nerves alone. With the help of meditation or relaxation methods, body therapy, a balanced diet, and proper nutrition, she can accomplish miracles with her prodigious motor.

Health-conscious, organized, healer, worrier

Virgo tends to be impressively organized and may have a file for everything from recipes to child-care techniques. She may keep a diary of lovers and rate each one precisely on her own Kinsey scale.

Because of her peculiar nervous system and her low self-esteem, the Virgo Woman tends to fret a great deal. She frequently attempts to guard herself against worry by organizing everything precisely. In this way she tries to eliminate the likelihood of confusion and the pressure of conflicting demands.

She is inclined to be conscious all her life of her own mental and physical health, and that of her intimates; her concern with the emotional/spiritual aspects of health usually comes later. In time, she is apt to haunt health food stores (she will know the best bargains); to be superbly informed on preventive medicine; to have comparison-shopped a slew of therapists and doctors; and to be as up to date on every new potion or herb as on each ailment of her loved ones. She may be an overprotective mother, and she is usually available to tend the sick. She also has a talent for it.

The positive Virgo Woman can pioneer a holistic approach to health and self-healing. She is a healer herself, provided that she properly channels all her energies—mental, spiritual, and physical.

Humane, responsible, good teacher

The Virgo Woman is loyal and reliable. Whether in the context of home, hospital, or charity work, she is trustworthy and follows instructions to a tee. Thus, she may do an exemplary job admitting a patient or satisfying a client; she is also unlikely to forget the human side, to neglect to wipe a brow or hold a hand.

She is a stickler for the letter of the law, and she tries to follow its spirit as well. She is usually as good an instructor as she is a follower of rules. When the occasion arises, Virgo has no match in teaching the "how-to" to anyone. She has every tool at her disposal to be a brilliant debater, orator, or teacher.

Critical, efficient, has character

Virgo is so busy teaching and carrying out the law that she is frequently intolerant of those unwilling to do likewise. She believes she is always right and would be hard put to remember the last time her criticisms missed the mark. She may be moralistic and preach a return to absolute simplicity; the Rousseauian natural order would have appealed to her.

She is disciplined and dislikes wasting anything. She therefore tends to be efficient, targeted, and task-oriented. She believes time is of the essence and may try to bend life to her philosophy. Free-flowing, unfocused, undisciplined people tend to make her uncomfortable. She needs to remember that they can teach her a lesson, act as a reminder of the necessity to relax her structures and loosen her strictures.

She is precise with words and can put a fine point on any argument. She is often good at, and enjoys, the precision and artwork of petit point. She may create her own needlepoint designs. She works with surgical precision, and if she is a doctor, she is in fact most often a surgeon.

The Virgo Woman must remember, or perhaps relearn, to love herself. No amount of accomplishment and good deeds can fill the hunger that plagues those who are not at peace with themselves. Virgo tends to learn a great deal in her life and to be an important member of society. She is most frequently an admirable person, a woman of quality. She has integrity and character. She must take care not to let her wish to conform bar her from standing out and shining as a glorious woman in love—with life and with herself.

Virgo relationships

The Virgo Woman deeply needs to benefit her partner, to sustain him, to be his all-important lover, friend, and ally. Indeed, she is often attracted to people who are in trouble, on the fringes of society, or seriously handicapped. She tends to thrive on being a man's indispensable savior or at least his full-time helpmate.

Her outstanding characteristic in a relationship is her beguiling directness, along with her disciplined devotion to her man and their partnership. She honors her commitments. She is apt to do everything in her power to make life smooth and comfortable for her lover and closest friends, to enable them to function at optimum capacity. She may be more discerning about the needs of others than about her own.

She is no clinging vine. Rather, the Virgo Woman is a commander of forces, both emotional and economic, marshaling them to attention and preparing them for action. She is strong but does not resent playing second violin if her husband is soloist or conductor. She is often at her best when her man needs her most.

The Virgo Woman has a tremendous need to criticize. She seems to have undertaken a lifelong crusade on which she leaves no stone unturned. But her criticism is more a result of an overflow of anxiety than of a deep-seated wish to transform people. It is frequently more a symptom of her restlessness than an accurate indication of another's shortcomings.

Paradoxical though it may seem, hypercritical Virgo is basically one of the most accepting of all the ladies of the Zodiac. She is consistently, deeply loyal and seldom dreams of remodeling people. She is more likely to appreciate their virtues, accept their faults, and stand up for them at any time.

The Virgo Woman can be a charmer. She is usually an actress with mimetic talents; her imitations draw people out and make their eyes twinkle. She is a one-woman union who can accomplish more than a plant manager with the mere lift of her eyebrow. She collects resources, understands how to utilize them, and is systematically able to employ them for the welfare of her loved ones. She tends to have many friends, but there are also those who try to take advantage of her. She must learn the difference between being a user (mostly in the positive sense) and allowing herself to be used. This is sometimes a bitter lesson.

Outwardly the most moderate of the true romantics, inside the Virgo Woman is as starry-eyed as any teenager. She seems like a cool customer, but romance is of the essence in her life. She spreads her rationalism over her sentimental yearnings as if she were throwing an old, gray blanket over a whinnying, exuberant, but untrustworthy filly.

Sadly, she tends to withhold sexually, and her seeming emotional disinterest often creates insecurity in others. Deep down, Virgo often fears she is unworthy of being loved—and perhaps that is what drives her so hard.

Childhood

On the whole, our culture does not teach people to live vibrantly and confidently. Because so many parents lack self-confidence and the ability to express affection, their children often feel misunderstood and unloved; they grow up without adequate examples of love, self-esteem, and *joie de vivre.* Beer drinking, golf games, and television can never replace a warm hug or a caring query.

Typically, the Virgo girl is excessively receptive to being "programmed." She often feels overwhelmingly burdened, consciously or subconsciously, by her family's values and demands. Usually a very good girl, she is apt to be the oldest, or the only girl in the family, or an only child. In any case, she is often the child who provides her mother and father with a training ground for their role as parents, and who bears the consequences of the classic mistakes of adults practicing the parental role.

She usually grows up strongly identified with her mother and may have trouble breaking the tie. Though independent, she tends to adopt her mother's beliefs and may later experience a severe identity crisis (age twenty-eight may be especially difficult).

Sylvia grew up as the only child of two hardworking, wildly successful musicians. She was a spoiled child, went to excellent schools, and had the best after-school tutors, mostly in the arts. She responded well to growing pressure to please her parents, mostly in the role of a budding genius of some sort. Her grades were perfect, and she usually managed to look impeccably clean and ladylike. All in all, she seemed an exemplary child, fully in control of her gifts and destiny.

When Sylvia came to see me, she looked as if she had gone for a swim and hastily reassembled her costume on the way to my office. Gone was the faultlessly groomed prodigy. In her place was a young lady of twenty-three, nervous, unsure of herself, feeling as if her life had been a waste, a joke. This is how she described her situation:

Until last year, I was a model daughter. I did everything my parents had raised me to do: I was the wunderkind they had wanted. Suddenly, just after my twenty-second birthday, I started smoking, drinking, and wearing bohemian clothes—you know, with frills and shawls—instead of tailored skirts and tucked blouses. I stopped pulling my hair back into a tight little bun and let it grow out.

It seems to me I am entitled to a little fun and a life of my own. I am tired of living out other people's dreams. I have yet to find out what really makes Sylvia tick.

The Virgo Woman's girlhood is apt to be overloaded with "shoulds." She is very often raised to have puritanical values, taught to fit into the mold, to be task-oriented and efficient, to withhold her feelings, to fear sex and intimacy. This early repression frequently is the bane of her existence in later years.

How the Virgo Woman relates: lovers and other intimates

Virgo is often irreproachably correct in her manners and interactions. She does all the right things, or at least looks as if she does. It is difficult for others to show disagreement or hostility in the presence of a paragon of virtue who seems to know it all, and perfectly at that.

Like a good quarterback, the Virgo Woman usually has a game plan and generally evaluates things correctly. She is a staunch defender of her ideas, and a convincing debater. She frequently has control of her amorous relationships, but she is clever enough to disguise it. She is not above playing her woman-of-virtue role to the hilt, thus eliminating potential opposition but also creating guilt in her partner each time he feels he is being selfish.

At the same time, the Virgo Woman is a true romantic. She usually tries her best to give; she seeks love and passion pure and uncomplicated. What she often gets instead is a life so busy that it leaves her little time to relax and spend a passionate afternoon. She is typically up to her ears in activities, friends, and hangers-on, and she is frequently a vestal virgin dreaming of lust rather than a flesh-and-blood woman thirsting for a tryst.

She loves fully but never easily. Virgo passions may take time to heat, but they take eons to cool. She tends not to be unusually possessive and normally lives with her jealousy as she might with an unwelcome, persistent insect. Her insecurity periodically fuels her jealousy, and she may then make scenes that seem out of character or hand down a mandate about how she expects things to be.

She tends to be choosy, meticulous, and systematic, though at times she may throw caution to the wind and enter into an uncharacteristic stormy romance. Mostly she calculates the pros and cons of every relationship, perhaps drawing up a list to keep in her night table. She is admirably rational in her decision making, and her talents as a perspicacious puzzle solver also work in her favor.

The Virgo Woman usually knows how to get her man. She knows how to flatter, cajole, convince; she can also make him see that he needs her. She can intuitively make herself into the very person he quickly feels he cannot live without. She has the gift of making each person feel that, by extension, he or she could be the center of her life.

Because she is more a specialist than a generalist, Lady Virgo tends to choose one man at a time. To her credit, she is almost always totally honest with him. Virgo does not play games, especially in love. She is likely to inform her prospective intimate of her opinion. If she wants him, she'll let him know. If she is unsure, she will tell him.

A pragmatist, she is bound to analyze each issue. She is likely to ask herself, Am I doing it right? Will it work? She wants faith but seldom has it. She knows intellectually, but rarely truly accepts, that love is imperfect.

Repression in the Virgo Woman

The Virgo Woman tends to have very sharply defined views of right and wrong. She has an unquenchable thirst for knowledge in every area and a tendency to make inflexible judgments. Her strong mental nature molds her beliefs. What she perceives as beneficial for her is in fact right.

One cannot repress an emotion one does not feel, but one can repress the thought that would lead to the formation of a feeling one does not want to admit. The Virgo Woman frequently represses the interpretive thoughts or value judgments that lead to her emotions. For example, if Virgo is envious of a friend who excels in her career, and if her envy is an unacceptable emotion, she may punish herself for the unconscious envy by repressing her feeling of elation when she later hears of the same friend's demotion. She will rush to her friend's aid, and what is more lethal, she may use her friend's misfortune and her own guilt about envy to repress her own ambition.

Virgo's repression, like all repression, is a subconscious mental process that blocks certain ideas, memories, identifications, and interpretations as unacceptable. What she blocks depends on her value structure. If it has been automatically copied from her parents, she will have automatically learned to block the same constellation of responses.

Repression breeds a system of automatic avoidance reactions that are habit-forming. These reactions also tend to spread, so that one restricts not only feelings of envy but also feelings of elation. Repression in the Virgo Woman is at first like a shot of Novocain that numbs a localized area; it may become like a general anesthetic that gradually affects her entire range of emotional expressiveness. She may engage in behavior that separates her from her loved ones, and she may do so for reasons of which she is not aware.

Agnes came to see me when she was forty-three. She had sacrificed her desire for a high-profile career in health administration to her children and to her husband's desire to keep her at home. She had no interest outside her family. She was aware of occasional terrifying scenes with her children, during which she hurled abuse at them and threw glasses at the kitchen wall. She would then forget these scenes.

She was horrified to discover one day that she felt contempt for her weak-willed husband, who stayed out of these fights; and that she also periodically felt real hatred for her children. With each such realization, she threw herself into the role of perfect mother and wife with renewed enthusiasm. To the world the image never wavered.

When she came to see me, her problem was twofold. She no longer enjoyed sexual realtions with her husband, and she had begun to drink heavily during the day when she was alone. Agnes was repressing feelings of hatred for her children and disdain for her husband. She needed to acknowledge her real feelings to herself, without running away, so she could take responsibility and change.

The Virgo Woman's emotional repression cannot help but color her life, make her outlook grayer than it need be. If she represses unacceptable feelings such as envy, fear, guilt, anger, and hatred, she is also apt to repress feelings of joy.

Coping with repression

The Virgo Woman needs to be as acutely aware of her value system as she is of many of her (and other people's) faults. What makes her believe, for example, that exercise and psychotherapy are beneficial while homosexuality and frozen foods are harmful? Until she comes into her own, she may well base her judgments on adolescent thinking.

What made Agnes accept her husband's decisions, and what made her resist her own feelings so completely that she was driven to drown them in drink? It was her belief that it was unacceptable to defy her husband, that to be a career woman under the circumstances would mean being a bad wife and mother, ergo, an inadequate woman—all values she learned as a child.

Virgo, you must learn to evaluate the validity of your concepts of right and wrong, moral and immoral, in your life as it is *now*. I suggest the following exercise to help you become aware of why you feel as you do. It is a self-evaluative list of questions. A word of advice: be honest with yourself, and expect to change your answers from time to time!

1 What are my five top priorities in life? Why?
2 Have I done what is most important to me? If not, why not?
3 Do I enjoy life? What do I love about it, and what do I dislike about it?
4 Do I enjoy my sex life? If yes, in what way? If no, how and why not? Do I want to change it?
5 What do I really feel about my relationship with my husband or lover? How important is it to me? What do I like, and what don't I like about it?
6 In what ways does my behavior with my husband or lover resemble my mother's with my father? What parts of my behavior do I like, and what parts do I dislike? How would I want to change it? Can I expect cooperation?
7 Who is my best friend? What do I see in this person? What do I give, and what do I get? Am I satisfied with this friendship? If not, what is missing?
8 How often do I relax? Is it often enough? Do I need to change my lifestyle? How?

The Virgo Woman in love

Virgo is a labyrinth, a paradox of feelings. She is romantic and conjures magic with her walk; her body telegraphs a knowledge her mind may not catch. She may be a creature of ambivalence, a heated body with a cool mind. She makes the art of love into a craft, fashioning relationships slowly, with delicate fingers, body, and smiles backed by an incessantly active and practical brain.

Whatever Lola wants, Lola is apt to get, but she also gives Larry his due. She is typically a dedicated, serious lover. Hers is not to reason why; the how interests her more. How does it fit into the framework of her life? How will this relationship work? How does he like her best? How would he be as a husband, father, friend? These are questions she always asks herself.

The Virgo Woman has a hunting, eternally youthful quality unless she mars it with skittishness or nagging. She is often love's servant and happily complies with her own desire to cater to her husband and to his whims. She arrives at dates ahead of time, buys his favorite records to play in her bedroom, scrubs the bathroom and sprays it full of his favorite perfume.

She is most eager to please and to learn. She is genuinely curious about him. She wants to know everything, from his favorite baby foods to his boyhood baseball idol. She wants to know his current preferences precisely so she can cook only what he likes. She queries him about his taste in women, films, television, and brands of beer, wine, alcohol, and cigars. She will probably want to know his preferred sleeping position and schedule. Most likely, she'll commit every scrap of information to memory forever. Only her desire for romance exceeds her curiosity.

She is bound to pamper or mother her man. She may prefer a man who needs to be educated, reducated, or healed in some way. She may correspond with prisoners and fall in love with a parolee; she may meet her fiancé in a hospital ward or play Florence Nightingale to her own doctor.

She is flexible to a fault. Many a Virgo would accompany her man anywhere—to a California hot-tub party, a disco, a punk rock concert, a nude beach. But she will draw the line at sharing her man with anyone else unless it is her last chance and her only way of holding him. She can overcome a lot of jealousy and inhibitions in order to do what she deems necessary to make the relationship work.

She is generally astute, devoted, curious, and caring enough to make relationships last. It is her goal to do so once she has found her man. She is usually monogamous and makes it unnecessary for her mate to stray. She also has a natural protective instinct and may cover her lover with a careful shield against illness, poverty, or other ladies.

The Virgo Woman is almost universally a die-hard perfectionist. Nothing short of the best is good enough for the man she loves, and she aims to make sure he gets it. In addition, she is a perfectionist in her own needs for fulfillment. She wants what she wants from him, and if it is not forthcoming, she is likely to criticize him into helpless alienation. She may find herself deeply in love years after her marriage, but her man may build defenses against intimacy as well as against criticism, so that without their conscious knowledge an emotional distance is created.

Patterns in the Virgo Woman's sexual relationships

The Virgo Woman's sexual relationships tend to display the following patterns; to some extent, they apply to her platonic ties as well.

1 She has a highly internalized, often repressed sex drive for which she compensates by daydreaming. She is usually a late bloomer.
2 She tends to hold back from "getting emotional" and from making commitments. She may dislike experimentation on a wide scale, considering it beneath her, but a few Virgos go to the other extreme, as if in an attempt to outwit the archetype.
3 When she falls, she falls very hard, tumbling into a whole new dimension much as did Alice in Wonderland. She tends to have one man at a time, is intensely romantic, and may think that each new relationship is "it." She may have a great need to justify sexual activity to herself, and being in love may be the only way to do so.
4 She often attracts losers, hangers-on, the stray, or the sick. She likes to play nurse; it brings out her need to take care of people.
5 She usually marries early in a fit of passion that may surprise her. She frequently marries her childhood sweetheart and tends to believe it is forever—and it may be! Sometimes, though, it may take will power, coupled with guilt about divorce, to survive the roughest bumps.
6 Her relationships tend to have quality and depth, but they often lack spark. This may engender hostilities in later years. She is ill equipped to cope with these and may ignore or internalize them, which is unhealthy.
7 If she divorces, she is apt to be unusually bitter and disappointed. Some Virgos stay single for the rest of their lives

and rather enjoy it. Others may engage in simultaneous love affairs for the first time.

8 The best type of Virgo relationship is one where both parties work at jobs they love and come together by mutual agreement. She may want to have a precise contract stipulating how, when, and for what purpose they join.

Lovers and Husbands

The Virgo Woman needs a man who is perfect. Short of that, he should be charming, sensitive, exceedingly industrious, honest, and capable. She enjoys a man who is a mirror image of herself, except that he must have more flair, humor, and spontaneity. These are qualities she admires and often lacks.

While she may adore inadequate males who need her desperately, she is best off with a male who is highly competent and secure both in his vocation and in his sexual prowess. She will not respect him if he is not a hardworking person, and she needs a sexually ardent and sensitive man to bring her out.

Virgo needs a man who is tolerant and easy going. She probably doesn't have a lazy bone in her body, and she may be a dynamo who only stops to recharge her batteries once in a blue moon. She needs a man to slow her down, help her to run without excessive nervous energy. Her man should be a relaxed sort, a lazy pussycat on weekends, a take-it-easy fellow who means it. He should be a vital man with open attitudes, less critical than his mate, judging not on appearances but enjoying the diversity of human nature.

Virgo prefers a man who is stable and scrupulously honest. She does not want a schemer, swindler, con man, or adventurer. Errol Flynn, Warren Beatty, and other legendary playboys rarely appeal to her. She is more comfortable with a man she trusts, a man of the down-home variety.

She needs a man who is willing to work extra hard to understand her. Since he may have to help her open up, he should be sensitive to and unusually aware of feelings, and unashamed of his own. She needs a man who can help her transform her nervous intensity into stable self-love that can irrigate her passions.

She needs a man who understands freedom and can give it to her. She wants space to be free and self-sufficient, but she has such a strong need to be needed that she can be manipulated by others. The man who is best for her will never take advantage of this trait and will help her to balance her need to give with her need to run free.

He must be clean, well groomed, and neatly dressed. He need not look dashing or expensively attired, but she appreciates quality in the smallest details. She has the eyes of an eagle and will probably notice every cigarette ash, stain, or wrinkle. The man who does not wash regularly or forgets to shave before making love, whose apartment is normally a shambles, can forget about her. She is extremely sensitive to odors, and something as intangible as his smell can make all the difference.

Virgo sexuality

The Virgo Woman has learned our cultural messages about sex only too well. She tends to develop technical proficiency before she develops sexual soul. She is apt to be disciplined, strong, and high-minded, and she is often repressed. It is seldom easy for her to overcome sexual guilt or the fear of being inadequate.

In our culture, sex has ceased to be a natural function. Our sex education is largely negative, subliminally imparted. Seductive but unreal and unrealistic billboard, movie, and television ads and figures; hushed conversations in the powder or locker room; cryptic remarks, "naughty" clubs, and adult bookstores—these are not part of a healthy sexual climate. We learn early and thoroughly that sex is an activity that falls somewhere along the continuum from questionable, dirty, and unavoidable to sinfully pleasurable. I have never met anyone who has not grown up with some sense of guilt and fear about sex.

The Virgo Woman, because she is often a good girl and a perfectionist, frequently absorbs a double dose of the messages passed on by her mother and by the times. Her sexual identity runs mostly along conservative lines; her greatest goal is frequently a stable marriage to the most suitable man. She is probably better prepared to fulfill her marital duties in the nonsexual sphere, playing the role of partner-wife-hostess-matron, than she is to play out the fantasy of being her husband's whore in bed.

At times, she may react to her repressive background by rejecting it and adopting a bohemian lifestyle. This may be her way to break out of confining stereotypes. She may join a commune, travel, have an illegitimate child, or just "hang out" and live by her wits. Whichever route she takes, the underlying dilemma of psychic repression is likely to reappear at a later date. The Virgo girl is generally too conscientious and sensitive to be able to overcome her heritage without either a painful coming-to-terms or a self-protective course of avoidance that is likely to make her feel more repressed, confused, or physically ill.

The truth is, however, that once Virgo is freed from compulsive taboos, she is a giving, generous, deeply loyal, exciting woman with impressive cosmopolitan tastes. Liberated, she has a potent sexual aura, a scintilliating charm and freshness, an indefatigable body. When she wants to be seductive, she is irresistible. She has the air of a proper lady who promises to turn delicious tramp.

Virgo's opposite sign is Pisces. The Virgo Woman's subconscious nature resembles the emotional, poetic, romantic, self-doubting nature of Pisces. After many years of observation, I suspect that some Virgo women cover their Pisces qualities with self-discipline and an aloof, hard-to-crack veneer that is pure self-protection.

The key words in understanding the Virgo Woman's sexuality are *technical sophistication* and *emotional bondage*. She likes to perfect her skills. She has a systematic approach and a disciplined mind that she applies to every task. She picks up her sexual knowledge as she might search for books or pick apples—practically, persistently, persuasively. But she cannot transform sexual know-how into happiness until she accepts herself with all her flaws and comes to view sex as a natural, joyous function.

Early sex experiences

Many Virgo-type girls grow up in moralistic, loveless households. They are often reared to be traditionally feminine, supportive, sexually passive, and closed. They expect to depend on a man for satisfaction. Sex is generally not discussed in the home, and the parents are unlikely to communicate to their daughter positive sexual attitudes.

Bred to be a dutiful, obedient daughter, Virgo also harbors a stubborn streak of rebellion that may drive her away from home and into an early marriage. Her pent-up needs for adventure and experience may be expressed in a search for unconventional jobs or lifestyles.

In high school, she is apt to carve out a niche for herself and earn people's respect. She is usually popular and has serious responsibilities as president of a club, head cheerleader, top speller, or intellectual in residence. She typically has friends of both sexes, but she remains guarded and is not an easygoing, superfically friendly person. She is seldom a toucher, usually preferring to relay her point or her affections verbally.

She often has a fabulous fantasy world that provides a delicious secret escape. She yearns for glamor and excitement, and deep down she may dislike the atmosphere of carefully controlled sensuality that surrounds her. She may devour sexually oriented material in secret, sneak into porno movies, and discuss sexual positions with her friends. She wants to *know*. She may also be excited by breaking taboos.

She may be asexual in adolescence, or she may be a glamour girl, sex symbol, or bohemian artist. She may be compulsively clean or, at the other extreme, revel in being sloppy. The loss of virginity is a rude shock and may precipitate a crisis of conscience.

The Virgo girl may flirt with homosexuality or, less often, with bisexuality. She may have lesbian affairs or mad crushes that remain fantasies. She tends to be insecure about her sexuality and about men, and she may prefer all her life to have exclusive female confidantes.

She often admires her mother much more than her father but also is bound to resent her. She tends to internalize her mother's doubts or sexual guilt, and later to transfer these feelings unknowingly to her own relationships. Since the Virgo girl is unusually precise and dutiful, she is especially prone to unconscious limitation of her mother's virtues as well as her difficulties. The best remedy for this is self-awareness.

She is unusually fascinated with pure and perfect romance. She tends to idealize love and may fall in love with love itself rather than with a person. She is bound to adore all the showy accouterments of romance and is easy prey for a gift-bearing suitor with imagination. Few young men are equipped to fulfill her dreams of perfection, however, and she may not fall in love happily until long after she has given up her virginity.

Love and sex

Virgo would certainly have agreed with Freud, who said that the normal person should be able to do two things well, *lieben und arbeiten*: to love with the generosity of intimacy and to engage in sexual/genital love; to work productively without losing one's capacity to be a sexual and loving being. The Virgo Woman must have both outlets, love and work, in order to bloom. She needs to give and to serve, both personally and professionally. And she is least demanding, restless, and doubting when she is in love.

The Virgo Woman in love is a beautiful being, disciplined yet emotional. She has faith to sustain her, and enough pragmatism to survive. She is balanced. She tends to be a giver, but when she is in love, her receptivity also emerges in full force. She may experience a glorious sexual expansion and see herself as more feminine than ever before.

If she has been guilt-ridden or afraid of sex, she begins to relax. Her natural resilience and avid curiosity propel her to try new avenues. She resembles a fresh flower smiling with iridescent dew. If she has been mistrustful of men, falling in love is a boon, a unique new puzzle she must learn to solve. She may toss the new pieces into the air, juggle them, and fashion an original pattern. Never mind the old one; it has outlasted its usefulness.

She is endlessly interested in her own sexual responses, rather like the child seeking new delights in a candy store. She may be discovering her body's pleasure potential for the first time—its curves, the texture of her skin, the purring feeling of being female.

She may embark on a sexual binge with the appetite of a chocolate enthusiast. Bonbons filled with liqueur; Swiss truffles; French milk chocolate; strawberries, walnuts, almonds, and oranges dipped in dark Dutch chocolate—these suddenly catch her fancy. Scissors, woman superior, man on top, doggie style, sixty-nine, taiwan baskets, mirrors on the ceiling, egg-shaped vaginal vibrators, peacock feathers, dildos, benwa balls, sensuous condoms—these may be the antipasto, entree, or dessert in her sexual meals.

She is likely to try whatever appeals to her with fervor and precision. She will want to share it all with her partner and make up for lost time. Her sexual appetite is likely to increase in proportion to her enjoyment. She can lose herself in pleasure with the same intensity she devotes to work or duty. Still, the old repression sometimes colors her new freedom. The early years of motherhood, for example, may bring conflict. Motherhood is considered asexual, and Virgo may find it hard to combine it with a free-flowing sex life. She will probably find it exceedingly hard to relax with the baby in the next room or to vocalize during love-making with a toddler around. Weekend trips, time off with her husband without the children, and private time to meditate, shop, or have her hair done are very important to her.

What kind of lover she needs

The Virgo Woman who wants to have a rich and exciting sex life needs a lover with a free mind and body. She seldom takes the initiative and usually needs a man to help her over the first blush of embarrassment. In particular, she needs a man who is subtle yet sophisticated. The head-on macho approach is likely to frighten her, and she dislikes boasting or vulgarity. She needs a lover who, despite his obvious range of knowledge, retains a charming air of innocence. She does not want to be outclassed, but she needs to be led.

She may seem demure, but she usually has a fancy imagination. She is a bit slow to let her man know just how fancy, but the more forward he is, the more she tends to open up. She wants her man to have taste and class, and above all he must be meticulously groomed and washed.

She is apt to dislike messy sex, though the line between acceptable and unacceptable tends to blur with experience. She may like oral sex in all its varieties. The ideal male for her would be the lover in the film *Swept Away*. Virgo likes to be coaxed, opened, and perhaps possessed. Her favorite fantasy may be to be seduced against her will. She often imagines herself bound with silk stockings, spread on a bed, teased, caressed into semi-oblivion, reaching climax as soon as she is entered. Foreplay is important and, as with many women, is necessary for regular orgasms.

Virgo needs a man who is sure of his sexual techniques and enjoys introducing her to new ones. If he is a sensitive teacher, he is apt to find Virgo an excellent student. She will probably want to know the exact length of intercourse necessary to bring him to climax, the precise positions he favors, and the bath oil he likes best. She is unlikely to inform him as minutely of her own sexual patterns, however, and it may be because she has yet to familiarize herself with them.

She needs a lover who respects the role of emotion in sexual satisfaction. She needs him to be a catalyst for her emotions, to enable her to feel comfortable in expressing them. A man who is uptight, silent, and quick is not her cup of tea. Worse, he may make her doubt herself.

She may enjoy sex at odd times during the day as a way of transcending routines. Unusual episodes and meetings in strange places may excite her and make her feel she is more passionate.

Her body image is usually good in the areas of health, self-discipline, and cleanliness (barring the few extremely sloppy ones), but mediocre to poor in other ways. She rarely considers herself pretty or sexy and has to work hard at raising her sexual self-esteem. She needs a lover who will help her to do so. Masturbation, about which she is apt to feel guilty, may be an excellent aid.

Her lover should respect the limits she wishes to place on her sex life. If she does not enjoy porno films, skin magazines, or vibrators, he should understand. Simplicity may give her the most pleasure, and if the missionary position is her very favorite, he may not be able to convert her. On the other hand, if Virgo is a technical expert, her man must be prepared to keep up.

The Virgo Woman has a kinky, rarely seen, but extremely powerful dominatrix side. When she allows this character to emerge, she becomes an entirely different sexual being. She will participate in group sex and enjoy organizing and dominating the scene as well as the men. She is often turned on by women and is frequently the seducer. She adores spike heels, heavy makeup, and parties. Bondage and trios may appeal to her; kinky sex, unusual dress-ups, outré aids, and weird scenarios are to her taste; and she may enjoy big-city activities such as gay bars, the S-and-M haunts, and bathhouses. When Virgo throws off her restraints, steamy sex is often the result. Her man should be ready for it.

What she needs to learn

The Virgo Woman needs to learn that there is more to sex than intercourse. She must break through her limitations, first in her brain, then with her body.

The most basic limitation she imposes on sexual loving is that she tends to equate it with genital sex. But she, like all of us, has a choice about her form of expressing love and of sex. The ecstasy of being in love stems from a feeling of loving life, of being in love with flowers, with the blue sky, with people, and with being silly. Virgo's love need not be limited to her mate or to her family, and sex need not be limited to genital intercourse. When she liberates her idea of sex, she will be liberating herself.

Here are some sensuous hints for the Virgo Woman who finds starting sex difficult:

—Send your lover a poem.
—The next time he sweats, wipe his brow. If this leads to cuddling and then to loveplay, don't be surprised.
—Pay him a compliment, caress his neck (More than once, of course).
—Buy him a new after-shave or eau de cologne. If you love it, all the better.
—Propose a midnight walk under the stars.
—Talk to him about some of your erotic fantasies. Perhaps you can play a few out.
—Have different kinds of massage oils and bath oils available. Suggest a relaxing bath followed by a massage.
—Act silly sometimes; for example, play doctor or wear your favorite "dress-up."
—Eat dinner together . . . semi-nude.
—Read to him from one of your favorite books. Kahlil Gibran's *Prophet* is a romantic, love-filled book that also has erotic overtones.
—Visits friends who collect and share erotic films.
—Jump in a sauna or hot tub together.
—Put dimmers on your light switches; you can then signal a romantic mood wordlessly.
—Fingerpaint each other.
—Listen to your favorite records together.
—Pick each other up in a singles bar.
—Wash and brush his hair. You can cut it, too, if he'll let you.
—Record your lovemaking. If you hear silence, it's time to change your style. Nothing turns on your partner—and perhaps you—more than to hear you open up and vocalize pleasure.
—Go slow-dancing.
—Have sex for breakfast, lunch, or dinner.

Virgo, you must treat your whole body as a sex organ. Your attitude is crucial: an attitude of awareness and curiosity is best. Sexuality involves your whole being. The average person in our culture lives out of touch with her or his body and sexuality. This need not happen to you. Do not live in your brain, or more precisely, in the part of your brain that worries and calculates. Do not expect to play roles and give a performance when you make love. Do expect to let go, to experience sex as a miraculous healing force, a unique bridge to the most sensuous and vital part of yourself—and of your partner.

Virgo anger

The Virgo Woman's greatest problem with anger is that she seldom recognizes it. Her other main problem is that she fears expressing it. But she is not alone. Anger, in general, is considered socially unacceptable, and for this reason most of us are taught to repress it. Violence and poor emotional functioning often result. So-called sex crimes, such as rape, are extreme examples of the explosion of pent-up violent anger. Rape has nothing to do with sex. It is an act of rage.

Recent research sponsored by the Department of Health, Education and Welfare has shown that war-oriented and patriarchal societies, such as ours, tend to repress various forms of physical pleasure. Research has repeatedly proven that the limitation of sensory pleasure and stimulation causes rage, insanity, severe depression, and other types of emotional disorders. Lack of touching can even result in death, as was shown by studies done on continuously neglected babies.

Anger and sex are found in a reciprocal relationship. Repressed sexuality produces anger. Repressed anger numbs feeling, resulting in inadequate sexual functioning. The woman who holds back her anger is destined for the bleak landscape of an unhappy emotional life, inhibited sexuality, and chronic mental or physical pain.

Anger is a basic human emotion, though we have not really accepted it as such. Feelings are facts. We love someone, we feel sad, jealous, greedy, elated, happy. We have angry times or moods. These are facts. Drinking, in many cases a symptom of repressed anger, is condoned, but anger overtly expressed frightens us. We do not want to mar our already flawed, cracked, civilized masks with it.

We tend to call anger by other names: depression, stress, anxiety, resentment, hostility, irritation. We project personal anger on groups of people: women, Jews, Chicanos, blacks, unions, strikers, foreigners, the government, radicals; the list is endless. Because we fear it so, we have limited the expression of anger to ritualized channels such as war and sports. This leaves women without a socially sanctioned way to express hostility. Rage in war, as in Vietnam, is acceptable, even rewarded by medals. But as thousands of veterans found out, rage at home must be turned off even if it becomes depression. It is a well-known clinical fact that depression is most frequently caused by unexpressed anger turned inward.

The woman who shows her anger is quickly called a bitch. She has no roles, and no role models, to help her transform anger into a positive force. Yet anger causes blocked communication. It also can cause low self-esteem, physical illness, psychosomatic illness, or outbursts of temper that may result in the loss of a job or a friendship and can even cause divorce. Anger is also a huge obstacle to healthy sexual expression. The angry woman closes down sexually. She may justify this as a means of punishing her partner or all men, but she is most of all hurting herself.

The Virgo Woman is likely to be ignorant of the basic steps to take in coping with anger: the identification of anger, and its proper expression. I came to this conclusion after interviewing a number of women who are Virgo types or who were going through a Virgo phase. Here are some of their comments, typical of the Virgo attitude toward anger:

1 "Anger? I don't think about it. I mean, if I think I might be getting angry, I just think of something else. I'd rather think of something pleasant."
2 "I used to hate shopping with my mother when I was a little girl and a teenager. I found it boring and humiliating. I could never fuss about it but I was really in a rage. I've never told my mother this, but I get depressed now every time I have to go shopping for anything bigger than a sack of groceries."
3 "I remember being teased a lot in school for being so prim. I guess I was sort of a prude by their standards. I was really shy, but I think now that I just became, more than anything, angry."
4 "I have never once been angry. My life has always run smoothly. I have everything I want. Why should I start ruining it now?"
5 "The recognition of my anger, I think, has probably destroyed my marriage. So I feel ambivalent; maybe it's good, maybe not so good to know you are angry. Each woman has to decide if it's worthwhile to dig in. You can find an awful lot of frightening emotions in yourself, and once you open Pandora's box, anything is possible.
6 "I've recently learned in your seminar on constructive uses of anger that people see me as a placid, contented person. My classmates have told me that I smile when I seem to feel uncertain. I'm just learning about how I really feel, and I know I

don't feel placid and happy inside. I am *outraged* at what has happened to me, at what I *haven't* done with my life. And I have nobody to blame but myself; that's the hardest part of all."

The first woman has the quintessential Virgo attitude prior to *enlightenment* (the term my classes have used to denote the point of no return in a person's self-awareness). After enlightenment, only forward movement is possible. This woman has pushed her anger down and is not sure when she is angry. Her use of the word *might* indicates how tentative she feels about being angry. She would rather "think of something else." Anger, however, is not a thought. It is an emotion. It cannot be cheated or ignored out of existence.

The second woman learned thoroughly and efficiently early on that she was not supposed to show her anger. Even now, she seems to turn anger inward against herself, and this results in depression. The Virgo girl who is taught not to fuss, to be prim and proper, to please by being a perfect little girl, often pays for it by the suppression of emotion. Anger is one of the toughest for her to unearth, for she is often taught to feel guilty about feeling angry, guiltier still about expressing it.

The third woman takes it on the chin for being a typical Virgo girl. However, she seems fairly aware of her own angry reactions and of her suppression of anger out of fear. Virgo fears rebellious behavior and is often teased by peers for following parental dictums. She is often an emotional prude, not deigning to touch on feelings she considers dirty or unwanted.

Though I'd like to give the fourth woman the benefit of the doubt, it is probable that she has been trained, and has trained herself, out of recognizing her anger. Her priority is to have an unperturbed life. I believed her when she told me she had everything she wanted, but I also believe she had something she did not want: anger. No human being can exist without feeling angry sometimes. She had probably suppressed the thoughts, memories, and associations that would lead to anger. In a later interview, she intimated that her sex life had never been a source of joy to her, but she said this was unimportant. She was not sure she had ever had an orgasm either.

I admire the fifth woman for her courage and honesty. When a Virgo Woman wants to be honestly analytical, she has more insight than the Delphic oracle. She is fair, precise, and self-critical without self-pity. This woman made a very good point. Each person must decide what she wants to know about herself. Many people elect to live with their eyes closed to all but a few facts and feelings. Some have been raised to ignore everything their upbringing did not sanction. A few break out; others more or less happily muddle through. But life is full of options, and one even chooses not to choose. One cannot choose well without knowing oneself.

The sixth woman covers her feelings with a smile. She is not realistically in touch with what she feels, and she has been largely unaware that the clues she sends out are so much at odds with her inner state. The woman who wants to be in charge of her life and to live it as she wishes must understand how she appears to others. This is most important in a professional situation, where she has to learn to balance her image: brains with beauty, femininity without submissiveness, strength without bossiness that others might find frightening. Expressing her anger is also a matter of fine-tuning her self-control. She must learn to lose her temper just enough to be heard—not so often that it's like crying wolf, but often enough to make a difference. Releasing anger *and* losing face doesn't help.

Coping with anger

During her youth, the Virgo Woman was probably overpraised for being good, sweet, compliant, and ready to cooperate; or perhaps she was shamed or forced into it. Her expressions of anger were ignored or rebuffed; she may have been made to feel guilty and been manipulated into silence. Virgo probably got the message early: feelings are not as important as good behavior, and anger, especially, is not an acceptable part of proper behavior.

To increase her self-awareness, the Virgo Woman must be able to identify her anger. She can then decide to get rid of it, hopefully in a healthy way—perhaps through caustic literary essays, athletic contests, controlled fights, rearranging her staff when it's high time, or changing her furniture.

The most obvious sign of growing anger is a tightening of certain body muscles. In the Virgo Woman, the intestines and lower stomach are most likely to be affected. Acid indigestion, butterflies in the stomach, gas pains, constipation, colitis, stomach spasms, an accumulation of mucus, and heightened nervousness are sure signs that negative emotions are being held prisoner in the body.

Another clue to anger is facial expression. If Virgo is unaware of her own, it may help to do an occasional self-check. The lines in her face are a kind of after-image of the range of her most frequently expressed feelings. Anger and worry, sometimes fear, cause the brow to crease heavily. Constantly pursing the lips causes tiny lines to appear around them. Setting the chin in anger or grinding the teeth may make extra visits to the dentist necessary. Laugh lines around the eyes can rim an angry look, augmented by a vertical furrow between the eyebrows. A generally tight, pinched look is often the result of a mountain of unspoken angry words, and a martyr's look may cover anger hidden from the self.

The body language of the angry person may be subtle or violent. Nobody can miss the rage of a shouting, screaming maniac, but it is more difficult to spot subtle clues to anger. Clenching the fists is often a sign of anger or of extreme frustration. Sucking in the stomach and intermittent, slow, or shallow breathing are signs of anxiety and often of repressed anger. The anxiety may be caused or augmented by unconscious anger.

It is important to learn a person's style of anger. Many people fall ominously silent when they get angry; others start to scream or shout. A few seem to get so carried away that they throw things, fling papers across the desk, wildly buzz their secretaries, or phone someone else in your presence and give them hell. The Virgo Woman tends not to use strong body language to show anger. Rather, the signs are most often internal.

A subtle but fascinating puzzle is to try to guess from another person's reaction what "vibes" you are sending out. An old metaphysical law assures us that whatever subtle energies we emit will return to us. Thus, if we telegraph beauty and positive attitudes, others react well to us. If we are hostile and fearful, others tend to do ugly things to us. Similarly, we can to some extent perceive our anger by intuitively measuring how much anger others telegraph to us. Obviously, an angry cab driver is bound to be mad at the world or at the last passenger who did not tip him, and his anger may have nothing to do with us. But watch his anger subside if we are in a good mood. Conversely, his hostility will increase if we react with anger, even wordlessly. Anger fuels anger, whereas peaceful thoughts diminish it.

Honest anger, appropriately expressed, can help the Virgo Woman get more of what she wants out of life. It can make her feel better about herself. It can help make her relationships lighter, more trusting and meaningful. It can help relieve mental and physical stress. Anger can also whet her sexual appetite, excite her, energize her and her mate. Repressed anger can cause a kind of female impotence, robbing her of orgasm, limiting her sexual desire and pleasure.

Anger, constructively used, is a catalyst. It can be a signal for necessary change. It can revitalize Virgo's motivation to confront herself, to reevaluate her life. From time to time, such self-examination is imperative. Anger, far from being a forbidden, inhuman feeling, is very much a human emotion, and it is vital that she recognize and use it in the best way possible.

After she recognizes signs of anger in herself, the Virgo Woman is free to acknowledge when she is angry, then to decide what to do about it. Sometimes she may find it best to work out her anger alone or talk it over with a friend or therapist. Other times, a good talk or a series of discussions with her mate may relieve her anger.

Virgo, in terms of anger, you need to:

1 Clearly examine your feelings, including anger, and learn to recognize them.
2 Accept conflict and anger as inevitable and necessary for growth.
3 Accept your own upbringing as largely responsible for creating tensions in you, tensions that can be highly productive if channeled correctly or highly destructive if repressed or used to criticize and blame others.
4 Accept without self-blame your right to your feelings.
5 Be aware that anger is caused by holding certain values, and know what those values are.
6 Be aware of your options, and choose those that benefit you and enrich your life.

(For specific communication skills, see "Libra Anger." For more advice on how to identify anger, see "Scorpio Anger.")

Virgo lifestyles

There are women who are content with monogamous marriage and never seriously consider taking a lover. There are women who fantasize about an affair but don't wish to bring the fantasy to fruition. Some women are so bound by their upbringing and the need to conform to societal sanctions that they do not admit, even to themselves, that they are bored, frustrated, and unfulfilled by unswerving, full-time physical and emotional exclusivity with their mates. Some women may "cheat" on their husbands and feel guilty; others may commit adultery and live happily. Many women practice serial monogamy. A few have an open marriage for some months or years, freely pursuing sexual and nonsexual friendships, supposedly without guilt.

I believe it is important to feel that one has choices in life. Victor Frankl, in describing life in a German concentration camp, theorized that the survivors were those who, by sheer will and creative genius, improvised imperceptible ways to be different. A human being needs to be aware of her or his individuality and to feel a degree of choice. Free will is part of life, and psychoastrology supports this view.

There is variety in every living thing, and there is variety in marriage. Marriage can be happy or sad, fleeting or long-lasting, arid or fruitful, hot or cold, open or closed—it has a thousand nuances. I think women need to be supported in their explorations, and I look forward to a time when we are unrestricted by economic dependence and the fear of pregnancy. I also support men in their investigation of options in life.

All the recent experimentation and choosing may, and in some minds certainly does, lead to confusion. The family does not operate as it did in the 1950s. Indeed, it has changed radically more than once since the beginning of the industrial revolution. It will surely change again, as will the social fabric as a whole. We do not live in easy times. Ours is the challenge of keeping an open mind, of seeing good where possible and averting doomsday thinking by dedicated action.

Monogamy and nonmonogamy

The Virgo Woman tends to stay faithfully married to one partner —or at least, one at a time. Hers is a mutable sign, and she often marries more than once (serial monogamy). She is capable of being fulfilled by a monogamous lifestyle, but because the world is offering her more options, and because the times seem to require a growing awareness, she has begun to question her lifestyle more than ever before. And because she has a compulsively inquisitive nature, she is apt to investigate thoroughly.

Monogamy is a lifestyle of sexual exclusivity with one's mate; by the strict definition, it includes emotional exclusivity as well. The Virgo Woman is totally in favor of monogamy, both in principle and in practice. If she discontinues the practice, it is often against her better judgment and deeply conservative values. Nonmonogamy is apt to create tremendous emotional tensions that she must learn to master and resolve creatively.

The following represent typical situations which could influence the Virgo Woman to become nonmonogamous:

1 Perfectionism. The Virgo Woman often marries the illusion of perfection in love and romance. If her husband turns out to have bad breath or small ambition, if he becomes too busy to generate the glamour or security she needs, she may get restless. She may pursue her illusion elsewhere, and with more experience and maturity, she may later settle back into reasonably contented domesticity, often with the original man.
2 Absolutism and judgmental attitudes. The Virgo Woman is exceedingly fond of absolutes and indeed may depend on them. To her, truth, beauty, love, and family life may have to fulfill a rigidly defined image and standard. This impulse toward absolutism is closely allied with her need for perfectionism but goes beyond it; it is more emotional and more directly tied to her value system. She may become nonmonogamous in reaction to the failure of any of the important absolutes in her life, and out of a growing, often petty spirit of revenge.
3 Fear of intimacy. The Virgo Woman may wish to guard her innermost self, particularly her fears. She may seek sexual partners who are less likely than her husband to penetrate deeply and truly get to know her.
4 Anger with her mate. The Virgo Woman often endures more pain than most, but she too has her limits. If her husband consistently hurts or disappoints her, she may seek solace elsewhere. Though she may be justified, she is still likely to feel guilty.
5 Pragmatism. If her husband leaves her high and dry in bed, or if he looks like a permanent loser, the Virgo Woman is capable of cutting her losses. She may look around very carefully, testing prospective suitors and mates for both pleasure and usefulness. She is apt to be a cool and rational decision maker, especially in important matters.
6 New age Lady Chatterley syndrome. Many a shy Virgo maiden

lives her life without earthquakelike orgasms or poetic ecstasies. When the opportunity repeatedly arises for her to experience these, she may profit. Sometimes she is swept away despite herself, though she may never see the lover again after one peak experience.

7 Sexual self-doubt. Nonexclusivity may be sought as a cure for this condition. The sexually insecure Virgo Woman may try shopping around, however briefly.

8 Search for new technical know-how, curiosity. Nobody can beat Virgo in the technical aspects of lovemaking. She has a knack for absorbing information about various sex positions, exercises, breathing techniques, and games. If her husband insists on sticking to a meat-and-potatoes sexual diet, she may find more sophisticated lovers who delight in uninhibited sexual play.

Alternative lifestyles

Single woman: There are some Virgo women who remain single all their lives, more or less happily; they may substitute work for pleasure, and they may rise to dizzying career heights. This is not an unusual lifestyle for Lady Virgo, either on a permanent basis or from time to time. She tends to like her privacy and is basically self-sufficient.

Intimate networks: The Virgo Woman might be curious about the *concept* of this movement, which advocates friendship with both sexes and neither rules out nor requires sexual involvement. In practice, though, she will probably resist it. She may prefer to keep her female friendships separate from her male friendships, each category precisely in its place.

Open marriage: The Virgo Woman tends to be too traditional for a sexually open marriage, though I have met a few who tried it as a last resort. Not one has stuck with it, however. This is an unlikely choice for her, but it may be an instructive experiment.

Ménage à trois: Virgo may try it, especially with her man and another woman if she has bisexual or homosexual leanings.

Group marriage: If she is exposed to this concept in the right way, with the right people, and in the right environment, it may appeal to her. It combines the opportunity for traditionalism with the chance to break out and experiment. It offers some protection and a limited but reassuring reliance on structure.

Communes: She is unlikely to get involved with this lifestyle. If, by chance, she tries it, she will probably want to see to it that the living quarters are clean and the administration is proceeding smoothly.

Gay/bisexual lifestyle: I have met quite a few Virgo-type women who have tried one or the other, but none that have given up on the idea of heterosexuality leading to a comfortable marriage. Virgo tends to be old-fashioned, and nowhere is this more evident than in her stubborn loyalty to the basic American dreams: success, family, heterosexuality, the survival of tradition.

Summing up Virgo

The Virgo Woman, with her keen insight and ability to tell the truth, can teach us a great deal about ourselves. She is a good model for loyalty, efficiency, analysis, and organization. She is valuable in a corporate context and is usually successful at anything she chooses to do. Personally, she has a great deal to learn.

She tends to throw herself headlong into a task and may be described as obsessive-compulsive. She combines low self-esteem with considerable self-reliance and self-sufficiency. If she must, she can function well in the world at large. She can take care of herself and of her own world as well. The trouble is that she is often stuck in routines; she may be so good at details that she neglects to see, and be involved with, the whole. Knowing the precise origin and configuration of each tree may prevent her from seeing the freshness, originality, and potential of the forest.

Virgo is usually a deeply loving person who, however, frequently finds it difficult to express love warmly. She is often anxious, but instead of learning to release her anxiety, she tends to overwork and to pick on others. She may be fussy, nit-picking, and demanding with her loved ones. Her greatest emotional task is to learn to love without criticism, to accept people as they are. She must also guard against a negative communication style. She often feels softer, more affectionate and vulnerable, more feminine and yielding than she appears.

She has a tremendous capacity to accomplish what she sets out to do. Thus, in the long run, she is a winner. She is emotional but realistic and has the magnetism and will power to attract whatever she needs. Should she wish to do so, she can turn any man's head and make him feel he is the only important soul in the world.

She is an actress when she wants to be, and many a Virgo woman makes acting her profession. She has lifelong youthfulness, the quality of a gazelle that leaps to and fro, charming and attractive.

When Virgo learns to let go and let others take care of her, when she finally realizes that trusting and loving other people, as well as herself, will bring about the tranquility she seeks, she can become a modern madonna.

LIBRA

CHECKLIST OF LIBRA TRAITS

Note: This checklist describes the traits of one *phase* only; if it doesn't seem to fit you, check other lists to find the phase you are in right now.

1. Seductive
2. Sensual
3. Attractive
4. Self-indulgent
5. Artistic
6. Sophisticated
7. Sociable
8. Melancholic
9. Sensitive
10. Procrastinating
11. Indecisive
12. Ambivalent
13. Compliant
14. Adaptive
15. Self-protective
16. Subtle
17. Paradoxical
18. Strong
19. Aggressive
20. Cooperative
21. Argumentative
22. Manipulative
23. Rational
24. Detached
25. Controlled
26. Cool
27. Team Worker
28. Multiple Relationships
29. Narcissistic
30. Ugly Duckling
31. Diplomatic
32. Dedicated to Causes
33. Popular
34. Polite
35. Self-doubting

Libra personality

And so the ugly duckling became a beautiful swan . . .
Children's Fairy Tale

General traits and background

The Libra Woman is charming, attractive, naturally elegant and charismatic, sentimental, melancholic, and mentally active. She has an innate ability to give and receive attention and admiration, if not always love. She usually gains a lot of experience in the realm of relationships.

Her astrological symbol is the scales, usually held by a female who symbolizes balance: human justice, cooperation, and orderly law. Libra is the seventh sign of the Zodiac, Cardinal Air. It is primarily concerned with partnerships, marriage, and all *open* associations (Pisces deals with secret relationships).

The Libra Woman is one of the loveliest. She often has an undulating grace and the movements of a sensualist. She tends not to flaunt what she has and instead wears her looks like a subtle but solid charm bracelet. One can be sure there are countless charms attached, golden, glittering, and jingling with quiet pride.

The Libra Woman's often stylish facade just as frequently covers an intense preoccupation with impressing people. She is usually extremely concerned with how things look to friends, partners, associates, lovers, and would-be mates. It seems to be her lot in life to be continuously compelled to try to balance the "I" with the "Thou." She may become polarized, especially early in life when she has not yet learned the art of creating harmony. She usually errs on the side of overdoing the imagery, perhaps at the cost of inner development.

The Libra Woman's personality is described by the checklist of traits at the beginning of the chapter. The woman who has thirty or more traits is the Libra *type*, at least right now. A woman can also be going through a Libra *phase* characterized by the following:

1 Intense, especially mental preoccupation with all aspects of human relations.
2 Involvement in the arts, humanities, music, beautification projects; consuming interest in how things look; work in decorating, remodeling, refurbishing.
3 Seeking approval, order, and harmony above all, in all relationships; alternatively, the Libra phase can mean constant nasty warfare on all fronts.

4 Pleasant contacts with many people, spanning generations and geographical distances; however, these often lack depth.
5 Gentle feelings of inner peace and harmony—the ultimate Libra goal.

Professions that are particularly associated with Libra are the following: fine arts, fashion, women's apparel, floristry, beauty industry (parlors), boutiques, human relations, jewelry (especially work with copper, coral, cornelian, opal, quartz); law, litigation, the courts; interior decorating, dress, furniture or fur design or sales or promotion; music, poetry writing or publishing; diplomacy, politics, peacemaking; medical work specializing in the spine, ductless glands, or urology; tailoring, warfare.

Until she reaches emotional maturity, the Libra Woman tends to live off balance, swinging from one extreme to the other. She is often contradictory though she would rather be a perfect blend.

Seductive, sensual, attractive

You might imagine Libra as a curvaceous, pretty woman whom an artist would capture in sensuous ebony or pink jade. In each hand she would hold a gem-studded scale, perpetually tipping. Her look would invite and reject.

Libra Women are famous for their beauty and sex appeal. Brigitte Bardot, still sexy and youthful well into her forties, was born a Libra (sun in Libra). Her gorgeous backside made her a celebrity after Roger Vadim splashed it across the screen in *And God Created Woman*.

The Libra female is skilled in the art of seduction and expects to be well appreciated for it. Another Libra sun sign, Rita Hayworth, knew how to parlay looks and sexiness into fame and fortune, and capped it all off by marrying the Aga Khan, a millionaire.

Libra is often sensuous, lazy, and feminine. She is wise and naive, young and old. She tends to charm and manipulate life and people like an ageless Lolita.

Self-indulgent

The Libra Woman enjoys the power with which her beauty, sensuality, and air of distinction endow her. She tends to think she deserves the very best. The world, she believes, owes her for what she brings to it.

She may spoil herself. She buys gallons of bath oil, the latest in makeup, vintage wines. Nothing is too good for her. She enjoys gourmet food and is apt to be plump. She often dresses exquisitely and trendily and is sometimes overperfumed. She shops passionately for the latest in chic and buys everything from rare pearls to pleasure cruises.

She is especially content in the lap of luxury and looks for means and men to provide it for her. She may be a sucker for flattery and gifts. She usually adores the good life. She is naive or optimistic, depending on your point of view, and she trusts fate to deliver what she needs. Things have a way of turning out well for her.

Artistic, sophisticated

The Libra Woman is responsible for her own luck, for she has the right touch. She can transform a shack into a love nest, bad "vibes" into good. She selects music, wine, and food to make an evening a memorable success. If Libra is in charge of a dinner party, you can expect silver candelabra, a soft glow from the candles, tall, sensuous roses in vases, embroidered napkins on the table, and a plush shag rug.

Her sophisticated taste extends to all details of her life and the lives of her intimates. The look of things may be more important to her than smell, sound, and taste. She is aware of trends in art and fond of beauty and nature. Her gift for pleasurable living is her prime contribution to the art of love.

Sociable

The Libra Woman tends to make social contacts easily. She is a supportive friend and an admirable lover, ready to share her abundant assets. She gives lovely gifts and can be a super matchmaker. She remembers birthdays and likes to celebrate all kinds of anniversaries: first dates, communions, openings. She does not mind life's details. She generally enjoys people and likes doing things for them.

She usually enjoys parties and is outgoing. She can talk endlessly on subjects that interest her: people, art, social theory, law, beauty, history, ethics, and various worthy causes. She is often more conjugal than maternal and prefers company to solitude. She is rarely consumed with ambition and needs a partner to provide support and push her in the right direction.

Melancholic, sensitive

Libra has a hidden side to her nature. It is the reverse of the often gorgeous garment she displays to the outside, a sort of gray melancholy and morbid sensitivity. The Libra Woman from time to time tends to be passive, depressed, and slightly paranoid. She may fantasize that people are only pretending to like her and believe that no one knows the "real" her. She may be caught up in the feeling that her life is all sham, window dressing with little permanent substance. In essence, she may feel quite sorry for herself.

Fortunately, this is normally nothing more than a passing phase. She can snap out of it when she receives a gift, a bouquet of lovely flowers, or any little token of affection. A word of warning to Libra: you can put so much energy into building an image and creating an association or an environment that you leave too little for self-nourishment. If you get depressed often, you should consider consulting a professional. Style is not a substitute for true self-esteem.

Procrastinating

One of the Libran's biggest problems is her tendency to put things off. This reduces her self-confidence and her effectiveness. A passive decision maker, she most often allows choices to be made for her. She tends to take the path of least resistance and ride things out, to "wait until something happens." This works to a point, but when it ties her and her life up in knots, no one profits.

A word of advice: consider taking a seminar in decision making.

Indecisive, ambivalent

In business the Libra Woman can make decisions with competence. In her personal life, however, she tends to shy away from decisions that involve emotional risk. She does not want to be held responsible for hurt and pain. In order to avoid adverse results, she evaluates the issues carefully. She often spends so long weighing each side that the decision is usually made by default or by the other person involved.

She usually operates with the best intentions; her motto is "Justice to all." She wants to give everyone a fair hearing, but in practice her grand ideal is often devitalized by her own lack of action.

To be an effective decision maker, the Libran must know what is really important to her. She must first clarify what she wants and then work to achieve her aims. She can actually go about this by making a list and then jotting down the pros and cons of each issue. Such an approach will enable her to see if a decision is necessary to safeguard her best interest. Next, she must proceed with the decision and stick to it. The only way to deal with indecision is practice—make a decision, and then act on it.

Compliant, adaptive, self-protective

The hidden priority of the Libra Woman is to please others. This is usually far more important to her than, say, being the one to choose a particular film. However, in major decisions such as whether or not to have a baby or change her job, she *must* learn how to assert herself. It is also important that she be able to judge and differentiate between major and minor decisions.

The Libra Woman is usually raised to be a good girl. Her indecisiveness and delays may be the result of her wish not to offend, to abide by social regulations. She rarely says no, seemingly out of a desire not to hurt people, but her fear often covers the fear of being rejected herself. It is as if some Aries traits need to rub off on her to enable her to be more directly assertive (by the same token, it might be good for Aries to incorporate some Libra traits in order to be more diplomatic).

Sometimes Libra uses her indecisiveness as an evasion of responsibility. In this case, the adaptability that should ordinarily promote sharing becomes a source of annoyance to others and a potential sore spot in communications.

Subtle, paradoxical

Charm, softness, and the low-key approach may work best for Libra unless she gets angry. On the occasions when she allows herself to let out steam, she may turn into a staggeringly aggressive female who seems not to have heard of subtlety.

People are full of contradictions, and Libra is no exception. She is as paradoxical as the midnight sun. She can be superficial or substantial, decorative or managerial, subtle or blunt, complaint or forceful. Most often a highly appreciated person, she is all female, dedicated to partnerships, beauty, and pleasure.

Strong, aggressive

Though frequently a pleaser, contradictory Libra also has an innate aggressiveness. Many famous military figures have been

Libra types. The Libra Woman has a military streak that she holds in check, releasing it only on certain occasions. She may turn from pussycat to tigress when she feels backed into a corner or when a matter of principle is clearly critical to her. Cruelty and injustice madden her the fastest.

Her strength may be hidden from view. One might write her off as the eternal dilettante munching bonbons at a card game, but a Libran changes and pushes insurmountable obstacles away for a cause in which she believes.

Cooperative but also argumentative

The visage of the Libra Woman is usually pleasant, and she often has dimples, soft rounded cheeks, and an engaging smile. She cooperates on principle. She wants to get along with others but often ends up fighting them for the sake of her ideals.

Her argumentative tendencies are fueled by the fact that her daily life is generally overloaded with feelings of conflict. Libra seldom believes that it is all right to stop smiling or to express disagreement, so her disapproval takes the form of hostility.

She is often of two minds about all the great issues in life. As her lack of resolution mounts, so do her tension and hostility. Since she seldom says exactly what she feels (though she may stun with intellectual explanations of why she acts as she does), she becomes argumentative about petty things.

Manipulative

Though she will sometimes let loose, direct tactics make her uncomfortable. She tends to defuse charged situations before her real feelings come out. She frequently uses her fine sense of humor to avoid emotional scenes or confrontations. Good at punch lines, she will often deliver one just in time to keep a friend from boiling over with rage. She is able to keep a sexual upper hand, too, through a cool tone of voice and a "don't bother me with your troubles" demeanor.

She typically uses "feminine wiles" to get what she wants. The women's movement may have changed this some, but she still does not consider it in bad taste to compete with other women, even if it is for a man.

She tends to be obliging, adaptive, self-righteous and lazy. She can manipulate people to do all that needs to be done so that she herself is left with only the most necessary tasks.

Rational, detached, controlled
The Libra Woman may relate to her feelings as if they were a time bomb ticking away and ready to explode. She is a mental creature who tries to reason everything through, not once but ten times. She wants to *think* her way in or out of every situation without getting bogged down in emotions.

Logic and abstract thinking are her friends, irrationality and emotionalism her enemies. She tends to withdraw when tempers flare, though she can unpredictably become the aggressor herself. Possibly she does this to take control of the situation.

She is emotionally detached in part to protect herself from expected slights, but she is loath to confess this. She is ever ready to spin yarns and give reasons, but if you want to know how she feels, ask her. You will find she may not know herself.

Cool, team worker
Behind the exterior of the extremely feminine Libra Woman lurks the brain of a calculator. She bears comparison with Napoleon's mistress, who used her brains and body to help change the course of history. The Libra Woman knows how to use all she is, plus what she learns, to achieve her aims.

She is usually effective in business, prefers traditional methods of getting ahead, and is a good team player. Unlike her sister Aries, her opposite sign in the Zodiac, she is not one to blaze new trails or forge ahead by herself. She takes risks carefully and tends to consult her colleagues on every decision. She is excellent at strategy, understands power hierarchies, and instinctively works well with people. Her co-workers like her.

She dislikes disorder and illogic. She is precise and selectively organized. She can live in a sloppy apartment, for example, but it would be most unusual for her to allow her looks or her work to become disorderly. She can keep cool under pressure. If you observe a woman with a lovely but tense smile who manages egos and schedules that would confuse a First Lady, you are looking at Libra.

Multiple relationships
The Libra Woman is always searching for her ideal partner and is rarely happy with what she has. In any case, she generally doesn't like to get too deeply involved, preferring instead to contemplate a lover's or friend's potential. Deep down, she may be afraid that if

she looks too closely or reveals too much, no one will measure up to her fantasies. To avoid intimacy, she may keep three affairs going simultaneously, sometimes with both sexes.

She dislikes too much privacy, for she fears loneliness. She often depends on others for pleasure and motivation and usually has no trouble finding willing helpers. To avoid "heavy" commitments, she does her best to keep everything on an even keel, parceling her attention in many directions and clinging to her ambivalences.

When she does get passionately involved, she fears being hurt. In brief, she is rarely faithful but abhors fights and endings. When she *is* faithful, no woman on earth could be a better partner.

Ugly Duckling, narcissistic, diplomatic, dedicated to causes

As with many women, the Libra Woman's story is one of inner transformation. She is the original ugly duckling who grows up to be a swan.

The Libra Woman tends to be narcissistic, usually blooms late, and has strength but also self-doubt. She is humane but can be personally insensitive. She is compliant and yet aggressive on occasion. She is part innocent little girl, part untouched virgin, part revered love goddess, and part femme fatale. She is no ordinary woman. Nor does she wish to act like one.

Eleanor Roosevelt was a Libra type. Her life is a study in courage and achievement born of pain and insecurity. It shows what can happen when Libra casts off her self-doubt, her exaggerated wish to please and belong, and places her vitality, drive, and fighting spirit in the service of humanity.

Eleanor seems to have grown up feeling like an ugly duckling. Her lack of beauty (though she had her own kind), of traditional feminine charm and grace, must have conspired to burden her with a poor self-image. Typically Libra, she went ahead and built a *bond* with a man. She fashioned a personal *style* that became the independent yet attached woman's hallmark.

Franklin evidently never paid much attention to her as a woman, especially in later years; her children looked up to him but not as much to her, and she took to protecting strays. Did she feel they were like her? However that may be, Eleanor created a style that shows Libra at her best: fair, openminded, independent, assertive, effective, dedicated, and caring.

Popular, polite, self-doubting
The facade is unruffled, the smile in place. Her countenance is usually pleasing, her manners polished. No wonder the Libra Woman is well liked. She is a hostess's dream, and she makes any man proud to be seen with her. Yet she wears her beauty like a reversible garment. She has such a great need to be noticed and accepted that she is frequently anxiety-ridden about how well she has succeeded. Perhaps she fears that those who look at her carefully will discover the ugly duckling underneath.

Imagine the following scene. Libra is dressed for dinner and, as usual, looks smashing. Inside, she quivers with uncertainty. She checks herself in the mirror again. An unsuspecting observer would think she dotes on herself too much. The truth is she desperately needs reassurance. She tells her companion how she feels, and he give her the reassurance she needs. They leave, arms linked, and have an enjoyable dinner.

The alternate scenario has Libra pretending she feels great, swallowing her fears. Since in Libra the primary body stress spots are the lower back and kidneys, she is unlikely to enjoy her dinner if she keeps her tensions in.

It may seem paradoxical to advise sexy, artful Libra to appreciate herself—yet she needs to be told. She has confidence and inner strength under stress most especially in her professional life, but she needs to develop more esteem for her whole self.

True self-esteem will come from exploring, trusting, and learning about herself.

Libra relationships

All her life, the Libra Woman falls in and out of love with the idea of love. She believes in the magic bond and caretaking power of partnership, and she usually marries early and divorces at least once. Her sign is the median between emotionally restrained Virgo and hot Scorpio. She can be extremely aloof or languidly inviting.

Her relationships run in cycles. Pronounced highs and lows are familiar to her and her partner. She is driven by the need to find the ideal union; marriage to a great provider and soulmate is her goal.

Childhood

The Libra Woman grows up unaware of her sensual potential and artistic gifts. She doesn't know she exudes a powerful feminine aura. Her smile is as mysterious as Mona Lisa's and as mischievous as Marilyn Monroe's.

She often becomes her father's pet. Sometimes she is victimized by men who are threatened by her sex appeal. With the onset of menstruation and biological maturation, she becomes aware of her father's reaction to her development. Her father may respond to her budding sexuality by withdrawing from her. The Libra adolescent then reacts by feeling that something is wrong with her, and she carries the scar for the rest of her life.

Ages twelve to fourteen are more difficult for the Libra type than for any other. This is because she often experiences double rejection—first by her father, then by her mother. The Libra is frequently resented by her mother. She may adore her mother, but the underside of their relationship is often colored by her mother's jealousy. She is not aware until ages twelve to fourteen that she is "different," that she is often prettier, sexier, or more appealing than other girls her age. This precise situation may not apply to all Libra Women, but its essence is the fear and distrust every Libran feels for her own sexual attractiveness. A common result is the Libran's attraction to particular men who can give her the mothering she never had.

The Libra Woman is usually conditioned by her childhood experiences to expect attention but to distrust emotional closeness. Like all air signs (Gemini, Aquarius), she is usually more comfortable with rationality than with emotion. She has a "push me, pull you" approach to the head-versus-heart issue and is in perpetual motion trying to integrate the two.

How the Libra Woman relates: lovers and other intimates

Above all, Lady Libra has style. She may be anxious, insecure, or annoyed, but one thing with which she is plentifully equipped is class. In her relationships, she tends to play the roles of the following three characters:

1 *Diplomat.* The Libra is a mediator in family disputes. She is a master of survival tactics such as indirect suggestion, compliance, sublimation, anticipation, evasion, and subtlety. She stands her ground, neither winning nor losing, but sharing with both sides in equal balance.

Instead of participating directly, she becomes the negotiator and go-between. She soothes ruffled tempers and bandages egos. She understands and empathizes with the feelings and arguments of both sides. She perceives the rightness and wrongness in each participant's attitude. Above all, she wants justice and peace to reign.

As an adult she is an accomplished diplomat and maneuvers through life using a skillful strategy. Her style is effective with her friends, who appreciate her charm and good humor and forgive her sudden aggressive displays. However, her manipulations with her love partner will eventually create blocks in communication. Many of the tactics she learned as a child serve her well. Others counteract the mutual honesty and give-and-take that are integral to achieving an intimate tie.

The Libran must be aware of her skills in diplomacy in order to use them constructively. She should not use manipulation to get others to act against their wishes, and she should increasingly try to be honest.

2 *Aloof Lady*. The Libra Woman is apt to choose the wrong man as a partner the first few times because she lacks the self-knowledge to make the right choices in love. She usually wants a man who can provide the maternal/paternal nurturing she needs, yet she also wants him to place her on a pedestal. Caught in a conflict, she wants her man both to nurture her and to be detached from her. She wants him to be close, but only when she beckons.

Internally Lady Libra is a vulnerable little girl, externally the aloof lady in control. She appears cool, calm, and collected most of the time. Others may think she is remote, someone with "a chip on her shoulder." She is uncomfortable with Mediterranean displays of affection. She controls her personal space and spreads it all around her like a buffer. She restricts body contact.

Because she is prone to overintellectualizing, she often keeps people away from her. She is always thinking, trying to balance her scales. She gives the impression that she wants and needs a close relationship, but she wants it only on her own terms.

3 *Tough/Fragile Woman*. One has a hard time understanding just what Libra's terms are, because she shifts often. She greatly fears loneliness, jumps into one relationship after another, and has some simultaneously. She often mistakes friendship for romantic love.

> It is as if her two sides were not quite connected. The one may ignore the other. The fragile part is dependent, eager to please and serve her partner. When this side dominates, she automatically subordinates herself. The other side, the tough part, resents this behavior. When it is in charge, she is manipulative, argumentative, and sometimes hostile. The hostility may be masked by cloyingly sweet behavior.

The Libra Woman seeks to be defined through others. She wonders, 'Who am I?" and "Who are we?" She takes criticism badly, and declarations of love with skepticism. Offended, she retreats into her aloof lady or becomes submissive and fragile. On occasion, though, a tigress will come roaring out.

She is naturally possessive but does not like to be. She is simply addicted to being bonded. She does not feel whole without that special someone, but she thinks that jealousy is in bad taste and that showing jealousy is worse. On principle she believes in freedom and equal rights. She may feel hurt by their exercise, but she will act unconcerned.

Unlike the mobile Aries or the agile perambulator Gemini, she does not seek new people or excitement. She is able to magnetize, to draw people and opportunities towards her. She actively waits—another contradiction very typical of Libra.

Patterns in the Libra Woman's sexual relationships

Generally, the modern Libra Woman displays the following pattern in sexual relationships:

1 She marries early. She also usually marries several times or, if not, lives with several partners.
2 She struggles to maintain the partnership and follow traditional sex roles. However, she eventually becomes restless and suppresses her feelings. Then she separates, divorces, or adopts an alternative lifestyle.
3 Between unions, or during an open marriage phase, Libra may try everything from group sex to lesbianism.
4 New relationships or lifestyles emerge.

Ending relationships is difficult for Libra, but if she gets divorced she often adopts a gay or bisexual lifestyle. She may also start another commitment, or she may experiment with the single lifestyle. In any case, she will not want to live alone for long.

Yet she is also strong and tends to be a survivor. She is on a merry-go-round looking for the right mate and the best lifestyle, and deep down she believes the brass ring is right within her reach.

Lovers and husbands

Since the Libra Woman is best paired with someone more attentive and indulgent than the norm, she sometimes forms love relationships with older men. Her man must want to cater to her and accept her needs for admiration and affection. He must not allow himself to become jealous when she excites other men through her exhibitionism. Who else but Lady Libra would wear a see-through blouse to the Christmas party at her man's office?

Her man must be tolerant and understanding. He should encourage her to break out of the rigid molds of her three poses. He must recognize, and help her to perceive, the reasons she assumes her roles. He can best help her and their relationship by encouraging her to be more spontaneous, honest, trusting, and open.

The Libra Woman is attracted to men who offer good conversation—sophisticated, intelligent men with taste. She enjoys impressive and informative discussions. She and her man are likely to engage in passionate verbal foreplay, discussing topics as diverse as the glories of Rome and fettucine, the latest disco craze, fashion and photography, styles in housing and erotic baths, the religious wars, and the breakdown of the legal system.

Libra's male must also offer her financial security. Money is important to her, for she correctly recognizes its necessity in the creation of a pleasant, safe lifestyle and ambience. Poverty simply is not her bag.

The first two years in the Libra's love relationship are crucial. It is during this period that she learns the greatest life lessons or loses interest in the opposite sex.

The Libra Woman has a dual nature. She is capable of loving and being sexually involved with both sexes. She can love and hate at the same time. She wants a mate more independent than she, yet when she finds him she resents him for it. She wants him to surround her with luxury and affection, yet she does not want him too close. Her motto is "Everything in balance." But until she herself is balanced, nothing else in her life can be stable.

From time to time, she may feel guilty over failed relationships. She then judges herself harshly, and a depression may follow. To bring her out of it, she needs tender loving care—along with perfume, flowers, and fine music.

In summation, the most frequent trouble spots the Libra Woman encounters in her relationships are as follows:

1 Unreasonably high expectations of another.
2 Inability to accept people as they are.
3 Lack of awareness.
4 Lack of assertiveness in gaining what she needs
5 Manipulation.
6 Self-denial.
7 Lack of self-esteem—and the expectation of attaining it through a relationship.

Once you decide to be in charge of yourself and of your love life, there are some basics you should follow. For instance, answer the following questions:

1 What are the top priorities in my life?
2 What do I want and need in a mate?
3 What do I want in a close friend?
4 What am I willing to give?
5 What do I want to accomplish within three months in this relationship?
6 What do I want to change about my life in the next three months?

These aren't easy questions, and the answers will also change from time to time as you change, so it's good idea to keep reassessing. You must not shy away from your real feelings as you answer the questions. You must try to clarify and understand your priorities, and to see them written down in black and white is a helpful confirmation of your aims.

Once she is happily settled with a partner, the Libra Woman is an angel. No woman on earth can be, or can make a man, happier. She is domestic yet comfortable in the outer world, soft and smart, skilled in the art of living and lovemaking. She has style as well as substance. She has an identity and has also mastered the art of sharing.

Her life may revolve around a central relationship, but happily so; or she may be balancing various equally important involvements. In any case, she knows how to extract the best and give the best. She stays young, pretty, and romantic. She enjoys walking hand in hand, throwing parties, and kissing under the mistletoe. She weeps over old films. Fine music turns her on. She likes to dance closely. She takes care of herself and does not mind the laugh lines. She stays cheerful, balanced, and busy and achieves a serenity she never had before.

Her identity, disclosed to the right people in the proper balance, becomes complete. And anyone who shares her life with her at this stage is blessed with a totally giving, receptive woman.

Libra sexuality

The pursuit of pleasure

It seems natural that a sensuous, feminine woman like Libra would enjoy sex, and it is true that the sounds, smells, and rituals of sexual interaction are pleasurable to her. But the verbal buildup to erotic play is essential to arouse her. She is also stimulated by a romantic movie, a candlelight dinner, music by the fireplace, erotica, and sexual fantasies. The screams of a passionate couple making love next door also arouse her.

She makes the creative pursuit of the pleasurable life an art—and she defines pleasure broadly. Plain intercourse ranks as a tiny fragment of her total satisfaction. To turn on sexually, the Libra Woman needs to be primed by words, strokes, cuddling, and comfortable if not luxurious surroundings. The vibes must be right.

She wants a sex partner who is agile, aggressive, alert, and impressive to others, one who takes the initiative and also follows through imaginatively. The desirable partner must have a vivid erotic fantasy life, a gift of gab, and superb techniques to match her own.

The Libra Woman is likely to be most aroused by an articulate, polished, refined, clean, well-dressed partner. Her ideal man never forgets to open the door for her and always takes her to the nicest places, to a smart restaurant rather than to a pub or dive. He must always have clean fingernails and hair, smell good, smile, speak well, and make love exquisitely.

Libra wants to be pursued, courteously wooed, and loved like Lady Guinevere. She likes to be persuaded into bed, for she is part reluctant virgin. She likes to tease, for she is part temptress. She is a goddess of love and beauty, a modern Aphrodite who wants to be admired by mortals.

She likes pretty things, for she is part little girl. She likes being spoiled with gifts as part of the courting, and she in turn spoils her lover. If she were living in days gone by, she would want the full romantic rituals of the times. She would have felt at home in the civilization of Pompeii. Theirs was an erotic culture in which sensuality was revered, not downgraded or exploited. The cult of beauty, the natural acceptance of the body, the established rituals of social and sexual interaction—all would have pleased her.

The ambience and interaction preceding sex determine whether she wants to consummate sexually. Intercourse is not necessarily her favorite pastime. She may prefer a sensuous picnic in bed before or after coitus, and never mind the bread crumbs.

It is very important for Lady Libra to look good. Though she battles with overweight all her life, she does take care of herself. She has regular appointments with the hairdresser and at the skin care center.

She knows instinctively how to keep sex exciting. She is attractive, smells good, walks gracefully, and has a particular brand of femininity that turns men on. Her knowledge of sexual techniques is often impressive, even though she may be reluctant to impart this information to uptight lovers. She wants to eliminate the old-hat feeling that renders sex dull, to abolish the sloppy habits that result in a lackluster feeling and a lessening of stimulation.

She caters to the man in her life, though she is not quite sure how far to go. She is reluctant to give herself totally, for in her mind there is always a certain fear of dependency. In her early years particularly, she wants her man to adore her as a sex kitten and make love to her as a sex goddess. She wants to be pampered yet idolized. At times, she wants complete control of the situation. She is afraid to give up this control and be dominated by her passion.

She shares with Pisces a deep, hidden fear of being engulfed by her partner, though she is usually not aware of this fear herself. To open up completely to a man sexually means running the risk of emotional vulnerability. She is frightened of losing her identity. Her actions might be interpreted as embodying the male idea of cool detachment. James Bond and John Wayne do not want to lose control either.

Sexual self-image

It is often true that the sexiest-looking women are the most sexually insecure. A number of Libra Women have a poor self-image, a negative body image, and deep sexual fears.

For a woman, the enjoyment of sex is tied to familiarity with the female body, with her own sexual response as well as with the male sexual response, and above all to her love of self. The Libra Woman relies heavily on the media, especially on best-selling women's magazines like *Cosmopolitan* and *Vogue*, to set standards of beauty and sexiness. She often feels that she is inadequate by comparison. Because how she looks strongly influences how she feels, this sense of inadequacy permeates her entire self-image.

In bed she may remain preoccupied with images of perfect beauty and sex appeal, thus blocking her feelings. She may try to assume positions that she thinks are most flattering to her, thus reducing spontaneous response and interaction. She may also suffer from the fear that at the moment of orgasm she will look unfeminine, or even ugly. Finding this unbearable, she will often clamp down on her sexual feelings, and as a result she may not experience the total letting go that is necessary for a satisfying climax.

So the Libra Woman may look great, but she is often lonely and scared. Because she is too shy to discuss her sexual insecurity, she suffers in silence. Sex, she decides, simply is not what it is cracked up to be.

A great problem in her sexual relationships is the buildup of unspoken tension and criticism. Because she is intent on keeping a calm facade and pleasing her partner, she may pretend calm where a storm is brewing. Erotic storms should be unleashed. If she attempts to contain hers, her sexual response may become poorer, not richer, and she may seek new partners for greater satisfaction. She ought to look within and begin sharing what she sees with a partner who can give valuable feedback and support.

One of her favorite sexual fantasies is that of being an abducted princess. Another is being Wife Number One in a harem. The perfect fantasy is to play the role of a madam, running a call girl ring and sadistically controlling everyone under her while she herself is secretly mentally dominated by an invisible, omnipotent chief—gender unknown.

Her search for pleasure may lead her to try group sex in order to validate her tastes or fuel her sex drive. She feels that contact with a number of people might make her more sexually assertive. She tends to avoid the choice of a male or female mate on a permanent basis, and group sex provides her with freedom from commitment. She might also enjoy voyeurism. She is an exhibitionist if given the right atmosphere. She enjoys dancing on tabletops, stripping in a friend's living room, and playing adult post office or hide-and-seek.

Whispered erotic words of endearment help her to let go, as does lewd sexually related language. Grazing fingernails, feathers on her thighs, and soft, sensitive oil massages during erotic play make for a good session.

She likes mirrored ceilings and enjoys X-rated motels for a day or a weekend of total pleasure. She might have her own X-rated room, complete with a soft rug, incense, hi-fi, special lighting, and video equipment. Her closet is well stocked with an array of perfumes and oils.

Dressing as a member of the opposite sex (cross dressing) also stimulates her. She appreciates transvestites and accepts them. One of her recurrent fantasies is that she is a man. This fantasy stimulates her to be an aggressive sex partner. In this mood, she becomes animalistic; she roars, teases her lover mercilessly, and may indulge in a bondage scene.

The Libra Woman has a strong bisexual element in her makeup. She is aroused by the soft touch and the mystery of the female body, and she finds security in being with another woman. She may also be stimulated by switching roles, going back and forth between domination and submission, and she finds it easier to take these roles with a woman than with a man, who might be more uptight.

She has definite ideas about sexual etiquette. She is not an early riser and is not usually in the mood for morning sex. Her peak arousal period is midafternoon through midnight, after she has had her beauty sleep, bath, and toilette. Woe to the lover who appears sloppy and disheveled. She is wont to throw him out.

Though she shies from deep emotional commitment, she is fastidious about remembering what her lover likes, and she expects him to remember her favorite flowers and perfume. She believes in fairness and equality, but these are merely concepts to her. In actuality, she adores being wined and dined and treated like a *grande dame*.

In short, the Libra Woman is a good lover and is highly desirable. The way she looks, feels, and walks gives her partner exquisite pleasure. But she may shortchange herself as she caters to her lover's sexual needs and downplays her own. She often denies herself the pleasure that comes from feeling deeply in a sexual relationship. She must learn to balance thought with feeling, giving with taking. She may at times take too much and not give enough for her heart.

The lesson she needs to learn in sex is feeling, allowing herself to let go fully during the experience. Body image exercises, communication skill education, and relaxation methods such as Tai Chi, medi yoga, and visualization may be all she needs to open up sexually.

Libra anger

Anger is a natural human emotion. We feel loving, greedy, lusty, jealous, sad, happy—and we feel angry.

The Libra Woman is a dove whose hawk side comes out unexpectedly under stress, usually in the form of pretended concern. She has an enormous problem with unacknowledged, repressed anger. She is first of all unlikely to recognize her anger. Second, she does not know how to express anger honestly and constructively. Lest she feel overwhelmed by the problem, she should rest assured that almost everyone in our culture shares it.

None of us are taught the ground rules for "integrity fighting." What we do know is "dominance fighting." The difference is that the first results in the removal of friction, while the latter increases it by leaving one party victorious, the other humiliated and hurt.

In our culture, we usually call anger by other names. We may say we are depressed, hostile, withdrawn, guilty, upset, worried, selfish ... and we might feel any of those emotions. But just as often they cover anger. And by now it is common knowledge that depression is usually the result of anger turned inward, never expressed.

Anger, like sex, scares us. We think it is like the genie in the bottle, that once it is released our anger will never again be controllable. And in the Libra Woman, what particularly works against the expression of her anger is the belief (our culture supports her in this view) that she becomes a "bad" person when she is angry. She does not yet know that if we learn to accept anger as a natural human emotion, like love, we can deal with it and use it constructively.

The Libra Woman's pleasant face seldom registers anger. She might be at war with herself internally, but externally all is calm. Her primary mode of coping with anger is to express it in the guise of loving concern. She "knows" that her husband is worried, that her best friend is suffering from an unhappy affair, that her child has done something wrong. While she pats people on the back, she fails to rid herself of her anger. Instead she projects it onto others and distorts it into worry, fear, and guilt. Unfortunately, the Libra Woman is unaware of her manipulation. She thinks that above all she wants to avoid hurting her partner, but the outcome does more harm than good. Her manipulativeness and avoidance of her real feelings endanger her and her partnership.

As a cardinal sign, Libra wants control. She tries to achieve it by withholding her anger and practicing manipulation. She appears solicitous but in fact may be ignoring the other person.

Anger and sex

The typical Libra almost never discusses anger with her partner. Instead, she persists in destructive actions.

Anger directly affects her sexual feelings and performance. As her hostility and her partner's hostility increase, she starts to suffer from headaches and backaches. She nags her man about her health, about petty details, about his lack of attention to her. Since everything she does and doesn't do sexually is affected by her repressed anger, she also represses the feelings necessary to promote healthy, active sexual relations.

For Libra, anger can work as a turnoff to sex but is sometimes a stimulus. An example of the latter is the story of Jack and Barbara. Jack and Barbara argued constantly toward the end of their marriage. They had passionate sex that was always connected to fights. After they divorced, Jack found to his dismay that he was impotent with other women. In therapy he discovered that in his mind sex had become linked to aggression. By using sex as an assault on Barbara, he felt more in control. When Jack did not feel angry at the woman he was trying to have sex with, he did not turn on. She did not deserve his assault.

Libra, here are some ground rules to help you express your anger constructively:

1. Be aware of when you are angry. Recognize, do not suppress, your anger.
2. Decide what is making you angry. Decide whether you need to

discuss it with your partner or with someone else. Sometimes a friend or a therapist can help. Sometimes shouting to the rooftops or into a waterfall does wonders to lift the anger.

3 If you decide to have it out with your partner, consider a time frame. Make an appointment to have a fight at a time that is mutually convenient.

4 Prepare for it. Clarify what the purpose of the discussion will be. Is it to clear the air? Is there a specific issue? What is it? Do you want to fight to win (dominance fighting is no good), or do you want to improve the relationship and remove whatever is making you angry?

A good opening might go something like this: "Look, Marty, there's something that's been bothering me for a long time, and I realize it's making me angry. If I didn't care about the relationship, I guess I'd forget about it or just scream at you about taking out the garbage or forgetting to give me phone messages. But because I care, I want to get the real issue out in the open and see if we can resolve it."

5 Stick with your own feelings and perceptions. Do not *blame* the other person; don't let this issue poison other parts of the relationship that are good.

6 Use role reversal to explain yourself. Try to help the other person step into your shoes. Here is an example: "Rose, maybe you don't know what it is like for me to constantly have to wait for you. Picture it in your mind. I am a cautious, fastidious person, and I hate to make people wait. After a half-hour of waiting for you, I am fuming inside. I can no longer imagine how I can enjoy myself. My parents raised me to be considerate. Whenever I'm late, I feel like a heel."

7 Understand the difference between one action and a person's whole personality. We should remember what we tell children: "You don't dislike him, you dislike what he did."

8 Do not assume that the other person intended to make you angry.

9 Think positively. Search for share motives, goals, and interests that promote communication and mutual respect.

10 Remember that you have the right to your feelings. Feelings are facts.

11 Finish by discussing what you have both gained. Reaffirm your care and commitment.

12 Remember that you can not "protect" your relationship by

repressing anger. Dishonesty will destroy the relationship you think you're trying to save. A healthy relationship is one in which you feel safe to express anything, including anger.

Libra lifestyles

The Libra Woman is partnership-prone and believes in marriage. She may want different traits in a husband than she wants in a lover. Sometimes she wants her man to be everything—Lothario, Don Juan, Don Quixote, and Willie the traveling salesman. As a mate, she is idealistic, moody, sensitive, demanding, accommodating, refined, romantic. She has a strong desire to do everything in her power to make her mate happy.

She is anything but Earth Mother. She tends to be ethereal and devoted to lofty principles. She is a romantic but a fighter for equal rights. She is an idealist whose adaptability to her mate's wishes evaporates in the heat of battle for a principle.

Monogamy and nonmonogamy

The Libra Woman is totally for or against monogamy on principle. Either way, she is unbending, self-righteous, and willing to argue vehemently on the subject. The Libra woman who opposes monogamy may not have more than one sexual relationship. It is often enough to take an ideological stance without practicing it. She believes in justice and equality, so why not in freedom?—freedom of thought, if not of action.

The following represent typical situations that could influence the Libra Woman to become nonmonogamous:

1 Search for a more perfect partner. The Libra Woman believes, sometimes unconsciously, that there is always a potentially more ideal partner or husband than the one she has. She is willing to wear rose-colored specs and live in the Land of Dreams for awhile, but when the glow and the dreams wear off, she is in the market for a new lover.

  You can tell when she's approaching this state by how attentive she is to her mate. If she looks around a lot, plays with her hair, or fidgets in her seat constantly when he is with her, danger lies ahead. But the most unmistakable signal is when she diets in earnest to buy a whole new wardrobe, or at least a new bathing suit.

My advice to her man is to redouble his attentions. Ask her what she is missing; try to lead her in a direction that will provide what she needs without amorous adventures. Since she is suggestible and appreciates being pampered, all is not lost.

2 Lady Chatterley. The Libra Woman can trap herself in the role of the refined lady or vestal virgin at home, leaving herself no place to go with her animal passion. The whore in her needs a man who forces her to get out of her head and her role. She is quite able to balance relationships with two men, and she may live out some raunchy fantasies this way.

3 Personal growth. Libra changes many times in the course of her life. She is destined by her sign to experience a great deal in relationships. In her early life she may define love as getting all she needs from a good man. Later, when she is more in tune with her higher self and with *eros* (see "Summing Up Libra"), she will need a man with whom she can share all of herself.

As she journeys on, she will have times of overlapping involvements, trying different kinds of men. She will do best to keep in mind that she is spiraling upward in her development, toward being a balanced, sharing, total woman.

4 Great appetite for life. The Libra Woman has plenty of *joie de vivre*. She wants to swim in Bali, ride a camel in the Sahara, ski in the Alps, drive in Monte Carlo, and make love on Telegraph Hill. If these opportunities come along, she will most probably take them. Thus, if she is without her mate and her ski guide is handsome and attentive, she may just have sex for lunch. She is unlikely to feel guilty afterwards, for she does not think it will hurt her marriage. Besides, she feels entitled.

5 Low self-esteem. Libra has many moments of high anxiety about beauty and aging. She may try to shore up her sagging ego by taking another lover, even a new husband.

6 Insensitivity from her partner. The Libra Woman is a complicated creature of many sides and moods. If her partner is unable or unwilling to accommodate her, she will sooner or later grow very disenchanted. She will have little desire to tell him exactly how she feels or where to get off. She may instead try to relieve the tension by having a new affair or a one-night stand. She may perhaps be faced with a situation in which her man is definitely not giving her the mothering she needs. She may then feel so empty that she is likely to have sex just to fill the void.

7 And others are doing it too. The Libra Woman likes to keep up

with the trends. If her social circle admires a liberated pose, she may feel obligated to open her marriage. Many models and actresses are Libra types. They may have commitments to one partner, but they may also have sex with others if this is expected of them in the world in which they work.

Alternative lifestyles

Single woman: The Libra Woman does not want to live alone for very long. When she does, it is likely that she is between serious relationships. In this case, she is bound to have a cat, many plants, and numerous *objets d'art* filling the space to make her feel less lonely. She may go through periods of asexuality due to a heavy work load or mere lack of interest, but these are temporary. Change is universal. Life never stands still. The Libra Woman is different in each phase of her life.

Intimate networks: The Libra Woman would be comfortable trying this movement, which advocates friendship with both sexes. It neither rules out nor enforces sexual involvement.

Open marriage: This arrangement is a very poor choice for Libra because of her insecurities. The Libra Woman is uninterested in talking things out. She is very interested in getting her way and usually believes that total honesty is undesirable and impossible. An open marriage simply would not provide her with enough control or reassurance.

Ménage à trois: The Libra Woman might well adore it. Unlike her Aries sister, who prefers two men with her, Lady Libra would probably prefer to have another woman. This would give her a chance to interact fully with another woman, which has long been one of her fantasies (in some cases also a reality). Libra will patrol her territory very cleverly, and it is likely that the ménage à trois will revolve, however subtly, around her.

Group marriage: Libra is usually too jealous, but she might be willing to try this for the possible richness it provides—materially, sexually, intellectually, spiritually. Verdict: doubtful.

Communes: Communes are a good choice for Libra. I know a number of Libra types who are trying out this kind of lifestyle in Israel, India, and the United States. Rotating chores, a variety of partners, contact with people in all social and age groups, lots of socializing, and the opportunity to learn new things make this an especially good possibility for the Libra Woman who is considering an alternative to monogamy. However, her jealousy may become a problem, especially if she lets it build up and eat at her insides.

Gay/bisexual lifestyle: The Libra Woman is a dual personality, and this naturally also manifests itself in her sexual life. Many are bisexual or lesbian. For a fair number of Libra Women, this is an interesting temporary lifestyle. For others, it is all there is.

Ugly duckling or love princess, sex goddess or wife, Libra is more likely than not to be charming and *très femme.* If she fails to experience pleasure in her relationships, she will continue to search for it. The search may take her through many new partners and lifestyles and may lead to a new sexual identity.

The limitation of sensory pleasure is strongly related to serious emotional disorders and to violent behavior. Research also indicates that the positive effects of touch on infants can be negated by the repression of various forms of physical pleasure, such as, for example, premarital sex.

The Libra Woman must have her love times and sensual highs. She needs her man, money, music, bath oil, perfumes, flowers, shag rugs, and satin sheets. The odds are that she will be blissfully happy—at least until she changes her mind.

Summing up Libra

The Libra ugly duckling is supposed to believe in herself and grow up to be a swan. She will then be able to teach out of her own experience and by her own example that *love is a properly balanced act of sharing.*

One way or another, the duckling managed to keep himself alive as best he could the rest of the winter. And at last, as spring returned he felt a new strength in his wings. One day he saw the same white birds on the lake. "I will join them even if they should kill me for my ugliness," he said bravely.

But even as he pleaded he saw his own reflection among the waterlilies, and lo, he was as beautiful as they! The old swans bent their heads in admiration and welcome. The ugly duckling had become a proud young swan!

In her coming-of-age, the Libra ugly duckling joins the human group as a full-fledged member.

SCORPIO

CHECKLIST OF SCORPIO TRAITS

Note: This checklist describes the traits of one *phase* only; if it doesn't seem to fit you, check other lists to find the phase you are in right now.

1. Complex
2. Practical
3. Mystical
4. Lusty, Passionate
5. Diurnal (A Day Person)
6. Nocturnal (A Night Person)
7. Intense
8. Vindictive
9. Prone to Extremes
10. Repressed
11. Compulsive
12. Self-confident
13. Capable
14. Psychic
15. Stubborn
16. Loyal
17. Curious
18. Adventurous
19. Insensitive, Dictatorial
20. Arrogant
21. Secretive
22. Self-indulgent
23. Manipulative
24. Torrid
25. Asexual
26. Possessive
27. Nonconforming
28. Iconoclastic
29. Leader
30. Lonely
31. Guilty
32. Self-destructive
33. Unusual Destiny
34. Undergoes Changes and Turning points, Emotional Death and Rebirth in Her Life (A Main Theme)
35. Power User

Scorpio personality

When she is good, she is very, very good,
When she is bad, she is horrid.
Nursery Rhyme

General traits and background

The Scorpio Woman is an eternally intriguing creature who, like the Sphinx, seems to know and guard the riddles of life and death. She either fascinates or frightens nearly every man. She is magnetic, lusty, and endowed with mysterious powers. She can devastate with a look or revitalize with the healing energy in her eyes and hands.

Scorpio is the eighth sign of the Zodiac, and it is Fixed Water. The fixed part gives her persistence, determination, and willfulness; the water gives her regenerative powers, intuition, mysticism, compulsiveness, and some paranoia. Each astrological sign is said to be "ruled" by a planet and its vibrations. Since Scorpio is ruled by Pluto, Pluto dominates the main themes in the life of the Scorpio Woman.

The Scorpio-*type* woman is one who has the sun or other important planets in Scorpio, planets in the eighth house (the natural house of Scorpio); a Scorpio ascendant; or a powerfully aspected Pluto. Scorpio types are also those who are temporarily going through a Scorpio *phase*. In this case, the person need have no planets in the sign of Scorpio. The Scorpio type is described by the checklist of traits at the beginning of this chapter. The Scorpio phase has the following characteristics:

1 An obsession with power, and the use of sex to obtain it.
2 A major illness, or the death or major illness of an intimate, which deeply alters the person's awareness and lifestyle.
3 A transcendence to spiritual attunement (Ghandhi comes to mind).
4 A transformation that results in a new self and lifestyle; symbolic death and rebirth in life.

Sometimes the Scorpio phase is characterized by destruction via fanatic sexual involvements, moneymaking, and manipulation of individuals or groups. Scorpio has had a bad press mostly because its potent energy has so often been used to gain personal power at the expense of others.

The Scorpio Woman lives on many levels, most of which are hidden to all but a few intimate, perceptive observers. You can identify her by her intensity, her will power, and her strong hypnotic aura. The Scorpio Woman enters the room quietly but commands it immediately.

She is all woman, and very real. No man could ask for more than she offers. Frankly, quite a few men would be more comfortable with less. These are the men who do not find it easy to love a woman who exudes power and understands how to use it.

Power is the ability to cause or prevent change. The Scorpio Woman has it and wants it. She effects major changes in people and in all vibrations she encounters. She can also block influences that would create change. For example, she is almost immune to opinion makers and will rarely change her mind.

To understand Scorpio, one must be aware of her needs for both privacy and power. She wants to make an impact on the world, sometimes at great personal sacrifice. She also demands secrecy. The conflict comes when she realizes that leadership usually comes at the price of her privacy.

A key word for her is *use*. As well as her own talents and resources, she sometimes uses people to gain her ends. She craves understanding but seldom is understood. She wants emotional peace but lives on the edge of compulsive excess.

Complex

Scorpio's sign is symbolized by the scorpion, the eagle, and the phoenix. She is as complex as her symbols imply. Her highest task is to achieve *self-mastery*. She must do this through self-reform. She has to learn how to pull herself up by her sandal straps from the lower scorpion existence to the higher level of the eagle. A few Scorpio Women reach the spiritual transcendence the phoenix symbolizes. As Joan of Arc was dying at the stake, a big bird is said to have soared over her head—an eagle.

Practical, mystical

The Scorpio Woman is a pragmatist but also a mystic. Though unlikely to shed many tears for the victims of Hiroshima, she may decide to become a doctor and heal the sick. Her mystical side tells her to search for a cosmic reason for the holocaust. She may seem cruel to people who do not know of or share her pragmatic, action-oriented beliefs, and who are not in tune with her mysticism.

She believes that no condition, habit, or relationship escapes change or ending. The pragmatic Scorpio believes that destruction is a necessary forerunner of rebirth. The mystical Scorpio finds hidden purpose in each tragedy.

Lusty, passionate day self—night self

The Scorpio Woman's is a lot like Molly in Fielding's novel *Tom Jones*, on which the film of the same name was based. She loves sex and abandons herself to all its delights. Her senses are highly developed, and she "feels" through all of them. She may roll in the hay as Molly does; she appreciates the sensuality of eating and can make a meal a ritual of seduction.

She hungers for touch and for a man's body. She delights in his shape, textures, and potency. She sniffs, traces, strokes, nibbles. When she loves, she loves with fierce loyalty. When she lusts, she longs for the meshing and thrashing of bodies from the depth of her being. This is her diurnal, or day, self.

Scorpio also has a nocturnal self. It is just as hungry and strong as her day self, but it lurks, waiting for an opening. It is her compulsive, inhibited, domineering, sometimes maniacally possessive or secretly sadistic side. Mata Hari, for example, was a nocturnal creature. She lusted only for power. She hid her true goal and used sex to get to it. This side of Scorpio is destructive and can end up destroying her.

Intense

Every Scorpio Woman glows with intensity. Her intensity is double-edged—a gift or burden, depending on what she does with it. It is a gift when, linking it to her powers of concentration, she serves a good cause. For example, she can concentrate intensely on the number of the winning horse in the next day's daily double and bring it to mind. Her mental powers enable her to visualize the man she wants—and he appears.

Scorpio's intensity, positively used, makes her a winner and a delightful challenge. Negatively used, it can turn into vindictiveness and vengefulness.

Vindictive

If anyone crosses her, her intensity turns into revenge. If you have ever been on the receiving end of the Scorpio Woman's stings and attacks, you probably have some unforgettable memories.

She will hardly ever forget slights, real or imagined. She even invites them by her own expectation of being crossed or hurt. An old law is that you get what you think you'll get, and plenty of the good and bad comes her way. If she does not rein in her negativities, she can turn into a mean witch indeed!

Scorpio, I advise you to stay away from petty intrigue and avoid inflicting hurts. Remember that if someone has wronged you, it ultimately becomes their karmic problem, not yours. The corollary of the rule above is that you get back whatever you send out, whether it returns this year or at the end of your life.

All or nothing: she is an extremist

The Scorpio Woman prefers to wipe the slate clean and begin anew rather than limp along patching up old habits. Her life is a roller coaster through eternity. Unlike the Libra Woman, who swings from pole to pole because she can't decide what to do, the Scorpio Woman *wants* to experiment and live life to the fullest, from extreme to extreme. She goes from a torrid affair to asceticism, from artist to business woman, from occult study groups to spiritual isolation.

Her motto is that if one does something important, one must do it completely. She is almost incapable of taking the middle road, even under the pressure of public opinion. She is usually able to maintain a cool pose while waiting to pull off a coup. She can metamorphose in just a short time from passive observer (or so we think) to key mover and shaker.

Scorpio energy almost always manifests itself through opposites, and here is why. Deep down, the Scorpio Woman knows she is in life to transform, to fly like an eagle. She has an inner knowledge, harbors a vision of how to recycle herself. She knows how to emerge from the ashes of pain and defeat. On her path, she relentlessly pursues extremes of joy and suffering, creation and destruction. It is our perceptions, shaped by heredity and early conditioning, that define her behavior as extreme.

Repressed

The Scorpio Woman must learn to cope with one of the results of her all-or-nothing nature, her repressed emotions. She often acts as if she had a stopper in her throat. When it blows, she can go to shattering extremes to let off steam. She can swallow years of domestic abuse and then one day walk out without a nod to her husband. She can tolerate battles on the job with no sign of misery and then down her boss and colleagues with a devastating attack to the gut. She is as good at repressing emotions as she is at planning and launching barbs and raids where they hurt the most.

She can get ill from allowing her feelings to fester inside. Though the Scorpio Woman has a sturdy constitution, when she gets sick she holds onto illness as tenaciously as she once held onto her health. Her recovery is usually slow and long.

The weakest part of her body, the point where she feels the most stress, is her first chakra, or the sex center. Any emotional repression goes directly into this sexual area, immediately causing sexual problems and related physical complaints. The stopper-in-the-bottle syndrome can also bring ulcers, periodic explosions that traumatize the family environment, throat discomfort or disease, and sometimes nagging lower back pain.

Compulsive

Leaving little to chance, the Scorpio Woman tries to arrange everything around her to run according to her plans. Perhaps she does this to prevent herself from coming on too strong. By prearranging life to suit her, she feels she may avoid blowups. She kneads life as if it were dough for daily fresh bread. She wills, desires, manipulates, organizes, categorizes, transcends, grabs, exploits, holds on, lets go, attracts, and repels experience.

She has a secret inner force that compels her to gamble when she would rather play it safe, to be a catalyst when she would prefer her life to be staid. She may dislike change, yet she cannot live without risks and revolutions. Her compulsive activity and her search for secrecy go hand in hand.

Self-confident, capable

The Scorpio Woman is probably the most self-sufficient, strong-willed, self-confident woman in the Zodiac, except when she is in one of her crises. Usually, her drive for significance is unrelenting, her will to power formidable, and her ability to seize an opportunity and play a hunch astounding.

If self-esteem is born of knowing what she wants and how to get it, she brims with it. For her, the problem is not so much to get what she desires as to choose and use constructive means of doing so. She is confident about her ability to dominate the forces of nature and to surmount obstacles. In truth, domination is a game to her, one she feels she was born to win. Tasks that require confidence and endurance challenge her. Because she is confident, persistent, thorough, and intuitive, she can be a capable engineer, physician, or military leader. She is a good manager. She likes to work, and she is usually good at it. The positive results reinforce her self-confidence, which in turn enables her to tackle new tasks with confidence. The more she does, the more confident she becomes. She short-circuits only when she turns to revenge or any other underhanded expression of unvented fear and anger.

Psychic

Scorpio's self-confidence is heightened by her psychic powers. She relies on them; though our culture represses psychic gifts, she tends to be clairaudient, telepathic, and perhaps also clairyoyant. She sizes people up quickly and accurately, and she can wait to act as her judgment dictates.

She usually psyches out her opponents. She has a good sense of timing for attacks, too, because her senses process data accurately. She misses little of what goes on, and though she is psychic, she is seldom tuned out to a dreamy never-never land. Usually, she is right in the thick of a situation, feet on the ground, eyes carefully observing, mind questioning and evaluating.

Stubborn

Scorpio is bound to go wrong when she gets too stubborn. Hers, after all, is a fixed sign, and so she is capable of getting stuck in ruts, psychic or material. Especially in early adulthood, she feels insecure enough that she tends to stick to arguments beyond the point of no return. She often digs in her heels to prove she is right, though deep down she may know she is wrong. Sometimes she fights just to vent aggression, and the more wrong she is, the more she may battle to win.

Loyal

The Scorpio Woman is loyal and chooses her commitments carefully. Normally she selects a small circle of friends who, once hers, are hers for life. She is cautious in allocating her affection, as she expects others to be. She neither likes nor understands flighty people or quick friendships. When she opens up to someone, she expects to have that person around for life. If something goes wrong, she is bound either to withdraw without explanation or to lash out.

Scorpio, I advise you to try to voice your expectations about friendship and loyalty. Interpretations of such things vary widely. If you count, for example, on having a Gemini type for a friend, you may be disappointed. State your hopes and needs clearly and early. Listen carefully to the response, and decide whether you are in the right place to give and get what you need.

Curious, adventurous

The Scorpio Woman is drawn to adventure, knowledge, and intrigue. She is always interested in tapping new resources. Sexual and artistic experimentation, detective work, metaphysical investigation, healing workshops, competitive financial tangles, and complex mental puzzles attract her.

However, her curiosity is never merely bookish. She wants to live out her adventures and is willing to be a guinea pig. She is very curious (but never yellow). She adores unraveling intrigues and sniffing out the skeletons in peoples' closets. She is a natural detective who believes that things are seldom as they appear, and who is willing to put time and effort into finding out just what lies below the surface.

She is usually more interested in the heart of the matter than in its appearance. The submerged part of human life and behavior challenges her. As befits a female Sherlock Holmes, she has a knack for asking embarrassing questions. Sometimes one has the feeling that Lady Scorpio has made up her mind way ahead of the questioning and presumes to know all the correct answers herself. Her curiosity and her blunt, bull's-eye interrogations can turn to cruelty or arrogance.

Insensitive, arrogant

The Scorpio Woman is fascinating but not always easy and likeable. She can be a bitch who rides roughshod or a condescending amateur who pretends to know more than the specialists. When she is especially determined to probe, or when she is out for revenge, she can be hell on wheels. She does not even remotely resemble the "nice soft female." She neither uses traditional feminine wiles nor is in any way willing to be submissive. She goes straight for the jugular, and heaven help those who cross her path at such times.

When she wants her way, she is insensitive in that she cannot bring herself to see another's point of view. She is also remarkably able to detach herself from the feelings of those she may have hurt. This detachment makes her different from other water types, who are far more likely to end up emotionally protecting even their enemies.

The Scorpio Woman has no great need for approval, and this frees her to do her own thing. But she must learn to discriminate between pushing straight to her own selfish goals and embarking on a more valid search to accomplish goals important to her group and to humanity. She is best off using as talents both her insensitivity and her detachment.

Secretive

As a born detective, she seems to feel entitled to be a mystery person herself. She is not likely to reveal anything too personal. She would probably enjoy wearing a one-way mirror allowing her to see others perfectly, but no one to see her.

She is naturally secretive. At times she acts as if she were the keeper of universal secrets; her divine mission being to keep herself the biggest enigma.

An important key to understanding her personality is to know that she trusts neither herself nor others. Because she mistrusts, she becomes fanatically self-protective. She is likely to pull a Garbo on most of us.

If pushed, she has been known to fabricate answers which later turn out outlandishly incorrect. She also plays games to waylay ardent detectives.

However, it is a mistake to think she is indifferent deep-down. Her embers never cool. It is much safer to assume she is biding her time until the right moment comes to enter the game and rig the dice in her favor.

Self-indulgent

Because she is so fascinated by life, she experiments beyond traditional limits. Like her sister Pisces, the Scorpio woman is attracted to dangerous forms of self-indulgence.

There is always a part in her that both fears and courts self-destruction. Many a Scorpio Woman has recurrent problems with drug and alcohol addiction; many wash out too early. Scorpio's overindulgence periodically results in health problems. From time to time she is apt to suffer from mysterious ailments that come and go without proper medical diagnosis—gout, rheumatism, and even malaria and typhoid. She is also bound to complain of elusive internal inflammations. Bouts of high fever may also come and go.

It is lucky for Scorpio that she has steely will power. When she wants to, she can usually kick any habit and recoup lost energy.

Torrid or asexual, possessive

The Scorpio Woman uses sex, first of all, to control. She likes to dominate a man and channel her passion for the purpose of possession or exploitation. She may mistake love for ownership. She has two sexual faces. One is the face of a fantastic, demanding lover. The other is the face of an ascetic, asexual woman. She will adopt both sexual lifestyles more than once in the course of her life.

In her torrid phase, the Scorpio Woman has a whore's vocabulary and the lust of a sex-starved mariner. She drives a man wild with desire. She is a virtuoso who makes sex worth living for. Sex fuels her in a way nothing else does. Even the inexperienced Scorpio Woman intuitively knows the art of lovemaking. The sex experience, even without love, is familiar to her from other lifetimes. She enjoys it even though she may calculate precisely with whom to mate in order to best advance other causes. Love and sex may be separate entities to her.

The Scorpio Woman also goes through periods of complete withdrawal from sexual activity. She may do this out of guilt over her "promiscuity." She may channel her energies into mental pursuits alone. She may suddenly find that sex falls far short of her extreme expectations and give it up in disgust. Sweeping changes are her style.

Sexual lust is always part of her makeup, for she is a very physical person. But she also has the capacity to turn it off. There are times when she is engaged in a spiritual quest for the celebration of life through universal love. She may go overboard and forget that universal love may very well include physical passion.

The spiritually aspiring or evolved Scorpio Woman, the eagle or phoenix, has more than a bit of Joan of Arc in her. Sex is not just the way to land a promotion or the richest Rockefeller. Sex can become for her a way to release sacred passions. In later life, her sexual energy may be used to reach the pinnacle of strength and integration or to achieve a religious coming together with another human being.

Nonconformist, taboo breaker, leader

The Scorpio Woman is drawn to three areas that society still considers taboo: power, death, and money.

She is a nonconformist by virtue of the fact that she is a woman who enjoys using power in a culture that still reserves this domain to the male. She is an individualist who believes that life beyond death does exist. And she is a frank debunker of myths concerning money.

She knows that sex is power and power is money. Her sexual exploits are well known, but we know a lot less about her involvement with money, because money is still a seldom-discussed topic.

People's resources, taxes, and inheritances belong in Pluto's domain. Therefore, the Scorpio Woman has the privilege of experimenting with these, using her own special intuition. She does well as an investor for others, as a real estate agent, antiques dealer, or stockbroker (especially when dealing with underground natural resources), as tax expert, or as an attorney specializing in deeds, bequests, and inheritance cases.

Scorpio can also work especially well within the "death industry." She can be a good funeral parlor administrator, embalmer, counselor for the grieving, religious leader, or cultist. She can break through traditional notions of death and dying and share her own deep wisdom with others.

It is profoundly important for her to examine her own values regarding these areas, for only when she is clear about them can she be effective in teaching others. At her best, she can help dismantle harmful notions about money, sex, power, and death. She can become a great demythologizer of harmful old notions, and a harbinger of an expanded and more helpful vision.

Lonely

The path of the nonconformist is never easy. Whether or not the Scorpio Woman becomes a public leader, she is often lonely and misunderstood. In some ways, she is way ahead of her times. She is usually out of step with her neighbors, family, and friends. Also, she changes so radically in her life that it is hard for others to keep up with her.

She is a private person, and her own person. In many ways, she feels she does not really need other people. Of course, she is human, but she dwells in the depths, sees into the future, and sometimes lets the present weigh her down.

It may be her pride that keeps her from reaching out to people and asking for sympathy. Or perhaps she feels just plain mean and nasty and prefers keeping her secrets and her devious methodology to herself. She has a great need to feel strong and self-sufficient. She often affects a female macho pose and seems to resent anyone worrying about her. "Who needs it?" she seems to be saying.

Despite her appearance of fearless indomitability, she craves acceptance and understanding. Nobody is a more loyal friend once she finds that you accept her funny ways and "odd" streaks. Nobody can be a more faithful ally than she once she believes you have done your best to understand her.

Guilty

The Scorpio Woman does not carry the problems of the world on her shoulders, but she has a strong puritanical streak. This makes her a part-time believer, depending on her mood, in the ethic of productivity. In this view, sex is for procreation, and time is never to be wasted in idle pursuits.

Since she is an extremist, there are times when she adopts a puritanical belief system and becomes as fanatic about duty as she had been about pleasure. In this phase, she experiences guilt over her sexual passions and activities, and she may swear to forgo them. She may become a model suburban wife and mother, denying herself sensual avenues of self-expression. If this proves satisfactory, more power to her. But for most, it is only a temporary phase, usually riddled with intense frustrations and longings.

Self-destructive

Pluto power may be turned to purposes of self-destruction. The most common avenue for Scorpio is to practice lifelong self-denial. In this case, the stopper-in-the-bottle syndrome is doubly strong, and she experiences many bouts of physical illness. Her mental powers are so strong that whatever she thinks can become her reality. She can sell herself on anything, including everything that is bad for her. She can make herself lead a life that may be great for others and hell for herself.

Taking drugs and alcohol to excess, pursuing certain goals single-mindedly while denying all other needs, ignoring pleasure in favor of duty, removing sex from its natural place as a great source of communication and joy and transforming it into a means of manipulation—all are ultimately self-destructive.

The Scorpio Woman's sensual nature is so strong that when some of her basic needs are unmet, she literally consumes herself with illness, frustration, and anger. For example, if she wants a promotion, she may ignore her love affair. Secretly, she knows she is doing herself harm, and unless she changes directions, this knowledge drives her further into the depths.

Scorpio, my advice is: be sure you examine carefully what you are after; be sure that what you want is really good for you on all levels, because you, as a Scorpio Woman, will definitely attain the object of your desires.

Unusual destiny

The Scorpio Woman makes life bend to her wishes. She has the concentration, personal power, talent, intuition, capacity for judgment and action and for leading or following, that make her a stunning winner or a desperate loser. She is a magician who never chooses a gray path; she is either magnificent or she is horrid.

Her habits, appearance, and "aura" bear testimony to an unusual life. No matter how routine her experience may seem to an observer, you can be sure her inner life would make fairyland seem drab by comparison. She is an artist, a white or a black witch. She may behave like the last puritan and live in a bordello. She paints life with the odd stroke, in extreme color combinations, and hides her secret code under the obvious. She is like a Rembrandt painting that has suffered under the palette of lesser masters, only to come into its own at the proper time.

Never underestimate the Scorpio Woman! If she is a wallflower or an impotent career woman now, she may be transformed by your next meeting into a riveting, clever go-getter. On the other hand, she may be at the top of the heap now, but land in the obituary columns just awhile later.

When you live as close to the edge as Scorpio does, you constantly run the risk of falling off. The challenge of the Scorpio Woman is to make the edge bend to her needs so that she is able to deliver the goods she has promised herself. She is a powerful woman born for her own special purpose—to change certain taboos, to teach people secret knowledge in the realm of sex, death, and resources.

Scorpio relationships

In dealing with the Scorpio Woman's relationships, we must once again look at the definition of power. For it is power she wants, and until sometime later in life, she may use sex and intimacy to get it.

Power means "to be able," in whatever domain. For centuries, women have embraced a kind of psychic, sexual, and economic impotence. Even today, female sexuality is thought to exist only when summoned forth by a princely embrace. While the male sex drive is openly acknowledged and widely condoned, females still lack the power to admit to an abstract, independent female sex drive. The concept of a sexually independent woman still seems to many people sordid and unimaginable. And I believe that it is women themselves who withhold the largest chunk of permission.

Women as a group have also been unable to bring themselves to play an important role as agents of political or economic change. We have not yet taken equal risks and equal responsibilities in high-level decision making. Most of us continue to think of ourselves as oppressed by the system and its top dogs, men. We would do better to look at our own oppression of ourselves, our own fear of expanding roles and responsibilities.

Though most of us have thought of intimacy and relationships as our domain, lately many of us have been unable to safeguard the happiness and stability of our marriages, of our "primary relationships." Change, it seems, may have gotten out of hand even for us domestic experts.

The greatest challenge for the Scorpio Woman is to be fair in love. She must find an outlet for her scheming ambitions outside her relationships. She is always tempted to play top dog at home as if to compensate for the historical imbalance between men and women. She is purposeful, goal-oriented, and dictatorial. Lady Godiva, Bella Abzug, and Scarlett O'Hara rolled into one may not equal the fierce passion she uses to guard her seniority in relationships.

"All's fair in love and war" is her motto. In friendship, she feels entitled to a lopsided loyalty. In romance, she wants an exclusive attachment that simultaneously strengthens her libido, her bank account, and her status in the community, and puts a gleam in her eye and a sway on her hips. In marriage, she wants double of everything.

The Scorpio Woman is a very ambitious person. She may become an example of the miscarriage of personal power in relationships. I advise her to involve herself in work, competition, or serious study throughout her life. She must find ways to feel meaningful and gain some recognition outside the domestic and intimate spheres. If she does not do this, she is bound to turn into the type of shrew Liz Taylor portrayed in *Who's Afraid of Virginia Woolf*?

Childhood

A depressingly large number of Scorpio types grow up in a climate of emotional or physical hardship. It is as if they chose an early Golgotha of obstacles. The attempt to turn such experiences into growth, to build on life crises, to overcome distrust and fear of further hurt, is a part of Scorpio's love life.

Over the years, I have seen almost everyone I know, live with, or work with experience a Scorpio phase that brings a total life change. Evidence shows that people with heavy Scorpio influences in their natal chart had childhoods with one or more of the following: divorce of the parents; early death of a close friend or relative, usually in strange or tragic circumstances; alcoholism in the family; or extremely psychic people around them.

Nothing comes easly to the Scorpio Woman, and even as a child, she has an extreme relationship to at least one important adult. Usually, she grows up feeling strongly polarized about her mother. She either idolizes or hates her.

Susan illustrates the first case. A handsome, dark woman in her late twenties, she was the oldest in a family with five children. In school, she was a straight-A student, a cheerleader. She was a virgin until she married at twenty, and she remained Mommie's good little girl until her divorce at twenty-nine. Susan had this to say:

> I never knew I could live a life different from my mother's and from what I imagined she wanted from me. I really became my mother all over again—a super-mom, super-wife, and super-daughter, all in one. I ran myself ragged, but eventually my husband tired of my compulsive needs for approval. He said he felt like he was married to an immature robot.

When Susan was twenty-eight, Tom left her and her mother died suddenly, two events that represented a strong Scorpio phase in her life. Suddenly she was faced with having to build a completely new life on her own.

How the Scorpio Woman relates: lovers and other intimates

Scorpio can get her hooks into people by her magnetism, that "certain something" she exudes, her strength, depth, and persistence. People often feel that she can impart secrets worth knowing.

Until she rises above her initial tendencies to be possessive, manipulative, and secretive, she may fall into the trap of conducting relationships as if she were trying to win a battle. But even Napoleon met his Waterloo, and the Scorpio Woman is no exception. Long-term intimate relationships do not lend themselves to warring strategy.

She usually has few friends, and of these, most are bound to be men. She lacks the empathy and easygoing qualities other women seem to want in female friends. What she herself fails to realize is that she could control a lot more territory if she cultivated female friendships.

The Scorpio Woman is bound to experience many intense friendships, mostly with men, and several stormy romantic breakups. She may also have, or narrowly avoid, an emotional breakdown. Mountains and valleys are the terrain of her romantic wanderings. She burns a lot of bridges behind her, sometimes needlessly.

Ruth was in therapy with me. She repeatedly warned me (really herself) that she expected a "blowup" between us at any time. She was then in a Scorpio phase, tying up loose threads, going through a divorce, and recovering from a hysterectomy. Our therapeutic relationship never blew up. What this taught her experientially is that she could not only get along with another woman (a rare experience for Ruth), but that she also need not cut herself off from old contacts when entering a new phase.

All too often, the Scorpio Woman appears haughty, jealous, and demanding when in fact she is covering up insecurity. She suffers from deep feelings of mistrust and isolation. She may lead on a man by her mysterious calm. She may test him mercilessly with sudden twists and turns of behavior. She almost never discloses her expectations of him, and he may be trapped into failing to match them. But if he knows nothing of what she wants, how can he measure up?

The Scorpio Woman often acts like the Queen of Hearts in *Alice in Wonderland*. She holds back, watches for transgressions, and without explanation shouts, "Off with his head!" No wonder people are bewildered by her.

She is constantly testing the limits of the loyalty of friends and lovers. She may also alienate many people in the process, though deep down she may continue to need their support. I have often wondered if what drives her to test and to cut ties so drastically is her deep fear of losing in relationships. As long as she still considers them a battle of loyalties or of the sexes, she will continue to try to win at any cost.

Scorpio, I advise you to take a close look at (1) your expectations of people; and (2) what you give in return for what you expect. Also, *moderation* is a key word. I suggest you tack it on your mirror, kitchen cabinets, or windshield until the meaning penetrates.

Jealousy

Jealousy in the Scorpio Woman's Achilles' heel, her very own double standard. She may have sex with more than one partner, but she will not tolerate the situation in reverse. We don't know if jealousy is a learned or inborn behavior, but it seems to me that in Scorpio's case it may be a double portion of each. Her jealousy is written in large letters, in indelible ink that never seems to rub off.

Often her jealousy lies dormant until some small thing lights the fuse. An explosion can be ignited by a passing remark from the Scorpio Woman's lover about Jacqueline Bisset's chest. If her man watches the waitress cross the restaurant or lingers at the neighbor's, Scorpio may conclude that he is straying. Fireworks may be easier to cope with than sulking, but both may occur with regularity.

Coping with jealousy

The Scorpio Woman can cope with the green-eyed monster only by detaching herself. To practice detachment, she must change her thinking.

Scorpio, my advice is this: *think*. Your mate is almost certainly *not* doing things to annoy you. He is simply engaging in behavior that is pleasurable or familiar to him. He may not even know how much it bothers you. Communicate and be more tolerant. It is another thing altogether if your lover is playing on your natural jealousy, however. In this case, you might explore with him whether he is feeling angry with you or insecure in the relationship. Using someone's weaknesses is destructive and has no place in a healthy relationship.

Another step in detachment and mental reprogramming is meditation. Meditation will help you overcome the source of your jealousy—your own ego. What follows is a simplified recipe for self-hypnosis. I recommend a weekend seminar on the subject for further exploration. Remember, too, that any form of meditation is not a cure-all; it may take some time for the effects to show, and it is in no way a substitute for therapy.

Self-hypnosis is a good start on the road to self-healing. To practice self-hypnosis, begin by sitting comfortably. If you can, use the lotus position. Program the length of time you wish to spend meditating. Choose a quiet time and set a timer. The usual duration of this exercise is three to five minutes, though some people meditate for much longer. Look at three objects of your choice, then slowly reduce your concentration to one alone.

1 Very slowly, letting the words drone, tell yourself you *see*, *hear*, and *feel* three things:
   a I see a candle, I see a house, I see a book.
   b I hear music, silence, a child.
   c I feel cozy, warm, happy.
2 Repeat, but with only two things.
3 Repeat again, but this time with just one thing.
4 Be quiet for a time.
5 Focus on your hands and see which one seems lighter. Let the lighter hand come up and touch your face.
6 Tell yourself you like yourself and also your lover. Tell yourself this three times. Then . . .
7 twice. Then . . .
8 just once.
9 You may repeat this, substituing *love* for *like*.
10 Blank your mind, breathe evenly, remain in the same position as long as you can.

You can use this self-hypnosis program to decrease jealousy (envy, fear, guilt) and slowly substitute positive sensations. The root of good feelings is self-love. Work on that, and give it lots of time.

The Scorpio Woman in love

When she is in love, the Scorpio Woman can be a sexy pussycat. She is a giver. She can organize life to suit her man. If he wants his pipe by the easy chair, his slippers by the fire, dinner on time, and sex galore, she'll make sure he gets it all.

Eliminate her jealousy or anger, and the Scorpio Woman is miles ahead of the rest of us in her use of will power. Even with her problems, she is fascinating and effective.

Among the roles she may choose to play to please her man (and incidentally to further her own interests) are those of an exquisite hostess, a nurse, a wife, a partner, and a lover. If her husband dislikes making decisions, she will make them. If he dislikes decisive females, she will make decisions indirectly if she wants to.

Almost nothing fazes her. I once knew a lady who must have been a Scorpio type, judging from her devotion to making herself her husband's indispensable ally. When he took up balloon racing, she took up sky diving in the same club. I know a lumberyard that is completely owned and managed by Scorpio sun signs. The wife of the owner helps her husband cope with nervous customers, represents the company at marketing meetings, and still goes home to fix dinner and keep house every day. As long as she chooses, she can be as diplomatic as Libra, as patient as Taurus, as intensely ambitious as Capricorn. But please be aware that this is a phase. She must want to do it of her own free will, and she must be paid back for it, sooner or later.

You can never discount the Scorpio Woman's hidden motives. She is savvy in planning the best of everything, and her ultimate goal is to safeguard her own interests. In love, she will make sure to guard her man against other flirtations. She will protect her loved ones from disease, injustice, inconvenience. A note to remember: she likes to make others dependent on her. She usually operates out of a calculated strategy and retains a deep, secret core of separateness.

In short, the Scorpio Woman has mastered the art of being indispensable. Within reason this is healthy. She tries to design her present as well as her future, for she believes that if she does not protect her interests, no one else will. However, the Scorpio Woman can easily cross the thin line between self-protection and permanent manipulation of others for her own ends, She must be constantly *aware* of what she is doing and why, and she must incorporate open communication into long-term contacts.

Scorpio may reserve the right to please herself above all. Those recently come of age are more able to do this than an earlier generation that was brought up on the lesson that selfishness is all bad.

Patterns in the Scorpio Woman's sexual relationships

1 An unusually large number of liaisons from early adolescence on, or else a very delayed sexual coming-of-age.
2 Sudden early infatuation leading to a surprise marriage, or else an unusually late marriage. Scorpio marries once and tries to marry for keeps. Though divorce is more prevalent now, she will not give up on a troubled marriage or primary relationship until, and unless, she has tried everything to keep it going.
3 Extramarital sex sooner or later, or, if not, obsession with work, food, alcohol, or sexual fantasies.
4 Crisis in her main relationship. She must anticipate this and work with it rather than play ostrich. Crisis in relationships is a fact of her life. Her ultimate destiny is to transform and purify her love and her sexual nature. Whether the changes are good or bad is up to her, but changes she will have.
5 Survival of crisis and attainment of a higher level of consciousness. If this happens in the context of a relationship, that relationship will totally change it. If it dies, another relationship will come along, often completely different from the last.
6 Continuation of cycle. She may go back to step 3 and start all over or swear off sex for awhile.
7 Attainment of a new stage of holistic living. Here, she can harmonize power urges and personal fulfilment (see chapter 13, "The Cosmic Woman").

Lovers and husbands

The Scorpio Woman above all needs a strong, intuitive, and tolerant male. He must be physically strong to keep up with her libido, emotionally healthy and intuitive so as to facilitate her own liberation.

She needs a man who does not have overly rigid expectations of her and does not attempt to *judge* her by his expectations. She is intuitive enough to be made uncomfortable by a man who is heavily judgmental. She is also apt to change radically too often to stay with a man who will not change along with her.

She is too ambitious to stay with a prissy, insecure male who needs a mother figure. She likes to be needed, but she also has mighty sexual needs that would not be satisfied by this type of man.

She needs a man who will help her balance her unbalanced nature, who is neither a psychic sadist nor a vampire nor an emotional masochist. Give-and-take, strength and tolerance, are keys to a successful connection with her.

She needs a man who is powerful in his own right. He need not be on a crusade to change the world, though she may be. He should be like Gary Cooper, possessing a quietly macho sense of self that neither threatens nor gives an inch.

The Scorpio Woman needs a man who will stand up to her but will also cater to her femininity. If they go out to dinner, for example, she wants him to have a game plan. If he did not phone ahead for a reservation, he should at least insist on the restaurant and the time, and advise her about the menu. Or if there is a question of a move, she expects him to put himself ahead of her (to her, proof of masculine strength), but she will bitterly contest his doing so. They may fight the issue past the breaking point, but if he tells her he will forgo a promotion because of her, she will think him stupid for passing up a good chance. After all she herself would not have.

She needs a man who can stay one step ahead of her nimble games but never rub it in. She expects to win the games she plays, but heaven help the man who loses too often.

She needs a man who understands how to be and feel positive. The man who is good for her will use techniques like meditation and will constantly help her to focus her psychic powers on constructive things.

She needs a man who is highly sexual and whose repertoire, stamina, and interest in sex match hers. If she is sexually repressed (see "Scorpio Sexuality"), she needs a man who will bring out her latent animal passions and help her to time-release deeply buried hostilities.

She needs a man who is more trusting than she, who will cut through her defensive armor, who will never hide in a corner when company comes or sink into resentful silence when he is upset. She needs an articulate extrovert with a sunny nature. She needs a man with a child's sense of humor.

My advice to her men is as follows:

1 Beware of making her your enemy. Should you break off stormily, go back and patch up the friendship later.
2 Be aware that most of her relationships before age thirty-five are based on some kind of battle plan for control or power, even if she herself doesn't know it.
3 If you are her friend or mate, I suggest you take a good course in self-assertiveness and couple communication. It is likely that you'll have to lead her to engage in fair discussion, frank self-revelation, and active listening.

The Scorpio Woman must make a special effort to carry out the "continuing acts of self-revelation" that are the backbone of a good relationship. And she must learn to opt for love instead of ownership.

Scorpio sexuality

Scorpio is synonymous with sex in people's minds—and for good reason! The sirens in the *Odyssey*, the Queen of the Night in Mozart's *Magic Flute*, Marguerite in Goethe's *Faust*, Joan Crawford, Ava Gardner, Indira Gandhi—all have the Scorpio Woman's smoldering sex appeal, earthy shrewdness, unusual looks, and hypnotic tones.

The Scorpio Woman is an enchantress with a hot body and a cool mind. Her magic telegraphs the promise of instant, permanent arousal and deep, far-reaching sex. She may not be a traditional beauty, but the potent vibrations she radiates add up to drama, stature, and mystery.

Scorpio sexuality has reached the proportions of myth. Mention that you are a Scorpio Woman to people at a party and see them react! They may draw back, giggle, wink at you, or start an inquisition. Tell your son's teacher that you're a Scorpio, and she'll shoot you a look of reappraisal. For to be a Scorpio Woman instantly transforms you from "Chuck's mother" into a woman with the sex drive of a truck driver and the versatility of a geisha.

The Scorpio Woman has quite a sexual legend to live up to. It is also one that she expertly continues creating. Depending on how comfortable she is with her own sexuality, the Scorpio sexual myth can be a lifelong burden or a boon to her social life.

Sex is still the most potent attention-getter in our country.

Money ranks a close second, death a distant third. The Scorpio Woman is as much at home in the land of amours as with the affairs of the dead. No one could ask for a more multidimensional woman.

She is intense and polarized about everything in her life, including sex. Her sexual potency can be compressed or repressed under certain circumstances, or released in an explosive, lush sensuality.

We hear much more of her insatiability than of her sexual problems. Yet the fact is that she can carry her sexual inhibitions to an extreme. She suffers from a hidden, deep-seated insecurity; a periodic need to escape into sexual abstention; and an underlying obsession with "purification," which can lead her to asexuality (no sex) or masturbation.

Her opposite sign is Taurus, and her subconscious nature reflects the still, deep well of self-doubt associated with this sign. After many years of observation and psycho-astrological work, I suspect that some of the Scorpio Woman's frantic sexual activity is a cover-up for her streak of Taurean insecurity.

There are two key words to help one understand her sexuality. *Variation* is one. She needs variation in her sex life. She is as dependent on it as a jet is on a clear runway. Landing and taking off, bumpy and smooth rides—the Scorpio Woman desires varied sexual experience.

Power is the other key word. Her biggest sex secret is that sex is almost never her real goal. It's power she's after. The Scorpio Woman often uses sex as a means to an end. However much she enjoys sex, she rarely forgets that it is the most potent weapon in her arsenal of tools for domination and survival. She wields sex to score points, vanquish an opponent, gain entry, or increase her influence. She uses sex to hook her mate into exclusive dependence or, just as often, to boost herself higher on the ladder of success.

Early sex experiences

Nothing the Scorpio Woman does is simple. There are always two extreme paths for her, and her sex life is no different. As an adolescent and young adult, she is either extremely repressed and avoids sex altogether, or she is an early devotee of a full range of sexual activities. She may be a professional virgin or a sexual sophisticate.

The late-blooming route is taken by the Scorpio Woman who is brought up in a sexually inhibiting environment. Most often, it is a religious home or school where she is encouraged or forced to channel her energies away from sex.

If she is abused or grows up in a home without warmth, she is bound to withdraw into a secret world of fantasy. She may dream of wild adventures, of daring rescues or of bad princes who abduct and rape her. She may be depressed or sick throughout her teenage years. But repression and submission are seldom permanent. Sooner or later, she learns how to snatch mundane victory (status or leadership) from the jaws of sexual defeat. She is likely to rehearse it all in her dreams first.

The Scorpio girl may also choose the other extreme and develop sexually by age twelve. She may throw caution to the wind, rebel, and get to the bottom (or peak) of the much-touted experience we call sex. She may take risks that drive authorities wild. Rizzo, the leader of the female street gang in *Grease,* engaged in this kind of behavior and ended with an unwanted pregnancy.

The Scorpio girl is apt to be unpopular with other girls and usually has only one confidante. She is secretive and suffers in silence. Her sexual activities in her youth and later may be a partial compensation for the loneliness she almost inevitably feels as a teenager.

She often develops a mad crush on a female teacher at twelve or thirteen and then transfers it to a male. Most teenage girls do this, but the Scorpio female (or the girl in the Scorpio phase) does it to excess. She may be ridiculed for it.

As an adolescent, she usually broods a lot, is preoccupied with death, and may be convinced that love will elude her forever. Because of the inherent nature of Scorpio, she is also bound to be exposed to some unusual sexual situations. Incest, hidden affairs, sexual cruelty, drugs, and associations with undesirables may all be part of the scene around her.

Scorpio is usually infatuated with unrequited love, which seems to allow her to indulge her latent masochism. She is almost uniformly, totally heterosexual. She frequently loses her virginity by the end of high school. If she resists temptation, she may do so out of the mistaken belief that chastity will help her control her desires altogether. In fact, it may do the opposite. Bottling up sexual tension can create a Mount Vesuvius inside her.

By twenty, she has usually wrapped some mesmerized males around her fingers—or thighs, as the case may be. She is well on her way to flowering into a sexual activist. She is willing to dish out sex and take it in return.

Love and sex

She was born for sex and power; love does not necessarily enter into her calculations. She may truly love her primary partner, but she will always keep the door open for times when she may desire variety or a more long-winded performance. She tends to outdo her lovers in stamina and the need for variation. Orthodox faithfulness is not her bag.

Mostly it is she who is in charge of the sexual relationship. She casts the roles, choreographs the movements, chooses the decor and the timing. She is a sex star, and though her body may run to fat later, she will keep it supple enough to imitate the positions taught in the Kama Sutra.

She is a demanding, lusty lover and—let's face it—hard to satisfy. Faint-hearted men need not apply. But most people would also agree that she deserves a round of applause for her unfailing attention to sex and generally honest expression of her passions.

The most positive aspect of her sexuality, however she employs it, is that she herself truly prizes it. She seldom has to be persuaded to have sex despite herself. She rarely gets "headaches." If she gets grumpy about menstrual cramps, she will try to follow experts' advice and relieve them by climaxing. In respect to sexual desire, she is a liberated woman.

The Scorpio Woman is inquisitive and experimental. She is nearly compulsive about having to try things. Standard props in her head or in her bed include S-and-M equipment, dresses, panties and bras that titillate, leather outfits, bondage accessories, drugs, candles—everything that saturates the environment with eroticism. She may be a groupie who adores the feel of satin sheets, the smell of marijuana, the beat of music, and a different sex partner every day.

She is wired, emotional, selfish but fiercely loyal, and more sensitive than we might suspect. She would probably be the first to nod approvingly at the notion of female superiority. In the area of sex, she thinks she is probably light-years ahead of her sisters. I won't dispute her.

Once the Scorpio Woman turns on, she hardly ever wants to stop. It's as if she harbors an eternal flame that keeps her lit and ready. And the more sexually aroused she is, the more uninhibited and dominant she becomes.

Her sexual response during intercourse seems to take the following pattern:

1 Initial reluctance before getting aroused.
2 Sudden arousal (she may then flip her man over and make love to him, though moments before she appeared cool and remote).
3 Total involvement; uninhibited building to orgasm.
4 Intense orgasm (some have a pattern of sexual peaks and valleys, and report that later orgasms are the most satisfying).

What kind of lover she needs

A man who is beside himself with passion, whispers obscene words in her ears, lets go with grunts and heavy breathing, and provides lots of stimulation in the pelvic region is the Scorpio Woman's idea of sexual heaven. It helps if he has vast reservoirs of physical strength.

She usually likes oral sex, and a few have told me of having orgasms while performing fellatio. Others have said that words alone can be so arousing as to put them on the verge of orgasm. The Scorpio Woman usually likes hard thrusts and cervical stimulation by the penis. She may become an aficionado of anal sex.

She wants a man who has a high sex drive and has learned total control of his own responses. A multiorgasmic male is a sure winner. Her fantasy male is a combination of Charlton Heston, Charles Bronson, James Bond, and John Travolta. A bit of sadism, a lot of visual appeal, hair and macho, a dash of sensitivity, and total sexual expertise will surely capture her.

She dislikes a man who is reluctant in oral sex and uneasy about her ambitious sex stragegy. If he is physically impotent, she may be patient with him because she wants to give herself total pleasure—via him. If he is psychologically impotent, she will drop him. She seldom tolerates a weakling, a man who crumples under pressure.

The Scorpio Woman enjoys sex in exotic places, at least in her fantasies. The back of a hearse, the seat on a night flight to Istanbul, the toilet of a 747, a public beach with a conveniently placed sand dune, a phone booth—all are great locations for her sexual fantasies. She may well turn these fantasies into reality.

She likes strongly scented lubricants, kinky sex aids, home porno films, pleasuring condoms. She often gets turned on by hard-core sex catalogues, erotic sculptures, sexy records. I suspect that a Scorpio is responsible for that ingenious recent invention, the flexible shower hose with power nozzle. How else could a woman masturbate to her heart's content in the bathtub?

The Scorpio Woman is interested in exploring sexual taboos. Her body image is usually fair to good unless she is in one of her slumps. In this phase, nothing can convince her she is attractive, but just as surely she'll make a comeback. If she is preorgasmic, the earth will truly move and comets cross the sky when she releases her blocks and finally explodes with orgasm. (There are now groups around the country to help preorgasmic women. There is also an excellent manual called *For Yourself*, by Lonnie Barbach.)

Scorpio's inner sexual conflicts center around her emotional sadomasochism. *Forum* magazine receives more than fifty thousand letters a year from readers all over the world. Of these, it is estimated that more than thirty percent come from readers involved with S-and-M. It is clear, then, that large numbers of people are into sadomasochism, whether in fantasy or reality.

The Scorpio Woman is naturally a slave driver. She compels men to serve her. She uses everything from her hypnotic eyes to her beckoning thighs to make a man submit. She satisfies more of his desires than he ever knew he had, though she may also drive him crazy with her demands, jealousy, and crises.

She wants to find a man who is her equal in all domains, and she tests him endlessly. The testing is done mostly through attempts to dominate him sexually. She will try to break her partner in, and in some cases to break him down. She goes for broke.

The Scorpio Woman has an inborn dominatrix side. She is interested in some of the basic S-and-M practices, either in fantasy or in reality, often taking the role of the mistress. Some basic S-and-M fetishes and fantasies concern legs, feet, nylons, and clothing made of fur, leather, and rubber. Some of the men she fantasizes about or actually dominates may wear lipstick, long fingernails, and long hair. Others want to be walked on with spike-heeled shoes or boots. But bondage is most common. Her bondage scenes or fantasies range from tying a man to a bedpost with nylons while she takes over and runs the scene to tying and stretching him on a medieval X-shaped contraption to simple spanking. In reality, the limits would be set by the man, for such scenes are controlled by the masochist.

The Scorpio Woman, even if she is an inexperienced housewife, is capable of dreaming up elaborate sexual scenarios in which she has the star's control. She is also likely to fantasize about the feel of rubber or leather on her as she controls a man who is acting out her fantasy. She is nothing if not a totally sexual creature, with the balls to carry out anything any man dares her to do—if of course, it also pleases her.

But, in spite of her brash roughness, she has her masochistic side too. She is no stranger to unfulfilled longing and pain, and this affects her sex life. Typically, her earlier suffering has programmed her to incorporate the subconscious expectation to suffer. She may act this out by letting herself be spanked, tied, or forced to submit to her mate's wishes; or she may desire to have sex that leaves her bruised and limp with exhaustion.

Masochistic fantasies or acts may also have their root in guilt. No Western woman as dominating as she is escapes the guilt that arises from her own power.

What she needs to learn

The Scorpio Woman must be aware of all her sides and not expect a perfect mesh. Until she understands herself, she will be victimized by her own desires. She may deny her masochism and compensate by being female macho; or she may deny her strength by going with her need to submit to domination.

The Scorpio Woman needs to learn to remove the "bad" labeling this culture has taught her to attach to some of her most basic drives. For example:

—She is highly sexed, but not a whore.
—She is competitive, but not a frigid career woman.
—She wants to win, and she needs to accept this.
—She likes primeval sex play, and she must realize that deep down, just about everyone likes to let go and be pleasured.

Scorpio anger

The Scorpio Woman accumulates anger slowly but surely. Usually holds it back as securely as she would tie a baby to her back. She appears as cool and calm as the eye of a storm. But the calm of the eye has never yet stopped the storm from raging. When she finally lets her anger out, it explodes and causes a domestic, interpersonal Pompeii. Egos get buried and relationships sometimes die as a result of her inability to cope with her anger. She is a grudge bearer; don't let her secrecy and outward calm deceive you.

On anger

I interviewed several Scorpio women, and here are some typical responses:

1 "I try not to get angry. When I do, I feel so outrageous that I'm sure I'll get mine."
2 "I'm almost never angry. It wasn't until your questions made me think, that I realized that for me to be angry is cataclysmic. The moment I am angry, I become a total bitch."
3 "I'm never angry at the things I should get angry at, like social injustice. Instead, I get angry and kick the dog when he eats his bone on the carpet. I seem to get angry mostly over petty things."

The first person is indicating that she feels guilty whenever she acts angry. This woman has a strong religious background, and was raised with the idea that anger, like any "sinful" behavior, can only bring down the wrath of authority. When she joined one of my classes on the constructive uses of anger, she was having difficulty reaching orgasm during intercourse. She was highly orgasmic while masturbating, however. It became clear during the course of the class that she was going through a typical Scorpio phase. She was angry inside almost all the time, and the anger was catching up with her now that she was under the general life stress of separations and endings. The accumulation of old, unvented anger directly affected her sex life.

The second woman, Beth is a sophisticated person in her mid-forties. Her upbringing taught her that anger means being a "bad girl," so she chooses not to get angry. I asked her what she does with her pent-up anger. At the start of our acquaintance, she told me that she handles anger by ignoring it. But two months later, she came to see me visibly upset. I found out that her mother-in-law had been visiting and had stirred up feelings of hostility that Beth thought she had controlled.

You cannot ignore anger and hope it will go away. It just shifts ground. Eventually, angry people develop sexual and relational problems. These may show up in family interactions, body image, or sexual functioning (difficulty reaching orgasm or lack of sexual desire, for example). In Beth's case, her sex life had ground to a halt.

The third speaker, Lila, is overweight, bright, and quite angry. Her husband is out of work, and she must support both of them. She dislikes her job, is upset with her husband, and wants to go into business for herself. However, she has no time to develop her plans, and she never has enough money, either. Lila is displacing her anger onto "safe" things. It is safer to kick the dog than her husband or boss. The dog may growl at her, but he will not have the power to divorce or fire her.

As long as Lila refuses to confront the real issues that make her angry—which she must eventually do if she is to change her life and be happier—she will continue to vent her anger on "petty" things. Incidentally, she is not turned on by her husband at all right now.

These three women are typical of a pattern. Their parents probably sent them to bed without supper when, as little girls, they displayed anger. They were probably all raised in a religious or puritanical atmosphere. Left to sit alone and contemplate the "wickedness" of their anger, they grew up believing that showing it is sinful and dangerous. In their subconscious, anger probably became linked with another area that almost all of us are raised to consider sinful and dangerous—sexuality. We know from recent research that jailing people often begets *more,* not less, aggressive behavior. This goes for little girls, too.

The Scorpio Woman was probably trained to be sorry for her anger whenever she showed it. Typically, she grew up feeling guilty about it and fearing it. But because she is a very intense woman who harbors an emotional volcano, she can no more deny herself expression, be it of love or of anger, than we can tell the moon to forget about influencing the tides.

Anger is particularly poisonous for Scorpio because it attacks her sex drive first and foremost. This is because, as I mentioned before, she is most susceptible in her first chakra (the sex center). Rob the Scorpio Woman of her sex drive, and you will see a sorry creature, bereft of her mightiest source of power and energy. I strongly advise her to relinquish her hold on guilt and fear when it comes to the expression of anger.

Expressing anger

Scorpio, the following is a basic guide to help you deal with anger:

1 Learn to identify your anger. Use the following as your best clues:
   a Your body language. If you are leaning forward, flashing your eyes, pointing your fingers, and jabbing the air, you are probably angry.
   b Your verbal expressions. Learn to identify the expressions you commonly use to disguise or communicate anger.
   c Your feelings of stress. What part of your body does it hit? Are you sick right now? When did it start? See if you can figure out a pattern for times you feel ill or angry.
   d Whatever is going on in your life right now. Is there anything you would think might be making you angry?
   e Other people's reactions. These provide a mirror for you. Are people treating you patiently and lovingly, or are you inundated with hostile vibes from others? If it's the latter, take a look at some of your own.
2 Identify what kind of anger you feel. Anger can be:
   a Situational (impersonal, professional situations).
   b Family (interpersonal).
   c The wall (free floating; does not seem to be situational or family-related).
3 Determine what can help you cope with anger on the job:
   a Establish your goals, both short- and long-term.
   b Define your resources (or power leverage):
      i Credentials
      ii Past contributions
      iii Personal power
      iv People you work with
      v Connections in your field
      vi Savings that make you feel able to take a risk and leave the job
4 Determine what can help you cope with anger in personal situations:
   a Have a sense of humor.
   b Maintain a positive attitude.
   c Develop detachment.
   d Stick to specifics when discussion begins.

e Speak up; do not remain silent.
f Cry
g Relax.
h Do not become threatened or take the other's reaction too personally.
i If you must throw a tantrum, try to do it alone. If you must scream and your partner is there, preface it by saying, "I am going to let steam out because if I don't, I'll burst. Please leave the room if it bothers you. We'll carry on after I'm finished."

The most important thing to remember when you are trying to cope with your anger is this: *Anger is a reaction. When you feel angry, it is because something in your personality or belief system tells you that you ought to react by being angry. Anger, like love, is a choice you make based on subconscious needs and values.* In other words, the most effective intervention spot is right in your own belief system.

If a construction worker whistles at you, you can get angry, or you can smile. If your mother tells you you don't raise your kids right, you can get angry, you can try to meet her for lunch and explain your point of view, or you can detach yourself from her perspective. Any time you can control your reaction, you are in charge.

Whenever anger affects her sex life, the Scorpio Woman must first recognize what is happening and then take action. The most effective action is to prepare to discuss what is happening with her mate. If Scorpio cannot control her anger within any rational guidelines, she might consider a therapy that will allow her to express it physically. Primal scream and bioenergetics are two therapy approaches that encourage unloading anger directly and powerfully.

Scorpio lifestyles

I do not believe marriage is obsolete. Most of us are still looking for love, and marriage is still the most popular place in which to find and sustain love. The divorce rate in America may be unprecedentedly high, but I predict that the marriage rate, too, will increase in the 1980s.

The Scorpio Woman is not ideal marriage material, for orthodox faithfulness usually eludes her. But if someone wants an earnest, loyal, intensely involved mate with fascinating surprises in store, she is all that and more.

She may marry too early or too late to fit the norm. That is, she may jump into a hasty marriage before twenty or wait until midlife. If her husband is a better general than she is, her marriage will probably last, though it will sustain many crises.

She may drive her husband crazy because she is sex-struck and she can't get enough; or she may drive him wild because she suddenly enters a drought and no amount of water can revitalize her thirst. "All or nothing" remains her motto.

The Scorpio Woman is often a model wife at the start of her marriage. She caters to her man, is faithful, involved, and always on his side. He may think he has picked the most remarkable woman on earth. This may be true—if you stretch the definition of *woman* to include some critical changes.

Scorpio often seeks sex outside her love nest once the initial glow wears off. She wants deep, endless passion in her man. If her husband falls short of her wishes, only guilt or illness will hold her back; but like a phoenix, she may rise above those too.

If she picks a sex partner outside marriage, she wants lust, thrill, abandon, endurance, and a teasing possessiveness. She would like to pretend she is her new man's one and only, even if he is Number 5 on her list.

Lady Scorpio can routinely split love from sex. She can keep her love, economic status, and security needs safely bound to her home life while she unleashes her sexual passions on other grounds. Lady Chatterley is not far away.

Monogamy and nonmonogamy

Monogamy is defined as a lifestyle of exclusivity with one's mate. We now use the word to denote *sexual* exclusivity, though the dictionary includes emotional exclusivity as well.

Monogamy means that extramarital intercourse is out, though friendship between the sexes is permissable. On this definition, anything short of intercourse still keeps one monogamous. (I've always wondered what to do with our sexual fantasies. If a woman makes love with her husband and only fantasizes about her neighbor, is she still faithful?)

The Scorpio Woman usually remains monogamous when she is in the honeymoon phase of her marriage, when she is transiting a masochistic or asexual phase, or when she is suffering from guilt and tries to make up for it by suppressing her libido. The honeymoon phase can return several times during the course of her marriage, and it usually follows a major turning point.

Few men can keep up with her emotional and physical demands, or with the roller-coaster life she leads. Therefore, few Scorpio Women stay sexually faithful to their husbands all their lives.

Somewhere in the depths of her being, the Scorpio Woman harbors a vision of an ideal sexual experience—torrid, spiritual, and so unifying that it defies verbal description. Someplace inside her, she is constantly on the alert for her soulmate, possibly from another lifetime.

If she falls in love with a man who is not her husband, she is bound to be tortured by guilt, for she is usually a devoted mate. But though she knows she runs this risk, she usually ignores it if a very desirable man knocks on her door, approaches her at a party, gives her a promotion, or dreams up an appealing fantasy to capture her. She can rarely resist verifying whether far-out techniques in seduction equal prowess in bed.

The following represent typical situations which could influence the Scorpio Woman to become nonmonogamous:

1 Search for new sexual experiences, for variation, for better lovers.
2 Sexual or emotional starvation.
3 Use of sex as a power ploy.
4 Need for reassurance about her own powers.
5 Misplaced anger at her mate, or free floating anger.
6 Fear of death. She is highly psychic and is drawn to death and destruction fantasies. She believes in goblins, gremlins, ghosts and the bad witch. In the course of her life, she may turn to prayer, psychic seances or healing, or new sex partners to exorcise her dark thoughts.
7 Drug addiction, and possible use of sex to acquire drugs.
8 Submission to a powerful fantasy man, someone who can dominate her for a time.

Alternative lifestyles

Single woman: When Scorpio is into this, she is wholly committed. When she is ready to change it, she'll throw herself headlong into a new lifestyle. For a time, this option is good for her, especially if she is very involved professionally or in nursing her wounds after a love affair. However, she should not stay alone for long if she is depressed. Scorpio Women are periodically suicidal and need others to brighten their lives.

Intimate networks: This movement advocates friendship with both sexes, neither ruling out nor enforcing sexual involvements. For it to work, the Scorpio Woman must overcome her inhibitions and her distrust of females especially; she must also stop seeing all men as potential bed partners and loyal sex subjects.

Open marriage: Scorpio is not a sharer, and though she may want the adventure of open marriage, the experiment won't last.

Ménage à trois: It's fine for Scorpio if the third person is a man or a female who's into submission. In all, a possible temporary adventure.

Group marriage: Scorpio is far too jealous for this lifestyle to work, in spite of the possible security, sexual variety, and emotional richness it can provide. Unless she is a very wise and detached Scorpio Woman, it won't work.

Communes: Here Scorpio has the same problem she encounters in group marriage. I will add, however, that as we enter the Aquarian age, such groups are becoming more popular. In the long run, this may make a difference, but for now Scorpio is normally too ego-bound and possessive to enter a commune.

Gay/bisexual lifestyle: The Scorpio Woman is one of the most irrevocably heterosexual of women. She may not totally reject bisexuality, because her yen for sexual experimentation is alive and well, but she almost never is interested in the gay lifestyle. She links sex with power, and it's still men who have the latter.

Summing up Scorpio

Integrative power, or the power of cooperation and love, is probably the most universal goal of people who have lived, survived crises, and developed some awareness of self and the meaning of life. Achieving integrative power is the particular challenge of the Scorpio Woman. She has the power both of healing and of destruction, and both to an extreme. She is at once impotent Cassandra and raging Clytemnestra (as all women are, to perhaps a lesser degree).

Integrative power does not arise from trying to fit someone else's model. Integrative power is found only in a deep awareness of one's own being and potential, only in a profound respect for the earth on which we live and depend.

We are each on earth for a purpose. Each of us has the potential to live a life of significance and meaning. Our purpose will be realized neither in the abdication of power (Cassandra) nor in the brutual seizure of power of the wrong kind (Clytemnestra). The special task of the Scorpio Woman is to overcome the misuse of power and arrive at the point where she uses power in the service of love, the truly integrative force.

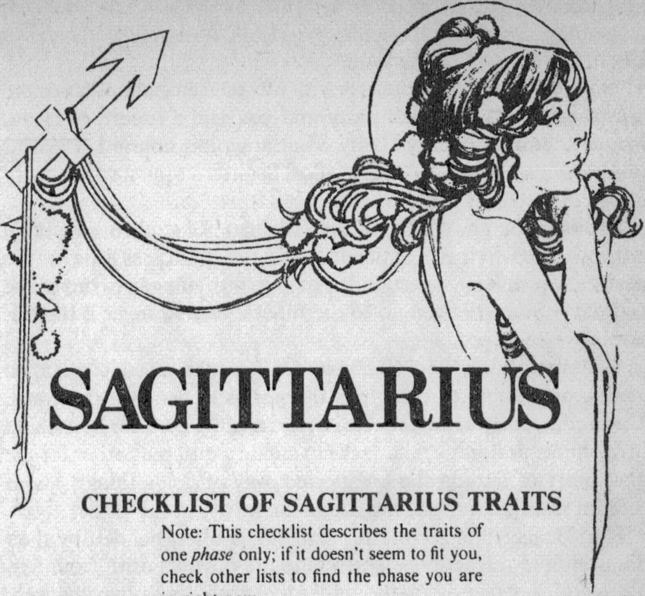

SAGITTARIUS

CHECKLIST OF SAGITTARIUS TRAITS

Note: This checklist describes the traits of one *phase* only; if it doesn't seem to fit you, check other lists to find the phase you are in right now.

1. Expansive
2. Always in Motion
3. High-spirited
4. Jovial
5. Blunt
6. Trustworthy
7. Gullible
8. Eager
9. Joyous
10. Optimistic
11. Lucky
12. Extravagant
13. Giving
14. Enchanting
15. Charming
16. Flashy
17. Exhibitionistic
18. Adaptable
19. Versatile
20. Scholarly
21. Pompous
22. Slapdash
23. Impulsive
24. Intuitive
25. Good Judgment
26. Musical
27. Cultural Patron
28. Independent
29. Progressive
30. Explorer
31. Far-out
32. Inspirational
33. Patriotic
34. Philosophic
35. Spiritual

Sagittarius personality

General traits and background

The Sagittarius Woman pulses with life and sensuality. When the crowd parts at a cocktail party and you feel a breeze of clean, woodsy, animal energy, Lady Sagittarius has entered. Idealist, philosopher, and lusty conquistador, Sagittarius pursues her every desire in the spirit of the centaur.

Even on the go, the Sagittarius Woman is a study in perpetual motion. She will travel at the drop of a hat. She cares little for the destination as long as it sounds exciting, intriguing, and out of the ordinary. She will even go to the funeral of a stranger if there is noplace else to go.

Sameness bores her. She continually seeks greener pastures, sometimes failing to recognize the jewels in her own backyard. She is constantly in the process of rearranging. Be it her household furnishings or her life, she seeks to create a different order for the possibility of finding the one perfect way of doing things. She is seldom satisfied that she has found the way.

Her ideals shine so brightly that she is often blinded by their diamondlike refractions, which hide the obvious truth from her. She espouses causes of the underdog, truly loves her children, cherishes her family, yet sometimes loses herself and her causes as she pursues the ideal state of things.

She has a strong sense of propriety. She shops at all the right stores, reads all the right books, belongs to the right clubs—anything that enhances her social status and sense of self-worth.

The Sagittarius Woman monitors her actions very carefully, for she has one of the most conservative of natures. She believes in conserving everything from the nation's natural resources to string and old wrapping paper, but she does not want to be offensive in doing so. Her drawers will be stuffed full of odds and ends that she is keeping for just the right moment. She is very personal in her habits and will never make an issue out of her saving; she assumes that everyone else will share her high ideals.

Jane Fonda, a New Age Sagittarius, typifies the high ideals and determination of the Sagittarius Woman. She seeks to operate within the existing structure, although her ideas are of a kind that would bring dramatic change to society. She seeks to be far ahead of the crowd. She is a perfect example of the progressive, committed Sagittarius Woman. Her political ideals carry over into her artistic and personal life, and she uses all her talent and influence to raise the consciousness of her audience. Her inquisitive, independent mind and above all her fresh, direct, and supple sensuality have set a new standard for her sex.

Sagittarius is the ninth house of the Zodiac, and it is Mutable Fire. Her mutability imparts a love of people and a versatile, adaptable quality to her myriad relationships; the fire provides her intense energy and her often revolutionary spirit.

Each astrological sign is said to be "ruled" by a planet and its vibrations. Sagittarius is ruled by Jupiter, the largest planet in our solar system, and the symbol of expansion and personal liberation. Historically, Jupiter has often been linked to the sun's brilliance and life-giving energies. Like Venus, Jupiter promises good fortune and material gifts, with the added attraction of long, exciting roads to explore.

The Sagittarius-*type* woman is one who has the sun or other important planets in Sagittarius, planets in the ninth house (the natural house of Sagittarius), a Sagittarius ascendant, or a powerfully aspected Jupiter. Sagittarius types are also those who are temporarily going through a Sagittarius *phase*. In this case, the person need have no planets located in the sign of Sagittarius. The Sagittarius type is described by the checklist of traits at the beginning of this chapter. The Sagittarius phase has the following characteristics:

1 Reliance on intuitive insights that flash through the mind and are usually right.
2 A high degree of versatility, the need to have more than one major task in life. She may conduct two careers or relationships simultaneously.
3 A heightened sense of energy and optimism, or of restlessness and boredom.
4 Provocative behavior, often to the point of abusiveness, or an unwittingly blunt and tactless manner with friends and lovers.
5 A deep desire for travel and exploration, whether geographic, sexual, or spiritual.
6 A sudden indifference to family ties in favor of dramatically different friends and lifestyle.
7 A deep interest in people, with many, many acquaintances but few friends.

The Sagittarius personality responds to the song "Don't Fence Me In." Where her relationships or her personal space is concerned, she becomes claustrophobic when in the corral. All fiery energy and purpose, the Sagittarius Woman pursues her goals with the clarity and vision of the archer.

But expansive Jupiter can dissipate her energies with the love of excessive food and drink, an inability to keep secrets, a brilliantly sarcastic wit, and even a violent temper, if she allows restlessness and boredom to overtake her. She may gallop after her skyward arrow into an extremely eccentric way of life.

The great Sagittarian determination can uproot these tendencies, however. She has the courage to perceive and transcend her own imbalance, and the strength to become a visionary her many friends and lovers will admire and follow. However, she will not allow others to place responsibility on her. She must choose to accept it herself.

A key word for Sagittarius is *illumination*. She seeks to know the truth that underlies the universe. Whether in music, art, or literature, she seeks to bring light where only shadows exist. The Sagittarius Woman subscribes to the proverbial "'Tis better to light one little candle than to curse the darkness." Her optimism is legendary. She observes people very carefully to gain a better understanding of why they do what they do. She learns from experience and seeks to experience all things that will help her unravel the secrets of the universe.

Another key word is *obedience*. She respects power and obeys what she feels is right, especially what she has learned from authority figures. She follows the laws of the land, the pressures of her peers, and the cultural dictates of her heritage with equal zest. She is very practical in her obedience to the societal rules, for she knows that this is the path to respect, success, and security. Although she is independent and avant-garde in her thinking, she is very conventional in her actions (excepting sexual actions), and she presents the image of a busy bee to the people around her.

Expansive, always in motion

The Sagittarius Woman is always on the go. She rarely sits still and usually requires a tremendous amount of exercise. This is especially true if she is bored with her work or is under pressure; you will often see her jogging at dawn and on the tennis courts at lunchtime.

She particularly loves field sports or any activity that allows her full freedom to roam. She often has horse fever as a child, and to this day, her greatest pleasure is a gallop through the open country. Not the type to tap her foot if the party is too slow or crowded, she may lead half your guests into the pool or up to the roof for a midnight game of volleyball.

The gypsy of the Zodiac, she moves with the same grace and power across a room or a continent. *But,* move she must. Stagnation, restlessness, and boredom will actually make her physically ill. The ailing Sagittarian can do more for her health with a quick and stimulating change of pace than with any rest cure or prescription.

The Sagittarius Woman dreams of expanding her influence as far as possible. The last Dowager Empress of China, Tsu Hsi, provides a good example, for through her intuitive power plays, she came to rule one-fourth of the world's population. Such is the extent of the Sagittarius Woman's dream if she becomes obsessed with power. She can become so attached to doing things in a big way that she neglects human needs.

High-spirited, jovial

The Sagittarius Woman loves people, and in great quantities. Her address book is like a city directory and is always completely up to date. Like Gemini, her opposite sign, she loves to mix and mingle at parties. Groups outings such as picnics, ballgames, and trips out into the country are even keener pleasures for her. She often finds enjoyment even in committee meetings since she measures her effective social standing and personal power by the sheer number of people she knows on a first-name basis.

Her sunshiny, jovial nature and her spirit of adventure will get the most grumblesome Cancerian to join in the fun. This type of gallivanting is so much what she loves, however, that she can fly off into a boisterousness that borders on the obnoxious. She may gallop headlong into an abrupt or unwitting remark and send that sensitive Crab packing. When the party is over and she finds herself alone with her balloon, crushed and dismayed in an empty arena, she will wonder what on earth went wrong.

Blunt

Sagittarius is the sign of the truth seeker, and the Sagittarius Woman is very, very honest. Honesty goes beyond the point of pride with her; she is constitutionally unable to lie without blundering. However, she far more often blunders with the truth, for honesty is the Sagittarian blind spot. She is unabashed about what she knows or feels, and she often seems to have the sensitivity of a Mack truck.

I once heard a Sagittarius Woman refer to a homosexual man she worked with as a "faggot." She immediately turned to a gay friend at the same party and said, "Of course, *you* aren't that type of gay *at all*." Once again, her bluntness had overtaken her good sense, and she was desperate to make amends.

Another side of the notorious Sagittarian indiscretion is disdain for dishonesty in others. She'd much rather blurt out the real truth "to set the record straight" than cope with her own discomfort in the face of someone else's illusions. This is especially true when her own life is filled with uncertainties. In her restless and irritable state, she can project her confusion onto everyone around her until her every remark cries out, "Can't you see?" In reality, she is the blind one, and until she takes herself in hand, she may make life miserable for everyone around her.

Sagittarian indiscretion is not cruel. The Sagittarius Woman doesn't make the razor comments her Scorpio sister might offer as "truth." But like a true archer, she will lose sight of all else at the moment of insight, and she'll let her arrow fly with little, if any, thought for what attendant emotion might be in its path. She is not insensitive, but rather insensate, at the "moment of truth." Anyone who recalls Agnes Moorehead as Endora in *Bewitched* knows this brand of "calling a spade a spade."

Those close to a Sagittarius Woman will do well to remember that she is, at times, still a wilderness creature, aware of human feelings from the heart up, but not necessarily below the belt.

Trustworthy

Sagittarius is as incapable of betrayal as she is of lying. Though you might be wary of asking what she thinks of your new hair color, you can trust her with your life—and in most cases, with your man as well. When she breaks a date with you, rest assured that it is for precisely the reason she states. If it is because she must watch over her sick dog or, equally likely, watch a soccer playoff on television, she will assume that you realize the importance of her excuse.

She is extremely loyal and will keep friends long after they have outlived their usefulness. Woe to the easily offended or the jealous; the suspicious and mistrustful lover should think twice before becoming involved with a Sagittarius Woman.

She is certainly trustworthy, but discretion is hardly her long suit. It is difficult for her to keep a secret. She so enjoys displaying her knowledge that she is apt to blurt out the most embarrassing information (told her in supposedly complete confidence).

The Sagittarius Woman also expects others to be trustworthy. When they don't live up to her standards in this respect, she becomes very disillusioned. If such problems cause a relationship to fail, she can become vindictive and sarcastic, telling the whole world all about it. She seems to don horse blinkers and trample over the feelings of those she feels deserve it.

Gullible

The Sagittarius Woman is as gullible as she is trustworthy. She will accept what you tell her at face value and never look beneath the surface for hidden meanings or intent. Again, woe to the shy, repressed, or indirect! You may never make your message clear to the Sagittarius Woman, who, quite frankly, can't see why people hem and haw as they do.

Undeceiving as she is, Sagittarius is often far too easy to deceive, though her strong intuition and her sense of independence protect her from most overt kinds of manipulation. More dangerous is the kind of confusion and conflict that may beset her relationships if she lacks the fine tuning to discern the subtle messages of her lovers and friends.

I worked with a Sagittarius woman who was involved in a particularly disjointed relationship with a Libra man. Her lover was unusually gentle and refined, with quiet manners and a delicate sensibility. Though their attraction was in most ways one of opposites, their shared love of culture and reportedly glorious sex life were a powerful bond. The problem lay in the fact that my friend couldn't take a hint (in fact, she needed little less than a point-blank statement) about any aspect of her conduct or their life together. Her man's approach was always veiled suggestion or broad hints, and she seemed to ignore his every remark and continue on her headstrong way. He began to express his irritation and resentment delicately; finally they both blew up. He decided that he couldn't bear her blind selfishness; she concluded that she couldn't stand his mealy-mouthed behavior; so they parted ways. To this day, she has no idea how something that had seemed so right ended so abruptly.

Eager, joyous, optimistic

The Sagittarius Woman rises early to embrace the sun. She welcomes each dawn as the beginning of a new adventure, with the potential for great challenge and discovery just around the corner. The prototypical Pollyanna, she will never let yesterday's disasters taint the possibilities of this morning. Tomorrow is indeed always another day for her, and each day presents a clean slate and a bright future. She will bound out of bed and out the door for a stretch and a walk, grabbing a handful of berries or fruit on her way. Even the city Sagittarian can be seen on her terrace, nose pointed skyward toward the sun.

One of Jupiter's great gifts to this sign is an endless, buoyant optimism that will forever influence her destiny. Life for the Sagittarius Woman rarely involves a struggle or challenge that is not of her own choosing. Her ruling planet is a Queen Isabella whose patronage opens whole continents of freedom and discovery to her exploration. Mary Martin, whose bright and bouncy roles endeared her to audiences around the world, typifies this aspect of the Sagittarius Woman's personality.

Lucky, extravagant, giving

Optimism comes naturally to the Sagittarius Woman; she's downright lucky! Money is rarely, if ever, a problem for her, and the bottomless coffer is filled from many sources—work, friendship, or "fate." She always seems to be in the right place at the right time. She will move to a new city and find the ideal job within a week; her new lover will inherit a small fortune; someone will hand her a lottery ticket that turns to gold. If she *is* temporarily at sea, with no prospects, her sparkling personality and magnetism will bring her an invitation to summer in a villa in the south of Spain.

When in her (frequent) states of independent comfort, she spends extravagantly. She loves fine clothes, music, and especially wonderful food and wine. She never hesitates to exercise her taste for her finer things in life; she somehow feels certain there will always be "more where that came from."

The Sagittarius Woman's generosity to her friends is in much the same spirit—it is easy to share wealth that seems as endless as the world's resources! She is an enthusiastic giver of gifts large and small, and she never thinks twice about a loan. Above all, she loves to share the good times with lavish exotic parties. She is as generous with her friends as with her possessions, and you may meet Polish counts, French ski champions, and Eastern mystics at her table or punch bowl.

Enchanting, charming

The Sagittarius Woman is a fabulous hostess. She entertains with an exotic flair that is as much a result of her guest list as of her menu. She is a world traveler, at the very least in spirit, and your fare will consist of an ingenious and piquant combination of foreign dishes. She may give you a creamy Italian pasta dish with hot, spicy Chinese eggplant, and elegant chilled Portuguese fish as your main course. Her hors d'oeuvres will be inspired by the Middle East, and dessert will be irresistibly French.

The usually accomplished Sagittarian will create a brilliant effect with lights and atmosphere, and you may well spend a good deal of your evening out under the stars. If her plan *doesn't* work—if you hate the food or the mood seems wrong—she will impulsively reroute her bash by ordering cases of champagne and a cake for eighty, and then jumping into the pool without her clothes! Insensitive though she may be to individual feelings, she reads group reactions like a Geiger counter. She is often the catalyst of a rollicking good time.

In spite of her disastrously blunt moments, the Sagittarius Woman is the ideal guest. Her sunshiny personality and the frankly sensual, inquisitive look in her eyes will quickly break the ice at any party. She will often open with a provocative remark—be it political, sexual, or philosophic—then bring as many into the act as she can. She is enthusiastic, widely read, and interested in everything. Above all, her buoyancy and movement will inspire a burst of circulation, and she will end up introducing half your guests to each other—whether she knows them or not!

Flashy, exhibitionistic

The Sagittarius Woman is often very exotic. A traveler/explorer by nature, she often has unique and exquisite clothing that she brought back from foreign ports. She loves silver, gold, and stones more than cut jewels. Her taste in adornment is often primitive; her bronze Tanzanian collar and feather earrings may create a sensation.

The young Sagittarius Woman displays domestic adventurousness, and she loves faddish clothes—the more outlandish the better, so long as they enhance rather than inhibit her sense of freedom. If she succumbs to the temptation of purple six-inch platform shoes, you will as often find them slung over her shoulder like sneakers as on her feet. She will wear a skin-tight Mylar skirt if it's slit high enough to accommodate her long strides. She loves glittery make-up and glitzy shirts. She may paint her nails green and her lips black for fun. She is proud of her supple, athletic body and will show it off in cellophane, dyed leather, and brilliant jewel-toned silks. No matter how gorgeous or outrageous, if her clothes cramp her style, they will simply come off.

Adaptable

Her native restlessness and energy make the Sagittarian Woman highly adaptive. As the Traveler of the Zodiac, she is a whole-hearted believer in the motto "When in Rome, do as the Romans do." For her, not only is it interesting and practical, it is usually more fun!

She is always ready to try new ways—eating couscous with her hands Morroccan style, or joking her way through a first messy meal with chopsticks in a Chinese restaurant. She is very well coordinated and an excellent mimic, so you won't see her fumbling for long. She picks up new methods and manners quickly be they of another culture or of a particular social set. This is a major component of the great Sagittarian charm—when she chooses to turn it on.

She makes a perfect candidate for membership in the Peace Corps. She absorbs different cultures, languages, and customs like a sponge. She is so much at home in a foreign land that she is often stopped and asked for directions. She's likely to make a friend during a mere stopover on the way to her destination; on trans-oceanic crossings, the ship becomes her domain instantly. Her fellow passengers will be talking about her antics long after they return home.

The flip side of the Sagittarius Woman's adaptability is her capriciousness. Though at times her mutable spirit makes her seem docile as a lamb, she is more like a cat, cooperative when curious, independent and restless when bored. She doesn't bore easily—she's interested in everything—but it's difficult for her to settle down, much less conform, for any length of time. Again, her constant need for stimulation can get in the way of completing long-term projects or tasks that smack more of obligation than of fun. This can lead to ominous backlogs of unfulfilled responsibilities and create a truly nervous Sagittarius.

Nervousness is most likely a tendency for the Sagittarius Woman, and she must learn not to accept responsibilities she cannot handle. Her capriciousness becomes skittishness when onerous jobs pile up, and many a Sagittarius Woman hears the passionate call of the wild if she allows the situation to reach a breaking point. She'll have to learn how to rein in and discipline her ever-restless mind if she intends to enhance her sense of responsibility.

Sagittarius should recognize the benefit of travel as an expansion of her consciousness, one that will ultimately help shape her life goals. Too often, it becomes travel for travel's sake, a thinly veiled excuse for rejecting responsibility and/or boredom.

Versatile

A good deal of the joy of discovery for the Sagittarius Woman lies in her ease of mastery. It seems she can do anything well. As a child she was often a musical prodigy, beginning piano and dance lessons at age three. Her coordination is excellent, and throughout her school years that natural athletic ability, coupled with her bright curiosity and warm, enthusiastic personality, makes her a very popular girl. Her talent, self-confidence, and natural leadership abilities frequently make her class or club president (never secretary or treasurer—at least, never more than once!). Her ease and assurance elects her Most Likely to Succeed, and she leaves high school in a blaze of glory and high hopes.

Though she is not likely to recognize it as such, the biggest challenge for the Sagittarius coed is to choose her major. Like a true Renaissance woman, she studies everything from higher mathematics to Dutch poetry with equal passion. From early childhood she is lauded and encouraged in so many directions that she feels no urge to narrow her field as she approaches adulthood.

She may remain in the academic community for years, studying subject after subject, and teaching to support her continued explorations. More likely than not, wanderlust will be the force that propels her from the confines of institutional education to the myriad realities of worldliness. When she does depart, it will be with great sentimentality and with a general degree that is often of limited marketability.

Versatility is a blessing, especially in our twentieth-century society, but the life of a dilettante may be a frustrating one for the Sagittarius Woman. Her ceaselessly expanding possibilities will finally make any real career or life choice an exceedingly difficult one, and her deeply rooted indecision will often fragment her life. She will feel her energy dissipate, and she'll grow increasingly restless. Vacillation is a likely consequence, but it can torment her, for she possesses enough fire and energy to do five things at once.

Scholarly, pompous, slapdash

The Sagittarius Woman has a fantastic mind. In addition to her explorer's spirit and general enthusiasm for life, she has an impeccable memory for facts. She may, however, become the absent-minded professor, so involved in her intellectual musings that she forgets her keys.

Sagittarius needs mental exercise to match her high level of physical activity. Listlessness and boredom are at the root of mental depression for her, and intellectual engagement is the cure. Again, discipline is a crucial factor often lacking in the Sagittarius Woman's education. She gets concepts but lacks patience with detail. She may rely on her superficial knowledge, becoming quite pedantic and pompous when her opinions are challenged.

Because she quickly grasps ideas and facts and can play with them, she may assume she knows everything. This kind of intellectual snobbishness only feeds her gullibility. Her mind is less encyclopedic than she thinks, and it is very easy to lead the condescending Sagittarian down the garden path.

Brilliant she certainly is, but the Sagittarius Woman must remember to ground herself with the proper information before she launches her opinions. Her love for discussion may lead to buffoonery if she doesn't first get her facts straight.

Impulsive, intuitive, good judgment

Impulse for the Sagittarius Woman arises out of her intuition. She often feels she knows immediately what to do when confronted with the need for a decision. In a flash of insight, she can get to the heart of the matter, though it is nearly impossible for her to describe her methodology. The Sagittarius Woman who is in touch with her intuition has unerringly good judgment.

She is happiest when she acts on her impulses. Whether buying a car, taking a trip, or visiting a relative, she waits for the spirit to move her. The rational side of Sagittarius can run interference here. Because she is unable to articulate the process, she may mistrust her lightning-quick realizations. This can cause her to talk herself out of the proper decision and into one that is as inappropriate as it could possibly be. Her opposite sign, Gemini, will operate off the top of her head, often mistaking intellect for intuition. The Sagittarius Woman, on the other hand, will use her intellect to rationalize her intuition out of existence. If you ever meet an "unlucky" Sagittarius Woman, this tendency is most likely working strongly in her life at the time.

Saggitarius intuition serves as a counterbalance to her more "masculine" intellectual capacities. She must learn to trust both modes of operation before they can function harmoniously in her life. She must also trust her intuition while screening it through her intellect to see if it is indeed sound.

Musical, cultural patron

The Sagittarius Woman is exceptionally musical, and her talent is usually discovered at an early age. I have known Sagittarius girls who began piano lessons at age four after demonstrating a keen ability to plink out sophisticated tunes on the family piano.

Even if her musical education is neglected, her infallible ear and sensitivity to rhythm make her a latent musician or, at the very least, a potential connoisseur. Many Sagittarians are great partrons of the opera or of their local symphonies. Sagittarius's ear for the exotic will lead her to appreciate jazz and modern forms in addition to the subtleties of Japanese music and the intricate patterns of the Balinese gamelin. She sees no conflict in enjoying both a Joan Sutherland aria and a Dolly Parton ballad.

Her appreciation of art goes beyond music. Her fine sensibilities and love for the uniquely beautiful lead her to collect art of all kinds. When possible, she will draw artists into her circle of friends and promote their work incessantly. Painting and sculpture are intellectually stimulating to her and, in a sense, less ephemeral than her love of music. The combination of aesthetic and mental stimulation found in the cultural world holds a profound attraction for her. Even if she doesn't pursue her own art form, the role she plays will be a highly creative and visible one.

Independent, progressive

Whatever her philosophy or beliefs, you may rest assured that she has arrived at them herself. Nobody tells her what to do, much less what to think. She has her own system and approach to life, and she is indifferent to all criticism. Of course, she does love a good philosophical argument, mainly because she will always rise to the call of converting another soul to her political, spiritual, or philosophic views.

A good verbal battle is like an active baseball game, providing a chance to stretch her mental legs and take in some fresh ideas. The Sagittarius Woman's concerns are always future-oriented, and she will stress present responsibility for coming generations with unheard-of passion. Pollution, atomic waste, and the energy crisis are large and real issues to her. Her fire and zeal make her a brilliant lobbyist or politician.

Explorer, far-out

It is conceivable that a Sagittarius Woman combined the two words *wander* and *lust* to come up with the term as we know it now. She indeed has a lust for travel, for different experiences, for new places and faces. I've heard tales of a Sagittarius woman who, at sixty-eight years of age, took a correspondence course in hotel/motel management from her home in Sun City, Arizona. Before her family back in the Midwest could attempt to intrude their sense of reality, she was living in the mountains of Colorado, managing a resort during the winter months. Since her aging dachsund couldn't cope with the diminished oxygen at that elevation, the woman picked up and set out for Southern California to manage a nursing home.

The Sagittarius Woman has known since childhood what a bottomless reservoir of energy she has. This makes it all the more difficult for her to comprehend the importance of control and direction in her activities. She rarely wastes much time in a state of frozen indecision; instead she'll juggle six interests simultaneously and only partially satisfy each. Another tendency of hers is to go off on wild tangents in the belief that "anything worth doing is worth doing completely." She'll reverse directions just as quickly when her blind faith and native optimism crash into obstacles she is unwilling to surmount. The eccentricity of the Sagittarius Woman is a marvel to witness but often a hell to live with.

Inspirational, patriotic

Religion can hold an interesting place in the life of the Sagittarius Woman. She is first and foremost an idealist. The understanding so often lacking in her interpersonal relationships can reach amazing heights in her religious expression.

The young Sagittarius girl is often quite inspirational. She loves singing gospel hymns, and pledging allegiance to the flag is usually a profoundly moving experience for her. Many Sagittarius Women become deeply religious because of these early experiences. They make brilliant preachers, religious writers, and spiritual teachers because of their own powerful capacity to inspire others.

Philosophic, spiritual

The more mature Sagittarius Woman will shape her youthful religious fervor into a code of ethics and a system of beliefs to live by. This can range from "Respect nature and its manifestation in all creatures" to the complicated Freudian theory of psyche and soma. Whatever it is, you can be sure she will carry it to its furthest conclusions. Philosophy, in fact, is an excellent field for her, and fine analytical inquiry can well become the passion of her life.

The candle of her childhood faith will continue to glimmer through all the black holes and blind alleys. As her understanding ripens, her studies may take a mystical turn. Physics and the abiding laws of the universe fill her with awe and faith. Her blood bears traces of the woodland creature, and she instinctively feels the rhythm of the planet in her veins. This strong connection with nature pushes her skyward to a transcendent comprehension of reality.

Her head may soar beyond the clouds and into the stratosphere, but the Sagittarius Woman's feet are firmly planted in the practicalities of the earth, and her strong legs carry her forward. This is often the key to her spirituality. Every Sagittarian Woman has the teacher's gift and can actualize her cosmic understanding and regenerate the mundane rituals of our lives. She is called "the sign of the prophet." Hers is the potential to integrate, organize, and direct our human energies into a brighter future.

Sagittarius relationships

All mutable signs are endowed with the ability to make connections, and the Sagittarius Woman brings to her myriad relationships all the joy and enthusiasm of Jupiter. Her buoyant, undemanding, yet loyal nature makes her an excellent friend, and she is a friend to almost everyone she knows.

Her love relationships are far more complicated; she is joyful and true but idealistic and restless as well. This combination of traits makes her love life exciting and difficult by turns. Loving the Sagittarius Woman is sometimes ecstatic, sometimes painful, but always a challenge.

Companionship is key word for all Sagittarius relationships. In love, she is far less romantic than Leo or Pisces. In fact, many men may feel confused when they discover that their own response to her is far more "feminine" in emotional tone than hers is to them. Remember, Sagittarius is a masculine, positive sign. Her nature is somewhat like Aries'. The Sagittarius Woman has a distinctly male component in her mental makeup, though the brilliance of her intuition (a supposedly "female" gift) often belies it.

A dear friend of hers may have just died. She may be grieving very deeply, but she may never want her lover to hold and console her. More often, she will want his advice on how to handle the business arrangements that are left behind. She will feel the pain deeply, but her way of coping is to treat it like a business matter.

Independence is the Sagittarius Woman's watchword. Many a baffled man will envision his Sagittarian love as a Statue of Liberty staring off to sea with her torch held high. She must keep her separate identity at all costs, and there may come a time when the price is love itself.

Her independence is rarely hidden or blind, and the Sagittarius Woman who chooses marriage as her lifestyle will try hard to make it work. She may be employed full time or have a business she operates out of her home. We remember her from childhood as the mother who taught at the grade school, had her own beauty shop, or ran the Cub Scout troop! Even if her work involves travel or long sojourns away from home, she will remain faithful in all the important ways. The "long-distance marriage" is unquestionably a Sagittarian Woman's concept. All skeptics to the contrary, it does work if her mate is as game as she for the arrangement.

Her man needs to learn very quickly that her independence does not mean rejection. I knew a woman who wanted her home repainted. Her husband did this for a living. She did not bother asking him to do it but bought all the supplies and started doing it on her own. He was very insulted and hurt, but she was just doing what she wanted to do and didn't feel like bothering him.

The Sagittarius Woman loves children dearly because they have the same fresh, eternal curiosity about life as she does. She can make a wonderful mother once she learns to whisk through the drudgery of diapers and feeding schedules. Her house may be a shambles of messy beds, pet cages and sports equipment, but it will be a palace to her children, and the envy of the neighborhood. Her children and their friends adore her because she mothers like a big sister, never a matriarch. They trust her because she is a protector and guide with the energy and imagination of a peer.

Her difficulty with parenting comes when her children begin to break away. This is a difficult time for a Sagittarius mother. On the one hand, she is thrilled by having more freedom for herself; at the same time, the sense of losing control makes her feel very vulnerable and unwanted. She takes it as a personal affront to *her* freedom to choose, and she may literally feel that her rights have been taken away. She truly wants the best for her children but firmly believes her way *is* the best.

The Sagittarius Woman may have to rechannel her explorer's energy as she builds her family. But when she has established her marriage and borne her children, she will be off again, reaching out with both hands into the great world of possibilities beyond her threshold. She may get household help early, and by the time her children reach school age she will have flown the nest herself. Though always available (at least by phone), she will take up her own life at full swing. Sagittarius is not the self-sacrificing mother. Each family member will have her or his contribution to make toward the happiness and security of the home. Though she may seem to foist maternal responsibility off on an older daughter, this is as much the child's karma as it is her own expectation. Deep down, the Sagittarius Woman does not believe she is like other women, and in many ways she is right. Though conventional in some respects, her notion of family challenges the stereotype, and her family will either transcend it with her or fall victim to her quest for freedom.

The Sagittarius Woman is a loyal and generous friend. However, don't expect to drop by for a cup of hot tea and a word of solace when you're down—she won't be home! As with everything else, her notion of friendship involves activity. The only fireside chat you are likely to have with her is on a camping trip. She will share new ideas, activities, and friends; all she asks in return is a willing spirit and a sense of humor. Though she cultivates friends with high ideals, her heart warms to anyone who knows how to have a good time. You may never find her in time to help dry your tears or bind your wounds, but she can inspire you to new heights with her love, her vision, and her faith in you.

The Sagittarius Woman often has more male friends than female friends. She is not fond of gossip. She has little to contribute to the kind of fine emotional analysis that goes on in many feminine conversations. She prefers a straightforward discussion of political issues, filled with lofty philosophic concepts and historical analogies. She is not above sophistry. Abstract or high-flown dialogue is far more tempting to her than discussing John's motivation in seeing his first wife while Sarah was in the hospital with their new baby. She will leave the description of an antique auction to join a heated play-by-play recounting of a football game. She is simply more comfortable with men because her mind works more like theirs.

Today, her potential for friendship with women is much stronger since fewer women are trapped in the stereotype she rebels against. Still, her friends may find her uncomprehending on the subjects of the single career woman's loneliness, the motherhood dilemma, and even "the difference between men and women."

This basic difference in her perception will probably not come home to her until she marries or until she enters a long-term relationship with a man. As their energies begin to polarize, she will see the ways her own "feminine" side has remained in the shadows. Just as each of us are both *yin* and *yang*, we are each responsible for balancing the masculine and feminine energies with us. In this age of women's liberation, the Sagittarius Woman may seem ahead of the game when in fact the challenge for her is merely different, but equal.

Childhood

The most striking characteristics of the Sagittarius child are her high energy level and her intense curiosity. Few children ask "Why?" more times in a day! She can't bear to keep still, and her weary parents learn early that sports and vigorous outdoor play will insure less aggravation and fewer accidents. If hardier parents set her to piano lessons, they are in for a surprise. Magically, music will keep her in her seat—if nobody whistles outside with a catcher's mitt!

She spends a good deal more time with boys than with girls and may be the only girl allowed on the neighborhood ball team. Her closest friend, however, is apt to be her dog. The Sagittarius Woman loves animals. Their nondemanding, unemotional companionship is precisely what she wants and has to offer those around her. Especially when she is growing up, her pet will be the perfect confidant through all the confusing demands and conflicting expectations of her family and the society in which she lives.

Her culture-loving parents may despair in those early years, for her interest will often seem hopelessly superficial. Her intellectual curiosity develops slowly, and in her childhood it is somewhat that of a daredevil. Fearless in sports, casual, and carefree, she will extend her interest in math only as far as placing quarter bets on the Kentucky Derby. She rails against discipline, and if held in check too tightly, she will begin to physically cramp—with symptoms ranging from charley horses to vomiting! She is indeed a handful, but what many parents fail to recognize is how trustworthy and careful she is. She never lies, cheats, or does anything else she shouldn't—as long as she is given her freedom. Given her own set of keys and a code of behavior, she will honor her parents' trust and do them proud into the bargain.

In the traditional family structure, the Sagittarius girl is likely to identify with her father, though she may favor her mother, who is more apt to "understand" and plead her case regarding rules and regulations. Her mother may better know how utterly honorable this "wild" girl is, and she will defend her daughter staunchly in the face of all criticism. Her father may secretly rejoice that he has a kind of "son" to fish and play ball with; conversely, he may miss the subtle romance of having "Daddy's little girl." How the Sagittarius girl fares, and with which of her parents she most strongly identifies, will depend on their own notion of roles and freedom.

How the Sagittarius Woman relates: lovers and other intimates

The Sagittarius Woman does not equivocate in her involvements, at least not initially, and never for long. When she sees someone she wants, she acknowledges her attraction by direct pursuit. She will charm, provoke, and titillate the object of her desire in a direct and refreshing manner. Though she is not a coquette, she rarely is so aggressive that she scares her man away. She frequently makes the first move, but the man who draws her will be virile and independent enough to be fascinated rather than threatened.

The man who says yes to the Sagittarius Woman opens the door to a rich and joyful time for both of them. She is generous and free in love, and he will find himself luxuriating in her gifts of charm, intelligence, exotic excitement, and sophistication while retaining his own feeling of freedom! She will become his feminine ideal, and as he falls more and more in love with her he will wonder how he ever lived without her.

Phase two is the beginning of the bumpy ride, for ironically enough, the very qualities that drew him to the Sagittarius Woman in the first place now seem to be driving them apart. The sense of independence he has been feeling all along was not some feminine wile. His independence *is* intact, and so is hers. The Sagittarius Woman loves completely, but she will not be pinned down. On Friday, his anticipation of a candlelight dinner will explode when he finds her note on the door: "Special match race at Belmont 5.30. Back by midnight. Quick bite at Samantha's?" He may be tempted to respond with a comment of Lord Byron's about an ex-love: "To express it delicately, I think Madame Claire is a damned bitch."

He will often wonder whether theirs is a romance or a friendship, and with good reason. The Sagittarius Woman easily combines the two, and her dual expectations may leave them both in a muddle. She believes in honesty and spontaneity, and she will not "play the game" of courtship and fair maidenhood with him.

The Sagittarius Woman in love

For the Sagittarius Woman, love *is* sex. To her, "romance" is the mystery of a one-night stand. "love" comes out of friendship, because any continuing relationship with a Sagittarius Woman depends on mutual honesty and a high level of communication. She will only fall in love with a man who is her equal and who will grant her the independence she offers him. Sex for her is religion but is also a completely animal experience, for the animal is sacred to her. Her goddess is Diana the Huntress, and the Sagittarius Woman will constantly seek new heights of cosmic experience through her sexual nature. Her relationships are based on loyalty.

Hers is not a monogamous spirit; she will not lie to protect her lover. In this sense she tends to dominate their relationship, for she sets the terms. If he cannot stand it, he must leave.

Honesty

It is difficult to fault a person for honesty, but as we have seen, the Sagittarius Woman's candor can function both as a catalyst and as a stumbling block in all aspects of her life. She cannot pretend to be someone she is not. However, there are shades and qualities of honesty that she needs to examine and understand, especially in light of how she uses them in her relationships. To her, the "white lie" is as abhorrent as the bold-faced one; she is an absolutist where honesty is concerned. I am not suggesting that she learn how to use either form of manipulation. But truth telling has many names, and she should learn their differences and effective uses.

The following adjectives, all of which apply to the Sagittarius Woman, are synonymous with honesty:

1 *Sincere*—free from deceit, hypocrisy, falseness; earnest and genuine.
2 *Genuine*—possessing character or quality; authentic; free from pretense, affectation, or hypocrisy.
3 *Honorable*—principled, upright, noble, high-minded.
4 *Candid*—outspoken, frank, open; without reservation, disguise, or subterfuge; straightforward.
5 *Blunt*—callous, insensitive; dull, numb.

There are obviously more and less effective ways for the Sagittarius Woman to be honest in dealing with her friends and lovers. Born under the sign of the Prophet and Teacher, she has a mission to provide instruction in truth; but she must first learn how to get the message through without alienating everyone around her.

Sagittarius, this simple exercise will help you become more expert in dealing with your own honesty:

1 Have an imaginative lover or a friend make up a list of questions eliciting your opinion on issues personal, political, and sexual, ranging from "Do I look good in yellow?" to "Can open marriage work?"
2 Make up different answers for each question—one sincere, one candid, one blunt, etc.—until you gain a sense of the different possibilities inherent in each response.

3 Evaluate the quality of each response as to its effectiveness in getting your message across.
4 Finally, have your friend or lover check over your responses. Their observations may surprise you! You can learn from their reactions what kind of emotional response you can expect from others.

When the Sagittarius Woman learns that there is freedom in honesty, her relationships will take on a new quality of trust. The ambivalence and storminess she often experiences in friendship or love point directly to her tunnel-vision pursuit of truth. Honesty can be either an explosive stick of dynamite or a candle illuminating the world we all share. If we respect the flame of truth, no one need get burned in the process.

Lovers and husbands

The Sagittarius Woman has all the fire, energy, and idealism she needs to make her mark on the world, but she often lacks the empathy and patience to make long-lasting, productive, or creative connections with others.

She needs a man who has a sense of independence that matches her own. He must also have the ego strength to allow her equal freedom and must be able to withstand occasional tests of his will and faith in her. He should be idealistic, highly intelligent, and creative. If his sexual energy is high, she will settle for versatility or a background exotic enough to hold her fascination.

Her honesty tends to dictate the terms of their relationship; she will not tolerate subterfuge. A man who states plainly what he wants and expects will win her respect, if not her keys. There is a contract implicit in live-in relationships with the Sagittarius Woman. She will want to know exactly what strings are attached before she invests in matching towels.

It is through their shared sexual adventures that she and her mate will come to a deep understanding of each other's souls. With the Sagittarius Woman, rifts are more quickly mended in bed than in therapy or discussion. The more she balances the principles of *yin* and *yang* in the expression of love, the easier it will be for her to relate to everyone around her.

Advice to the man in her life

1. Know that you have met your match. Remember always that this woman is your equal in every way, and that she may be more like you than you think.
2. Let your feelings for her develop slowly, as hers will for you. Friendship, not conquest or bewitchment, is the key in relating to her. When you prove your companionability, you have won the better part of her.
3. Be prepared to reciprocate the gift of independence and freedom she offers you. It is sincerely and honestly given, with the expectation that you grant her the same.
4. Stimulate her mentally as well as physically (the latter goes without saying by now!). Engage her interest in your cultural and intellectual pursuits. You can share all of them with her fully, and they will bind her to you far more effectively than will offers of security, tenderness, or protection.
5. Respond to her honestly at all times. She will never play games with you, and she expects the same. Guard against role playing and manipulation at all costs, for she will sniff them out like a bloodhound and vanish.
6. Don't allow her to test your will with constant surprises or demands. If you can't stand her behavior, deal with her firmly and directly. She will only love and respect you more for your strength.
7. Look forward to a life of constant travel, excitement, new faces, and new ideas, as well as frequent spells apart. Domestic bliss is not in your future, but glorious adventure is.

There are many challenges in loving the Sagittarius Woman, and she is worth the effort of meeting every one of them. You will learn more about independence by sharing it with her than you could possibly learn alone. Her relentless honesty is a scourge, but it is also a prism reflecting your every motivation and desire. Use it to examine your own nature, and let it purify you.

Above all, trust her and return her loyalty. She will never lie to you; you can believe whatever she reveals about her life and her feelings. So long as you respect her, she will honor your love and trust. In her special way she is the truest, deepest soulmate you will ever find.

Sagittarius sexuality

The genes of the Sagittarius Woman carry an ancient secret. She is a centaur, cousin in spirit to Pan. Half woman, half glen creature, she has the sex drive and purpose of a female satyr.

Sagittarius is not shy, and she will trumpet her adventurous sexuality loudly and openly. Her perpetual state of motion derives from her need for constant stimulation—and she is, in fact, in a semi-aroused state most of the time. Like the centaur, she is half beast, half human, and never is her animal energy more alive than on the dance floor. The music courses through her veins like a second, familiar heartbeat, and the hundreds of undulating bodies around her are sensual magnets. This hypersuggestive atmosphere can become unbearable for her.

She seldom allows herself to fall in love, preferring the freedom to follow the dictates of her roving eye. Very few details of a man's anatomy escape her gaze. She assesses bulges and musculature with the eye of a practiced horse trader. However, when she falls, she falls hard. Her whole universe becomes wrapped up in her beloved. Even after her ardor cools, she carries the memory as long as she lives.

The Sagittarius Woman loves orgies. Group sex is a powerful aphrodisiac to her, and she barely comprehends the meaning of jealousy or shame. The caresses and ministrations of more than one person, in any gender combination, electrify her to the very core. She senses such possibilities instinctively in any crowd of people, whether or not she has tasted the pleasures of group sex. This true "animal magnetism" will draw many men and women to her in her lifetime, even when the attraction isn't mutual.

In the diffused sensual atmosphere of the dance floor, the Sagittarius Woman will experience many peaks and valleys of arousal. As the night pulses on, temptation grows, and she becomes increasingly excited and frustrated. This buildup can actually cause her to lunge at some leering (and more repressed) stranger—or she may find herself in trouble with someone else's date. She would do better to echo Cher's "Take Me Home" to a loving friend or available stranger who is more likely to satisfy her bursting desires. One Sagittarian friend of mine became a brief disco legend for her record number of gentle "bouncings." Now she occasionally visits the more outrageous discos, but her reputation has gained her entrée into a more select society of afterhours clubs where she can give full rein to her fantasies.

The Sagittarius Woman is often ready to tumble in the hay with a stranger, and many a comely, well-endowed man has been actively pursued by her. No matter how anonymous the encounter, her partner will never feel used. Rather, he will feel *chosen* as her companion for a blissful sexual idyll. Her gift for turning lovemaking into a celebration of life and beauty will electrify her lover and leave him in a cloud. The animal force of her libido is matched ounce for ounce by her powerful artistry and grace. For the Sagittarius Woman, each act of love is performed on the altar of Bacchus.

There are three keys words that provide a greater understanding of Sagittarian sexuality. The first is *expansive.* As with everything else in her life, this daughter of desire loves to stretch out sexually, with plenty of room to move. She is anything but inhibited, and a cozy candlelit chamber makes her choke with claustrophobia. Far more arousing is a long stroll on the beach, preferably nude. The more space around her the better, and the beach at sunset is a glorious setting for love with the Sagittarius Woman. She thrills to the sound of nature around her, and the crashing waves will surge and resound in her and her lover as they play among the elements, cavorting in the sand.

Her love of adventure makes her a willing playmate in the woods, in an abandoned house or the loft of an unoccupied barn, even in an empty ski lift, with all the unzipping and mitten stripping it implies. She loves to take her sex with exercise and as exercise. She never feels more gloriously alive than when she is active, and activity stimulates her in all ways.

If she ends up in a hotel, she will want a suite with a king-size bed and a view. Her own bedroom is large or gives the impression of tremendous space.It is light, airy, and simple, and her bed is enormous. Lovemaking is the dance of life for her, and a sense of freedom is the only requirement for her performance.

The second key word is *direct.* Sagittarius is not coy. She will not tease her lover with "go away, come closer" games. Her sexual interest is often aroused first, or at least simultaneously with yours. There is no need to pursue her; you are likely to collide! She knows who she wants, and her signals will be clear. In fact, more often than not, she will simply tell you. She appreciates the same kind of directness in her lover, and making love with her often involves a good deal of erotic conversation. She would rather you speak your desires than try to second-guess you; in turn, she will let you know exactly what feels good. She loves sound effects, too; groaning, shouting, and even well-chosen four-letter words will only spur her on to greater heights. She rapidly grows impatient with too much pussyfooting around. Rubbing knees under the table is more apt to irritate her than turn her on—unless your dining room is large and private and you can proceed directly to the couch.

Finally, for the Sagittarius Woman, sex is *aesthetic*. For all her directness and energy, she does not want roughness. She thinks of sex as a union of equals with slightly different apparatus; she holds the act of love to be the highest form of art. She is willing to share the orchestration of their movement, and each may by turns become the conductor of their private symphony. She worships the body of her loved one as a glorious creation, and the dignity of her self-love transforms them both into gods. The lover of a Sagittarius Woman is a very lucky person indeed.

Early sex experiences

The young Sagittarius girl is very precocious, though often not in the way she seems to be. She is usually a very active child, constantly seeking new stimuli for her quick, curious mind and her powerfully physical body. She may never lose that "polymorphous-perverse" quality of the human infant, whose whole body is an erogenous zone. She may have masturbated for as long as she can remember. She is also likely to have early erotic experiences with pets, sitting with her purring kitten beneath her skirt or letting her dog lick her "special place." She is naturally a great horse lover, and often her earliest crush is on the shaggy Shetland pony she rides bareback in the paddock.

On the other hand, some Sagittarius girls seem totally oblivious to their sexual natures. They are nonetheless very active, and their sexual energy is sublimated into sports and extracurricular activities like music lessons, drama club, and the school newspaper. But whether she is sensually oriented at this age or not, her energy and independence set the Sagittarius girl apart from other girls her age.

She often prefers boys as playmates. Doll parties drive her crazy, and she considers most of the girls she knows "sissies." She would much rather build a tree fort and is usually the only girl the neighborhood boys will tolerate. As she grows older, her tomboyishness may earn her a reputation for being "fast." The fifteen-year-old Sagittarius girl cannot imagine what's wrong with playing football with the guys past dusk, and she is likely to be out past dawn on prom night, careening off for a summer swim in the wee hours with two boys and another terrified female classmate.

The assumptions made about her behavior by other girls and their parents will only confuse her. Boys have long been her favorite companions, and besides genuinely liking her, they are often relieved to find no coy or threatening undertones in her actions. It will take a determined and experienced boy to awaken the sleeping sensuality of the energetic young Sagittarian. It is not *her* fear that postpones her initiation, but rather her boyfriend's. He may well find her sunshiny personality like a bracing cold shower. She can remain oblivious to the whole sexual process unless she hangs out at a breeding farm or has a randy dog. At this young age she is especially blind to sexual nuances, and most of her male peers are too self-conscious to teach her.

The Sagittarian girl is apt to take her initiation into her own hands. She may learn about the promised pleasures through her girl friends (she has lots of them—primarily teammates—by high school). Or the great revelation may occur to her while she's watching the neighborhood dogs grunt and roll on the playing field. In any case, she often decides when, where, and with whom she will have her first sexual encounter. It may be an "older man"—a college boy or someone from outside her sphere. Or she may tackle the issue head-on with her boyfriend by asking him directly to make love to her. Often, this comes as an enormous surprise to him, since she has always resisted his snuggling before, wanting a hard kiss and a squeeze, but none of that "icky stuff." Now she wants the real thing, and it may all be too much for him. If so, her loyalty may postpone her education even further. But she will be very disappointed, and she won't wait around for long.

By the time the Sagittarius girl reaches her early twenties, she will often be an accomplish lover. After her initiation, she will enthusiastically launch herself on a program of self-education. She is a fast learner; her athletic ability combined with her strong aesthetic sense makes her a glorious partner in the act of love. Her joyful sexuality and her independent spirit give men license to love her with no strings attached. Many men will find her, at least initially, their ideal.

Love and sex

For the Sagittarius Woman sex is a celebration, and she brings to each encounter the appetite and anticipation of a feast. She looks for a companion spirit in her sexual partner, a fellow traveler with whom to share the cornucopia. Like pilgrims in a foreign port, they may enjoy only an evening's repast. She simply seeks a kindred spirit, not lifelong commitment, and in a brief encounter "fellow feeling" means more to her than the illusion of love.

Sagittarius is capable of keeping love and sex quite separate, and she is very comfortable with the one-night affair. At breakfast, she will be happy and relaxed, full of humor but clearly ready to walk out the door after a wink and a sincere kiss. Even in her longer affairs, she prizes friendship more highly than love. Sagittarius is a masculine sign, and no matter how womanly the Sagittarian may be, there is a "comradely" quality to her affairs with men. One thinks of Garbo as Ninotchka, and of the poor Polish lancer who underestimated her. When she remains with a man, it is out of admiration and respect for him as an equal. Love is often the last thing to flower in her as the relationship continues.

This masculine quality of thought and action can result in great misunderstanding and confusion for the Sagittarius Woman. She may be pursued by cold or weak-willed men who wish to dominate or be dominated by her. Unlike her Scorpio sister, she is not titillated by power games to any great extent. Though she finds mild forms of subjugation and mastery in sex play intensely pleasureable, the master-slave dynamic utterly contradicts her notion of mutual independence.

Particularly in this New Age, she may turn to women for her primary relationships. She may choose a partner more outwardly feminine than she herself is, though role playing is not her style. She will look for a woman who matches her in energy, independence, and sexual appetite. Above all, she seeks equality in affairs of the heart. She would no more seek a wife in the kitchen than be one herself.

Her sexual response pattern in lovemaking seems to be the following:

1 A glorious sense of freedom or personal expansion, most likely the result of some limbering, "warm-up" sort of exercise, like a nude swim, horseback riding, or yoga.
2 A frank, direct approach that orginates either with her or with her lover. She likes clear interest and admiration, a "no-games"

approach including blunt talk and four-letter words—but no "bathroom jokes." This is not a woman who considers sex dirty in any way!

3 Firm, strong, powerful intercourse. The Sagittarius Woman is all there, and her movement is wholehearted, timed to the stroke. She loves strenuous intercourse and will make love all through the night. She wants most of all to be totally spent, and it takes a great deal to tire her!
4 Multiple orgasms through the night. The Sagittarius Woman experiences many peaks of pleasure, and after a blissful orgasm she will rest peacefully for several minutes—and then start all over again. This is yet another reason why orgies appeal to her so; if one of her partners is exhausted, she can continue elsewhere.
5 A feeling of peace, warmth, and oneness with the universe. When she's finally satiated and spent, she will lie back, dreamy and distant, and seem to commune with nature, the stars, or her own mysterious inner spaces. It is best to leave her alone in this reverie, and let her "come back" of her own accord. She will be serene and loving when she does.

What kind of lover she needs

Like Jupiter, the Sagittarius woman is expansive and joyous in her sexual expression. Her first priority in a lover is that he match her enthusiasm and high sexual energy. She will even ignore power-hungriness or the urge to dominate—at least for one night—if his lust has a sense of humor in it.

Though many different types intrigue her, she wants a man who is all male, in the best sense of the word. She cannot bear Milque-toasts; she hates caveman types just as much. She loves a man who is forthright, strong, and even very directive, but he must be gentle as well. Above all, the act of love is art to her, and she glories in a man whose movement expresses grace, sensibility, and power.

She loves any kind of intercourse—anal, oral, and vaginal. She is not fond of scented creams, though she loves olive oil. She never needs amyl nitrate, but if it helps revive her lover, you will certainly find it under her bed! Sex for her is as natural as the great outdoors, her favorite place to indulge.

Her great love of animals (dogs and horses especially) leads her to sexual fantasies that may in fact stem from her childhood experiments. Those early memories may lead her to become an aficionado of anal sex and vaginal intercourse from behind. Anyone involved with animals—horse trainers, dog breeders, even veterinarians—will hold an immense attraction for her. Of course she is drawn to athletes and dancers of any sort. She considers men who sweat and train to be in ripe condition for her kind of play.

She also loves travelers and foreigners of all nationalities. Her own spirit of adventure will lead her to investigate the physical proportions of an Ethiopian ambassador or the legendary sexual prowess of an Indian yogi.

For the long term, she wants a lover who is strong but equal. Many men cannot, in fact, match her staying power between the sheets, and this is another factor that may turn her to women. She may find another lady with the virtuosity and stamina to fulfill her in a way no man ever has. This, coupled with the lack of implicit formal structure and societal expectation in gay relationships, may make lesbian life the ideal alternative for her.

Again, freedom and independence stand above all other considerations for the Sagittarius Woman in love. She is certainly loyal but not necessarily faithful. She will never become embittered by the man who first adores her, then berates her, for her independence. She will simply leave him.

Whatever her lifestyle, the Sagittarius Woman chooses to keep love at arm's length. She fears intimacy. Although she may be the one to initiate sexual action, she is the first to put the brakes on when her partner gets too close. She knows her own weaknesses and doesn't want anyone too near. It takes a very special person to gently fan the smoldering embers that lie hidden in the crucible of her sexuality, beneath her outwardly cool and blasé attitude. When the fire ignites, she falls deeply and completely in love.

What she needs to learn

In spite of her basically conventional nature, the sensibility of the Sagittarius Woman is strictly New Age. Her free spirit and joyous, emotionally undemanding sexuality have led men to respect and admire her for generations. She genuinely loves and respects them in return, but on her own terms. She loves her independent security and she *will* maintain it, even if it means spending a good deal of her adult life alone.

Through hard experience, she may learn that the very independence and casual companionship she offers her men will lead to accusations when they find their love will not "change" her. She must never allow her own honesty to be held against her in this way. If her man assumes she has been playing a game with him from the beginning then he obviously does not know her well. But it is her responsibility to make the message as clear as possible. Sagittarius does not lie. If her man so mistrusts women in general that he does not believe her, she must read *his* message loud and clear as well.

In the New Age, she will find living alone less difficult but also less necessary. Already many of her sisters are learning the joys of freedom and self-sufficiency, and men accept more easily the kind of casual relationship and open lifestyle that has long been the Sagittarian mode of operation.

As men grow more comfortable with their own "feminine," receptive sides, the Sagittarius Woman must take care not to increase her masculine dynamic in relating to them. She dislikes weak men so intensely that she may try to force the issue with a man who is just learning to recognize his vulnerability. A man may be drawn to her openness, independence, and kind heart in his effort to strike a new balance in love. The insecure Sagittarius Woman who drives and tests the virility of her man may trample on his fledging efforts at real emotional communion and send him packing in a fury. In short, she can become the new Shrew!

The Sagittarius Woman must remember that her *animus*—her masculine nature—may well be stronger than her *anima*, or feminine side. An interesting facet of her new relationships with men in the challenge of growing more feminine *with* them. Of course no one wants a clinging vine, male or female; but exploring tenderness and empathy, and sharing the deepest kind of intimacy, is often as big a challenge for the Sagittarius Woman as it is for her man. When her spirit of adventure turns upward and inward, she will become the ideal mate for the New Age man.

Sagittarius anger

When the Sagittarius Woman is angry, she channels her forceful energies into restlessness, irritability, sarcastic wit, and snide comments. She fears this important emotion in much the same way that she fears intimacy. She doesn't want the varied passions that accompany close contact with others.

The Sagittarius Woman may stomp her foot occasionally,

shout, and even cry when she is angry. However, such displays always embarrass her; she doesn't want to appear weak or out of control. Her reaction to her anger is more intellectual than emotional. She seeks to protect and shield herself from the demands and emotional needs of her friends and intimates.

Paradoxically, while fearing one-on-one relationships, she does care about people in general and about her immediate environment in particular. Dishonesty, cruelty, betrayal, or injustice directed at groups or anonymous individuals will instantly ignite her temper. She feels their rejection and disappointment on a global scale. She makes a great humanitarian, a true crusader. She picks up the banner and marches forward with little regard for the extreme negative reactions she is likely to encounter or create. She always has a deep commitment to improving life and conserving society.

The Sagittarius Woman directs her anger at insensitive conglomerates and at people who turn away from the problems humanity now faces. However, she finds it difficult to express her personal anger and direct it positively. Jane Fonda, for example, can and does use her anger to defend the rights of others; unfortunately, she often doesn't speak up in her own behalf.

A great challenge for the Sagittarius Woman is learning to experience and understand the complex personal problems of those closest to her. She can be a great humanitarian (like Margaret Mead, a Sagittarian who dedicated her life to solving the mysteries of the human condition), but she rarely becomes involved in the problems of her own mate.

The Sagittarius Woman uses her talent for quickness to immediately move away from inner feelings of doubt and anger. She judiciously protects her social image and works very hard to project a friendly, outgoing, and liberal facade. She attaches greater importance than is necessary to her standing in society and relegates her self-doubt to a less prominent place in her mind. She is motivated to display her anger only when she is personally threatened. She can be a worthy opponent in a battle over her freedom; her keen sense of survival often dictates the outcome.

She removes herself from angry confrontation more often than not. It's rare to see her remain and fight an issue to the death. She must learn to channel her energies, to be consistently analytical. There is much she can learn about the expression of anger, and if she applies it constructively, she can effect positive changes in those around her.

If anyone tries to block her efforts or control her actions, she seeks to remove the impediments with vigorous, determined drive. She becomes very intense, raises the pitch of her voice, and renders the offender helpless. Her quick "surprise attack" is most effective, but she is apt to walk away from the situation without evaluating the effectiveness of her angry display.

If unpleasant situations confront her and she finds no solution, she often becomes overwhelmed and slips into depression. Since she is not very self-analytical, she may have difficulty understanding the roots of her problems and remain confused for years. Eventually she will snap out of it, but she may never gain the valuable insight into why or how. Many Sagittarius Women find in the study of psychology or human relations a way of intellectually understanding and coping with their anger.

The Sagittarius Woman doesn't often experience hate. If she does, she often lets go of the people who aroused the hateful feelings and dismisses them permanently from her life. Her anger is quick and violent. Like sparklers, it bursts into flame and quickly dies. It is over, forgotten almost as soon as it is spoken.

The Sagittarius Woman solves many of her problems with laughter. She is a great wisecracker, and if she interacts with someone she doesn't care for, she becomes a master of sarcasm and offhand, snide comments. She seldom comes down from her lofty position to get involved in a messy fight. Not particularly emotional, she tends to be more philosophical or intellectual.

She loves to explore the feelings and emotions of others while keeping hers securely under wraps. A Sagittarius friend and I were having dinner with a group of colleagues, and during the course of the evening she managed to coax all the "bigwigs" into divulging the details of their first sexual experience. Everyone was telling outrageous tales, trying to top each other. Not once during the conversation did she share her own experiences.

The Sagittarius Woman often uses her anger to create excitement during periods of boredom. She knows that if she can get people angry, she can spend many hours trying to work things out. She uses this ploy on the job and in many of her social contacts. She keeps on the go constantly to avoid expressing her negative emotions, and she especially seems to want to outdistance anger.

The Sagittarius Woman must watch for signs of tension in those close to her. Early in life, she often lacks the empathy to identify with another's hurt, and the experience to deal with her anger or others'. Often she cannot even communicate it. A resentful comment or critical remark from a loved one often causes deep pain. She needs to let it register, acknowledge her hurt, and then approach the issue with a relaxed and openly friendly attitude.

These issues are particularly sensitive where her lover is concerned. When the air is cleared, however, they can get down to the basic issues together. It may be as simple as the amount of time she spends on the phone, or as complex as her continued friendship with a former lover. If the present relationship is worth it, the two of them will work it out. Sagittarius must be sensitive to her lover's needs and must explain the kind of information *she* needs in order to behave considerately. Then, if the message is not coming through, it isn't her fault; it's a flaw in the communication system between the two of them.

Sagittarius lifestyles

The Sagittarius Woman often works to make her lifestyle match her current infatuation. If she's a devotee of est this month, her life will have to revolve around the principles of *that* philosophy.

As a perennial student, she is apt to adopt a transient lifestyle. Portable furniture, portable housing, portable friends, and portable values appeal to her. She doesn't like the idea of being tied down; often she rejects the conventional three-bedroom-two-and-a-half-bath-family-room abode for something a little more to her tastes. She has a deep sense of community, but again, that community is more apt to be a community of the world—a global village, if you will—than the suburban sterility so popular during the past few decades.

It isn't unusual for her to marry young and divorce soon thereafter. She's often caught up in the philosophy of marriage, just as she's philosophically entrenched in other matters. However, if the first man she chooses to settle down with doesn't have her spirit of freedom, doesn't allow her all the space she requires, or doesn't grow and change with her and the times, she will move on. She can be a terror in the household, and many a man has thrown his hands up in dismay and given her permission to divorce him.

If she chooses to remain single, either from the beginning or subsequent to a disillusioning marriage, she'll probably move to another area of the city or to another city—or to another country, for that matter—and "start all over again." She'll become a devotee of singles bars more than likely, since they offer the perfect meadow for her sexual grazing. Her gullibility, however, will make it difficult to escape the shallowness and dishonesty that are so often found there.

She may create a "family" with her friends, adopting their children, their pets, their well-stocked cupboards. She can thus remain independent of family ties but enjoy a familial atmosphere. She makes an excellent friend, trustworthy and cheerful most of the time. One must develop a fairly high level of tolerance for her nervous energy, her blatant, often hurtful honesty, and her sometimes holier-than-thou attitudes to really love her deeply.

She tends to take up with people who will automatically allow her freedom of expression and who aren't overly protective and jealous. There are times in her life when a little protectiveness from friends and intimates would do her good, and she should learn the difference between caring and inhibiting. Too often she mistakes the advice of friends as an attempt to slow her down, to bring her closer to their values.

The Sagittarius Woman will try almost anything once. If she hears of homesteads still available for those interested in growing Christmas trees in the wilderness of Montana, she'll be on the phone to Washington, D.C., to apply for one. She won't, of course, be concerned with all the minutiae involved. Bureaucrats and red tape rank high on her hate list.

I know a Sagittarius woman who married young, on the farm, and dutifully bore her husband four children. Before they were grown, she left to pioneer in the war effort of the 1940s. She met yet another man who offered her the opportunity for adventure, this time in the cabarets of a war-era boomtown. After his death, she waited a respectable year prior to marrying yet another man. He offered her the hope of new life in a new city in a new state. Theirs was indeed a stormy marriage, since his idea of a wife was one who would cook, clean, tend the home fires, and forget the world waiting outside. After his death, she vowed never again to "marry a damn man," and she pursued many, many affairs with men both younger and older than she. Her seemingly irresponsible ways alienated her children, and as she approaches true senior citizenship, instead of bitterness and regret, she embraces anything new. She has found the perfect cloak to hide behind—she's just a batty old woman to those who misunderstand her.

Unlike her Aquarius sister, the Sagittarius Woman takes little stock in what the folks back home think about her. She's flashy, extravagant, and impulsive, and to those who deride her she merely offers an invitation to join in. She has probably pioneered more alternative lifestyles than any other woman in the Zodiac. To her, open marriage isn't a lifestyle—it's a necessity. She was forming communes and espousing the need for getting back to nature long before it was in vogue. Her sense of optimism and her sheer luck make any alternate way of life work for her.

As Sagittarius grows and evolves, she must learn that embracing different life arrangements means more than merely joining. It takes work and a certain amount of long-term dedication in order for any new growth movement to succeed and achieve credibility. She will have to stick around longer than she's accustomed to—and longer than she cares to—in order to actualize all that is possible.

Her magnetism will be a positive force in getting more people involved in exploratory lifestyles as we face the New Age. She *can* harness her wanderlust and ultimately serve as ambassador-at-large for her compatriots, spreading the word that there are alternatives to being locked into unproductive and unfulfilling stereotypes.

It is extremely unlikely that a Sagittarius Woman could embrace a down-to-earth, monogamous relationship with a man who didn't at least have a sense of adventure. She may find herself in this type of marriage at one time or another, and if alternatives do not present themselves, she will become nonmonogamous easily and discreetly. In cases of nonmonogamy, she may sometimes find it difficult to wait until the time is right, and she can become embroiled in some fairly bitter divorce and adultery situations.

The Sagittarius Woman's expansive nature dictated that she reject the traditional role of women long before the idea became broadly accepted. She has a good, positive effect on the women around her. She makes being comfortably liberated seem so easy that the seeds of liberation are often sown amongst her women friends and co-workers effortlessly. Women can learn a valuable lesson from her: the scope of their travels and the richness of their lives needn't be confined within societally assigned roles. She often demonstrates that women can be wives, mothers, and productive members of society and still have experiences long afforded only to men.

Alternative lifestyles

Single woman: This lifestyle affords the Sagittarius Woman freedom to roam and experience life as it comes to her, without a commitment to a husband and family. She often remains single much longer than her contemporaries; she also often remains single after a particularly difficult divorce. Her talent for making friends and her loyalty to them often provide her with a substitute family to satisfy the need for that experience. She seldom feels lonely, which is one of the great pitfalls of being single.

Should she decide to remain single, she must first ask herself some questions: Are the benefits greater than those found in traditional family situations? Am I afraid of the commitment, or am I being realistic about my own needs and foibles? Will I have the personal strength to endure the last part of my life alone? Are children really the poverbial "comfort"? Am I willing to become a member of, or to form, an extended family to satisfy the need for belonging to someone and sharing family-type experiences?

Intimate networks: This is an arrangement in which one has friends of both sexes, and which neither encourages nor prohibits intimate sexual encounters. The Sagittarius Woman thrives wonderfully in such situations, if for no other reason than that they satisfy her needs for expansion, giving, intuition, and exploration. She functions well in relationships that discourage jealousy and possessiveness. She will have to keep her independent spirit and bluntness in check to be a part of *any* relationship, and that is a real necessity in intimate networks.

True to her nature, the Sagittarius Woman will probably have been involved in many intimate networks long before now. It's the kind of friendship she looks for, one without the traditional "you do for me, I'll do for you in return" requirements.

Open marriage: It will be to the Sagittarius Woman's advantage in the long run to enter *any* marriage with openness in mind. She should carefully inspect the true motives of her intended partner and completely educate him about hers *before* making a marriage commitment. She is often misunderstood, partly because she doesn't make her needs clear enough and partly because she changes so rapidly.

Open marriage satisfies not only her need for multiple sexual experiences but also her need for travel (though it may only be to the other side of town). She must have a firm grip on the concept of primary relationships in order to remain married and enjoy the benefits of open marriage. Should she develop a sense of commitment that is strong enough to withstand her travels, the expansion of her philosophies, and the harshness of her personal sense of honesty and integrity, she'll be able to weather any turbulence that many come her way in this lifestyle.

Ménage à trois: Probably the only thing that the Sagittarius Woman would really enjoy more is a good orgy. She sexually welcomes others to join in her personal adventures and delights in showing them the way. She has strong, assertive sexual tendencies and must be careful not to take charge of the other two people. This arrangement dictates that all three share in the joy, the discovery, and the satisfaction of sex; if one or both partners are less strong than she, she will naturally take over to insure the results she requires. She should let it flow and take its course naturally, without prodding or asserting herself unequally.

Group marriage: This is an ideal situation for the Sagittarius Woman who has evolved and who has learned the value of self-confidence. She'll probably want to take the entire group on her distant travels and explorations. This concept provides the perfect stage for her exhibitionistic talents and progressive spirit. Again, she must take care not to overtake and outdistance the other members of the marriage. She must also be sure that they are sincere in the endeavor; too often her gullibility makes her a prime target for those seeking too much power.

Communal living: The Sagittarius Woman's life is the essence of communal living! She likes nothing more than sharing experiences, learning new talents, perfecting charm, and spreading joy. The sheer numbers of people involved in true communal living insure that she will seldom be without new stimuli and an audience for her exhibitionistic tendencies. She is a born teacher and leader, something often in diminishing supply in our culture. She believes in personalizing things, in conserving and in embracing nature. Her intuition is invaluable in a communal setting, and the expansive, progressive nature of this lifestyle means that she'll do well.

Again, she must polish her bluntness and extreme sense of honesty in order to protect the feelings of those with whom she lives. The intimacy of communal life is also something she'll have to get in better touch with. Her eagerness and optimism will help boost the spirits of others when the going gets rough—and then, of course, there is her abundance of luck!

Gay/bisexual lifestyle: Although the masculine side of the Sagittarius Woman often becomes stronger in gay relationships, she is a likely candidate for this subculture. Often men present problems of sexual frustration and are unable to satisfy her enormous appetite; they also have a tendency to traditionalize her role. She is progressive enough, for sure, to embrace this alternative to the traditional societal norm. She must restrain her tendencies to control and must allow the differences between gay lifestyles and heterosexual lifestyles to prevail. She rejects role playing and games with men; she must not embrace them with another woman, either.

Summing up Sagittarius

The Sagittarius Woman's greatest natural resource—her boundless energy—is also perhaps her greatest challenge. To learn to channel that energy she must learn to control it. But before that can happen, she must learn that control does not necessarily imply inhibition. For her, control will have to take on new meaning and emerge as a force that directs her movements and disciplines her mind. Only then can she achieve the higher goals she is forever seeking.

She must redirect her pursuit from the distant star to the closer reality of life itself. She must also learn to dream dreams that aren't quite so impossible; then she will have a stronger, self-instilled sense of mission.

The Sagittarius Woman can forge a strong sense of identity by becoming less fearful of losing her independence. As she grows, she will find her foallike legs, which now carry her from stone to stone across the river of life, developing and gaining the strength to gracefully propel her into a strong leadership role in the New Age.

CAPRICORN

CHECKLIST OF CAPRICORN TRAITS

Note: This checklist describes the traits of one *phase* only; if it doesn't seem to fit you, check other lists to find the phase you are in right now.

1. Purposeful
2. Appetite for Life
3. Ambitious
4. Determined
5. Skilled in Crisis Management
6. Loyal
7. Sense of Responsibility
8. Dedication
9. Contradictory
10. Passionate
11. Critical
12. Highly Sexed
13. Vulnerable
14. Materialistic
15. Moralistic
16. Attracted to Structure
17. Rigid
18. Conformist
19. Traditional, Glamorizes the Past
20. Insecure yet . . .
21. Confident
22. Regal
23. Selective yet . . .
24. Scattered
25. Self-sufficient yet . . .
26. Seeks Protection
27. Cautious, Dislikes Risks
28. Practical
29. Realistic
30. Organizational Ability
31. Long Memory
32. Humorous, Sarcastic
33. Moody, Depressive
34. Long-lived
35. Successful (is long-term winner)

Capricorn personality

All my life I wanted to be somebody
Only to find that I am!
A friend

General traits and background

The Capricorn Woman is blessed with a deep hunger for living, for achieving, and for triumphing over the odds. She is an expert at coping with crisis and adversity, and during her usually long life she has plenty of chances to prove herself. She is a survivor, a loyal lover and friend; she frequently manages the affairs of others with more flair and perspicacity than she runs her own.

Her health and happiness usually increase with time. She may not feel really sure of herself until about age thirty-five. Her greatest friend is joy, for being born in the darkest days of winter seems to create in her a need for sunshine. Her worst enemy is her hidden self-doubt, which can lead to frequent depression.

The Capricorn Woman has Olympian ideals and expectations. She rarely is satisfied with herself or with the way things are. She reaches beyond the rainbow; and when she is not chasing a dream, she is usually in rigorous training for the next assault on Mount Everest.

Taurus, Virgo, and Capricorn are the three earth signs of the Zodiac. Capricorn is Cardinal Earth, the tenth sign. The Capricorn type is described by the checklist of traits at the beginning of this chapter. The Capricorn phase has the following characteristics:

1 Geared for action and self-assertion. The key words for Capricorn are *apply, utilize,* and *success.*
2 The value of all important things in life must be carefully measured. She sifts her priorities as finely as she would flour, always mindful of how each fits into the total scheme of her ambitions. She rarely loses sight of her goals.
3 She has an affinity for words and is a champion verbal magician. She is forceful and articulate when she wants to be, but she rarely tells more than she deems necessary. If it suits her purpose, she can be downright secretive.
4 Capricorn is astrologically ruled by the planet Saturn. Saturn is traditionally associated with duty, responsibility, delay, restriction or constriction; metaphysicists consider Saturn the lord of Karma. It is said that because her astrological ruler is a

fair authority and judge, Capricorn herself is meant to be impartial and just.

5 She is certainly born to rule and even as a child is frequently observed to have a regal demeanor and queenly bearing. Authority is important to her, particularly as an ingredient of success.

Capricorn energy is pregnant with the potential for outstanding achievement. But, as with every aspect of living, it is the *use* and *application* of energy that determines the quality of the life experiences.

People with Capricorn strong in their charts, or those going through a Capricorn phase, usually reap the exact harvest of their thoughts and deeds. Positive, they can conquer any peak; negative, they can expect a long, painful struggle ahead.

The young Capricorn Woman, or a woman going through a Capricorn phase, has a tendency to work hard, play hard, pay for every mistake, be very money- and "thing" -conscious, and have difficulty relaxing. The positive Capricorn Woman hitches her wagon to a star, and never mind the material worries. The negative Capricorn Woman hitches her wagon to a fence post and may get mired in the mud.

Positive, the Capricorn Woman is a wizard of forms and rituals. She can work magic with thoughts—that is, heal the sick and wounded. She can wave her wand and create a beautiful and comfortable environment. She can incorporate rituals into her life and the lives of her loved ones so as to facilitate communication, accomplishment, and optimism. She can feel right at home with ancient traditions, translating and assimilating them to today's world.

Negative, she can be materialistic to the point of excessive worry or avarice, rigid, critical, fearful. She may alienate many people by her harsh tone and judgment. She is bound to be hypersensitive to criticism and may suffer from pessimism, doubt, and periodic depression. Sometimes her depressions become a way of life—an ever-present danger in the Capricorn phase. Born to carry out the law, she may mistake her mission in life for that of a dictator. It would be helpful to Capricorn if she let her natural forbearance, not her fears, color her unfolding fantasies.

The Capricorn Woman has the substance to make her dreams come true, but she must work to develop the style. She may, in fact, be a slob or a klutz. She may neglect details of personal appearance and image. She is very intrigued by people more glamorous and chic than she, and may even be envious. She benefits from efforts to match her magical inner nature with an equally compelling outer image.

A night owl, she is usually serious, a lone dreamer of great dreams. What ultimately makes her so fascinating and distinguished is her inborn courage, ambition, persistence, and capacity to make her fantasies real.

What follows is a representative sample of the negative and positive aspects of Capricorn energy. Traits common to all Capricorns appear on this list, but the individual Capricorn Woman must remember that she has free will, or variable choice. She must decide which list describes her more accurately in this phase of her life. Positive Capricorn traits are: emotionalism, independence, ambition, fondness for beautiful things, thriftiness, persistence, courage, respect for tradition, caution, control, regality, dignity, humility, responsibility, trust, confidence, organizational ability, and will power. Negative Capricorn traits are: moodiness, overdependence, one-upmanship, greed, acquisitiveness, miserliness, depressive fears, rigidity, procrastination, repression, haughtiness, imperiousness, false pride, domination, distrust, self-doubt, authoritarianism, and obstructiveness.

The primary body stress spots for the Capricorn Woman are her knees, spine, the skin, joints, ligaments, cartillage, tendons, the teeth, gall bladder, nails. The professions most especially associated with Capricorn, or ruled by Saturn, the ruling planet of this sign, are the following: architecture, building contracting, bricklaying; chiropractice, counseling, land ownership and speculation; farming, grain dealing, civil engineering; ranching, sculpting, tanning, time keeping; business in general, carpentry, a business of scientific branch of metaphysics; government, politics, large scale administration, watch making. Some of the best professions for her to enter are: crafts that produce tangible products made of leather, stone, metal, or wood; auction work; self-employment as a jeweler or owner of an antique store, dress shop, or restaurant; real estate; the food industry; anything connected with mining, plumbing, or the use of lead; antiques; collecting for museums or patrons of the arts; bookbinding; stage craft or design; acting or producing; cartooning or humor; accounting; administration of large projects; working as a bone specialist; dentistry; professional organizing.

Strong sense of purpose and direction, appetite for life

When an interviewer asked Capricorn film star Faye Dunaway when she had first become aware of wanting to be an actress, she replied, "Always!"

If Scarlett O'Hara is the typical Aries fireball of the movies, we might say that the women Joan Crawford played in her most famous films were all Capricorn types. Her characters were clever and poised, regal, persistent, achieving, upwardly mobile; they knew how to advance their ambitions, faced many obstacles, but in the end were successful, at least professionally. The common theme of these films is still relevant to women everywhere, and most especially to the Capricorn Woman: Can a woman combine acute ambition with personal fulfillment? How?

Sex and love are supremely important to the Capricorn Woman, but they do not fulfill her need for worldly recognition. Even as a little girl, she is usually a dedicated thinker and planner. The typical Capricorn knows what she wants to do when she grows up—she wants to be an all-around winner in the stakes of life. If she suppresses this knowledge, she is likely to have experiences that shake her up and remind her of her destiny to be someone. The definition of *someone* is hers, but she must be satisfied by her own achievements.

Ambitious, determined

The Capricorn Woman's astrological symbol is the goat—sometimes the mountain goat, sometimes the sea goat. The mountain goat is usually depicted on a rock, scaling the heights, surefooted and alone. The sea goat is half-goat, half-fish, representing the ability to go far and feel deeply. Her ancient symbol was the unicorn. Its single horn symbolizes the Capricorn Woman's single-minded determination to reach her goals. She has intense powers of concentration, and she never quits any race that is important to her. She may be the tortoise instead of the hare, but we all know who won that competition!

She is persistent in her aims, though she may adapt her methods to the circumstances. She is a good judge of opportunity and will take advantage of it too, though she has a problem deciding things quickly. Some people think she is an opportunist, but this is often a sour-grapes evaluation.

She has grand designs hidden in her multilayered psyche. For one, she harbors visions of entering the establishment and making big money. She often imagines her name in neon on Broadway. Universally, her goal is to be recognized by those she respects. She may want to be remembered in the history books as a powerful political figure, or she may choose to be the power behind the throne. If she takes the strict domestic route, she will surely push and encourage her husband from her rung a step below.

Skilled in crisis management, loyal

If you're in a scene straight from *The Towering Inferno* or in divorce court crying your eyes out, or if you've just been invited to go to Stockholm for the Nobel Prize ceremonies but your husband is hospitalized with ulcers, call your Capricorn friend. She is superb in emergencies. Nobody is better equipped to take the reins calmly, soothe your nerves, and make your decisions for you. And nobody enjoys it more, either!

You may occasionally resent her for her know-it-all attitude, but the fact is that she does know how to cope—especially in a crisis. She is happy when everyone needs her and no one has time to resent her. She loves to come into a tough situation and make order out of chaos. She enjoys ruling situations.

Sense of responsibility, dedication

The Capricorn Woman is thoroughly loyal, a dedicated friend and employee, and a responsible human being. She is ambitious, and she has a good heart. She is also dedicated to herself and seldom loses a battle unless she has just calculated that it may be necessary in order to win the war.

Nobody, except perhaps Taurus, is as reliable as she at keeping the books and taking care of money or property. She likes clipping coupons, too, and always uses them. She gets the best value for her money and is an incomparably shrewd shopper. But one must remember to show appreciation for her efforts, or she may start brooding over the lack of recognition.

Contradictory

Who would ever think that Capricorn, with her self-reliant collected air, is a bundle of contradictions? Perhaps the Cheshire cat in *Alice* knew her secret, but most of us are still trying to decipher the chemistry of this lady's high-potency time-release formula.

In fact, she is as passionate as she is critical and cautious. She is highly sexed, but when love turns sour, she becomes a dutiful sex partner and grows to resent sex. She is emotional yet restrained. She is optimistic about her own chances except when depressed, yet pessimistic about human nature. She is selective about partners and sex positions but goes through phases of being receptive to quick affairs or one-night stands. She is a high achiever, yet she is doubtful of herself. She is generous yet thrifty; giving and loyal yet temperamental and jealous. She is self-sufficient but likes her man to protect her. She gives all in love, but it may take her a lifetime to find her true love.

Passionate, critical

The Capricorn Woman treads lightly on new territory, never jumping into commitments without long rehearsals, but once she loves, she loves totally. Her passions, once released, know no bounds. Unfortunately, her faultfinding tends to increase along with her love.

She hesitates on the brink of commitment because she normally fears rejection. But she also stalls in order to have time to figure out all the answers and calculate all the risks. What, she asks herself, will this love mean in terms of status outcome, sensual satisfaction, family approval? What will be the price and advantage of my surrender? Sometimes she hesitates so long that the opportunity is lost. She may also create distrust in others, especially in those with little patience. She needs to learn that life has no guarantees, not even in the short run.

Highly sexed, vulnerable

The bane of the Capricorn Woman's existence is her constant fear of getting hurt. Perhaps it explains why she frequently finds fault with her lovers. She may reason that as long as they fail to deliver the perfect goods, she is entitled to withhold her total love. When she lets the ice melt and the flames leap, she often becomes too vulnerable for comfort. It is then that her other side emerges. From behind the queen in control, a child peeks out, vulnerable, delightful, fragile.

The Capricorn Woman probably feels vulnerable because she is inexperienced in sharing, in emotional give-and-take. She cannot give halfway if she really cares; and so, to protect herself, she holds back until nearly sure of the other person. When the die is finally cast, she can be swept away by the intensity of her feelings, open and enthusiastic.

Sometimes she explodes with the intensity of a pent-up volcano. In bed, she may act like a puppy who has finally found enough space to run free. She is intensely responsive to a sensitive man who has emotional strength and resilience, enough intelligence to cuddle her, enough sexual experience to last.

Materialistic

The Capricorn Woman fights a running battle with herself over her attraction to wealth and its glamorous trappings. She craves money and prestige; she may also be a puritan and feel guilty about wanting or having it. She periodically dreams of sable coats, yachts, jewels, and country homes. She wants to wrap material security around her, as if to protect herself from the cold winter day of her birth. In fact, the warmth she needs is the sunshine of self-acceptance and love.

The danger of Capricorn's materialistic tendencies is that she may invest herself in the quest for gold and glitter at the expense of her total development. She may become a female Babbitt. She may take security as the only reality. For example, she may give up a promising career as a young artist or dramatist for a career based solely on material gain. She is also capable of marrying for money alone and being sorry later.

The world, and life too, is a *process* in change and flux. The Capricorn Woman may still hold the old-fashioned view that the universe and life in it are strictly physical fixed entities. Remember, Capricorn, Einstein came up with a new world view. You must strive to embrace the relativistic concept of life, of your own fluid self. Do not be so involved in *doing* or *having* that you forget *to be*.

Moralistic, attracted to structure, rigidity

Puritanism, with its narrow and rigid moral code, could be judged a Capricorn phase in our history. The Capricorn Woman is born with a strong sense of ethics. She thinks she knows right from wrong, and she does not plan to deviate. Even as a baby, she probably organized her toys into categories, communicated with measured feeling, and preferred clear, repetitious household routines to an unstructured lifestyle.

She usually grows up a very proper young lady. She may wear gloves and a hat when other girls do not, and she often radiates a cool magnetism. Early in life she usually holds absolute views of sexual right and wrong. She can be downright prissy, haughty, and judgmental.

She is the type of person who generally sets her daily schedule at least a week in advance. She seldom likes change and disapproves of "abnormal" habits. "Abnormal," in turn, may be anything she disapproves of. Fortunately for her, she usually relaxes her social and sexual standards after living for a while and having a few affairs. In some cases, it takes a failed marriage and nasty divorce to teach her flexibility and tolerance.

Conformist, glamorizes the past and tradition

The Capricorn Woman respects nothing so much as the past. She sees it as full of grandeur, invariably more glorious than the decadent present and the precarious future.

She is usually in love with durability, permanence, safety, and roots. In her desire to make everything in life conform to her views, she may surround herself as much as she can with objects that have an aura of permanence. She prefers antiques; she wants solid furniture. Brand names are important; she wants only the best, for it gives lasting value and status.

She is highly appreciative of family values and is usually more knowledgeable about the family tree than are her parents. She may try to inculcate old-fashioned manners and morals in her baby brothers and sisters. She has been known to get heavy-handed and to invoke her right of seniority, in which she firmly believes.

As a little girl, she frequently helps old ladies across the street, nurses sick or old animals, and is never too tired to read. She has the unfortunate habit of reading by dim light, as if to conjure up a past in which there was as yet no electricity. She glamorizes faraway places, success stories, and older people. To her, the secret of life lies in keeping traditions and reaching an old age. In many ways, she resembles her opposite, the Cancer Woman, also nostalgic, materialistic, traditional.

She would like to have guaranteed permanent relationships. However, she may have such rigid, outmoded definitions of good and bad that almost every relationship will sooner or later suffer from her moral ideals and judgments.

Insecure, confident, regal

The Capricorn Woman is a fascinating maze, a veritable Daedalian labyrinth. Somewhere there is a point of access, but it takes patience and ingenuity to figure out the path.

She is confident that time is on her side, and rightly so. She counts on her own durability in reaching her goals. She knows she is strong and competent, and she expects to be recompensed sooner or later. She has a sense of destiny, and she is willing to work hard to fulfill it.

When it comes to the area of love per se, she is less secure. She subtly courts intimacy, yet she usually shies away from it. It may take a megadose of affectionate pursuit to catch her, even briefly. Larger than life, splendiferous, she is the rare pearl in the oyster. It will take more than a grain of sand to get through to her; it may take a sirocco!

Selective, scattered

The Capricorn Woman's strange brand of confident insecurity inspires many dramas in her life. She is familiar with crises, with loss, with peaks and valleys. She is extremely choosy, yet in her need to be connected she consistently reaches out for real intimacy, often to the wrong people. She scatters energy trying to help the needy, the stray, and the elderly. At times, restless and hungry for physical touch, she may have empty friendships and affairs.

She may find intimacy too threatening, but her inborn confidence tempts her over and over to try every avenue. She may settle for quantity instead of quality. At times, when she is depressed or disgusted, she may forget her own royal inheritance and want to be a bum or live in a slum. But a new event almost always forces her to change course, and she may head upward, full of dignity and discrimination once more.

Self-sufficient yet seeks protection

The Capricorn Woman is probably the most able to be independent, yet she is healthily old-fashioned in her need to have someone she can depend on. She may be the president of her company or of the local League of Women Voters, but she will still want her mate to decide if the house needs refurnishing, if Johnny should go to private school, or if her mother should be moved to a nursing home. She also prefers that he pay.

Cautious, dislikes risks

The mountain goat is surefooted but careful. It is well aware that a heedless step could cause a fall that might temporarily incapacitate. The Capricorn Woman experiences frequent hurt and delay. She tries to anticipate this. She moves forward gingerly, putting one foot in front of the other. She never tries to swim, either, before she is an expert at all the strokes.

Capricorn, you have the practical wisdom and skills to direct your own life. But remember—even you cannot control the future, so don't overdo your cautiousness. Take some calculated risks, especially in human relations. Don't keep score. The law of Saturn, your ruling planet, is universal justice, and you will not be left out.

Practical, realistic

The Capricorn Woman is a pragmatist who rarely loses sight of her short- or long-term goals; she is prompt in sizing up the pros and cons of each situation. Will buying a new coat wipe out her savings? Will staying late at work now net her a raise? Will going to the movies with Sam be followed by bed, or is it too soon? Does Sam make enough money to take her to a nightclub next weekend, or should she wait for John? Lady Capricorn keeps a running score in her head that would impress the most avid tournament bridge player.

She is as realistic about her prospects with her lover as with her company or her divorce case. She comes well prepared and takes no chances. You will not see her wildly pedaling her bicycle down the highway, for the odds she previously calculated ran against her doing so. If you see her at the gambling table, you can be sure she has calculated that it's her day to win (she may have used biorhythms, computers, astrology, palmistry, dreams, or mood charts).

She usually tries to back her intuition with what she considers factual evidence in her favor; she tries to anchor all her activities in practical reality. If she sells jewelry, she will know the history and original location of each stone. If she grows plants, she will be well versed in the amounts of sunlight and nutrients each plant needs for maximum growth—after all, the profit (pleasure too) depends on the plants' health. If she is an astrologer, she will be an encyclopedia of useful household hints in just about every area of life. If she is an administrator, she is most likely to manage projects that make practical use of the earth's resources. She will be concerned with basics such as housing for the elderly, clothing, or food.

Organizational ability, long memory

The Capricorn Woman is more organized in business than in her personal life. She will service her accounts efficiently, but her own bedroom may look like an antique shop before liquidation. No matter how cluttered her own digs may be, she usually keeps things straight in her head. Ask her where last year's geraniums were replanted, and she'll direct you to the exact square foot in the garden. If you are looking for a pin you lost weeks ago, the thread to match your new chartreuse outfit, or a book that has been out of print for decades, ask her. She'll direct you to it.

She collects information and has an elephant's memory for the smallest detail. She also collects old pins and chartreuse thread in case there is ever a need. She is somewhat of a hoarder, but who is to judge the difference between a collector and a hoarder? She'll swear that her broken-down metal tub with Victorian feet is worth twice what you'd get if you sold your late-model, Italian-designed, gold-fauceted tub. In a few years, she will probably be proven right.

In terms of efficiency and loyalty, she is an outstanding mother or nursery school teacher. Kids listen to her, and she can organize them in no time for games and activities. She manages everything and everyone, or at least she tries. If people resent her officiousness, they admire her competence. She may try to categorize life a bit too neatly, but this will usually right itself.

Her retentive memory, though a blessing, may also be a source of grief to her at times. She rarely forgets a slight, never a criticism, and she has trouble filing painful memories in the wastebasket.

Humorous, sarcastic

The Capricorn Woman adores practical joke as long as they are played on others. She will gladly pair her brother's socks with glue, mix the gerbil's food with your dinner, and put stuffed mice on her grandmother's chair.

Humor is a lifesaver for her. She uses it to channel her hostility all her life. She is great at barbed one-liners and usually throws them at people who make her angry. She seldom "owns" her anger, but she almost always manages to get the message across, and release some resentment, through a joke. Of course some of the jokes are suspiciously similar to put-downs, but that is for others to worry about.

The Capricorn Woman has the potential to be an excellent comedienne. She has a precise, well-developed sense of timing. She blossoms on stage or even in an enforced spotlight as she rarely does without an audience. She is found of political satire, and her favorite cartoons are those with acid and "meat," i.e., pointed social commentary.

Moody, depressive

Humor notwithstanding, the Capricorn Woman lives in a mood elevator. She is stricken by moods as suddenly as the rest of us are stung by bees or caught by a coughing fit. She may be calmly watching television, then suddenly storm out of the room. She is no stranger to fits of sadness and sudden crying jags. Very often, there is no known explanation for her mood changes, but they are very real and persist most of her life.

Her biggest problem is that she does not know how to be happy. She has to learn it. She has sadness in her soul. She is prone to long periods of depression and corrosive self-doubt. These may flare up because of heavy reprimanding by a parent, criticism by a teacher, the loss of a friend, or fear of failure, but they may also strike out of the blue.

Her high expectations are bound to cause disappointment and may be one explanation for her moodiness. After all, nobody can constantly live up to high ideals. Living too much in the past may be another problem. But mostly she must accept her sudden mood changes as a factor in her makeup and work with them rather than resisting. Crying on the full moon or slamming doors every once in awhile may be tolerable, but she must find ways to combat longer depressions.

Long life span, successful

Most Capricorn Women do not really come into their own until age thirty-five or later. It is almost inevitable that they will have to work for their money, pay for their pleasures, and go through many lessons in love and life. They develop plenty of character formed in part by adversity.

The most outstanding characteristics of the Capricorn Woman are her abilities to mold life to fit her mature needs—success, independence, inter-dependence—and to age magnificently. The grand old lady whose eccentricities are the talk of the town while she is its favorite toast represents the best of Capricorn.

Capricorn relationships

The Capricorn Woman is often likened to a fortune hunter. Prestige and money are, in fact, very important to her. She usually wants worldly status, security, roots, an orderly life, and polite children. She also wants her ideal man, though this may be a lower priority.

What is often unknown about Capricorn is that she harbors a deep well of love; she also hides a gargantuan streak of loneliness. Moreover, she secretly longs for glamour and excitement and from time to time may be willing to give up security in order to obtain them.

She fears love, yet she needs it intensely to complete her, lift her out of her loneliness. Time weighs heavily on her, and she hates to waste it. She is a busybody. She may invite love and then grow cool and reject it.

Intense though controlled, the Capricorn Woman attempts to brake her emotionalism by an air of distinguished competence. She would love to have her relationships predictably in the palm of her hand, much as in a business deal.

She is full of surprises. She herself may not know what she will do next. She lives with a cacophonous inner dialogue maintained by her own warring voices. Sometimes she listens to an inner voice that tells her, Go ahead, take the risk with Ed, John, or Harry. Another voice may caution her to wait and protect her turf to avoid being hurt. Just when she appears to have clearly settled for a life of prestige and passionless security, she may fall in love with a struggling painter. She may make believe that he will be the next Michelangelo, however—especially with her help.

The important thing to understand about the Capricorn Woman is that while she may be off chasing rainbows, her steady gaze is fixed on the ground. You see, she doesn't want to trip if she can help it, even while pursuing her dreams.

The Capricorn Woman's greatest challenge in relating to people is to trust them and let down her self-protective barriers. She is often defensive, expecting to be hurt or maligned. She may mock and refuse to take love seriously. But what scares her most is this: the truth about love may be that even love will not stem the tide of her loneliness. The fear and existential pain of a Mrs. Robinson is familiar to her. Sometimes the simple act of living throws her into despondency. What's the use, she wonders, of falling in love? There is no guarantee, and Capricorn seldom likes to shop without it.

The circle of fear and loneliness—needing love, reaching out yet fearing hurt, growing thicker skin as the years fly, questioning more and more the place and meaning of love in her life—is a typical pattern for Capricorn. She persists; she always gives as good as she gets, and sometimes more. It may well have been she who authored the phrase "It is better to have loved and lost than never to have loved at all."

Her main resources in sexual relationships are durable sex appeal, which usually increases with age; persistence; the ability to give as much as she gets; secret passion; tremendous loyalty; sense of humor; and survival ability. Like Capricorns Ava Gardner and Marlene Dietrich, she can be counted in for a long, long time. And look for a winner!

Childhood

The Capricorn Woman often grows up feeling very close to her father and uncomfortable with her mother. If she is not close to her dad emotionally, she usually admires him from a distance and accords him the respect she reserves exclusively for males. She rarely grows up identifying with her mother. In fact, she is more male than female in her orientation. She may be a tomboy in adolescence, or a proper little girl, but she is almost invariably more goal-oriented and desirous of worldly success than her girl friends.

She may elect to hide her lofty ambitions (and later her passions) behind an excessively proper and/or competent facade. Many Capricorn girls behave like little old ladies, and it is easy to imagine them in velvet rockets with crocheted lace blankets covering their knees, their most troublesome joints. Nobody may be aware that inside the carefully coifed, prim little head live the dreams of a grand schemer.

She rarely, if ever, plays with dolls and other symbols of growing up female. She may secretly resent being a girl, feeling that it cramps her style. She may rebel in her own way, but never without worrying about rocking the boat. Capricorn is not a natural rebel; she just won't tolerate being typecast as a second-class citizen—especially when it comes to the size and kind of rewards accorded her.

Eva is a case in point. The oldest in a family of six girls, she was Mother's little helper, the good girl who carried out Mother's wishes. Eva came to me when she was thirty-eight, complaining of insomnia and vague aches and pains in her joints. She was married, a mother of three children, and an amateur playwright. As we explored her feelings about her life, she gradually revealed (Capricorn types never do anything hastily) her dislike of her mother and timid adoration of her father.

> My father was not around much; Mother was the focus of the family. I was supposed to hold the fort while she had the other babies, and to help her. I grew to hate coming home after school because it just meant more and more work. I was a responsible little girl, but inside I was exploding with anger. And only my father was aware that I was different inside than my facade suggested. He and I had a strong, quiet understanding, and we shared the knowledge that, in the end, we would get our share of whatever it was we needed.

Eva grew up with an imaginary playmate to whom she spoke a strange language nobody else could understand. She called her playmate a "celestial twin." It seemed to me that her twin was everything Eva herself was but could not yet express. Her twin was ambitious, dynamic, sexy, pushy, rebellious, quick-witted, popular, and trendy. Eva was prim, proper, and submissive.

Eva had always wanted to be a journalist but was afraid to tell anyone. Eventually her father came to her rescue and sent her to college over her Mother's protests. At that time, Eva broke through her shyness and shared her dream with her father. It turned out that he too had wanted to be a writer but had acquired the business he still owned when the burdens of supporting a large family outgrew his income.

Eva became aware that her insomnia at thirty-eight was punctuated by dreams about her parents, particularly her father. It seemed she had repressed her love and admiration for him in favor of following her Mother into a traditional, family-centered life. Eva had been afraid of being her *whole* self. She had never acted on her ambitions. Though she was domestic and nurturing, she also derived pleasure from work, from conquering new intellectual territory and competing in a male arena.

Many Capricorn Women grow up feeling a distressing emotional distance from others, especially the females in the family. Because the Capricorn is so sensitive, she may take this very much to heart. She may even conclude deep inside that she is just too weird for people to understand, and perhaps to love.

The young Capricorn frequently feels in exile either at school, at home, in the family at large, in her times, or in her culture. This feeling of estrangement usually underlies her determined climb to the top later; she wishes by her success to prove that she belongs.

Often, the Capricorn girl feels she was born in the wrong era. She may wish she had lived in the eighteenth-century France of logic and humanitarianism, or she may think she might have been more at home in Victorian England. Her identification with past historical eras accounts for her love of antiques, but it also baffles her. She may secretly believe that nobody else feels as she does, that nobody would understand.

She may have more than one childhood experience that reinforces her sense of isolation. For some Capricorn girls, feelings of alienation may be exacerbated by the birth of a younger sibling who takes most of the parents' attention away. For others, it may be the parents' divorce. Quite a few experience near-drownings, sports accidents (especially affecting the bones and knees), or some confining illness that limits their activities with peers. Also, moves that radically uproot them and necessitate coping with loneliness repeatedly are not uncommon.

How the Capricorn Woman relates: lovers and other intimates

The Capricorn Woman's mode of relating is frequently colored by deep shyness and fear. A constant vigilance as to the motives of others, intermittent attempts at controlling the relationship—plus a deep capacity for love and devotion—normally characterize her relationships.

When she decides to love someone, she is bound to go all out. Neither lightning nor earthquake can shake her instinctive protection of her loved ones. It is essential to comprehend this about her: despite her efficiency and aplomb, what the Capricorn Woman usually seeks in an intimate relationship is to fuse with the other. She may want *inter*dependence, but her ultimate desire is almost sure to be fused synergy, a harmonious and complete blend with her lover.

The Capricorn Woman often has trouble resolving her dependence/independence needs; this conflict manifests itself in her relationships in the guise of extreme devotion to her lover alternating with emotional withdrawal. She may have an exaggerated fear of dependence in any form and a high intolerance for parasites or weaklings, yet she may plunge into total commitment to the point of temporary obliteration of her needs.

She may often give to the wrong men, those who have nothing to give her in return. She may pick losers time and again, eventually learning her lessons thoroughly. She may also take from the wrong people—people who may love her very *conditionally*, keeping scores of hidden demands, or who may be incapable of loving as fully as she. Though it may not be hard to take advantage of her in her early years, it is usually impossible to make her forget she has been wronged.

A flurry of contradictions, she may find love and fault simultaneously. She may penny-pinch in love until she trusts enough to let herself go. If she is immature and unbalanced, she may economize on love at various turns and squander it at others.

She'll combine a sexy invitation ("Come up and see me sometime!") with a daring smile designed to taunt her seducer. Capricorn likes to dare would-be intimates to prove themselves, would-be lovers to warm her up and then equal her unleashed ardor. She is also, however, willing to pay the price for what she wants. She pays her dues, collecting punishment as well as rewards along the way.

The Capricorn Woman who depends on her husband for all her identity and status will almost surely encounter serious problems eventually. Living through another person is not her cup of tea. Sooner or later, as in the case of Ruth, she will usually find the need and the energy to take her own self and career seriously. There are Capricorn Women who are able to stay home contentedly and tend the hearth all their lives, but they are in a minority. Most need a larger scope for their inborn ambition, and most have a burning, long-lasting need to prove they can "make it."

The Capricorn Woman must recognize that this drive is part of her natural makeup, that she needs to make provision for it in her lifestyle. If she chooses to live through and for her husband or her children, she is giving power over her life and future to another person. There is a strong chance that she will resent this sooner or later. Many Capricorn Women end up as secret drinkers, taking their troubles out this way, perhaps unwilling to confide in someone.

As a friend, the Capricorn Woman hardly has a peer. She is attuned to people's needs, meets emergencies and manages problems with efficiency and wisdom born of experience. She has heart, and she is often more comfortable showing it in friendship than in romantic love. She is usually generous and chooses gifts with intuitive care. She is able to help an intimate fulfill dreams by providing an example, support, or practical, energetic prodding.

She usually has friends of both sexes, though she will probably be truly close to just a few. She tends to change friends periodically, as she changes. She is scarcely at a loss for contacts, and she knows just how to nurture them. She may prefer female friends who respect her need to succeed, though they themselves need not share it. In fact, Capricorn can also profit from domestically inclined women friends who from time to time provide an undisturbed port in the storm. She has no trouble making and keeping male friends, for she can think as a male. She will rarely make a man insecure by accusing him of opportunism, for she understands his need to be a recognized member of the species.

Capricorn, I advise you to avoid the pitfalls of choosing the wrong partner. However, if you do err, retain a sense of optimism and consider it a good lesson. Let go before too much time has elapsed.

I advise you also to avoid the trap of vicarious living. It is for good reason that your symbols are the unicorn and the mountain goat—you are a winner, born to the magic of success. You may share it, but you must not hand it over to someone less capable than you.

As you go through life, remember that it is a process. You are continually balancing. If it seems like a trapeze act at times, it is that for all of us. Keep up your confidence, and don't give in to self-blame or depression.

Your great need for accomplishment and recognition is a wonder to behold. Though it runs counter to our traditional feminine upbringing, don't deviate from this path. Instead, enrich it continually. And balance work with fun, public success with private joy.

The Capricorn Woman in love

When she is in love, the Capricorn Woman seems to be an angel at large, a temptress in bed, a secure empress in company (she rules the turf); she may also for a time be a mirror image of her mate.

She is usually gifted with the powers of persuasion, anticipation, and old-fashioned courtesy toward her lover. She is prepared to smooth the way for gracious living and loving. She may make original, craftsy, funny items for her man's desk, to remind him of her. She may design their bedroom for comfort and passion. She will certainly learn to cook all his favorite dishes and serve them with elegance.

She will probably visit his mother to find out what pleased him as a baby, and she may try to recreate the past through stimuli associated with earlier pleasures. If her man loved breast feeding, for example, she will probably dress to enhance her bosom. If he is a leg man, she may buy slit skirts. If he grew up pulling on his mother's long locks, she may wear her hair long. If he feared the dark as a child, she will make sure to have extra lights and candles available. As a lover, she combines the practical with the romantic.

The Capricorn Woman is usually excellent at working with her hands. Handmade gifts or the transformation of a bachelor's digs into an instant love nest are among the signs of her affection. She is good at creating an ambience of safety and privacy to shelter her and her man. She is mindful of important details like having his favorite records and his preferred brand of liquor available and keeping a supply of logs for the fireplace. She may even buy a special cushion just for him. She may spend lots of time fantasizing about their dream house, and she may end up designing it herself. But don't look for her to clean the corners and crevices meticulously; she will not be interested.

She is a sensualist for whom being in love may provide the first opportunity to explore this tendency. Earlier she may have denied herself sensuous pleasures that may now sneak up on her and demand overtime. In love, she is glad to oblige.

She often becomes a gourmet cook and popular hostess. She basks in the attention of socially prominent people, and she wants to make her man proud of her. The shadow cast by her longing to be accepted, especially by men, is not likely to be totally erased.

There seem to be two main Capricorn reactions to partying and socializing. One type of Capricorn lady adores parties and can barely tolerate being alone. She may react to every crisis in her or her mate's life by throwing a big bash. Nothing is too fancy or costly for her, and the more frantic the party giving becomes, the deeper the trouble may be. The other type goes to the opposite extreme. She prefers to ignore invitations and would rather stay home reading quietly by her husband's knee. She wants home to be an inviolable oasis from the cares of the world, and she may resent anything she construes as an interference. Parties she may rank as a major nuisance, second only to her husband's overnight travels away from home.

As long as the merger works, the Capricorn Woman is the most loyal, steadfast, devoted, reliable lover on earth. No man could hope for a woman more in love. She has stars in her eyes and a rainbow painted on the bedroom ceiling in his favorite fluorescent colors. Musk and perfume fill the air, spring is always around the corner, the plants learn to sing back to her, the kitchen hums with secret self-indulgent delights, and the bed creaks with insistent regularity. She looks smashing, feels great, is bright-eyed with the promise of a never-ending, happily shared future.

If the merger fails, she withdraws her deposit and demands her investment back, with interest. This is a sad and bitter time indeed, as the cold winds of winter chill the affected hearts. But for Capricorn especially, there are many, many tomorrows!

Patterns in the Capricorn Woman's sexual relationships

The Capricorn Woman typically displays the following patterns in her sexual relationships:

1 *Delayed sexual activity and involvement.* The few Capricorn women who are sexually active earlier than seventeen or eighteen may run the risk of disillusionment. Capricorn's native puritanical streak and hidden romanticism usually demand devotional love, not easy flings.
2 *Crushes on older boys, and later on older men.* Capricorn is usually very careful about "going all the way." Most likely, she will reserve her soul, if not her body, for a very special relationship.
3 *Early marriage in the hopes of a total merger.* If she takes this route, she is likely to do so with high hopes but somewhat blindly. If not, she may marry quite late or stay single.
4 *Wrong choice of partner.* Capricorn is very likely to choose a man who, in the long run, will not be right for her. It may work

for awhile, until her needs change. When natural ambitions and restlessness come to the fore, the marriage too must bend and change, or it will falter. The Capricorn Woman finds it very difficult to let go of a marriage or any important relationship with a man, even if it is no longer working. Most encounter heavy going at some point in their lives and are forced to confront their own dependence/independence conflict. This must be handled wisely, or else much unhappiness results.

5. *Mid-life period of reexamination*. Capricorn has an especially strong need to take stock of herself at this stage in her development. In some cases, ending a relationship is necessary to make way for emotional growth.
6. *Maturation and blossoming*. Between forty and forty-five, the Capricorn Woman is most likely to come into her own in every respect. She is probably more self-confident than ever. This is probably the best time of her life, and the easiest from the point of view of lasting romantic relationships. If she no longer has the naive hopes of youth, she has the maturity of faith. By now, she has usually reached a point where she feels she can truly adapt, make it on her own without guilt or blame. The greatest love of her life may appear when she is least anxious and has given up looking.

Lovers and husbands

The Capricorn Woman is both a pragmatist and a romantic. She wants to make a solid investment when she contracts for a romantic commitment. Therefore, she wants a man worthy of it.

She is usually attracted to older men, perhaps as a result of her bond with Daddy, perhaps because older men tend to be more powerful. She wants a man who is a solid citizen, mobile and ambitious in his field. She wants to be proud and secure in the knowledge that she has chosen well. She also wants him to appreciate her efforts to prod and groom him for social and economic growth.

But money and social power are not likely to be enough for this secret passion flower. She usually also wants a man who is durable and passionate. She does not wish to be stranded on the shores of singlehood when she is blossoming in middle or late middle age. She wants a man with stamina who considers living—and living with her—a fascinating challenge.

Because she feels she lacks flair, she may wish for a mate who has it in abundance. Her ideal man combines pillar-of-the-community status with the irresistible dash of Valentino, the vulnerable, sexy charm of Travolta, and the spotlight-grabbing power of Brando. He is also a sensitive man who is nevertheless tough enough to be a winner. He may be difficult to find, and she may have to do plenty of grooming and prodding. Nevertheless, nobody can accuse Capricorn of giving up easily.

She wants her mate to take care of her financially and to wrap her in silk and fur against her own fears, mostly of poverty and loneliness. She makes plenty of attempts to find such a man and may do so. Yet when it comes to satisfying the romantic side of her nature, the Capricorn Woman has a harder time.

She frequently dreams of a business magnate or a famous poet with the money and prestige to make her feel protected and noticed, but she also is likely to want a man who will sit with her by the hearth and forgo extra work when she needs him. She desires a mate who knows how to let sex unfold in its own slow rhythms until her submerged passions rise to a crescendo. In brief, Lady Capricorn is bound to be looking for the rare successful man who is also sensitive in the area of romance and sex.

My advice to the young Capricorn on how to recognize the best man for her is this: try to be very clear on your *priorities*. Are you looking above all for security or romance? Be aware that your priorities, your needs, will change as you change and grow. You may want a "Daddy" to take care of you now, but if he proves to be too dull or stultifying in five years, what are the chances of the relationship surviving?

The young Capricorn Woman must also be aware of her latent quest for glamour. She normally considers herself sedate and on the conservative side, and she usually unconsciously seeks a man who has charm and a seductive, easy air of conviviality. He may be exciting and glamorous, but he may also turn out to be a cad. She may wish to have a fling with him, perhaps to glamorize herself, but I advise against her marrying this man. He will not fulfill her strong security needs and will probably be unable to keep her respect in the long run.

As a general guideline, using astrological *types* rather than sun signs, the Capricorn Woman can expect to make money with Aquarius, to be mentally attracted to Gemini and Leo (expect conflict), to have secret doubts and fears about Sagittarius, to be fascinated by and drawn to Cancer (expect lots of compromises), to be sexually magnetized by Virgo and Taurus. She may have to be careful with Aries and Libra, both of whom want to control as much territory as she does, and she may enjoy Pisces and dominate the relationship.

What Capricorn needs to learn

The Capricorn Woman is a born climber. She is bound to succeed in any area of life, but she must conquer her own black moods and their major source, her fear.

She fears many things. She is frightened of being unloved, alone, ill, and poor. She may fear life itself, with its risks and emotional demands. At times she may be afraid to love, for she has trouble letting go in the face of uncontrollable feeling without the guarantee of just return.

Saturn, her ruling planet, nearly universally ensures early struggles in love but also just about guarantees rewards for loving acts. Love under the influence of Saturn may be difficult but will eventually turn out to be binding and true.

Because Saturn has rulership of bones, the skeleton, teeth, and joints, the Capricorn Woman can normally measure her emotional flow by how lubricated her joints appear to be. Loose joints reflect flexible thinking and feelings; creaky joints mean inflexibility. If she has stiff knees and wrists, or other pain in her joints, it may indicate a crystallization in her way of life. Her system usually overproduces calcium, which is deposited in her joints in response to fear that in turn triggers stress. Capricorn is more often afflicted by rheumatism, arthritis, dental problems, kneecap troubles, and phlebitis (blood clots) than other astrological types.

The Capricorn Woman must learn to cope with the source of her bodily stress, her fears. I have discovered from long experience that Capricorn does not easily learn by listening to other people or reading advice in books. She learns almost solely from her own experience. In order to make her relationships work, she must find a way to eliminate her fears.

My advice to Capricorn is this: Capricorn, stop pushing the river. The later years are almost certain to be excellent for you. If you eliminate negative feelings, most of all fear, your youth can also be full of love and meaningful relationships. Release your anxiety about living, about money and security. Release your fear of uncertainty.

The following technique, *color mediation*, is something you can test yourself, experiencing its method and results. As presented in the next few pages, color meditation is an outstanding way for you to release any negative emotion, specifically fear.

The method of color meditation

1. Lie down or sit comfortably with your eyes closed. Make sure that everything is quiet around you and that you will not be interrupted for the duration of your meditation (anywhere from about seven minutes to over half an hour).
2. With your eyes closed, picture yourself standing at the base of a flat-topped pyramid. Stretching ahead of you and up are seven steps in seven colors. You will go up slowly, step by step.
3. Step on the first step, which is red. Imagine your body suffused with the color red. Stand there as long as you wish, just "feeling red." Let the red rise up through your body, from your ankles to your head. Your red should be clear and true, like a field of oriental poppies. Red is a vibrant, energetic color that denotes freedom, will, power, strength, determination, independence, honor, leadership, and courage.
4. Take a deep breath and let the color slowly creep down. Start by visualizing the red at the top of your head. The roll the color down across your chest, hips, knees, and finally back down into the step.
5. Take a deep breath. Mount the next step. It is blue. Feel the blue as your breathe. Let the blue rise slowly from your toes on up, until it goes right to the top of your head. Visualize yourself completely blue, a beautiful deep-sea or sky blue. Blue stands for love, wisdom, kindness, humility, gentleness, understanding, trust, forgiveness, compassion, mercy, sensitivity, humane detachment, patience, cooperation.
6. Take a deep breath and slowly let the color roll back down. Start by lowering the blue from the top of your head, then roll it slowly down your chest, hips, knees, ankles, and finally back down into the step.
7. The next step is yellow. Visualize yourself on a bright, clear, sunny yellow step. It must not be muddy. It is the color of a buttercup in early spring. Imagine the yellow color slowly rising in you until you have become completely buttercup yellow. Don't forget to breathe all this time. Allow the yellow to rise slowly until it has reached the top of your head. Just hold

it there while you breathe and relax. Yellow stands for joy, expression, discrimination, organization, evaluation, praise, active intelligence, judgment, ability. Let it all seep into you.

8 Take another big breath. Slowly bring the yellow down. Lower the yellow from the top of your head to your eyebrows, neck, chest, hips, knees, and all the way down to the step you are standing on. Get ready to step on the next step. Breathe. Relax.

9 Step on the next step, which is green. It's a vital grass green, or perhaps a sparkling emerald green. Visualize yourself green, and slowly roll the color green all the way up to the top of your head. Concentrate on being green. Breathe the green in deeply. Green has all the good qualities of yellow and blue, and it also brings growth, hope, expansion, acceptance, enthusiasm, sharing, energy flow, industry, sustenance, gratitude, searching, and nurturing. Green is the color of vitality, of living things. Breathe it in deeply.

10 When you are ready, slowly prepare to roll the green down. Start at the top of your head, and roll it down your neck, chest, arms, hips, knees, and feet until the green has gone back into the step. Prepare yourself for the next step. Keep breathing deeply. Relax.

11 The next step is orange, a bright orange like sunlight or like a healthy tangerine. Breathe in the orange slowly, carefully. Enjoy its energy. It should be warmer than the green, slightly cooler than the red. Imagine the orange color going up your body, all the way through your body. Start by visualizing it in your feet, then in your legs, your knees, genitals, hips, chest, neck, head, and on up until you are orange yourself. Now you are all orange. Breathe deeply. It gives you all the qualities of red and yellow, plus great courage, illumination, intellect, action, steadfastness, the ability to build forms, confidence, victory, harvest, striving.

12 Let the orange go through you. Get acquainted with its intense energy. Whey you are ready, begin to bring it back down. When it has reached your feet, get ready to step on the sixth step.

13 This step is purple-violet. It is a deep violet color, like velvety pansies, or a deep royal blue with an extra dash of red in it. Unfurl the purple-violet slowly from the bottom of your feet all the way to the top of your head. Do it slowly. Purple-violet has

all the qualities of blue and red, plus devotion, loyalty, service, responsibility, idealism, aspiration, understanding of justice, and royalty. Purple-violet is also an extremely healing color. Many psychic healers begin by spreading this color around their patients and around themselves. It is a protective color.

14 Breathe deeply, slowly. Enjoy the vibrations of this color. When you are ready, slowly roll it back down into the step below you. Get ready for the final step before reaching the flat top of your pyramid.

15 Mount the last step. It is indigo. Breathe deeply. Slowly raise the color indigo, the color of the midnight sky, up through your body. When it has reached the top of your head, visualize yourself completely covered in indigo. It should look as if someone has poured india ink all over you. According to healers, indigo is the highest-vibration color. It brings synthesis (merging), unity, ritual and ceremonial magic. It is a catalyst for spiritual growth and purification.

16 After awhile, bring the indigo back to the step. Start at the top of your head, and slowly roll it back down, past your chest, knees, feet.

17 Step up on the flat-topped pyramid. Imagine it as a bright, whitish crystal. You should be there alone, bathed in light, gloriously relaxed. Visualize yourself proud, loving, confident. Wipe out feelings of fear and anxiety. Focus on the light, the sparkle, and feel your own energy lightening. When you are on top of the pyramid, you become cleansed and relaxed. Now visualize yourself free of fear. See yourself flowing and beautiful. Talk to yourself about your wishes in life.

18 Since this is a powerful meditation, you must now remember to say the words "This is meant to be for the highest good of all." You do not want to manipulate others through the use of visualization. Its purpose is to help you to be healthy and to grow.

19 When you are finished watching yourself standing atop your pyramid in complete happy freedom, prepare to go back down. If you feel you have communicated with a source of cosmic energy, as eventually happens in many meditations, say, "Thank you." If you have requested help from anyone while you were up there, also thank them.

20 You will now go down the step in reverse. The colors in reverse are indigo, purple-violet, orange, green, yellow, blue, red. Go

down each step slowly. Feel the color of each step through you. Visualize yourself in that color.

21 When you have reached the last step, the red one, you have finished your color meditation. Open your eyes; enjoy the feeling of trust and relaxation.

Visualization means conjuring up pictures in your mind's eye. It is a powerful—and effective—means of designing your own reality. With this meditation, repeated once a day or a few times a week, you will achieve your objectives in time, as countless people I know can attest. A final word of advice: if you do not actually *see* pictures when you close your eyes, this is normal. It takes people weeks, or even months, before they can visualize with the inner eye. Relax, as if you were daydreaming. Put no pressure on yourself. The results are usually astonishing, magical.

Summing up

The Capricorn Woman is usually practical and romantic, an erotic realist. She can raise her man to the top, but she can also nag him jealously. She gives as good as she gets and is willing to pay the price for what she wants. She can be an angel or a partner, but she becomes aloof and hard to reach if she feels insecure or scared.

She wants security, order, and status, yet she is often subconsciously magnetized by glamour and fame. She is usually attracted to older men, perhaps because of an early bond with Daddy, perhaps because older men are able to give her more of what she wants.

She can be trapped by fears or by her own subconscious need to be more outgoing, stylish, and glamorous than she naturally feels. She can thus select a man or a number of men who are dashing but in the long run not beneficial to her. An awareness of her changing needs and priorities, of her whole self, and the ability to flow, are key to forming good, long-lasting relationships.

Capricorn sexuality

Capricorn is usually underrated sexually because not every observer is astute enough to penetrate her cool white-gladiola demeanor and detect her luscious red-rose core. The Capricorn

Woman flowers fully only when the occasion feels right. And she takes her time about deciding.

She may be a *femme fatale* with the wisdom of an old lady and the grace and ingenuity of a young colt. She is picky; she may blow hot and cold, but when she falls, she falls very hard. The case of the immovable object meeting the irresistible force describes the Capricorn Woman's infatuation or sexual falling in love.

Many a Capricorn is a young beauty who can expect to grow into an ageless enchantress. Others, however, refuse to take care of their bodies, gain weight, and age prematurely, this denying themselves the full realization of their sexual potential. Nothing is sadder than to see a Capricorn woman with a vibrant, dynamic mind inhabiting a stagnant, neglected body. When she takes pains to preserve her youth and beauty, she usually blooms endlessly, weathering peaks and valleys of sexual ecstasy and boredom. She exhibits admirable durability and usually manages to outlive her partners.

The Capricorn sexual destiny includes the ordeal of patient labor. She may have to teach her lover sexual techniques; more likely, she will have to teach him how to truly love. If she herself has trouble in either of these areas, which she may, she is bound to go through some tense relationships.

Her sexuality is a deep, enduring, intense bonding force. She usually feels that love and sex go together and are meant to last a lifetime. She dislikes "head trips" and will seldom discuss details, but she keeps on looking for the best romantic and financial combination. She may be downright secretive about her sexual longings and not much more open about her search for love.

This woman "feels things in her bones" and has a built-in body radar system. She scans the sky for changes in weather, and the horizon for her ideal lover. She anticipates moods, weather, and her own love affairs with remarkable, earthy intuition. Deep down, if she is really honest, she usually knows when she is involved with a man who is not contributing to her growth—but you may never hear her admit it.

She has a nearly phobic fear of depending on a man. Therefore, the more she falls in love, the more aloof she may try to appear. It is as if a magical threshold has to be crossed somewhere within her before she will permit herself to be publicly affectionate—and privately passionate.

Her sexuality needs to be nurtured by many demonstrations of romance, passion, interest, and old-fashioned courtesy. She is exceedingly cautious about falling in love; she would really prefer to make sure the man is in love with her before she lets herself fly. Thus, shoring up her sexual self-esteem may have to be part of a gradual opening-up process to help her to let go. Ultimately, the result is almost sure to be a delightful celebration of sex and the senses.

Lady Cassanova experiments aside, the Capricorn Woman tends not to be fully open and happy with her sex life until she has "grown accustomed to his face." She is usually the type of lover who wants and needs a shared life, a relationship with a history and a future. When she feels secure, she gradually opens up to reveal layer after layer of gorgeous, never-before-disclosed vulnerability and a lush and earthy sexual energy.

Ultimately, she is bound to have a rich and satisfying sex life. What she needs is to open up, to build trust and sexual self-esteem. She must strive to allow herself to be "real," to accept and share her own emotionalism and vulnerability. Capricorn has to learn to apply her flights of fancy in such areas as effectively as she has already done in the areas of self-control and professional striving.

Early sex experiences

Capricorn's early sex life is apt to be more a desert than a dessert. She usually blooms late. She is normally more interested in concrete rewards of the kind that marriage brings than in pure and less tangible sexual pleasure. She may not always know how to relax, being performance-conscious and quite shy.

From time to time, one finds a Capricorn girl who starts with the boys as early as twelve. By age eighteen, this young lady will be capable of authoring her own version of *Fanny Hill*. She is a fascinating exception to the Capricorn rule. One surmises that she somehow found the early key to her own naturally high sex drive, and authorities be damned! She may prefer earthy, sensual pleasure and intense exploration to the usual cautious Capricorn path of slow sexual maturing combined with increasing material or scholarly concerns.

Capricorn usually dislikes doing things halfway. Thus, our young explorer may be every bit as open and sexually sophisticated as faster-maturing types. She is likely to do things thoroughly, so she will have covered every angle. And, unlike others of her type, she may be ready to move on to a marriage or business partnership at eighteen or twenty-one, just when the typical Capricorn female is learning the meaning of that special smile.

The Capricorn Woman is usually most comfortable in a monogamous relationship. She is frequently jealous and generally demanding. She must carefully examine her sexual (and other) expectations before entering a serious relationship.

The typical Capricorn girl has at least one big crush on a female upper-class member or a teacher, but she is probably too embarrassed to talk about it. She may secretly fear homosexuality even before she knows what to call a same-sex attraction. Of the many Capricorn girls who experiment with homosexual relationships, most come to accept them as a state in their sexual growth.

The Capricorn female must be wary of drugs and alcohol. She is secretly attracted to them in the hope that they will loosen her up. However, alcohol is a depressant, and recent research suggests that even marijuana is habit-forming and affects one destructively in the long run. Thus, Capricorn would be better off trying to relax socially by finding ways to express herself and increase her self-esteem and her communication skills. Drama, reciting poetry, sales, promotion work, and hostessing are all excellent training grounds for her.

What kind of lover she is

The Capricorn Woman usually thaws out much more quickly than many who initially give the impression of being fireballs of sexual energy. If she is mentally stimulated, she can turn on very quickly indeed. Though taking the initiative is not her forte, she somehow manages to get things going her way. Her lover may quickly find himself under her as she rides him to happy oblivion.

She does not relish complicated sexual moves. The man who must have his woman in a leather or rubber outfit, who adores slinky, tickly condoms for pleasure, who prefers the frills of sexual congress to the filling meat-and-potatoes approach, is apt to disappoint her. What matters to her is the length of his performance and the force of his thrust. If she never saw a vibrator or wore a sexy peek-a-boo bra, she'd be just as glad. She likes order, even in her sex life. She would probably prefer scheduling her arousal to coincide with his lusty peaks—ahead of time, of course.

She likes to have a lot of control over potential areas of friction, and happily sex is one of them. Normally, however, she does not make the mistake of dominating a man overtly; she goes about her sexual business with devoted, considerate passion. Try to find out what she thinks, and you are likely to witness an enigmatic, fleeting smile unadorned by words. The Capricorn Woman knows how to keep her counsel, which is why her sexual passion is rarely discussed. To her, the proper place for sex is in her bedroom, preferably with the man to whom she has committed herself for life; few words are necessary.

She is not usually interested in one-sided activity. That is why "69" is one of her favorite sexual positions. She likes oral sex that is mutually pleasurable. She also favors the wild bronco ride of woman on top. When she lets go, you can usually hear her shout, scream, and perhaps scratch with abandon. She may like to nibble or bite. She does not mean to hurt, but she gets carried away. Her gladiola cool may burst into hothouse orchid delicacy and passion.

The Capricorn Woman may go through alternating phases of sexual passivity and sheer animal lust. She is somewhat unpredictable in sex, as she is in the rest of her life. It may seem as if two women lived behind her gloriously controlled facade, each doing a slow burn her own way.

In her passive phase, the Capricorn Woman may choose to go without sex, or she may allow a man to make love to her while she withholds participation. If she is unhappy in the relationship, she is likely to treat sex as an irritant, a chore. She may also use it as a reward for virtue or as a bargaining chip. She is apt to have periods of sensual starvation. She may appear unapproachable—too cool, self-sufficient, or magnificent. She may radiate an aura of such success and self-dependence that men are scared away and her love life remains a desert.

At other times, she may have so many suitors and lovers that she can barely keep up. In her love life, when it rains, it usually pours. During these high sexual cycles, she is bound to experience pure, old-fashioned lust. When she lets go, she can be rowdier than a soldier on leave and more magnetic than an iridescent butterfly. In fact, she herself acts like a butterfly first out of her cocoon.

She may be surrounded by playboys or gigolos, ready to entertain her. Middle-age Capricorn Women are not too shy to pair with a professional escort, especially when they are between marriages. I've know quite a few who enjoyed this lifestyle more than their former domesticity. Free sexuality and glamour may be so repressed in the life of the average Capricorn Woman that if and when she gets her chance to unearth these drives, she may go all out to make up for lost time. She may try bisexuality but is more apt to be thoroughly heterosexual.

The Capricorn Woman is probably happiest and sexiest when she is in love, for she is then able to channel both her emotionalism and her high sex drive without any qualms or regrets. The tremendous bonding power of sex is important to her, the more so when it is allied to love.

What kind of lover she needs

The Capricorn Woman wants a man who is responsive and responsible. She wants a man who has old-fashioned values and takes the hearts-and-flowers approach, and if he subtly wears his heart on his sleeve, all the more exciting. She herself surely will not.

He must be able to bring out her restrained sensuality and appreciate her tongue-in-cheek seductiveness. If she sits on a barstool next to a man who looks as if he sprang from her dreams, she may overcome her natural shyness and approach him with self-deprecating wit. Alternatively she may turn the barb against him, daring him to match her.

The man who exhibits the proper signs of genteel upbringing, a dash of macho strength, and plenty of upward mobility has a slight chance with her. In addition, she wants her man to exude two hard-to-define attributes: class and sexual magnetism.

In bed, he should be a gentleman who accedes to her needs and cleverly hears her silent demands. She wants him to anticipate her moods and know her erogenous zones better than she knows them herself. But he must be more than a gentleman; she would like him also to be earthy, demanding, and unabashedly male. In her heart of hearts, she will respect him more if he doesn't cater to her every wish. Sometimes, he should make her do more work in bed than she, princesslike, has ever been willing to do.

She also has a hidden wish to be subjugated sexually. S-and-M is not usually her thing, but she secretly hopes to find that the man she is in love with can wield as much power in bed as he does in the corporate boardroom.

Capricorn anger

Anger is a natural, basic human feeling. We feel loving, sad, happy, jealous—and we feel angry. Most of us, however, have learned so well to ignore and bottle up our anger that we call it by other names or deny it altogether. Occasionally, we may explode with pent-up, irrational rage, out of control and destructive.

Our culture has taught most of us to label anger by such names as irritation, frustration, depression, or sadness. But *anger is anger,* and no amount of psychological game playing can keep our systems free of its toxic effects. The best thing to do with anger is to recognize it and learn to channel it constructively: into work, athletics, or the fight against social ills. At best, our anger can jolt us out of ruts and trigger us into taking necessary actions.

Anger is a major block to healthy sexual expression. It is one of the causes of low self-esteem; it is a frequent result of feeling unimportant or powerless. If we lack self-esteem, we allow hostility and anger to flourish. Sex in an angry relationship becomes a battleground rather than a pleasurable bond.

The Capricorn Woman generally has less trouble with repressed or improperly expressed anger than other people do. Still, her anger can be a blockbuster and a threat to her happiness. Typically, she deals with anger by rationalizing it. She may also use barbed wit to dissipate it or establish rituals of social intercourse as safeguards. Then again, she may ignore her anger altogether.

Focusing on the subject of anger, I interviewed a number of women who are Capricorn types or have gone through a Capricorn phase. Here are some typical responses:

1 "I have been married a long time and seldom find myself angry. I learned many years ago that I could not change my husband and have resigned myself. I take out my occasional frustrations—or anger, if you wish—by working at my sewing, in my garden, or sculpting."

2 "I used to think I seldom got angry, until I got to really know myself. It wasn't until my thirties that I recognized the enormous load of anger I had been carrying around, trying to get rid of it in well-controlled pieces and places. I used to act and found it a great way to unburden myself. Looking back, I mostly did comedy and preferred to play sharp-tongued shrews. It felt good to be hostile and be able to make people laugh about it. I

guess I best express anger now when I feel it will not be rejected or disapproved."

3 "I used to be explosive over little things, but I could rarely express anger at what really made me angry. Lately, I have been involved in my work, my business is growing, and I feel a success, so that I have not been aware of any anger. I think I may be too tired and contented to be angry."
4 "I am angry when I think I have *cause* to be angry. If I have been given no reason to be angry, I am never angry. The main cause of my anger is usually the incompetence or unethical behavior of other people. It seldom has anything to do with me."
5 "I find that socializing, dancing, and drinking usually take care of my anger. I may not actually *face* my anger or do anything directly with it, but I manage to get rid of it by going out to parties, cruises, picnics. They make me feel safe; they take me away from myself."

The first woman has chosen to ignore her anger or to divert it into useful pursuits. It sounds as if she has grown wiser and kinder to herself through the years. The second woman is "acting out" positively to cope with her anger. She acts literally—on stage. She also uses humor in a controlled setting to release hostility. The Capricorn Woman usually has a fine sense of humor and may excel at witty, derisive comments which barely veil hostility. She may have a Don Rickles streak.

The third woman sounds realistic. She has found a way to channel her aggression and anger into work. Her feelings of self-esteem are high, and she feels successful. Success, for the Capricorn Woman, takes care of more stress than it creates.

The fourth woman seems to have rationalized her anger. She does not seem to know that feelings are facts and need not be justified. When we feel angry, we need not marshal evidence as to why. We don't need to document why we are happy, so why do we so often seem to feel that we have to have "good" reasons for our anger? This lady needs to examine her value system. It seems to me that she lives with very strict *shoulds*. She shows intolerant, inflexible notions of how people *should* behave and what life *should* be like. She probably pictures herself as rigidly controlled—just like her expression of anger.

The Capricorn Woman very often reasons her way in and out of anger. Just as frequently, she assigns outside causes for it, taking very little, if any, responsibility herself. She often feels it is others and their unreasonable, quirky behavior that "justifiably" make her angry.

The fifth woman uses the ritual of partying as a safety valve for her aggressions. This is all right up to a point, but as she herself points out, there is the danger of running away from herself. I call this the "Peter Pan syndrome." She is choosing to escape the reality of her anger by frenetic activity. This woman is not accepting full responsibility for her emotions, in this case, anger.

Four of the women (the first, second, third, and fifth) were willing to discuss their sex lives openly. All four have experienced sexual difficulties, reporting both cycles without any sexual desire and cycles of intense sexual activity. All had had times when they found orgasm difficult to reach, *especially* when they felt upset or angry.

None of the women had been fully aware of their anger until our interviews started, so it was impossible for them to clearly define the role of anger in sexual problems. Only the fifth woman was able to see that the more frantic her partygoing became, the less interested she was in having sex. She also said that controlling her anger often meant inhibiting her sex drive.

I found it fascinating that the fourth woman, who seemed so sure of herself and so righteous about causes for her anger, refused to discuss her sex life altogether. I had the feeling she did not have any.

Identifying and expressing anger

The Capricorn Woman must become fully aware of what she feels in every area, including anger. Is she angry? With whom? How much of her anger might be the result of her upbringing, her temperament, or problems in her current relationships or lifestyle? What old scripts are still alive in her head? Is the "good girl" or "class valedictorian" syndrome strong? What do they have to do with producing anger?

The main source of anger in the typical Capricorn Woman is a sense of powerlessness. She usually defines it as *a feeling of being ineffectual*, especially on the job. The Capricorn Woman is so driven to achieve that her anger is often interwoven with her ambitions. Even if she does not work, she may be angry about ERA not passing or about the lack of good childcare for working mothers or perhaps about the small percentage of women in the professions.

As a woman, she is bound to encounter job discrimination. This will particularly fuel her anger, because Capricorn often derives much of her sense of self-esteem from aspiring toward and realizing professional goals. If she does not work for pay, she is almost surely striving for leadership in volunteer work, community causes, or the family.

Capricorn, there are a number of techniques that will help you come to terms with your anger. For a review of basic communication skills to help you cope with expressing anger, see "Libra Anger," page 245. For suggestions on how to identify your anger, see "Scorpio Anger," page 280.

Beyond that, you must specifically:

1 Realize that conflict is inevitable and anger is real and acceptable.
2 Know that anger is manageable and that it does not have to be ignored as an unworthy, irrational reaction.
3 Accept that continued resistance to acknowledging anger may create further problems.
4 Know that feelings of exclusion, jealousy, powerlessness, and injustice typically trigger anger for other women as well as for sensitive Capricorn.
5 Not give in to feelings of isolation and "poor-little-me-itis." There are others in the same boat.

The Capricorn Woman suffers from the following specific blocks to expressing her anger:

1 Vulnerability. Her ego is large and sensitive. She often does not want to show hurt by reacting with anger.
2 Fear. She is afraid of the other person's disapproval, rejection, or ridicule and of her own destructive powers.
3 Guilt about being angry.
4 Desire to please, to be perfect.

Acquiring communication skills and practicing meditation will help immensely in these areas. And her sex life need not suffer either, as long as she *expresses constructively rather than represses her anger*.

Ours is a patriarchal society. The Capricorn female has a strongly male side herself. A recent government research study found that patriarchal societies like ours repress sensory pleasure, physical touch, premarital sex. It indicated that the stronger the sexual repression in a culture is, the more warlike it becomes.

A similar phenomenon occurs on the personal level, where the relationship between anger and sexuality is reciprocal. Repressed sexuality increases anger. Increased ambition at the expense of sensory pleasures eventually creates problems in love. A woman who is deprived will become angry, and an angry woman may do some very self-destructive things. She may short-circuit her own pleasure, hurting others in the process, and hurting her own love life.

Since lasting love is based not on the denial but on the expansion of good feelings and sharing, the Capricorn Woman must learn how to nourish her love. She must have the tools to keep the poison of anger out of her life and her bed.

Capricorn lifestyles

The Capricorn Woman is excellent marriage material. She needs and wants a sustained relationship that fulfills her social, material, and emotional needs. She is probably one of the best candidates for a good old-fashioned "pleasure bond" stemming from a long-term primary relationship. However, it usually takes her awhile to get there. She may be looking for marriage or a strong primary relationship, and she may not wish to separate sex and love, but she is normally a late bloomer in finding happiness. She is usually also late in achieving self-awareness and developing the kind of skills it takes to make a relationship work.

There are some women whose needs are best fulfilled by a dual lifestyle, marital and extramarital. The Capricorn woman has varied interests, but she prefers to focus her energy on one main relationship which will hopefully satisfy most of her needs.

In her early years, usually through her twenties and perhaps even into the thirties, she is bound to experience multiple love affairs; she may then experiment with varied lifestyles, or she may be married and monogamous. Her life is apt to break into definite cycles during which her entire sexual behavior changes.

The typical Capricorn pattern in terms of changing lifestyles is as follows:

1 Early adulthood, from twenty to twenty-eight, but sometimes as late as twenty-five to thirty-two. She is apt to be immature and insecure. She may either withdraw into a totally monogamous

relationship that makes her feel safe or go to the other extreme and spend years running experiments to broaden her skills and horizons. If she marries young and is of the old school, she is most likely to stay monogamous all her life. I have, however, seen an increasing number of Capricorn types who break out of a stagnant marriage in their fifties and start to live again.

2 Middle adulthood, usually starting at thirty-five and continuing as late as sixty. This is a period of great individual variation, and its only common theme is predictable upheavals, especially at thirty-five, forty-two to forty-three, fifty, and fifty-eight to sixty.
3 Late adulthood, from sixty on. The Capricorn woman is typically at her best in this phase, *provided* she has not formed crystallized habits. If she has given in to fear and depression, she will have serious physical problems. If not, she blooms with the advancing years like a rare, precious flower.

Monogamy and nonmonogamy

The following represent typical situations which could influence the Capricorn Woman to become nonmonogamous:

1 Bitterness or disappointment with her life and mate.
2 The feeling that life has cheated her and that she must do something radical about it; the feeling that life has passed her by.
3 The search for glamour and excitement. She often feels these qualities must come from someone else, for she believes she lacks them herself. If she views her mate as also dull, she is almost certain sooner or later to try to find a man who will let a bit of glamour "rub off."
4 The search for a male mentor (espeically in the case of a very upwardly mobile Capricorn career woman). This is most likely to happen if her husband does not have an interest in her work.
5 Loneliness in her marriage.
6 Transference. If she is having emotional problems, she may blame her contemporaries, possibly including her husband, and turn to an older man.
7 Misplaced anger at herself or at her mate.
8 The search for new sexual knowledge.

Alternative lifestyles

Single woman: From time to time, this is a good lifestyle for her, but she must be careful not to let it go on too long lest her tendency to depression reassert itself. She needs companionship and cheerfulness, and living alone is not always good for her.

Intimate networks: A very good possibility for the Capricorn Woman. She tends to have friends of both genders and does not feel threatened by this situation as long as sexual involvement is not the norm. She dislikes any group or lifestyle that pushes people, and she simply becomes unyielding if anyone gets on a soapbox to try to convince her of anything. She'll make up her own mind, in her own time—and this goes for sexual acts.

Open marriage: As far as I know, this arrangement, popularized in the 1960s, has not caught on with many people. It is just about impossible for Capricorn. She is possessive, and her need to be exclusive is permanent. She is quite happy with monogamy, the more so if it is the socially accepted lifestyle of the times.

Ménage à trois: This arrangement, whereby couples may share their bed with a third person, is fine as a temporary exploration of her potential for relating. She should stay away from Aries, Leo, Aquarius, and Gemini types.

Group marriage: Capricorn likes insular lifestyles. If group marriage is formed in an atmosphere of trust and financial and emotional security, she may give it a try. (Group marriage in small, select communities whose members have come together intelligently and with preparation may be one of the lifestyles of the future).

Communes: These differ from group marriage in that a bonding ceremony may have been omitted and they are not based on couples. A commune has about the same potential for Capricorn as a group marriage, and it may work, given the conditions above.

Gay/bisexual lifestyle: I have seen very few Capricorn Women openly living in it, but I suspect there are many who would like to try. The Capricorn Woman's male side is often more highly developed than her female side. She may wish to try to open up her femininity by living with other women. However, she is generally so desirous of being accepted that she is unlikely to depart from the norm.

Summing up Capricorn

The Capricorn Woman's experience is formed deep inside the cave of winter and is best brought forth in the summer of love, self-love, optimism, and the development of the higher self.

The axis of material/physical versus emotional/spiritual growth is at the heart of her challenge. Will she go on a power trip at the cost of learning to love? Will she develop her head at the expense of opening her heart? Will she learn to overcome her self-doubt, her pessimistic bent, and learn to live for today instead of worrying about tomorrow? Will she enjoy her youth and middle age as much as she is almost certain to appreciate her old age?

These are questions only she can answer. The first step is to understand the challenge. The second is to be aware of her tremendous potential to do anything she wishes with her life. The third is for her to move toward emotional growth and learn to trust. If the heart is open, and the mind disciplined, the physical will take care of itself.

Lady Capricorn is truly an empress, born to a high station in life. Where the Leo Woman is born to rule the masses from her lofty throne. Capricorn is born to wield authority. She can be the voice of knowledge, wisdom, affirmative tradition. She can convert yesterday's goods to practical use today. Misguided, the Capricorn Woman will want to reenter or bring back the past. Enlightened, she will want to bring the beauty and bounty of the past to enrich the present, and she will ready herself for a starring role in creating the most humanized future for all of us.

AQUARIUS

CHECKLIST OF AQUARIUS TRAITS

Note: This checklist describes the traits of one *phase* only; if it doesn't seem to fit you, check other lists to find the phase you are in right now.

1. Reformist
2. Quirky
3. Offbeat
4. Quixotic
5. Unpossessive
6. Nonmaterialistic
7. Freedom-seeking
8. Avant-garde
9. Attracts Abrupt Change
10. Mental
11. Opinionated
12. Self-confident
13. Dutiful
14. Altruistic
15. Truthful
16. Courteous
17. Civilized
18. Tense
19. Lonely
20. Talented
21. Driven
22. Proud
23. Group-conscious
24. Inquisitive
25. Experimental
26. Unbiased
27. Fears Intimacy
28. Shy
29. Humble
30. Compartmentalized
31. Informal
32. Aloof
33. Friendly
34. Sexually Broad-minded
35. Erotically Inhibited

Aquarius personality

General Traits and Background

Understanding the Aquarius Woman requires adopting a new frame of reference. She is a fascinating maze of traditionalism and futurism, a blend of approval seeking and nonconformism, logic and intuition, eccentricity and dogmatism. She considers the brain the most important sexual organ, and indeed, she filters every aspect of life through her diligently perspicacious mind.

The Aquarius Woman is a harbinger of cultural concepts and of lifestyles yet to come. She could easily step onto the set of *2001* and feel at home. Mind control is abhorrent to her; she wants mind liberation. She is for peace, harmony, understanding, sympathy, and trust for all of humanity, exactly as in the lead song from the musical *Hair*. She wants freedom, equality, liberty, and sisterhood, in a slight variation on the slogan of the French Revolution. She is looking for equal and complete unions between enlightened males and females, as Susan B. Anthony, herself an Aquarian, projected. And she wants it all on her own terms.

Aquarius is the eleventh sign of the Zodiac, and it is Fixed Air. It is called the sign of the waterbearer, and its name leads many to wrongly assume that it is a water sign. But Aquarius is air; therefore, Aquarian-type people rely first and foremost on their minds. They often live in the mind, trusting it far more than the body. Many are intellectually outstanding, emotionally aloof, and predictably unpredictable.

Each astrological sign is associated with, or ruled by, a particular planet. Aquarius is quirky in more ways than you can count, and its first eccentricity is that it has double planetary rulership. The planet Uranus, discovered in 1781, is associated with Aquarius, but so is the planet Saturn. Aquarians are said to have qualities conferred by both: saturnine conservatism, seriousness, and ambition blended with uranian Mad Hatter inventiveness, originality, impracticality. The Aquarius Woman may be completely nonmaterialistic yet drive fifty miles to get a bargain on a can of green beans.

The Aquarius-*type* woman is one who has the sun or other important planets in Aquarius; planets in the eleventh house, the natural house of Aquarius; and Aquarius ascendant; or a powerfully aspected Uranus. Aquarius types are also those who are temporarily transiting an Aquarius *phase*. In this case, the person need have no planets in the sign of Aquarius. The Aquarius type is described by the checklist of traits at the beginning of this chapter. The Aquarius phase has the following characteristics:

1 Sudden flashes of insight and intuition, visions, telepathy, or dreams concerning the future, especially the future of society.
2 Absorption with scientific research and inventions, especially with the use of electronic machinery. Far-out technological advances are also Aquarian.
3 Temperamental, eccentric demands for freedom and privacy; a loner's lifestyle that alternates with involvement in groups, not with an individual. Many Aquarians adopt a futuristic lifestyle.
4 Humanitarian commitment to a group philosophy (perhaps combined with living in a communal setting) in order to bring about a new order. What distinguishes Aquarius from Scorpio in this respect is that Scorpio is concerned with dissolution prior to rebirth, while Aquarius is more concerned with building or rebuilding a better, more idealistic world.
5 Repeated difficulties with emotional closeness; extensive emotional armoring.
6 Experimentation in almost any aspect of life, combined with nonmaterialism.
7 Teaching and sharing knowledge, with far-reaching consequences (especially true of the developed Aquarian).

Aquarius has something special, a different flavor and a mystery. She is the fifty-second state, the eleventh planet, the eleventh disciple. She is not only complicated, she provides no access. She is a bit like a one-way mirror. She looks out and analyzes, but she rarely removes the shimmering reflective cocoon that encases her. Her very coolness creates a charm. She usually has an offbeat sense of humor, a tense but powerful ability to concentrate fully on the person or task at hand, an intriguing intuition that frequently makes the leap to precognition. She can be absent-minded, impractical, undemonstrative, aloof, irritable, inhibited. She can also be devoted, loyal, friendly, refined, penetrating, idealistic, nonaggressive, nonconformist, enlightening. She appears to be a step ahead, and you suspect she would not want you to know how she does it. There is also a streak of jealousy and envy in her makeup. She really doesn't like her friends and close associates to have possessions that she covets or that are of a higher quality than those she has herself.

The Aquarius Woman lives in many different parts of her mind. She can compartmentalize to the point that the various segments may appear unconnected. She is singularly untouched by the stormy emotions that can drive others to blazing outbursts or fits of depression. She tends to be controlled, and she reaps the benefits and pays the price of her control.

To love her is to let her be. To love her is to provide protection so she can spread her wings. To love her is to be available when she feels lonely, without demanding equal time. To love her is to be frustrated, fulfilled, curious, mad, scared, and forced to be more tolerant, inquisitive, flexible, intellectual. To love her means to face forward, forget the past and one's fears of the future and of freedom. To love her means to glimpse a New Age.

The Aquarius Woman challenges her friends and lovers to be on their toes. Revising old concepts is natural for her. Platonic love is comfortable, passion all right as long as it's not overwhelming; intellectual battles whet her appetite. In the end, she hooks you with her multifaceted, softly aggressive sparkle. She surprises you continuously; her dogmatic moralism and libertarian views go hand in hand. She is neither too shy nor too outgoing, neither too personal nor too detached. She is all of these and none of them.

She is all woman with a male mind, again challenging our definition of both. What she wants is to be turned on and upside down, to fall head over heels in love—with you, with life, with herself. What she seeks is the approval of the community, intellectual leadership and fulfilment, a romantic but measured love affair. What she needs is to let go, let down, and let up. And the inner battle lines are drawn.

The following body parts or functions are most acutely affected by stress or distress in the Aquarius type: calves, ankles, bones from the knees down, circulation, breath, eyesight, Achilles' tendon, blood, and lymph system. The most common Aquarian health affliction is varicose veins, and the second most common is circulation problems.

Aquarian professions are the following: aeronautics, anything connected with flying; being an announcer on the electronic media, broadcasting, radio and television; architecture, automobiles, astrology; chiropractic, congressional jobs; cooperatives, counseling, electronics, engineering; exploration of any dimension, mind or body; faith healing; grant work, philanthropic or club work; instrument or furniture manufacturing; inventions, legislation, mechanics; motion pictures, motors, motorcycles; navigation, neurology; new teachings and occupations, i.e., nuclear physics; pearls, photography, progressive works; psychology, radiology, radiotherapy; reforms, revolution, science, socialist movements, spiritual movements; telephone, telegraph, television, X rays.

The Aquarius Woman wishes to collect data so as to understand everything and everyone deeply and thoroughly. She herself resists being understood. Outwardly she demonstrates a coolness, a control that is equaled by few. Inwardly, however, she may be at loose ends mentally. Often she is vulnerable, one of her greatest fears. She lacks self-confidence and may put on quite a facade. She has her own kind of magic, full of paradox and mischief liberally sprinkled with misunderstanding. She is probably the most humane and humanitarian of all the Zodiacal types, and yet she is also one of the most emotionally detached. She tends to be a spectator on her own life, even her lovemaking. Only when she decides to take the risk of true intimacy does she come close to her ideal of universal, loving brotherhood and sisterhood.

She is often political in her dealings with groups and organizations. She seldom allows herself to be placed in a position where she might seem to be less than her idea of perfection. Hypocrisy is often her compromise. Her internal beliefs may sometimes lack any resemblance to her public stance on an issue. She desperately needs to develop good two-way communication. Unlike her Gemini sister, she often doesn't care to exchange information on a one-to-one basis.

Reformist

The Aquarius Woman is part Helen Keller, part Peter Pan, a dash of Minnie Mouse, and a pinch of Madame Curie. She is not only complicated and unpredictable, but she keeps one foot in the future and has fantastic faraway eyes that see much and reveal nothing.

She is an activist to whom causes may be more attractive than respectable, middle-class mores; she will at some point feel compelled to pursue freedom or fight sexism or join the diplomatic corps to do an "inside job." She is a doer with a visionary mind and missionary zeal, for she believes in the good of the common cause and in group destiny.

She may seek quantity instead of quality in her relationships and often tries to escape from herself into the crowd. She may belong to everyone, and in the end, least of all to herself. She has a periodic need to hibernate but also a strong drive to pull people together, to demonstrate the validity of her beliefs, to create a different way of life for some people. Jules Verne, an Aquarian type, saw into the future, and he entertained as well as educated his readers with his imaginative futuristic world.

The Aquarius Woman tends to have enlightened ideals in selected areas that can range from child raising and sex education to human rights and prison reform, from medical revolution to personal liberty. She always reserves the right to dissent, though she prefers to do it peacefully. She is usually attached to her version of the truth, and she is invariably ahead of her times in some manner. Often her lifestyle is middle-class, but she will have one or two shocking concepts. She may be a churchgoer, for example, yet also a devout nudist, a Sunday school teacher who supports the right to abortion. Part of her is always open to reform. Human rights, not just according to the letter but in the spirit of the law as well, are quintessential to her. The right to happiness, including a good education and medical care, is something she defends to her grave, though happiness in the sense of deep, personal, emotional fulfillment and total inner serenity frequently eludes her.

Quirky, offbeat, quixotic

The Aquarius Woman defies traditional descriptions; she blows hot and cold. One day she is a cookie-baking mother with no greater aim in life than to do the wash and repot the plants. The next morning she may be marching at the head of a demonstration, wildly supporting women's work rights. That night she may read a Gothic novel until three in the morning, and the following week she will probably take up horseback riding and archery. She can be outgoing in the morning and reclusive at night, a politician as well as a visionary.

She will greet you with enthusiasm on Monday, indifference on Tuesday, absent-mindedness on Wednesday, open arms on Thursday, an intellectual discourse on Friday, and a passionate invitation to a midnight ball over the weekend. She may be the most helpful neighbor you've ever had, always ready with aid and advice. On the other hand, she is probably the only person you know intimately (you thought) who will drive right by you as you struggle with a flat tire. It's not that she doesn't see you; it's just that your plight doesn't register as her problem.

The Aquarius Woman tends to be offbeat in her moods, tastes, and habits. She dresses to please herself, though a strong part of her hungers for approval. Nevertheless, she is just as likely to wear gypsy skirts as Victorian nightgowns, mother hubbards as the latest in Italian chic. Though she can't explain how she chooses her styles or what prompts her to swing from image to trend, one thing she never lacks is individual and avant-garde flair.

Unpossessive, nonmaterialistic, freedom-seeking

An outstanding and unusual Aquarian trait is lack of possessiveness, both of people and objects. Aquarius seeks to live by her own views. Her relationships will work best when she is respected, when her quirks are accepted. She is interested neither in owning people nor in accumulating possessions. Security or showing off is not nearly as important to her as giving a good performance, as adopting unusual aims and methods and making them work. She tends to be far more possessive of the techniques that help her to reach success, and of any pets she may have, than of people and possessions. Money is important to her mostly as a tool, a resource to give her independence. She wants to be able to do whatever she wants, on short notice, without having to waste time to account for her motives and aims. She would prefer life to run smoothly, without requiring too much maintenance and administration. A jealous or possessive partner is intolerable to her, but she appreciates one who cooperates in providing the material underpinnings and intellectual cooperation for her to "do her own thing."

The freedom she seeks is still in the future. The Aquarius Woman cannot be typecast; she is not a radical feminist, bohemian, socialist, fan of free love, rebel, revolutionary. She may be bits and parts of all of them, but her urge for activity and unrestrained existence probably transcends even her own understanding. She *is*, her nature is the way it is, and she must accept it as such.

The Aquarius Woman mirrors to the rest of us our own needs for growth and freedom. She is at least potentially an avatar of a new consciousness, one that is not enamored of the past, transcends many of its own limitations, trusts the moment, and is gifted both in foreseeing and in creating a more civilized future.

Avant-garde, attracts abrupt change, mental

Aquarius may identify with the Wheel of Fortune in the Tarot deck, for she lives at the hub of eternal flux. The coming and going of her mental tide may not ripple her surface, but the Aquarian female's calculator is more active than any computer. She justly considers the brain the most important human organ. Everything, in her opinion, is ruled by the brain; its signals determine sexual arousal, illness, mood, and reaction. She shudders at the term "mind control" and will be much more interested in the burgeoning self-help movement when it is renamed "mind liberation."

She relies on her own mental power to stimulate and guide her, and it performs many a magic trick. In her life, the unconventional may become the norm, especially if her mind is open. She can be telepathic, clairvoyant, clairaudient; she is extremely proficient at the use of magic. Many Aquarian types become involved with some branch of metaphysics, and a large number are visionaries, astrologers with a scientific bent, or futuristic scientists.

Revolutionary thoughts and events that strike out of the blue characterize her life. Many an Aquarian has been forced to leave her town, country, and whole way of life on short notice, to start all over in a strange part of the world. She tends to meet challenge well though she rarely seeks it. The Aquarius Woman perhaps has a special telephone plugged into the cosmos, a kind of internal Bell System. I wouldn't put it past her to send subliminal messages to planetary headquarters asking for a thunderbolt or two when change is needed. She probably learns more from sudden and trying experiences than from all her mental perambulations; and so she needs such jolts.

Opinionated

Aquarius can vacillate and seesaw, but once she makes up her mind, she is decidedly opinionated. She can also marshal her arguments cleverly and be so convincing as to make her point of view difficult to resist. She seeks the truth and believes there is but one; her belief becomes the only belief, and her opinion the only valid one. She is the most likely to tell you, "This is how it is! Take it or leave it!"

Self-confident, dutiful, self-serving

The Aquarius Woman is bound to accomplish a considerable amount in her life. She can do pretty much as she chooses, for her mind is strong, her will steely. She has the ability to discern what she wants and the talent to attract what she needs, especially at unexpected moments. She is apt to have a few stormy, quixotic relationships, and she finds it hard to be able to give from the heart. But where her head rules, she is usually vastly successful.

She has the type of self-confidence many people envy. Nobody can mow her over; she is never a helpless victim or a retiring wallflower. Though she has inherent humbleness and at times is quite shy, she can rise above these traits when necessary. She is often more confident in her work achievements than in her personal life. She hungers for recognition and awards that mean she has made it, for they alone provide her with the type of feedback that nurtures her self-esteem. Without the feeling of having done her duty she has little self-respect.

She rarely gets rattled, and her mind works quickly, efficiently. Passion seldom traps her into foolishness, and whether she wants to make tracks or cover them, she can and will do as she chooses. At times lonely, usually detached, the Aquarius Woman appears to be very much in control of what she wants and of what she gets. Other women can learn a great deal from her in this respect. To a very large extent, she consciously creates her own reality. She seems to know earlier than most what she wants and why. She tends to accept conscientiously the values she is taught, despite a reformist streak in her nature.

She has a refined instinct for bartering, with herself and with those whose approval she needs. The deal she most often makes with herself is to work for the advancement of a cause that will better our species and to allow herself to have self-respect in return.

She can barely exist without feeling worthwhile, and she needs a communal rather than an individual stamp of approval. She is victimized mainly by her own wish to suppress knowledge of those traits she dislikes in herself. Because she finds selfishness wholly unacceptable, she may utilize her bag of magic tricks to deceive herself, thereby protecting her self-esteem. The danger of this is that she, who is naturally detached, can increase the distance that already exists between herself and other people.

Altruistic, truthful

The Aquarius Woman is bound to be a charitable, humane, fair person who gives people in general a fair shake. She may be a tireless worker and crusader, for she is fundamentally decent and wishes to give her best to any commitment. She tends to be conscientious, responsible, dutiful, kind, humane, and trustworthy. She often employs her talents to benefit others. She frequently has artistic gifts, such as painting, singing, or writing. She tends to be good with her hands and may enjoy sewing, crafts, and cooking. These activities are especially good for her; they balance her overactive mind and anchor her to the physical world.

She is as good as her word. She says nothing she does not mean, and if she has little to say, there is often meaning in her omissions. She can sometimes feel sorry for herself and become reclusive. She may fall in the trap of doing everything for everyone and nothing for herself. She can be a passive manipulator, but most often she tries to be honest, analytical, incisive, and active. She does not like to feel she owes people; thus, she tries to avoid situations that make her dependent on others. She may be happier working at home or working in a small business, perhaps self-employed, than in large, bureaucratic corporations. Though she can learn and do anything she sets her mind to, she usually prefers not to expend energy on power games.

Courteous, civilized

Though the Aquarius Woman can be a hellcat fighting for something she really believes in, she prefers treating people with courtesy and displaying a civilized demeanor. She is a woman of quality and likes to surround herself with more of the same. She usually has a subtle air of refinement; it is as if she were free of some of the baser instincts that plague people, such as grasping or envy. Her ability to detach herself from the passionate pursuit of materialism, and her frequent unwillingness to tangle with the tentacles of emotionalism in relationships, confer an elusive gentility. No doubt about it—she is different. She does not want to be caught in the webs and traps of living.

Tense, lonely, talented

Though it is a difficult generalization to make, it is nevertheless true that the Aquarius Woman invariably has a unique talent. In many cases she is loaded with talent, i.e., precognitive gifts, organizational ability, and humaneness.

She resembles a flower that closes at dawn and opens at night. The desert cactus seeking the moon instead of the sun's rays provides an appropriate comparison. Nighttime is her time, and she often lays plans then. She is often a poor sleeper, for she has a finely tuned nervous system and is extremely aware of vibrations. She has a built-in radio receiver she cannot turn off, though her transmitter only operates on command.

She is apt to be unidirectional, totally absorbed in her current commitment. She asks for the "why" of every phenomenon; she is born with the urge to catalogue behavior, to find out what really makes people tick (and where the bodies are buried), to research social and political trends, and to set a few herself.

She tends to carry a personal yardstick and to measure life by her own code—and it rarely resembles the usual one. The controlled, insightful, and individualistic overseeing of projects and phenomena is one of her talents, and she exercises it repeatedly. She often has scientific talent.

Whether she is investigating rats, discovering antibodies, wiping tots' noses, or reading her favorite book, the Aquarius Woman is coiled like a small spring. Slightly inhibited, watchful, always nursing insight from observation, she is apt to think and work very hard. Duty is important to her, and her talent and conscience, harnessed to a cause, often make her an outstanding achiever. She seeks privacy from time to time, as if it were her safety valve.

Driven, proud, group-conscious

Many an Aquarian has said the same thing to me: "I don't know what compels me to work so hard. There is something inside me that forces me to give of myself, a drive to help. Perhaps it is the old urge for immortality; I want to leave something behind me, to make a difference."

The Aquarius Woman may be oblivious to household chores, but she is unlikely to neglect anything she considers essential to the advancement of causes or to the good of the people. She is often a teacher, albeit not the conventional sort. She may be a publisher, lecturer, medic. She may teach by example and by conduct, by haranguing teenagers on a crowded subway about the ills of marijuana, by writing angry protest letters to politicians, by founding an alternative education or lifestyles network. She deeply believes in the potential for good in everyone. She would like to bring about enlightenment for the masses. Though she is secretly an elitist, she wants all people to better themselves. Self-actualization and group sharing are Aquarian ideals.

On the other hand, she often ignores the personal dimension. She forgets that a touch is more healing and may ultimately be a more effective teaching tool than an impersonal half-hour lecture. She is not exactly secretive, but she is unlikely to be self-revealing; she sometimes lies by omission. She can be a visionary humanitarian, a kind leader, a strong comrade. But she is often tactless and can defeat her grand designs by failing to work with the little people who make the big projects go. Thus, she frequently has trouble practicing what she preaches. She often finds it easier to envision ends than to find and adopt available means.

Inquisitive, experimental, unbiased

Aquarius tends to prejudge things less than the rest of us and to keep an open mind. After all, Newton's ideas were revised by Einstein, and Einstein himself may be succeeded by a new theorist. Dr. Spock was the rage among mothers in the 1960s, and look what happened to him! Aquarius wants to know and is always ready to reevaluate.

The Aquarius Woman is attracted to those who examine the options of today to create a new tomorrow. Choices intrigue her. New methods, lifestyles, cures, and goals stimulate her. She travels further in her mind in one month than most people do in a decade. But she has trouble finding conclusions in which to wholeheartedly believe.

She tends to be ideologically experimental. She may believe in astrological birth control, UFOs, nudity in families, life after death. But her conservative, approval-sensitive instincts restrain her in practice. She may believe, for example, that divorce laws must be made fairer to men; that monogamy is passé and that alternative lifestyles are necessary; that new technology can produce miraculous medical cures. However, she will probably fight to have the law on her side if she herself gets divorced; have serious misgivings if she strays or decides to try a "far-out" lifestyle; and refuse to be a guinea pig for any medical miracle or breakthrough drug.

Fears intimacy, shy, humble

The Aquarius Woman tends to use her mind as a security blanket. She may embrace large causes, groups, societies, and crowds to lose herself and avoid one-to-one, face-to-face intimacy. She may be an emotional virgin throughout life, or at least until she experiences her first irrational, uncontrolled urge to be with someone and pour her soul out—an experience that is apt to shake her to the core.

She is usually more experimental conceptually than experientially. She believes absolutely in freedom and in the necessity for change and growth. But human beings have a way of getting scared on the threshold of change, and Aquarius is no different. Thus, she often talks a better game than she plays. Her greatest conflict is masked by her broad-mindedness and experimental stance. These are apt to hide her Achilles' heel, fear of intimacy very often coupled with fear of failure.

The Aquarius Woman is apt to be timid and somewhat passive in personal relations. She is more willing to generalize than to personalize, especially about herself. Few people cross the Rubicon to her carefully guarded inner self. Even fewer seem to understand that her oft zealous public engagements are easier for her than intimate tête-à-têtes.

She has a strong and attractive streak of modesty. She can be a public servant who really serves the people with fairness and humility. Her inner eye appears to see and accept the insignificance of a personality in the large scheme of things.

Informal, compartmentalized

She tends to dislike formal presentations, repetitive rituals, and overburdening structures. She would rather go to the ball dressed as Cinderella than as the princess, preferring the offbeat and casual. She may like the flexibility of the latest Italian modern furniture, the informality of Japanese living rooms, the originality and functional beauty of Victorian bathtubs with claw feet. Modular everything, mobile furniture, housing, and lifestyles fascinate her.

She can tuck her job in one corner of her mind and her love life in another. If necessary, she will leave her home in a disorganized shambles to run down a new lead or hobby. She can detach herself from family cares so that they seldom distract her at work. One Aquarian friend of mine looked out her window one morning and saw her horse lying dead in the meadow. She called the police and the county animal protection board, calmly dressed, and left for a fund-raising luncheon in the city. The horse, of course, was taken away and disposed of during her absence.

The ability to split her mind helps her concentration. Success is usually within her reach, partly for this reason. She will rarely allow herself to be disturbed by the hobgoblin of little minds, consistency, or the food of dramatists, emotional conflict. She frequently uses overwork as an escape from intimacy.

Aloof yet friendly

The Aquarius Woman is more likely to be concerned with the welfare of the world than with individual lives. Of course she loves her family and is loyal to her friends, but she thinks in broad sweeps; the large canvas fascinates her more than the details. She respects the natural rhythm of events and considers the order of things more important, and surely more permanent, than her own smallish concepts.

In a way, she has the unique characteristic of having a normal-size ego. She is not nearly as enamored of herself as most of the people she knows. She is seldom narcissistic and always tries to be broad-minded and fair. Her emotional detachment can have healthy effects. She seldom plays the prima donna or creates domestic disharmony purely to feed an overlarge, undernourished ego. She leaves power games to Scorpio, self-pity to Pisces, manipulation to Leo. However, she can use any tool she wants when and if she sets her mind to it.

She is good in groups, for she can balance leadership with fellowship. She can blend and listen or lead and debate. She can synthesize what others say, give credit where credit is due. She tends to find more validity in statistical demonstrations of truth than in unwarranted emotional displays.

Sexually broad-minded, erotically inhibited

The Aquarius Woman seldom says no to demands for sexual freedom. You will not find her fighting for the abolition of porno movie houses and adult bookstores or against the open sale of contraceptives. She believes in personal choice and upholds people's right to be exposed to a variety of stimuli and to determine which they find most appealing. Conceptually, she is broad-minded and liberated. She is also nearly unshockable.

One of her most attractive traits in her nonjudgmental friendliness. She is capable of coexisting with people whose belief systems are vastly different from hers, and though she is a natural teacher and an often autocratic lecturer, she is not apt to try to convert everyone around her. If her best friend is having a different man every night while she herself is monogamous, the difference in sexual values and behavior will not affect the friendship. The Aquarius Woman is able to give people a lot of space, and she expects similar treatment.

She learns very early to keep her strong opinions on personal etiquette to herself and to share them only when absolutely necessary. She may seek a public platform instead. She may write books about sex or become a sex therapist, a counselor of alcoholics with sexual problems, perhaps a writer specializing in New Age human relations, a publisher with a liberated view, or a moviemaker interested in exploring how relationships and lifestyles are changing.

She finds it more difficult to be open and uninhibited in her personal life. The more emotionally involved and invested she is in a relationship, the more she tends to fall back on old-fashioned mores. She fears rejection deeply. She can split what her head tells her (that it's okay to live in an open marriage, for example) from what her feelings dictate. In her heart, she is apt to be scared of the limitless potential for good and bad that is inherent in personal freedom, and to allow that fear to restrain her.

Aquarius relationships

The beauty of love is that it encompasses everything. The problem of love is a problem of the soul.

The Aquarius Woman has many relationships in her life, few of which could be classified as truly close, intimate. She is conservative; thus, she wants love, a primary bond, and more and more a meaningful career. She is also avant-garde; thus, she wants to explore her own full potential and anything that helps her to attain it. She is the last woman to conform to anyone's expectations of old fashioned femininity, which is far too limiting for the modern Aquarian.

She is a strong woman of fixed opinions and rich assets. One of her assets should be a good education. She finds it difficult to change and to be vulnerable; yet she can be highly altruistic, even self-denying. She is sometimes as lucid and open as a clear pool; at other times she is closed, her arms wrapped around her like protective shielding. She both wants and fears intimacy. She wants it as part of her joy and growth; she fears it because of her resistance to risking exposure and giving up control.

She is a many-faceted prism finely chisled to varying depths. Her mind is her greatest attraction. It can be as brilliant as a crystal, as luminous as the full moon, as opalescent as pearls. Her body is often not as pure, for she frequently neglects it. Her spirit is wide open, reaching to the stars for insight, unusual information, and knowledge. Her soul is often more barren, parched for vibrant, spring-fed mutuality, for easy exchanges of interest and hope that are rich in feeling.

The greatest challenge for the Aquarius Woman is to conquer her fear of exposure and vulnerability. She cannot attain happiness in relationships until she confronts it. She will try various avenues of escape: work, humanitarian involvement, protection and love of animals, study, multiple relationships. In the end, she must recognize that the total evolution of a human being cannot occur without letting intellectual knowledge penetrate the layers, all the way to the inner recesses of the heart, where knowledge is transformed into caring and compassion.

"All's equal in love and friendship" is her motto. If she carries out her obligations, she feels, the relationship will tend to take care of itself. She is typically slightly eccentric, nevertheless—in her own way a devoted mother, wife, and friend, responsible and unusually imaginative. She can be the life of the party, the one with the humorous, odd ideas to make any social occasion memorable. Children adore her, responding to her zaniness, her willingness to share ideas and to treat them as complete, albeit smaller, human beings. She loves to inspire children; she sees them as valuable and necessary components of the New Age she knows we are approaching. She teaches by the inductive method, challenging them to ferret out answers to some of life's questions for themselves.

"You do your thing, and I'll do mine," the motto of the Big Sur scene in the 1960s, later adopted by a large segment of the human potential movement, would please the Aquarius Woman. Deep down, she would probably prefer to be left to her own thoughts and devices much of the time. She wants to run her own life and cannot abide anyone telling her what to do. She does not expect her mate to order her around, nor to interfere with the essential pattern of her life. This often gets her in trouble with macho men who simply cannot understand what game she is up to. It is no game; it is the Aquarian nature to strike a silent bargain. The terms are: she will do all she feels is necessary to be a good wife, mother, partner, or friend; in return, she expects to be respected, understood, and supported without in any way being restrained.

The Aquarius Woman is the best of friends in the worst of times. You can count on her to be there when you really need her. But don't count on her to cry with you, not even to carry a hankie in case, you need it. She is unlikely to be too emotional, to get so involved as to actually feel with you. She is bound to lack empathy, though she will learn to be sympathetic mostly as a social skill. Putting herself in another's place is not her forte, but leading the way out of trouble, lecturing all the while, is.

She might tell a friend in trouble "I told you so." Her self-righteous attitudes often hurt the feelings of more sensitive, self-castigating souls. She will probably find it hard to understand why people accuse her of being aloof, even unfeeling, for to her, matters stand as they stand. She can even dissect affairs of the heart with her mental microscope, and she masters the intricacies of the rituals that bind people. She frequently has astonishing insight into human relations, but she exercises it as if she were sitting on a hilltop watching with binoculars from across the road.

She probably won't volunteer much information, either about herself or about her analysis of people. She may consider it rude to speak of intimate affairs. She is likely to think that asking you how Fred reacted to your going back to school is too personal a question; and she is sure that if you want to tell her something, it won't be necessary for her to ask.

Her imagination covers a wide scope. It is delightfully free of traditional female or male limits. She won't confine her thinking to decorating or cake mixes or her love life. She will mentally roam the pampas of scientific research, Chinese history, Italian art. She most likely is interested in the stock market, scientific inventions, the change in the world's climate, and why people consult faith healers. Far-out subjects such as astrological birth control may interest her, and she is likely to blurt out in the middle of dinner that she has decided to train herself for out-of-body journeys.

She seldom shares her thought processes with intimates, which often proves very frustrating to those who are innately possessive and curious. She believes in fair decision making and fair fighting, so she tries to do better in these respects. She is usually clever and articulate, but she must not take her own communications skills for granted. Those with which she was born must be developed and constantly upgraded in order to help her make relationships work.

She behaves with extreme inborn courtesy that may verge on disinterest. She won't push people to report on their own motivations or life plans. She assumes that people know what they are doing; she often does! She believes in getting expert advice in everything. She is as likely to explore real estate investments with a paid professional as she is to discuss psychological problems with a psychologist (though the latter goes somewhat against her grain of independent thinking). She believes in leaving her personal problems behind closed doors when she ventures out in public. She tends to be a remarkably controlled and compartmentalized person.

She believes in some absolutes, above all in the right and wrong of any matter at hand. To her, there is always one best way, and it pays to observe her formulating her conclusion as to which one it is. She gathers her data by observation, reading, and experimentation, nearly scientifically; feeds it into her mini-computer; weighs every aspect; and finally consults potential supporters as well as potential enemies of her emerging plan. And once she makes up her mind, heaven help those who disagree. She is capable of very cool, dispassionate displays of anger calculated to reduce the opposition to total capitulation.

She is very fond of animals, and though she lacks warmth, she is highly hospitable. She is traditional enough to believe that certain things are done in certain ways, and among the things that should be done just right are entertaining and welcoming people. She has a sixth sense about which people will fit into her life and which will not, but she is usually a flawless hostess with flair who appears to judge everyone equally. She is often more comfortable at social gatherings of moderate size than in an intense tête-à-tête that requires self-revelation.

She is ambitious and generally needs an outlet to express her humanitarian ideals and boundless mental energy. She can benefit from being a perennial student. She may be very psychic, and if so, she can gain from learning techniques to use her psychic qualities advantageously. Her open mind endears her to friends, and she has an intriguing, quixotic, almost modest brilliance. She must be willing to open up and increase her ability to feel, to express emotions (eros) along with ideas (logos), and to be aware of the inevitable pluses as well as the minuses in her relationships. She tends to be an optimist, expecting free-flowing give-and-take; she must learn more about what it takes to make her love relationships work.

Childhood

The Aquarius girl usually has a closer link to her father than to her mother. She tends to respect his typically more logical and dispassionate approach to life, and she is drawn to his authority and power. She often develops a crush on her father and distances herself from her mother. Her feelings for her father must be resolved by the time she begins a potentially long-term romance with a man.

Over the years, I have heard many Aquarius women tell me that they idealized their fathers and had trouble being close to their mothers. Invariably, these women had problems trying to find a male who lived up to their expectations. A few rejected their father after a period of teenage adoration and consciously sought men who were visibly different.

Katherine illustrates the first case. A lovely, long-legged blond in her twenties, Katherine came to see me because she was considering divorce. The older of two girls, she had adored her father and been his pet. She was never close to her mother and in fact had resented her mother for intefering with her consuming love for her father. Katherine's father, a successful small businessman, had devoted his after-work hours and weekends to pleasing Katherine.

The bubble burst when she was fourteen. Her father lost all his money in a business venture. Her mother went back to work, and he started keeping house. Katherine was blissfully happy, for she imagined that she would now have Daddy to herself full time. However, Daddy soon started drinking and grew increasingly depressed. Though Katherine was growing up, he insisted on buying her stuffed animals (she never knew where he got the money) and speaking to her as if she were still eight years old.

The crisis came when Katherine discovered her father eavesdropping on her as she returned home from a date at age sixteen. They had a huge fight. Her father had been drinking, and he said things he later regretted. Katherine, in turn, found out that her father carried only one picture of her in his wallet. It was a picture that showed her at age eight, a lovely little girl wearing a pink ballet tutu. Shortly after the fight, Katherine's father suddenly died of a heart attack.

She told me the following:

I suppressed my anger at my father, and after he died I continued to idolize him as I had when I was still a child. I looked for a young man who would give me the same adoring, fan-club-like support. Eventually, I turned to older men who had money, had been hurt, and wanted to cater to a spoiled young woman. I played surrogate daughter to dozens of middle-aged men. Eventually I married Sam, the mildest man of all, twelve years older than me.

Now the marriage is on the rocks. I never finished school, and I don't know what I'll do to survive by myself. But I can no longer live on illusion. Sam has neither the strength nor the emotional honesty to grow. I've outgrown him. I hope I am finally ready to let go of being someone's little girl. And I've just recently begun a dialogue with my mother. She turns out to be a sensitive, strong person herself.

Katherine felt a lot of hurt, anger, and ambivalence about her father. She loved him, yet he had confused her and let her down, even by dying suddenly. She wanted to marry a man like her father, and in Sam perhaps she did. But then her needs changed. Sam, still the mild, adoring man he had been, was no longer enough to help her sustain her growth, her emerging confrontation with her adult self. Her father's business failure and sudden death, which she had minimized for many years, cast a long shadow. She seemed, in effect, to be looking for Sam to fail also. Realizing the pattern, she wanted to break it by divorce. Eventually, Katherine and Sam decided to try for a reconciliation.

The more the Aquarius Woman is able to blend her emotions with her intellect, the happier her love life will be. The more conscious she is of her complex, idealized tie to her father, the more likely she is to adopt a healthier pattern with other males.

How the Aquarius Woman relates: lovers and other intimates

Aquarius can attract people by any avenue she chooses, for such is the power of her mind. She typically has many more platonic friends than sexually consummated relationships. She prefers cultured, interesting, offbeat people to jocks or an erotic merry-go-round, and her appeal is likely to consist of pleasant physical attractiveness rooted in intelligence, curiosity, and an air of civilized concern.

The Aquarius Woman does not place as high a value on having sex appeal as many of her sisters do. Interestingly, she is often as enticing a puzzle as the woman who tries much harder to attract men. She has an elusive, slightly detached unconcerned attitude that will whet the appetite of hard-core chasers. She also possesses an innate modesty combined with a subtle intellectual arrogance, an elitism accompanied by a profession of humanitarian concern.

Until she overcomes her tendency to be intellectually free but emotionally and sexually restrained, she will fall into the trap of conducting romantic relationships as if she were solving a crossword puzzle. An encyclopedic and dispassionate mind, an ability to analyze bits and pieces of information and find the overall pattern, a cooly elegant, subtle, slow approach—that is her style. She fears rejection and won't jump into anything hastily. Yet from time to time, when she gets fed up with deliberation and analysis, she will suddenly change her stripes and go for broke.

Part of her charm is her unpredictability. She has two sides: the girl next door (albeit with a diploma from MENSA), and the exotic bohemian peeking out from behind the Little Mary Sunshine facade. She herself probably never knows who is up next for which role.

She usually has many friends, most of whom are little more than acquaintances. She tends to respect men more than women and indeed may not like women at all. She may feel superior, more cool than other women. She is the type of lady who is a lady all the way: she never neglects service people, is kind to her landlady, elevator operator, cleaning man. She may have a neighborhood fan club composed of tots and animals. She probably belongs at least nominally to a few clubs and associations, and she will never fail to do her part in any organization associated with her children's school or her husband's business.

As to real, honest-to-goodness friends, the type you can call at three o'clock in the morning when you've had a tortured nightmare, she may have few or none. Early in life there seem to be many she thinks she could cultivate or call in case of emergency. But as she fails to call on them and to grow closer, these friendships often dwindle away. Though she is stubbornly loyal, she is equally stubbornly self-protective.

The Aquarius Woman very rarely lets her guard down all the way. She does not want anyone, including her closest friend, to see her when she is down and depressed. She wants to conquer her problems herself, and in any case, she dislikes it when people saddle her with their "petty problems." Though she is available for counsel to others, she very rarely asks them to return the favor. She is a prime candidate for self-evaluation, self-counseling, self-healing.

Unexpected events mark her romantic life. She tends to have a split personality: she is likely to be scrupulously fixed in her primary affection, as if by oath. The principle is important. However, circumstances are likely to test her love many times over. Life, as it were, conspires against serenity.

Of thirteen Aquarius women I interviewed, eight had been separated from their husbands for a considerable time early in marriage by the intervention of war, revolution, or sudden family crises. Three had fallen in love suddenly with another man. One's husband died in the first year of marriage; one's disappeared from the face of the earth. A sample of thirty-seven, twenty-eight married, others "committed," yielded the following results: seven had remained monogamous and had survived the marital ups and downs in reasonable shape; twelve had had extramarital affairs as if "out of the blue"—unplanned, unpremeditated, even against their better judgment; six were leading a lifestyle we call open marriage; four were living apart from their husbands due to sudden career transfers; the rest were coping with absentee husbands (usually engaged in scientific research) or illness and were considering a variety of sexual lifestyles. There were also four women in this group who had divorced their husbands and remarried them—an unusually high statistic.

The Aquarius Woman can be everything to her man; equal, mate, partner, inventive lover, mother, teacher, pupil, sister, daughter. She can run his business or their house; she can be his colleague in the most complex enterprise, provided she wants to train herself for it. She can coauthor articles or books with him, carry on the family tradition nobly and proudly. She will welcome his sister, his mother, and possibly even his first wife, with grace and fair judgment.

She can protect him from the vagaries of fate by shoring up his ego, providing strength and sustenance when he most needs them. There is a part of her that seems untouched by the whirling chaos of daily living, hiding a golden nugget of wisdom. She can help her friends to see patterns, even to foresee events. She can help to detach them from passions that would mar their judgment, to lift petty jealousies that disturb the rhythm of their days.

She must be willing to examine herself. She should consider giving some space and love to the little girl who lives inside her, impatient, needy, and hungry for affection and attention. The adult seldom asks for either, but she must learn how. The Aquarius Woman tends to hide her doubts and insecurities more successfully than most; she is often so proficient at detachment that she forgets how to be involved. Her key relationship word and crucial experience is *intimacy*.

Intimacy

The woman who wishes to learn to be intimate must first become sensitive to her own capacity for feeling. She must not reject out of hand all that is traditionally feminine. Intimacy is *not* computing, wearing masks, playing games, pleasing others, manipulating, coercing, competing, worrying about the past or the future, acting out roles, using people, saying what we don't mean. Intimacy, whether or not it is sexual/genital, has a physical component of touching, hugging, and reaching out.

Intimacy is a caring contact, touching on all levels, tenderness. It is affirmative communication, sensitive listening, honest speech; empathy, openness, trust; an upward spiral of sharing on the emotional, spiritual, mental, and physical levels. Intimacy is an open-ended arrangement in which the parties give each other an unconditional yes, an affirmation unchecked by the limits society and religion have placed on most human feelings and activities. Intimacy precludes deliberate hurt, exploitation, withholding, and violence. It facilitates total, integrated being, becoming, and sharing. Intimacy has the potential to make a person happy; indeed, it is such a necessary ingredient of happiness that without it the immortal creativity of a Thomas Edison or a Sarah Bernhardt seems hollow and extracts an undue personal toll. Professional achievement tastes uncertain, even bitter, in the mouths of those whose personal lives lack intimate caring.

Problems of intimacy

The Aquarius Woman's Achilles' heel is her fear of intimacy; that is, of showing her real feelings, exposing her tender roots, admitting vulnerability, being prepared to share with other people (or one person) on a mutual, equal-to-equal level.

Aquarius has a low tolerance for traditional female tasks, behavior, roles, status. Having preferred her father's logical approach, his prestige and authority in the household and in many cases in the outside world, she would prefer to emulate him. Like him, she relies on her mind more than on her feelings.

The woman today continues to bear most of the responsibility for teaching the man she loves sensitivity, communication skills, and the ability to open up and be vulnerable. If she herself lacks intimacy skills, her relationship will lack an emotional leader and is not likely to work. And it may take the Aquarius Woman quite awhile to realize that deprecating femininity takes away some of her own self-esteem and diminishes her willingness to risk being the emotional pioneer in her love ties.

Strong identification with a male during the formative years makes it difficult for a woman to integrate and respect her own femaleness. She may react by distrusting other women, fearing them, competing with them. The Aquarius Woman must face the fact that in fearing other women, she fears part of herself.

The first and most important way for her to cope with her fear of "coming out" is to recognize that the fear is there. All air signs have this detachment from feelings to excess. If she is unwilling to own up to her fear, so much the worse for her.

The Aquarius Woman typically uses a form of self-concealment that Virginia Satir calls "computing." Computing is a technique whereby she hides her emotional needs behind a shield so as to avoid being hurt. Computing is assuming a detached, rational, low-key, controlled posture while confronting any emotionally charged situation. Computing is "I believe you are angry because I see your hands are trembling, and you have been seriously considering throwing a pot at me" or "This family needs to examine its rate of efficiency in communication."

Computing tends to create envy in others, and in fact the computer's hidden agenda is to mobilize potential opponents to ally with her. Computing serves to diffuse feelings, cover them up, and create the illusion that one is in total control of one's emotions at all times. Computing is also a game of superiority whereby the computer does not let the other person in or allow them to take the role of an equal. Computing is playing negative parent in a totally detached, intellectualized way.

Some telltale signs of computing are the following: your words are ultrareasonable; your body is calm, cool, and collected, or so you tell yourself; your insides are screaming, "I'm vulnerable!" When a woman is computing, she is very correct and reasonable and shows no feelings. Her body often feels dry and dissociated, while her voice may fall into a monotone. The impassive behavior of the mother in Woody Allen's *Interiors* typifies this syndrome.

Coping with fear of intimacy

Aquarius, to cope with your fear of intimacy, you must first evaluate the following:

1 What is intimacy to you? Do you want it? Do you have it?
2 If you want it and don't have it, what are you prepared to do about it?
3 How do your values in general affect your personal life? Do you feel close to your friends? Are you comfortable asking them for a big favor? Do you reveal yourself to your mate or your current boyfriend? What are some of the defensive distancing devices you use? We all have some, and we all use them just about automatically. They are like the techniques Shirley MacLaine devised to "conquer those feelings that made me uncomfortable."

There are some basic things we all tell ourselves that block our self-disclosure. Aquarius, you tend to use these as your first line of defense:

1 They'll find out I'm no good (a sham).
2 I might do it wrong.
3 They'll make fun of me, criticize me.
4 I might intrude.
5 They might leave me.
6 They'll find out I am not perfect.
7 They'll see how scared I am.

The need for intimacy is basic in both men and animals. If this need is unmet in infancy, our ability to function sexually as adults is impaired. This was shown dramatically by the Harlow experiments with baby monkeys.

In one experiment, the researchers put infant monkeys with two "mothers." One was made of wire and was the source of milk. The other was covered with cloth. The monkeys mostly played with the soft cloth mother, cuddling and asking for affection. They would leave only with great reluctance to obtain milk from the wire figure. These monkeys, raised without warm, loving, intimate contact, grew up physically, but in a sense they never became adults. They could not love and were sexually dysfunctional to the point where not one could even assume the correct posture for intercourse. The researchers concluded that intimacy is an essential part of an infant's sexual education and that sexual functioning depends on emotional wholeness.

Everyone has a hunger for love, touching, cuddling, petting, for emotionally satisfying physical contact. The need for intimacy, however, is rarely acknowledged beyond early childhood. Most of us learn to be dysfunctional, much as the monkeys did, by repeatedly absorbing our socialization lessons too conscientiously. We learn to block our own impulses toward tenderness, for we are taught to surrender them to taboos against incest, homosexuality, bisexuality, the Oedipus complex, the Electra complex, etc. We withhold affection for fear of spoiling our children and spoiling ourselves, for fear of being "unrealistic" or "overly emotional." Power struggles start in the cradle, where we are taught to supress natural emotions in favor of societal role playing.

The Aquarius Woman, being an outstanding student, learns these prohibitions against intimacy only too well. Perhaps one reason she instinctively seeks out large groups is so she can interact with as many mirroring personalities as possible. The bigger the group, the more social mirrors she has and the more she learns.

Aquarius, here are more practical suggestions on coping with intimacy. However, intimacy is so complex, such a charged interaction, that if you feel you have serious difficulties, I advise you to see a counselor or therapist. Some of the techniques that follow are in fact best done in a therapeutic setting.

1 This is a gestalt exercise. Take two chairs, and put yourself in one chair, your fear of intimacy in another. Talk to your own fear. Switch chairs each time you assume a different role (you or your fear alone). Record the session so that you can listen to your tape later and muse on the insight that is sure to emerge.
2 To learn more about your inner self, describe yourself as an animal, a cloud, a tree, a child, a color. Do this verbally to get the hang of it; then write it all on paper. Refer to your descriptions from time to time, especially when you are dealing with intimacy. Share them with your mate or friends.
3 When in doubt about how you feel, hum a song. Choose the words to it. If you are in an emotional bind, this is an especially quick way to tap into your real feelings.

4 Pay attention to the seemingly inconsequential thoughts that enter your mind, especially when you are discussing intimacy issues. Also try free association, with or without your partner. Completing the sentence "I fear . . ." is one way. What does this chapter make you think of? How does this section make you feel?
5 Be aware of how and when you hold back. If you want to reach out to touch someone and at the last minute stop yourself, be aware of this. You'll have a choice the next time: you can touch, or you can stop yourself from touching. Also be aware of how and when you hold back verbally. Exercises 3 and 4 will help.
6 Be as honest as you can about your secret thoughts and how they may affect your intimate behavior. Review past actions as old scripts need to be periodically updated and revised. Remember that guilt, shame, and fear tend to lift in the daylight of honest evaluation. (See "Libra Relationships" and "Scorpio Relationships" for further advice on specific communication skills.)
7 Here is a good exercise if you want to know exactly who is important to you. Grab all the pillows you can and place them within your reach. Put yourself in the middle of the room. Then take the pillows one by one, designating each as a person. This person can be alive or dead, as long as she/he is important to you. By the time you finish, you will know who has priority in your life, who is closest to you, who is more distant. You will tend to place each pillow exactly as close or as far as you feel to or from the person that pillow represents.
8 Sexual intimacy is an important aspect of feeling close. See "Aquarius Sexuality" for a discussion of this topic.

The Aquarius Woman in love

When Aquarius is in love, she feels "together" and integrated. Her heart opens up, and duty is suffused with pleasure. Her experimental nature invents all kinds of delicious ways to keep her partner interested, and she tingles with almost electric stimulation. Love sparks her whole being; her creative juices flow more than ever. She plugs into 220 volts and runs her sleek engine at a consistent, amazingly high rpm. She buzzes with plans and excitement. For once, she may feel the future is assured . . . at least for awhile.

She is miles ahead of everyone in her appraisal of the total potential of the situation. She seems to walk with her head in the clouds, and what she sees up there is anyone's guess. Probably the future, possibly life in other dimensions. Perhaps she is examining karmic ties. Whatever it is, she's not telling, at least not yet.

Secrecy and intrigue are part of her approach. She is a natural weaver of networks, both of people and of vibrations; she has an inherent mystique she wishes to keep and develop. She won't stand on the corner and shout her happiness to the wind, but she probably will subscribe to all the international journals that can teach her about human relations, sexuality, futuristic lifestyles, and options for the woman in love. She does not look for role models exactly, but she studies so as to be prepared, made secure by her knowledge and ready to try an exciting new path.

She pleases her man by taking on equal responsibility in any part of the relationship that seems to need it. She may choose to play the role of the sexual leader or the financial follower. She can cook, sew, shop, hold his hands, listen, and teach; she can be a good hostess, lover, partner, assistant, chief, or healer. She can be painfully firm, stubborn, and independent, even in love, but she will give her lover equal time if he asks for it. She is fair and tolerant of his foibles, and she will put up with more than will many other women. Problems seldom faze her. She is apt to treat them as mental challenges.

She can be a divine equal. She is ahead of her times in her ability to play any role, including the "male" one. She will not try to possess her man, to make him account for each penny or peccadillo. She gives a man space and expects the same from him. Subscribers to the double standard need not apply.

Even in love she keeps her head, and she can keep his above water in the direst circumstances. She has a deliberate practicality that never leaves her and that she can use to protect her man. She also can make him feel that she knows something he doesn't, but that whatever she knows she will loyally use in their mutual interest.

She is a stimulating, more or less eccentric lover. She has a streak of unpredictability, the courage and desire to stand out, to be unique. She wants to be different from other women, and she does everything she can to distinguish herself, especially in her man's eyes. For example, if he's a tennis nut, she will go out of her way to take tennis lessons so she can keep up with him. Cheerleading or waiting on the sidelines with sandwiches is not her style.

The easy way out, the predictable, never attracts her. And the man who is in love with her will be thrilled, not threatened, by this aspect of her personality.

The Aquarius Woman in love is at her most balanced. She gives in all the important ways as long as she communicates, clearly. What she defines as important is not always identical to what her man considers important. She receives all he gives her gracefully, discreetly, and with an exciting, "just-for-you," electric air of intimacy.

She makes her man feel "in"—the gifted, exhilarated sharer of secret knowledge. She creates an ambience of mutuality in which she is more than willing to shoulder her share. She is able to make her man feel lucky, to keep him wondering about what special, eternally changing, electric-magnetic cosmic energy he has plugged into.

Patterns in the Aquarius Woman's sexual relationships

In her sexual relationships, the Aquarius Woman seems to display the following patterns (to some extent, these apply to her platonic ties as well):

1 She tends to be an early bloomer, open to experience and experiments. The *idea* of sex turns her on strongly, and she is often spurred to action by rebellion or by the desire to show off and be different.
2 She is apt to have many sexual relationships before she marries. She likes her freedom and may try all varieties of lifestyles before she settles down. Deep down, she might like to delay marriage, at least the old-fashioned kind, forever; the possibility that it will become a cage frightens her.
3 She is fixed in her affections once they are seriously established. However, sex and love are different matters to her. Frequently she falls in love, only to find herself sexually attracted by (or at least interested in) other men. If she is married, she is highly likely to have extramarital affairs in secret.
4 In friendship, she gives a great deal, but her friendships typically have out-of-the-blue endings. She probably doesn't understand what happens herself.
5 She experiences a number of uprootings in her life, mostly unpredictable. This can play havoc with her relationships and often does. Things seem to happen to her, including divorce.

6 She tends to be emotionally unfulfilled. Her relationships, though various and stimulating, are seldom fully intimate, totally satisfying. Her aloofness, the emotional shield she carries, prevents closeness with most people and is the single most frequent source of her separations, both emotional and physical.
7 She may escape into or compensate by overwork. She has a tendency to avoid intensely charged emotional situations and may do so most of her life. However, she is often highly successful in her career.
8 If she breaks through to the depth of intimacy she needs yet seldom seeks, she can be the avant-garde avatar of unconditional love. All she needs is to trust and expand her emotional side.

What kind of man she needs most: lovers and husbands

The Aquarius Woman above all needs a tolerant, understanding, warm male. Her man needs to be tolerant because she is; also, her originality requires his open-mindedness. He needs to understand her methods, accept the way she relates to people on the mental, analytical level first. He must be able to tune in to her approach and complement it. He needs to be warm, for she can be chilly. He needs to know how to hug her, when to wrap his arms around her and bring out the suppressed glow.

She needs a man who in no way holds rigid judgments and expectations. He must be flexible, willing to keep a fair and open mind. He should be curious, inquisitive, excited about ideas (especially her new ideas). "Right is right and wrong is wrong" may work for Capricorn, but it will not work for the Aquarius Woman. Her man must not moralize, but he must have character. She respects the man who knows and stands on his own dearly held principles.

She needs an honest man, assertive and willing to force a confrontation if necessary. He must be able to see into her and to call her on any tricks that might be destructive to their relationship. She needs a man who helps her to relay ideas as well as feelings, who supports her in her optimism and hope that also wants action in the emotional realm!

Her man should be neither too passive nor too aggressive. If he is too passive, she may get so comfortable that she becomes too willing to compromise for the sake of domestic peace. If he is too aggressive, she will be turned off. Macho men are not her cup of tea.

Her man needs to maintain a harmonious equilibrium on many counts. She is never money-crazy; wealth is not the most important thing to her. Yet her man should care enough about money to help her make sure there is enough to live a life with some independence. He needs to complement and supplement her drive to be a woman who is recognized as a full-fledged human being.

Her man must be able to flow freely yet also to plan. He can't be too stubborn or too rigid. She wants him to accept her quirks, and she also wants him to watch for the details that make the relationship work. She is willing to phone for dinner reservations, to discuss the income tax, to buy his socks and do some of the laundry, but she expects him to pick up where she leaves off. Equality, shared leadership, and mutual responsibility are attractive to her.

Her man must be a leader, a teacher, in some aspect of their relationship. He may be a budding metaphysicist who turns her on to her own esoteric intuition. He may be a scientist who can help her to think in new ways. He may have a colorless job but a stimulating hobby, something she can share.

The man who is highly sexual, experimental, and experienced is a good partner for her. She will follow him every step of the way and may lead him in some. Together, they can create a magnificent dance of fervor and futurism, a sexual act that is never the same, an enticing, sophisticated, limitless splendor.

The man who is interested in mind expansion or cosmic awareness, who is ever willing to look at and redefine some worn-out, flat definitions, will excite her. The man with whom she can share it all, the one who finally captures her elusive trust, is the one for her.

Aquarius sexuality

The Aquarius Woman, due to her innate sense of curiosity and her experimental attitudes, has a propensity to explore all avenues of sexual enjoyment, fulfillment, and enlightenment. She will probably be most happy when her sexual life is a combination of the traditional and futuristic. Employing the missionary position during a videotape playback of *2001* in her bedroom suits her fine.

She believes that the brain is the most potent sexual organ in the body. She will use hers imaginatively, if not calculatingly, to extract hidden urges and fantasies in her lover. Thus, she is sometimes more a spectator or prompter in sexual liaisons than a participant on the same level. She hungers for approval in everything, and sex is no exception. If she can bring about a complete, exhausting and frenzied orgasm in her man, she feels she has accomplished what she was supposed to.

Her controlled attitudes toward life overlap with her passionate need for experimentation. One can imagine seeing her, fully unclothed, walking through piles of bodies at an orgy, and taking notes or giving helpful hints to participants. She is willing to be a part of sexual experiences that are societally "abnormal" but insists that she only perform to the limits *she* has established for herself. Of course, those limits expand considerably if she thinks her performance can be kept a secret.

Sometimes, in the middle of sharing the most intimate sexual contact, her mind will catch on something else, and alas, the magic of melding bodies fails again. Her aloofness and fear of vulnerability seem to force her mind to think other thoughts when sex becomes too close to union with *one* other person. The man who thinks he can trap her into divulging some of her well-guarded inner secrets by passionate touch, feel, kiss, bite, and nibble or deep, purposeful thrusting is fooling only himself. She seldom falls victim to this ploy; in fact, one imagines that she is more often the perpetrator of this game than the victim.

The fact that she trusts her mind far more than she does her body is frequently evidenced by the lack of care she gives her appearance. She can be downright unappealing at times, but the glimmer of the future in her eyes and the subtle modesty she projects often cause men to overlook the less-than-perfect condition of the package to find out what surprises it holds for them.

She often promises more than she delivers. The Aquarius Woman has a deep need to fall for a man totally, to be giddily in love and full of sexual abandon. In theory, as is true of many aspects of her life, she is a true lover. In practice, however, she is determined to keep passion just below the overwhelming point on the scale.

The Aquarius Woman likes her man (or men) to be available for her, but they cannot possibly demand equal time. She is perhaps one of the most frustrating of the Zodiacal signs—a true devotee of emotional armoring. She embraces the idea of union between men and women but is undemonstrative and demands her privacy when her imaginative and emotional fuel is in need of replenishing.

When the Aquarius Woman finds that the marriage she is involved in isn't what she thought it would be, she often turns to other men. In fact, all through her married life she finds other men sexually attractive if they are intellectually attractive as well. The fact that she can be dogmatically moralistic and old-fashioned causes much inner turmoil when her sexual mind wanders.

What is often labeled the "double standard" is not found in the Aquarius Woman. It may seem so indeed but is more than probably the result of her being ruled by two planets. She has many conflicts in her attitudes and impressions, and sex does not escape this confusion either.

Early sex experiences

The Aquarius girl is often more attracted to the power and intellect of her father than to the nurturing, maternal aspects of her mother. She can, and often does, develop a crush on her father that carries over well into her teenage years. She respects his wisdom and worldly knowledge and feels that she too must learn to acquire these traits.

The idealizing of the father (or older male members of the extended family) tends to create in her a deprecating attitude toward females in general. It becomes nearly impossible for her to have close, meaningful relationships with other girls, and in her search for a young man to live up to her father's image, she goes through half the male population of her high school.

She is an excellent student early in life (which later carries over into being an excellent teacher). The often traditional values and taboos inflicted during childhood are learned well by the Aquarius girl. Again the conflict: she may think that homosexuality, incest, sex-infested motorcycle gangs, and love-ins are wrong because that's what her mother and father taught her; but she will embrace all forms of alternatives in her search for knowledge and for the liberation of all people. The leader of the local gang will have terrific appeal for her, if for no other reason than that she can find out what makes him tick and may be able to pick up some valuable information that will enhance her own life. If necessary, she will even have sex with males her family deeply disapproves of; she doesn't feel she becomes "one of them"—she's just conducting a valid experiment in alternative lifestyles.

Boredom with staid scholastic lessons is often accompanied by daydreaming about sex. The thought of sex is often a turn-on for the young Aquarian, and she finds fantasizing a valid escape from the tedium of intellectual endeavors she has already mastered.

Her emotional detachment is often ingrained during childhood. The distance she establishes from her mother and the idolizing attitude she has toward her father can cause her to become fairly unemotional toward both of them. She is sometimes jealous of her mother for the attention she gets from her father and can become peeved at her father for "giving in" to her mother. As is the case in almost any conflict, she will withdraw, at least emotionally, to study the broader picture.

Love and sex

Herein lies the problem. The Aquarius Woman has a deeply rooted need for love, for closeness, for what we call intimacy. However, she has developed so many roadblocks that it often eludes her. She is so intellectually astute and independent that she even intellectualizes love. She feels that inhibiting the mind is close to the greatest sin imaginable. Thus, she feels that inhibiting the mind sexually is also wrong. Coupled with her early lessons in monogamy, true love, and happiness (with 2.3 kids), this attitude yields a gigantic conflict. She needs to learn how to ask for and receive affection.

She needs to develop *close* relationships with one person at a time. She frequently has few one-on-one experiences, probably due to her fear of becoming vulnerable or attached (read "intellectually inhibited"). She also fears rejection by those she becomes close to. She sees vulnerability and romantic inclinations as potential cages that she can't escape from. She needs to recognize that her mind, with the power it has for her, can get her out of any real cage she may find herself in. Romance, closeness, and intimacy are natural and necessary emotions, even for animals.

Her often opinionated attitudes become even more rigid the longer she denies herself true closeness. It's as if she is afraid she won't learn anything from intense one-on-one relationships, that the back door of escape will be forever bolted. She loves her mate and her family, but she will nearly abandon them in search of a new bit of knowledge, and new experience, an opportunity to help those less fortunate than herself. Little does she realize that often her family and her mate become the very "less fortunate" she seeks to help. She has the power and the scope to embrace *both* her family and the masses; she must learn to balance the attention and love she gives to both.

Sexual intimacy

It's hard to imagine an Aquarius Woman lying back in a heavily scented love nest and allowing a man to fully possess her and her vast reservoir of passion. She wouldn't go for the trappings since they imply "caging"; she wouldn't go for the surrender either since she equates it with losing power.

Aquarius, you need to learn that you don't give up any space when you give someone true intimacy; you expand both yours and his. The masses you embrace don't often reject you; what makes you think one person is more apt to? You're willing to ask the state legislature for help, the school board for more understanding about sex education, the women's board for more money for Biafra—why are you afraid to ask the man who loves you for something (like affection, like protection, like love)?

Liberation is a key word for the Aquarius Woman. The liberation of conservative minds is a goal she never loses sight of. The liberation of women from the traditional roles they have been thrust into is of prime importance. When Aquarius learns that she, too, needs some liberation, she will become an even more powerful force for the liberation of others. Self-imposed emotional exile is indeed a tough prison to escape from, but when she realizes that there is a whole new frontier of intimacy and closeness awaiting her, she will find a way to unlock the door.

What kind of lover she needs

A man who will share equally all her intellectual adventures and her zeal for embracing the New Age is a man she will align herself with forever. Again, the mind is the most important organ in the human body for her, and if he has a good one, one as active as hers, he will be immediately attractive to her.

The Aquarius Woman has a tendency to share all aspects of her life equally with her family. She will stand by her man through thick and thin, and she will no doubt provide the sustenance for him to pull himself up by the boot-straps when the going gets a little murky. She expects equality in return, and the wise man who falls in love with this futuristic, idealistic woman will give it. She makes an excellent housewife in the traditional sense if that's what she needs to complete her intellectual circle. On the other hand, the entire wardrobe of the family may be firmly ensconced in the laundry room hamper for days on end if she feels her energies would be more wisely spent elsewhere. She is a bundle of contradictions, of vacillating priorities—with one exception. Her mind and the development of mental powers in others is always primary.

Her unpredictability is also part and parcel of her sexuality. She can be torrid at times, a sexual leader, but when she needs her privacy and hasn't the mental space of sex, she will become, at best, dutiful in bed. Her man needs to be able to see these times coming and respect them. She won't ask for much in terms of affection, love, intimacy, so he should be willing to court her aloofness by asking her to ask for warmth. He's surely taking a risk by forcing her into anything, but if she responds, she will learn the lesson quickly and well.

If he can be futuristic in his sexual attitudes, she will be futuristic in her responses. He shouldn't be afraid of experimenting with her, for her whole life is based on experimentation, on testing the waters that flow just out of her physical reach. She will provide him with tips on what routes to take, and when the sexual trip is well on its way, she will take over the wheel and drive them both to a sexual destination that is unbelievably full of satisfaction and further craving. If he can convince her to hand over the keys to her little box of stored-up sexual secrets, he will have accomplished the near-impossible. She is capable of surrender, and he will no doubt profit from his labors if he can maintain the pace.

What she needs to learn

Most simply, Aquarius needs to learn how to trust. She also needs to learn about life on a more practical plane. Theoretical principles and ideas are the tools for a better future, but concrete acts of closeness, sharing, and intimacy are the things people are made of.

She needs to cultivate the ability first to feel, then to feel as others do. She is likely to develop her own brand of feeling and declare it adequate, if not superior. She shares other things with people, like information and learning; so she can also learn to draw upon some acceptable and established theories about feeling.

Her competitive skills are honed to a razor sharpness. She can be unconsciously hurtful if that's part of getting results. Often when she competes with men, she employs castration-type tactics to gain a sense of dominance. The Aquarius Woman is good enough at winning that she needn't resort to unfair fighting techniques with men.

Aquarius is a woman; whether she chooses to embrace that truth is her decision. She rejects much of what makes her the charming, forceful, and powerful person she is—her femininity. She has perhaps lost touch with much of her femaleness in search of her maleness. A balance must be found, or one will become too powerful. She fears rejection, yet by adopting a strongly "male" attitude while being in the body of a female, she opens herself up for it. Men naturally reach out to her, for she has a magnetism and a promise in her eyes that is equaled by few other signs. When she turns from men and judges them as sexists or opportunists, she confuses them. The promise she offers must be fulfilled; when she realizes this, she'll probably make more promises, since the fulfillment is so necessary for her.

She needs to let go once in awhile, if for no other reason than to find out what it feels like. She'll probably like the feeling well enough to try it again, but it does take practice. Being controlled can guarantee professional achievement but often causes personal fulfillment to wane. Aquarius, when you feel the urge to chuck it all and fall passionately in love with the man whose mind is so attractive, do it! You are generally strong enough to recover should you make a mistake. Mistakes are measures of success, . . . and you cannot always rely on feedback from your masses to prove your effectiveness. Prove it to yourself by taking risks, by opening up and letting go. The depth of your passion and the free-flowing warmth you'll feel from your toes to the outer reaches of your great mind will probably make you swoon.

Aquarius anger

Recognizing our capacity for anger, hostility, hate, and resentment is harder than recognizing happiness, generosity, and fear in ourselves. The latter feelings are condoned. It's okay to be pleasant, nice people, just as our parents always said. But we don't want to be rude and nasty, and so we routinely suppress our anger.

We are all naturally aggressive and capable of hate. Some experts even believe that hate is part of love. We all seek partners who have traits we wish we had ourselves, and from time to time, inevitably, resentment wells up. "Why can't a woman be more like a man?" asked Henry Higgins. A wise man once told me that many people divorce for precisely the same reasons they got married; at the end, partners hate each other and are angered by the same characteristics that had earlier been responsible for mutual love.

Aggression is necessary to reach goals, to remind us to keep on our toes and be on the alert. Aggression in the old days was a matter of life or death. Without it survival was not possible. Anger often results when we feel someone interfering with our natural aggression. Women who feel they cannot yell, who feel they've been kept on the farm or in the kitchen too long, are experiencing a natural hostility reaction to outside manipulation. The brain sends constant messages through the body, and the message of aggression is to prepare us for greater effort.

If we contain our anger though our body is on alert, disabling consequences are unavoidable. Ulcers, migraine headaches, backaches, and menstrual pain plague millions of Americans. I believe that in many cases they are suffering from repressed anger.

On anger

I interviewed several Aquarius women on anger, and here are their responses:

1 "When my husband starts pushing me about how I feel and I know I feel hostile, I tend to sidestep him. I guess what I do is I start talking about other people. I talk about Johnny's piano teacher, the neighbors' divorce, the scandal on the school board, or the latest gossip at work. Rarely, I may explode. More often, what I do is I get bitchy. Did he know, for example, that the piano teacher is probably a frustrated dyke? Did he want to hear about the principal's balding pate and his practically public affair with his secretary? Why, she's as skinny as a rail and probably never learned her back from her front. And, as far as the neighbors went, why couldn't they have picked better places for their fights? From the kitchen window, the scenes are clearly visible; and she sure is a dud if she thought she could win him back with that face of hers that looks like mashed potatoes."
2 "I defuse my anger with jokes. I have a stockpile of foreign

jokes, domestic jokes, sex jokes. I probably use the dirtiest ones when I am angriest, for their shock value. It gives me the feeling I am getting back at my husband without actually expressing my anger at him."

3 "I am a dancer. Anger is no problem. I just take my ballet shoes from the hook in the hall and stomp out. It's marvelous way to train my body and my mind."

4 "I don't know. I've tried everything, all the therapies—Freudian, Reichian, Jungian, primal scream, the one where they had me beating beds with a tennis racket—and none of them did me much good. The more anger I expressed, the more welled up in me. I even tried rolfing, but that was too painful. I spent time in California; that didn't help. My life hasn't improved. I still feel angry, angry at everyone, but especially at men. And yet, when I try to show anger with my boyfriend, all that comes out is a sort of pacifying voice, an apologetic try at releasing hostility. Besides, I don't think it's fair of me to be angry with him. It's not his fault I've been enraged since I was born."

The first woman seems to have selected a method whereby she parcels out her anger—leaks it, so to speak. She allows her anger to come out through bitchiness *at a third party*. She is unwilling to create an atmosphere in which she feels safe enough to be honest. Her put-downs of other people siphon off some of the venom of her anger.

When I questioned her about her rare-explosions, she said that the few times she had erupted, her husband became terrified. He seemed otherwise unaware of the anger his wife felt and habitually unburdened through her bitchy, satirical anecdotes. She admitted that her explosions caused such discomfort in her husband that over the years she had virtually stopped them.

She came to the next session with a glimmer in her eye. She told me she had discovered that their sex life improved vastly about two days *after* an explosion on her part and stayed unusually enjoyable for weeks. She said she would try to discuss this with her husband, taking a constructive approach. Also, she would investigate some form of art (which was her main interest) that could help her express some of the anger that now took the form of childish bitchiness. I suggested she could write jokes, short stories, or a weekly report on City Hall for the local paper. I also recommended a vacation for the couple in a romantic spot, with a tape recorder for their forthcoming discussions. She was basically healthy; she just needed some reorientation.

The second speaker is very self-aware. There was little I could say to her that she didn't already know. She was highly analytical and quite deliberate in her use of anger. What I wanted to know was how she *felt* inside. Was she really able to vent her anger, or did her jokes simply shift her anger around? She told me she had no intention of changing her style; whatever anger she felt, she could handle it. Clearly she wasn't ready to pursue the subject at the time.

The third lady, the dancer, is a self-disciplined, beautiful artist. She had conquered a variety of childhood diseases, a disapproving mother and father. She had survived two divorces, and now she was in love with life. I believed her when she told me she used dance to express anything from love to hate, beauty to anger. As a little girl, when she had been very ill, she had visualized growing up to be a healthy adult and a famous dancer. Everyone thought she would not recover her mobility and strength, but through mind power and strenuous exercise, she was dancing beautifully within a year.

Self-control can be a virtue; in her case, I believe it was. There is a very thin line separating the attempt to escape anger through frantic activity from behavior that is legitimately integrative. In the latter, people use anger as a catalyst to produce something that makes them feel joyous and worthy.

People's motivation is very difficult to understand and often irrelevant. What, after all, does it matter if Albert Schweitzer went to Africa to gain fame, to get back at his enemies, or to express his genuine love for people? His motivation was mixed, but the results were crystal clear. In dealing with anger, I don't ask why a person has been angry all along.

The fourth lady went through the 1960s trying all kinds of lifestyles, drugs, and healing methods. She can be a raging feminist on the one hand, and a placating, submissive partner on the other. This woman is a highly competent, assertive career woman who in her private life cannot bring herself to show overt anger. She seems to use some of her anger constructively by applying it to her work. She told me she sometimes felt she could conquer the world or build it in two days, and these were the days when she felt either full of love for people or full of anger.

At home she combines guilt about her anger with placating behavior. She excuses her boyfriend for actions that normally would make her angry. She is afraid of losing him. She is afraid that her professional strength is a threat to him. She thinks she has to protect his ego and so represses her anger.

I pointed out that she was ultimately protecting herself. It was she who chose not to deal with her anger in her most intimate relationship, out of fear of losing it, out of old conditioning that "a nice woman doesn't blame her man and doesn't get angry." Deep inside, she was protecting Harry even from his own feelings while she denied her own.

The Aquarius Woman's basic detachment serves her well in the area of anger. She can instinctively channel her aggression into useful causes. But she also harbors grudes and experiences downward spirals in her relationships. Anger cannot be ignored; she must face it.

Susan did a slow burn over her husband's leaving the toothpaste cap off each morning. She found bristles in the sink, and she hated the messy bathroom he left in his wake each morning. Her anger mounted. She thought, "If he really cared, he would be more mindful. The least he could do is to close the toothpaste and roll it from the bottom as I do."

Susan has been taught that she cannot love and be angry at the same time. But as the evidence of her man's lack of consideration mounts, so does her anger. And the downward marital spiral begins. Susan begins to get headaches more often. Sex becomes more mechanical, less fun. They both drink more, smile more artifically. They resort to new little rituals to shore up an ailing relationship. She buys peek-a-boo nightgowns she secretly dislikes; he suggests a marital enrichment weekend he's afraid of. They patch up with flowers, candy, dinner out. He never forgets to kiss her good-bye, and she doesn't forget to make his favorite meal. But the atmosphere grows chillier, and an absentmindedness sets in. After awhile, the little rituals fail to help.

Susan's man feels her anger instead of her acceptance. He feels her sexual cool instead of a ready glow. He notices she no longer cooks his favorite meal. She says he has gained too much weight. He feels rejected. She says he never takes her out anymore. He points out that she spends too much money on clothes. She feels rejected.

They go to a party, drink too much, and on the way home have a fight. An explosion begins, seems to subside, then erupts again. They don't trust each other. She no longer calls him to tell him where she'll be after work. He no longer comes straight home from his job. Anger on both sides chips away at the very foundation of their once lovely relationship. Sometimes the sex is better than it ever was—frenzied, wild, though never close. But more and more, sex feels cold, begins to wither and die.

Many couples at this point have extramarital affairs, or they may go into couple therapy or individual counseling. Some decide to separate or divorce. Some take the angry bull by the horn and begin to discuss their feelings honestly. Three things are necessary to do this: awareness; the will to be honest and to share anger without a win/lose attitude; and communication skills. The couple must decide, too, whether they wish the relationship to continue and in what form.

Susan and others like her will find it helpful to say, "I'm mad!" and then do something about it. Sometimes all she can do is go out for a walk or slam a tennis ball around. These things help, but they'll never repair her relationship. Susan may have to start with "I've had it. I'm angry, and I'm ready to do something about it. Let's see what's necessary."

Anger, constructively used, creates a confrontation between partners that can lead to a greater understanding, to the liberation of all feeling. Susan didn't just suppress her anger; she suppressed hope, love, and self-esteem as well.

In my classes on the constructive uses of anger, the students compiled a list of the basic ways in which they found anger useful and also harmful. Here are the lists:

Where anger has been most useful to me

1 As a signal to "work on myself."
2 As a signal about which specific area of my life I need to work on.
3 As a clue to what is important but needs changing.
4 Anger helps me to focus emotions.
5 Anger gives me the energy for survival.
6 Anger is a catalyst, a mobilizer.
7 Anger is a source of assertiveness.
8 Anger pushes me to destroy ineffective gender roles.
9 Anger gives me authority, the power to express myself so that I'm really heard.

How suppressing my anger has been hurtful

1 When I didn't use it or express it, I grew depressed.
2 It makes me vulnerable to manipulation by others.
3 It makes me detach and distance myself (this can also be positive).
4 It makes me feel alienated.
5 It gives me instant paralysis.
6 I used it as a weapon.

The problems most often linked with anger

1 Family relations.
2 Job change.
3 Changing gender role behavior; old scripts.
4 Home purchase.
5 Changing other people's behavior.

Regarding the last item, if a woman cannot change a situation, she can change her goal of wanting to change it; she can choose to leave it behind. It is a mistake for a woman to start a relationship with a man she wants to change. The frustrations that arise from wishing to change other people often turn into anger.

Final words: Aquarius, give up your goal of trying to change others. Assume responsibility for your feelings of love and anger. Put your energy into maintaining the quality of all your relationships.

Aquarius lifestyles

The Age of Aquarius is literally at hand, and who should be better at plotting and experimenting with New Age lifestyles than the Aquarius Woman? Her innate sense of liberty of the mind for all makes her a prime candidate for forming and perpetuating new lifestyles. Communes, open marriage, polygamy, and homosexuality/bisexuality are all lifestyles that seem to be emerging in the last part of this century. Aquarius can combine them and come up with something that embraces the good in each.

There are lifestyles to come that most haven't even given a thought to. Aquarius has. Her broad-mindedness and futuristic thought patterns promote good brainstorming in this area. Her need for acceptance and her civilized nature sometimes inhibit her from promoting much of what she thinks would help people and enhance their lifestyles. She is so group-conscious, however, that any alternative to the exclusivity of marriage and nuclear families appeals to her.

While she's chairing a fund-raiser for Southeast Asian refugees, she's probably thinking of a way to include them in her community. When she's ladling gravy for the evening meal, she is possibly thinking about how different it would be if she were serving her meal to a large group of people she has embraced as her family. Such are the powers of her mind. If she really feels intent on a problem or on the plight of some less fortunate group of people, it becomes an issue in her entire life, from cooking meals to having sex to buttonholing people at the shopping center. She has the self-confidence and drive to effect great changes in our lifestyles, and the originator of a new or emerging style of living is often an Aquarian.

The Aquarius Woman is especially keen on the plight of other women who have become bogged down in the traditional roles they have been assigned. She feels that liberating them from the humdrum of their lives is her task, and she will go to great ends to accomplish it. She feels that the right to choose a lifestyle has been taken from oppressed women and that she can spur them on to break away and create alternatives *within* the structures they have built. Aquarius is not much of a revolutionary in terms of destroying or annihilating what's presently here and replacing it with something new. She often believes in rearranging what you have to achieve more equality and embrace more of life.

Though she works hard to help others, her own life is sometimes in need of "rehabbing." She is inherently nonpossessive, but when her refined taste for quality and "good things" becomes prominent, she can get hung up on ownership. If it's hers, it's hers; she can even become rather greedy. Perhaps this is because she often spends so little time with her own personal life that when she does, it is rather like an obsession with privacy.

Alternative lifestyles

Communal living: Aquarius is an excellent communal inhabitant. Her need to show everyone the path to mental liberation, her abilities to convince people that there is an alternative to unhappiness, and her extreme diplomacy all lend themselves well to communal living. Her fear of the "cage" of marriage cannot exist if the marriage situation is shared by many people. She is an excellent leader and teacher; she'll be the one with the *Whole Earth Catalogue* in one hand and the materials to build a hothouse in the other. Of course, she expects the other occupants of the space to pitch in too.

Her idealistic nature tends to enhance the good life that communal living can bring about. On the other hand, her sometimes opinionated attitude can cause dissension. She will generally choose people who are pupil-like to share her commune; other leaders tend to challenge her and expose her vulnerabilities in the area of leadership.

She feels that having multiple "mothers and fathers" can only enhance the knowledge and learning of the children of the commune. She will want to share equally in the child-rearing activities and will be quick to point out those who are neglecting their share.

Problems she will encounter in a communal setting: her air of self-confidence, unless shared openly and intimately with the others, can cause self-doubt to emerge in others. She is tense, driven, and aloof, and this flies in the face of a more relaxed, informal, laid-back communal setting. Hard work is a necessary ingredient for the success of communes, but forced labor resembles the lifestyle so many people have fled, and it can cause disillusionment.

Single woman: The Aquarius Woman may experience this lifestyle early in her adulthood but generally marries and "settles down." This doesn't preclude divorce and a return to the single lifestyle; if things don't work out or if what she thought she was getting isn't there, she will change it quickly. She tends to have many sexual encounters before marriage. She functions quite well alone, and the complications that exist in marriage, along with the inhibitions, can cause her to remain so for long periods of time.

The problems she faces with loneliness can often propel her to marriage for the wrong reasons. Having someone to sleep with at night and children to look after seldom assauges her loneliness; she finds that her need for privacy is greater than her need for companionship.

Intimate networks: This movement fits Aquarius quite nicely as long as the friendships don't require too much intimacy. Again, in the truest form, this arrangement doesn't exist for her since she has great difficulty in establishing one-on-one relationships. When she evolves to the point of extending and asking for intimacy, she will make an excellent friend who, by the way, can avoid the sexual complications that are sometimes present.

Open marriage: Aquarius's lack of possessiveness, her need for space of her own, and her intolerance for jealousy all make her available for this option. Her shyness and her civilized upbringing can cause some problems, but I sense that if the world at large is none the wiser, she will indulge openly, freely, and successfully in open marriage.

Ménage à trois: Now, this arrangement requires some intimacy on two levels with two different persons. If she can find a three-way setup that doesn't require too much closeness, warmth, or intimacy she will try it. Although she is much more a mental sexual liberationist, she will involve herself physically when societal approval is not required. She will probably suggest this lifestyle to a friend who is complaining of boredom in her sexual relationship with her husband, and if Aquarius is a sex therapist, ménage à trois will rank high on her list of things to do.

Group marriage: As is the case with communes, she will fit in nicely, especially if she can overcome some of the sexual inhibitions she has. This arrangement requires her to function with more than one man at a time, both sexually and in a marriage situation, and this she is good at. It may be a good opportunity for her to learn intimacy and to ask for the things she needs. Her ability to accept the other women in her husband's life (mother, sister, ex-lovers, and ex-wives), also lends itself well to this lifestyle.

Gay/bisexual lifestyle: Her freedom-seeking nature, her avant-garde attitude, and her inquisitive mind can propel her into either of these lifestyles. She can accept the challenge of the homosexual lifestyle and the entanglements it can bring about. She is an excellent role model and spokesperson for gay rights since her courteous, friendly, and civilized traits make her highly acceptable. She will no doubt have the same intimacy problems with another woman that she has with men. She will also attempt to be the aggressive partner in a woman/woman relationship, which doesn't do much to teach her to ask for the affection she denies herself.

Bisexuality intrigues her since it is futuristic, New Age. She is quick to recognize the maleness and femaleness in everyone, and this affords her an opportunity to exercise the sexual duality that she knows exists. Much of her life will be spent with people involved in alternative lifestyles such as homosexuality and bisexuality. She considers this a valid way to live and defends the right of people to live it whenever she has the opportunity.

Androgyny: As the Aquarian Woman moves closer to the New Age, she becomes an androgynous prototype for her sisters. She is one of the first to achieve the balance of the male and female energies. Having recognized that both exist and that putting them in proper relationship satisfies her needs, she embraces the new attitude with great relish. (See "Cosmic Woman" for a more complete discussion.)

Summing up Aquarius

When Aquarius becomes aware of *all* her needs and learns that some of them will only be satisfied when she lets someone do it for her, she will have truly begun to emerge. Her futuristic concepts, her inventive and imaginative mind, her concern for all people, and her self-confidence make her a natural leader. She has the power to, and often does, make people very happy, allowing them the space to grow and learn. A little more attention to the home fires and to what makes her tick will energize her to help further. She has a unique opportunity to see the future age to come, to prepare both herself and her intimates for it, and to have a hand in how we all perceive it.

When she finds a man who will respect her, provide her with what she knows she needs (and what she fails to acknowledge she needs, too) she will blossom. Equality, honesty, inquisitiveness, and friendliness are some of her finest and most admirable traits. None of these will be diminished by warmth; in fact, warmth and closeness will only make her New Age star shine even more brightly.

PISCES

CHECKLIST OF PISCES TRAITS

Note: This checklist describes the traits of one *phase* only; if it doesn't seem to fit you, check other lists to find the phase you are in right now.

1. Mysterious
2. Beautiful
3. Romantic
4. Subtle
5. Elusive
6. Passive
7. Mutable
8. Adaptive
9. In Love with Love
10. Devoted
11. Gullible
12. Compartmentalized
13. Easily Hurt
14. Sentimental
15. Indirect
16. Dependent
17. Intuitive
18. Psychic
19. High Spiritual Strength
20. Dominated by Subconscious
21. Receptive
22. Depressive
23. Isolationist
24. Introverted
25. Unfocused
26. Escapist
27. Artistic
28. Brooding, Low Energy
29. Guilt-prone
30. Self-sacrificing
31. Low Self-esteem, Self-denigration
32. Procrastination
33. Compassionate, Humanistic
34. Nurturing
35. Messianic

Pisces personality

My first vision of the earth was water veiled. I am of the race of men and women who see things through this curtain of the sea.
Anaïs Nin
House of Incest

General traits and background

Like Dorothy in *The Wizard of Oz*, the Pisces Woman is full of magic and mischief. Her world is rich in emotional tornadoes; at her heel is a ubiquitous friend or suitor who remains blissfully unaware of her strength, resilence, and self-containment; ahead lies a path strewn with nearly insurmountable obstacles and unfathomable experiences; all around is a hostile world that nevertheless provides her periodic shelter and offers unexpected aid in rare forms. At the end of the journey is a never-never land visible only to those wearing the special emerald-green glasses with which every Pisces Woman is naturally endowed.

Pisces is the twelfth sign of the Zodiac, Mutable Water. It is ruled by Neptune and is one of three water signs in the Zodiac. As the last of the twelve signs, it is a composite of characteristics culled from the other eleven. Receptive, ultra-feminine, and intuitive, Pisces has magnetic beauty and great psychic and spiritual powers that are often shrouded by her own chameleonlike defenses.

The Pisces-*type* woman is one who has her sun or other important planets in Pisces, planets in the twelfth house, a Pisces ascendant, or strong aspects to Neptune. Pisces types may also include women who are now going through a Pisces *phase*. The checklist at this chapter's beginning describes the Pisces type. The Pisces phase has the following characteristics:

1 Confused, changeable emotions.
2 A tendency to withdraw into self-absorption, romantic dreams, or alcohol and drugs.
3 Repeated choice of disappointing or hurtful lovers.
4 An overpowering sense of obligation or self-sacrifice.
5 A new kind of spiritual understanding or awakening of faith.
6 A recognition of the joy of selfless service.

Two key words for Pisces are *suffering* and *service*. Neptune and the twelfth house rule the unconscious, and the Pisces Woman will always be at odds with herself until she confronts and accepts the tasks set for her in life. She will by turns flagellate herself with guilt and wallow in self-indulgence until she learns what giving really means. Her tendency is to rely on others for the answers, and they will always let her down.

The astrological glyph which represents Pisces shows two fish swimming in opposite directions. The unique task of the Pisces Woman is to choose the positive route and stick to it. Ideally, her destiny is to bring the vision of magical possibilities to others. Since a frequent Piscean tendency is to float and take the easy way down and out, Pisces women need support and education to use their tremendously fertile imagination and sensitivity productively. *They need to learn how to grow up without becoming dependent.*

Mysterious, beautiful, romantic

Pisces is beautiful, with limpid, soulful eyes filled with dancing lights. One can look into her eyes for a lifetime and never know the mysteries of their depths. Her magic is riveting, and one can't help but be attracted to it.

Her world is at variance with ours. She sees more and suffers more. She is the divine malcontent of the Zodiac. Her dreams are different, out of step with the cool rationality promoted by our culture.

It is not possible to gauge what is really going on inside the head of the Pisces Woman. She has a mask for each role and occasion, and she prefers it so. She tunes in to vibrations faster than a gypsy but shrouds her insights. She is as wise—and as inscrutable—as the Delphic oracle. The Pisces Woman has more unfulfilled dreams than Joan of Arc had visions. More dreams go wrong in her head than in reality, for many never see daylight.

Subtle, elusive, passive

In relationships, in love, in work, the Pisces Woman is elastic, fascinating, and full of surprise. She is tougher than she seems. She is different with different people. If anyone gets too close, she may just slip away.

She follows better than she leads. She investigates fashionable cults and religions, hoping to find in them the ideology or partner that suits her needs. She has more sides than Shakespeare could have pinpointed—gullible and savvy, naive and sophisticated, dependent yet strongly detached.

Mutable, adaptive, compartmentalized
Pisces is a New Age woman in the age of relativity. She stands as a symbol of Albert Einstein's view that we mistake verbal form for essence in our dealings with reality. She is a kaleidoscope in motion, never a still photograph.

Elizabeth Taylor has a Pisces sun. In terms of New Age Astrology, she varies between the Scorpio and Aries types, often in a Libra or Pisces phase. She typifies the Pisces Woman's extraordinary beauty, the Piscean tendency to choose unsuitable partners, and the Piscean ability to juggle the strands of her life and her changing identity. Her ability to create illusion (acting), her crisis-prone character, and her guts and gift to survive all are indicative of the Piscean character.

In love with love, devoted, gullible, easily hurt
Pisces needs to be needed. She is in love with love in her own special way. Given to sudden enthusiasms, she is not a passionate drummer but a delicate harpist capable of devotion from afar.

She loves in every way: spiritually, religiously, platonically, sexually. Ideally, she is happiest when she can pour out all her feelings. In fact, she is a demanding perfectionist and remains compartmentalized in her attachments.

I know a Pisces lady who had one father-figure lover, a second lover who explored her own deep, sensual seas, and a third with whom she had a tense, fraught, emotional relationship. She juggled these three for over a year, pitting one against the other in her mind. None was her ideal, but for awhile she was able to satisfy her different needs separately. Finally, in one dramatic act, she withdrew altogether, with a deep sense of having been betrayed by each lover.

The Pisces Woman seems bent on picking partners and mates who disappoint her—not surprising, because she is a dreamy idealist in love. She often projects the image of perfect soulmate onto her lover, then experiences intense anger and frustration when he falls short.

Sentimental, indirect, dependent
Pisces is a dreamer whose sensitive nature makes her unfit for direct action or speech. She has to learn to do both after she grows up. She also needs to learn *to ask for what she needs.*

In an intimate relationship, Pisces needs to make every effort to retain a strongly independent self. Otherwise, instead of an equal tie between two adults, she will form a symbiotic relationship reminiscent of the parent-child bond.

Intuitive, psychic, high spiritual strength, dominated by subconscious

The evolved Piscean believes in mysticism and reincarnation. She expects to survive worldly troubles and soar into more inspired dimensions. She is contradictory in that she accepts pain and tragedy as part of life but feels guilty if she sees other people suffer. She has a strong savior complex and consistently fights for the underdog.

She rationalizes her own suffering and neediness as natural life experiences, but she is often depressed. She believes in life after death and cosmic powers but would like to be reassured. She has insight but seldom trusts it. She lives in spaces others may never penetrate and keeps so much a secret that it is no wonder that communication gaps abound in Piscean households.

She does not thrive on challenge and change, yet she is dominated by the changing undercurrents she allows to carry her along. Introverted, powerfully intuitive, and committed to a mythology of suffering and beauty, of love with pain, the Piscean must learn to build bridges to the outer world. But to build those bridges, Pisces must accept and articulate her vast intuition and imagination. Depression is her greatest enemy. As any lay counselor knows, it is anger turned against oneself.

Receptive, depressive, isolationist

In the Pisces Woman, anger and depression are the result of frustration and a sense of impotence, of stifled ambitions and desires, of unborn dreams.

The Pisces woman is overinvolved with her feelings. Burdened by excessive fear, guilt, and anger, she also absorbs these negative emotions from others and has difficulty releasing them. She tries to cope by withdrawing, but this is not the answer. The Pisces Woman needs to get outside herself more, to communicate with others. She needs intimates who believe in her dreams, who act as midwives to her self-expression and catalysts of her creative energy.

She must cultivate a better sense of humor. She needs anchors to hold her to "normal" routines in living but never to weight her so heavily that she stops trying to make her dreams come alive.

Also, she can take more people into her confidence. She can discuss her strong needs and feelings. She can openly acknowledge to her lover and friends how hard it is for her to trust. She will find many who share her feelings. She can define and ask for the kind of relationship she needs in order to develop trust.

Introverted, unfocused, escapist, artistic

Pisces is the astrological sign concerned with hidden feelings, negative emotions, self-hurt, and all places of confinement. Pisces deals with *restriction*. Those who read standard astrological manuals know that Pisces is the sign/type considered especially vulnerable to escapism. Alcohol and drugs are two usual routes.

A Piscean of lower consciousness would rather not be tested and frequently avoids situations in which failure can be measured. She avoids success as well, and spends her life daydreaming, engaged in self-indulgent and self-absorbed activities.

She says little to others because she believes she is protecting herself. She has learned that the cost of being a shy, sensitive person, a poet, an artist, is high. But if not everyone appreciates her, many have the capacity to learn . . . if she will let them.

She can avoid escapism by having supportive friends and daily routines. She can establish a suitable balance of self-care and her commitment to groups, relationships, and causes simply by doing what "feels right." The Pisces Woman can afford to follow her hunches.

For the Pisces Woman who chooses to be upwardly mobile, apathy can be corrected by involvement in an outside cause. She can clarify her situation by setting clear, realistic short- and long-term goals. She must then persist in reaching them. The Pisces Woman may choose self-realization or self-denial. Whether she is on her way up or slipping, she sprays life with a rainbow-colored mist. Judy Garland was a Pisces type. Her life is a good example of the Pisces Woman's complexity and polarization. In it we find extremes of achievement and degradation, self-sacrifice and self-indulgence. She was addicted as much to failed relationships as to drugs. Her problems stemmed from miserably low self-esteem.

As befits the Pisces Woman, Judy Garland suffered from feeling misunderstood. Her admirers were always ready to help and defend her. She was loved by many, but she felt like a stranger in a strange land—elusive, distrustful, eager to love and to be loved, and ever close to pain and sorrow. Yet she was able to transmute her pain into art. She was a professional, a magnificent, charming, charismatic figure who brought Emerald City to millions.

Brooding, low energy

Never very energetic physically, the Pisces Woman must pay close attention to the negative emotions she harbors. She should understand their effect on her body. She should develop a better filtering system and release mechanism. She needs to permit herself more frequent rests from anxiety.

The holistic health movement is popularizing the concept that health means a balanced interrelationship between mind, body, and spirit. This is true for everyone, but because of her acute sensitivities, the Pisces Woman is extremely affected if any of the three is diseased. Personally and professionally, she can benefit by acquainting herself with the holistic movement in the United States. This movement is based on the age-old wisdom that the mind and the body are mutually interdependent and that physical health is an expression of mental health.

As a practical measure, she needs to create environments that promote a sunny, cheerful attitude. Colors, textures, music, flowers—the entire decor should be arranged so as to increase her self-esteem and energy.

Guilt-prone, self-sacrificing

Joie de vivre represents the direction in which the Piscean needs to expend energy. Pisces feels guilty about many things, but most of all about "selfish" pleasure. She often denies herself the very things she knows would make her happy.

The Pisces Woman especially needs to learn to love herself more. She must learn a healthy selfishness. She must *not* always put others' needs ahead of her own. She needs to nurture herself. She has absorbed only too well society's admonitions that to give is always better than to receive. To suggest to her that she be more selfish, more assertive and confident, is akin to heresy. Nevertheless, *she does have a choice*!

The Pisces Woman allows herself to be drained by many professional and personal situations. She needs to protect herself with detachment. She needs some of the qualities of her opposite, Virgo. One's opposite astrological type describes the traits one must develop to become a whole person. These latent tendencies need to emerge from the unconscious, to be seen in the light and allowed to unfold. The Pisces Woman needs Virgo traits of mental detachment, analysis, clear goal-setting, and rational judgment. She needs to engage in tasks that increase her confidence in her ability to perform and deliver.

The optimum attitude is cultivated involvement, or what might also be called detached involvement—a combination of empathy and commitment to doing for others, yet with an awareness of one's own needs. We live in different spaces and should never forget to cultivate our own gardens.

Low self-esteem, self-denigration, procrastination

The Pisces Woman's unhealthiest tendency is to disbelieve herself and to escape into apathy and confusion. Like everyone else, she faces an important question—how to attain self-esteem. Specifically, Pisces must define what she needs to do in order to strengthen the positive aspects of her nature and understand what gives her life meaning.

She should keep in mind that she is a worthy, acceptable human being as she is. Though we all long to be thinner or taller, prettier or sturdier, we forget that no matter how blemished we feel, we are each still unique and lovable. Pisces ought to remind herself constantly, in every way, of her positive assets.

The controlled demeanor of the Pisces Woman is punctuated by passionate crusades and disguises a deep fear of rejection. Sometimes she seems submissive, wispy, or indecisive, while at other times she appears strong and ready for battle. She needs to learn to speak up and say what she thinks and feels. She can learn to acknowledge her supersensitive nature and share her excellent insights. She will earn others' understanding and respect—and gain more self-respect.

The Pisces Woman can learn to love herself more by banding together with kindred spirits. She can build a communication group for the improvement of the human condition. This is a good way for her to be creative, responsible, other-directed. She will also receive positive feedback about her own unique contributions.

The Piscean is a procrastinator. She needs to select people who will propel her to action while treating her sensitively. She must learn how to recognize these types in order to reach her goals.

Compassionate, humanistic, nurturing

The healthiest drive of the Pisces Woman is to nurture. She does this instinctively. She sends you birthday cards long after you've turned forty; she calls if you are sick, even though you did not tell her (she sensed something was wrong and checked).

She nurtures her children overprotectively, supports her husband (whether he is the first, second, or third) wholeheartedly, and never forgets a needy neighbor or friend. The Piscean is nutrition-conscious; she is not physically robust naturally, but she works at it and in addition is concerned with raising healthy children.

Any Pisces mother knows that it is not the Band-Aid she puts on her child's scraped knee that stops the pain of injury. What initiates the healing is the feeling of caring the transmits to the child. She is an excellent homemaker who leaves no small detail of childcare or housekeeping untended. However, she can be swamped by minutiae and by her need to be perfect. She can slip into fantasy and go as far out as the astronaut in *2001*.

Pisces relationships

We all grow up looking for our fantasies to come true, expecting an ideal mate to arrive. We expect to have a primary relationship and share a lifetime of bliss with one partner. We think our relationships will protect us from the complex demands of self and the outside world. Though this is only fantasy, the devoted Pisces Woman comes close to success in cushioning intimates against stress. She protects them and helps them realize their dreams.

She makes a marvelous lover or mate as long as she feels loved and protected, but problems arise from the fact that she does not love herself enough. She may not, at first, attract men who support her. The situation can change, but it takes self-knowledge, self-esteem, time for change to occur.

The Pisces Woman who overcomes her tendency to brood, cling, and put all her eggs in one basket has excellent love potential. She knows how to turn people on to themselves. She is liked and loved widely, for people are attracted by her ability to help them love themselves. She also likes to please. She would walk on water if her partner asked her to, and she seems to float on the wings of romance.

The Pisces Woman needs a lot of love and protection but seldom seems to get it. She continuously creates stress-free environments for others, but she herself is drained, not enriched, by these efforts. *She has not learned how to receive.*

Pisces is a puzzle of independence and capability hidden under intense vulnerability. She is a woman of complex needs, needs magnified by her moodiness and fears of rejection. Contradiction is a cornerstone of her personality, and contradiction characterizes her style in relationships.

She catches friends and lovers by letting them pursue and catch her. She yearns to be captured and possessed, yet her spirit does not allow this. She needs friends who push and yet protect her. Impossible to predict or understand, she is Sarah Bernhardt reincarnated.

Muse, Mother, Whore, and Madonna are female archetypes conceived by men. She is all at different times, and at times she is all simultaneously. She is seductive and knows how to get the man she wants. However, Pisces in her thirties and forties is highly crisis-prone. That's when she realizes that she has fulfilled roles passed on to her by her mother and her culture, that she has played out her man's fantasies but barely knows *her own* needs, fantasies, and preferred roles.

Childhood

The Pisces Woman is frequently raised by a dominant mother who subtly or overtly denied herself pleasure in relationships. Absorbing this, the daughter too feels guilty. She is closely tied to matriarchal values. Being intuitive and receptive, she soaks up "vibes" and subliminal messages.

Among the harshest internal taboos she must deal with and release is her fear of men. It takes time for Pisces to recognize this fear. Releasing confusion and guilt, deciding what type of relationship she wants, and then totally recognizing her needs—these do not come easily to her.

The Pisces Woman is Everyperson, for she constantly goes through different phases, and her needs change accordingly. She grows up believing her mother is pure and perfect. Later in life she has enormous trouble allowing herself freedom of erotic fantasy and impulse, for these conflict with her internalized idealized version of her mother. The Mother appears untouchable, so the daughter finds it difficult to participate in deep sexual intimacy.

Adult love relationships consist, at least at the start, of a replay of the old pattern of dependency-anger-rejection the child enacts with the mother. The symbiotic tie formed with the mother (or mother substitute) thus forms the basis of all other intimate relationships. How one breaks that tie is a gauge of psycho-emotional maturity.

As she approaches adulthood, the Pisces Woman has little or no self-awareness and self-assurance. She is fickle, for she is unsure of herself. What she thinks she wants to do commonly turns out to be what her mother wanted her to do.

Early adulthood

In her early sexual relationships, Pisces is passive and dependent. Her submission to the male is a tactic she thinks she must use in order to catch and hold him. She quickly pours the contents of her erotic-emotional self into her sexual relationship. This paves a sure road to dependence and trouble.

The Pisces Woman tends to marry young and to marry several times. She needs much emotional assurance, but since she seldom asks for it she seldom receives it. Instead of confronting this problem, she buzzes like a bee from one source of honey to the next. She is a good candidate for serial monogamy à la Liz Taylor. She makes an ideal mate as long as a man protects her appreciatively—and as long as she thinks he is her best source of honey.

The young Pisces Woman resembles the sleeping Snow White. It is the tumult of new desires and the need to change that forces her to open her eyes. The clamor comes from the strength of her ignorance and repression. Pisces starts out in life repressing the needs of the male in her—needs for independence, self-sufficiency, ambition, achievement, recognition. She fails to see that everyone has such needs, including herself. Only gradually does she become aware of the heretofore unacceptable male within her. Eventually, she must also face her hidden fears of or hostilities to men in general.

Pisces does not wish to compete with her man. What she wants is male approval and protection. In a sexual relationship, she becomes exclusive and reclusive through her attachment to her partner. She adores her man in a potential climate of jealousy.

Eventual breakup may result in anger, if her mates seek other sources of affection. A child breaking away from the all-powerful mother, the single source of affection, has just as hard a time as the mate of the Pisces Woman, should his eye wander.

The Pisces Woman dislikes newly aggressive career women who use flashy clothes and status symbols to gain attention. She feels she can accomplish more by blushing than pushing. She wears floating skirts instead of pantsuits, and the only four-letter word is her vocabulary is l-o-v-e.

The first stage in an intense relationship with a Piscean may last two months or two years. Throughout, her man practically has to be a mind reader, long-distance runner, artist, and magician in order to keep up with Piscean unpredictability.

The middle years reaching emotional maturity

Pisces is a water sign, which denotes intuition, receptivity, intense emotions, imagination, and sensitivity.

The Pisces Woman goes through many stages in her important relationships. If the relationship is sexual, the following stages may be felt more intensely. If it is nonsexual, as with her children and friends, the phases may be expressed more subtly. Not every Pisces Woman will experience all these stages, nor will she necessarily experience them in the following order. Also, as she matures and makes new friends or remarries, she may have no need to go through the first three stages again.

1 Total devotion to the object of her affection.
2 Growing dependency linked with fears of being unworthy or abandoned.
3 Possessive attachment to the partner.
4 Self-awareness, bringing the realization that love and intimacy necessitate high self-trust; emerging need to relate to the other's process in new ways.
5 Attempts to change and take action, bringing turmoil and later change.
6 Resolution of some sort: a truce; and ending; a reshaping of the same relationship.

The Pisces Woman searches for relationships that make her feel hopeful and loving. She falls in love with and remains loyal to the people who make her feel joyous and loving.

What she needs to learn

Specifically, the Pisces Woman needs to distinguish between *commitment* and *attachment*, which produce different feeling states.

The mate or friend involved with the newly emerging Pisces Woman needs to support her search and her growth. He or she must accept the Piscean need to break some ties. It is essential to trust that her search will yield more self-esteem and that ultimately this will strengthen the relationship. The turmoil that accompanies the emergence of a new self is to be expected. But it is also possible, and desirable, for partners to respond to each other's needs, survive the turmoil, and grow from it.

The Pisces Woman must remember that no matter how rocky her relationships become or how many she views as failures, she has needed these experiences; they are challenges and signposts in her evolution.

The Pisces Woman especially needs to understand the concept of androgyny. Male and female, *yin* and *yang,* are energies that complement each other in living organisms. Their apparent duality is based on a holistic, natural unity. Thus, the two fish that symbolize her sign are intrinsically united though they appear to swim in opposite directions.

Commitment means "I love and accept you as you are and will do what I can to help you love and accept yourself." It means "I will do all I can to support your well-being."

Attachment means "I love you because I need you, and I want you to take care of me in turn. I want you to love me in my way."

The immature Pisces easily becomes attached. Because she mistakes attachment for commitment, she often feels unloved. The mature Pisces Woman can love her intimates unconditionally and feel they love her.

Because Pisces is so adept at nonverbal communication, she seldom discusses psycho-emotional needs. But as she is breaking her ties with the unhealthy parts of her past, she needs to emphasize verbal communication. She can avoid rocky times if she shares herself with friends and lovers and includes them in her growth process.

Her relationships thrive when they include at least two of the three *A*'s: Affirmation, Affection, and Admiration.

Pisces sexuality

During her lifetime, the Pisces Woman undergoes radical changes in her sexuality. A woman with multiple selves and varied needs, she is initially more openly concerned with social and moral issues than with psychosexual development. Sexually, she is a late bloomer. Her judgment in love is clouded. Often, she mistakes fantasy for love. She mistrusts men, has a martyr complex, and is repeatedly deeply hurt.

Like her sign, Pisces' sexuality is double-edged. Inexperienced, she is a delicate flower whose scent attracts those unsuited to her. Experienced, she is a discriminating and confident love artist.

The mature Pisces Woman is a sensitive, sensuous, unusually creative lover in control of her body and able to please her partner as easily as she pleases herself. She can be sexually liberated or old-fashioned and chaste. She plays out her lover's fantasies and mirrors his moods. She believes in the possibility of the total love experience and in sex as an exchange of ecstasy.

For the Pisces Woman, it is especially important to choose a lover or mate who complements and brings out her higher nature; for if she is not careful, she can be humiliated and lowered through her sexual unions. She has strong masochistic tendencies, and she is insecure. She is so closely attuned to a man's moods and needs that she often mistakes them for her own. She gives much of her power away and blames herself for almost anything that goes wrong.

For her, the total love/sex combination is a compelling need. Her internal struggles create a spiral—either up toward peak experiences in sex with love, or down into the depths of sado-masochism, exploitation, drugs, or total self-denial.

The Piscean sexual nature is protean. It never has a predictable, one-dimensional quality. On the contrary, it is forever in flux, ambivalent, rich with potential and forks in the road. The sensual appetite is keen, subtle, alternately self-effacing and lushly demanding.

The Pisces Woman has ethereal, out-of-body transports, ecstatic erotic experiences with the right man at the right time. He's as often her mate as not. The important thing is that she must feel he is a soulmate if she is to open up.

The Pisces Woman is one of the few who enjoy long-distance unconsummated affairs. She also enjoys long-distance sexually active relationships. She puts her lover on a pedestal and likes intrigue, veiled and difficult situations, tortuous, unpredictable paths.

She has a greater tendency than most toward bisexuality. She is attracted to the soft, receptive beauty of females and is often far more comfortable with a "feminine" kind of gentle lovemaking than with hard, male thrusting. Androgynous, poetic men are nearly irresistible to her. She wants to mother them, and she does. She wants to feel their hairless, youthful, lithe, textured beauty, and she does.

Her sex drive ebbs and flows. She can be insatiable for weeks or months, luscious, ripe for the soft and hard touch. She also periodically enters into an apathetic state. She then withdraws from all sexual activity and sublimates her urge in more neutral pursuits. When she is depressed, she loses all sexual desire, and the tumor of self-doubt spreads. Her personality stamps her sexual response; it is cyclical, in some cases marked by a highly compressed manic phase alternating with depressive tendencies.

The key words in understanding Pisces sexuality are *fantasy* and *esotericism*. The Pisces Woman fantasizes what sex is like and dares not separate the gold of her daydreams from the dross of her life. In the best times, her fantasy matches reality. She has esoteric tastes, talents, and potential. It is the best of times or the worst of times, but Pisces sexuality transcends definition. It operates on 110/220 voltage at the same time, a dual tempo, an ineluctable rhythm that outwits time and one's own preconceptions.

Early sex experiences

The Pisces girl who grows up under Mama's watchful and frequently unhappy eyes internalizes more than her share of sexual guilt and fear. Her life is never easy, and accepting sex as pleasure, with or without love, will never be completely comfortable for her.

She tends to be a good girl who may outwardly seem equally close to both her parents. Nevertheless, in my surveys, the picture that emerges is one suggesting a form of brutalization by the father, not always evident, not always physical. Combine this with the latent dominance of her mother, and the frequent outcome is Piscean emotional confusion and fear of men. Sexual guilt (see "Pisces Relationships") is also a strong force.

The Pisces girl works hard to do well, though she is often lazy. Nothing would appeal to her more than to play the role of the tragic princess. Instead, she plays the sacrificial lamb. She suffers for love and duty, and when everyone has gone to the picnic, she has herself a grand cry. Tears are a good source of relief for her, and she resorts to them often.

She is an actress from the cradle, a baby magician whose talents are often so brilliant that she is envied. On the other hand, she may be the scapegoat, the butt of her peers' jokes, the girl teased for being too nice and too good to be true. She really is nice, and she truly has a need to do good and offer her assistance to the poor, lame, lonely, mute, and blind. When the boys ask for her services, she is secretly flattered though fearful. All her life, she has trouble saying no. Her first sexual experience is as likely as not to be the result of her inability to deny a horny teenager's request.

She may suffer from neglect or from the opposite extreme, the reputation of being an easy lay. She cannot seem to find a middle road. Up or down, ecstasy or terror, the mists of illusion mark even her early, gullible years.

She is likely to discover masturbation early. She is a born sensualist. She adores being touched, and not even the most vigorous puritan training convinces her that loving contact should be denied to people after two years of age, and especially at the moment of genital caress.

The values she forms at this time bear the strong stamp of the Judeo-Christian tradition (provided she grows up in our society) and tend to detract from her naturally hedonistic nature. Somewhere early on, she is taught that sex is for procreation, that recreative sex shall breed guilt, that the body she so enjoys should be a source of shame to her. It will take vast amounts of reeducation and pain for her to regain her natural playfulness, body freedom, sensuality.

The young Pisces Woman tends to believe she is doomed to suffer no matter what—and so she does. She is frequently hurt because she expects to be. She picks the wrong men as though to prove the truth of her beliefs. From another point of view, however, it could be said that she picks the right men. They are men who, because they mirror her pluses and minuses, force her to confront herself. She is so intuitive that deep down she knows that she attracts the qualities she offers—and that should she wish to improve on the character of her men, she will first have to upgrade her own.

Early in her sex life, she fills up on information, variety, and diversity. She may become an avid reader of pornography or sex atlases. She moves through a confusion of love affairs with varying degrees of sexual interplay. Her budding sexuality takes her to places she did not know existed outside her imagination. Others may think she is promiscuous, but that is simply the label they project onto Pisces' tortuous, legitimate search for a soulmate.

Love and sex

Pisces has a subtle, electric intensity, like the glow of a low-watt bulb in an antique light fixture. Only connoisseurs detect her underlying, volatile, mysterious sexuality. She is a sexual artist whose love can fashion unsurpassable works. As she gains confidence, she creates *chefs d'oeuvre*, adds to her experiences, follows her intuition. She loves many men on her path to a harmonious life.

Pisces learns quickly. She gives with pleasure and accedes to her lover's demands. The more outrageous he is, the more she likes it. She needs a sexually expert lover who helps release her own inhibitions; the other option is a lover whose passion and love incite her own. She loves best the man who freely expresses his needs and fantasies.

Her demure appearance belies an incessant fantasy life in which she is pleasured by strongly dominant males. While the Aries Woman rejects rape as a turn-on fantasy, Pisces uses the idea of forced seduction for erotic appeal.

Pisces enjoys being possessed, yet she secretly aims to be mistress of the situation. She wants Prince Charming to woo her in the gentlest troubadour tradition, but she also wants a Jack the Ripper who forces her to open up and yield in agonized, ecstatic surrender. She lets a man dominate her but in turn takes possession of him by becoming his indispensable slave and ally, much like wily Scheherezade in *A Thousand and One Nights*.

She likes to cater to her lovers' fantasies, if only on the chance of seeing them lose control. She wins her lover's heart by making him feel special, by having him believe she is on earth expressly for his pleasure. However, she can intuitively assess the amount of power this gives her—and she fully enjoys it. She plays these love games to avoid being hurt. Her sexual education is colored by her fear of not measuring up. She needs a very special type of man who recognizes this, one who sees and loves the scared little girl inside.

Pisces likes sex to be playful, free, bubbly, imaginative, exploratory, rich in moods and variations. A depressive man cannot be a good lover, especially for her. A manic type would not be sensitive and considerate enough. The man who considers certain sexual behavior patterns "deviant," based on his moral scruples, cannot help her get over her own restrictions. When she is honest, Pisces admits that the one sexual act that is taboo to her involves extreme violence. She may find incest or bestiality unacceptable also, but if the truth be known, they intrigue her kinky side.

She enjoys wearing masks to bed, being surrounded by incense, candlelight, and soft pillows. She likes vibrators as added stimulation, and feathers for the teasing touch. She will try anything once, and once aroused, she likes most anything. Water games are a good bet.

The Pisces Woman in love gets carried away. She finally tells her lover how much she adores wearing high heels and a garter belt to bed, or that the whip in the closet intrigues her. Strange accouterments act as strong stimulants, but until she is secure in the relationships, she may not feel free enough to enjoy them (though she'll probably try).

Playing a whore is one of her fantasies. She'd love to go to a costume ball with the man she loves, each dressed as the other's favorite wet dream. Public sex may take some getting used to, but if her lover gently introduces her to California-style, hot-tub, under-the-stars ecstasy, she's likely to enjoy more than coupling *à deux*.

She likes her man to surprise her. If he comes over with a Chinese meal and eats it with her in a bubble bath, she will be his slave for the night; or she may just proceed to make love to him as he never dreamed a woman could make love. When Pisces takes command, she does so totally.

In addition to her sexual drive, it is her gift for survival that compels her to search. She wonders how she will find unity within and with another. What the Pisces Woman seeks in the unification of love and sex, in her union with another, is purity and harmony. Her biggest task is to turn her fear of confinement and rejection into love of life and love, and guilt-free sex.

What she needs to learn

The Piscean has the potential for sharing energy totally and equally with another being. We can all learn to transform early fears and hangups into life-giving feelings. The sexually aware Pisces Woman transforms her sexual encounters into a whole, soul-binding union with her special lover. She wants a sensory flowering that is complete and shared.

It is difficult to move from sexual repression to full sensuality. The first step recommended by today's sex therapists is knowing how to give pleasure to oneself. Pisces needs to get to know her own body well and not simply trust the ministrations of others. An artist in pleasing her partner, she can also please herself. She can then share the knowledge acquired through self-pleasuring. Though she is shy about private matters, it is essential in a growing relationship to communicate such information about oneself. (For specific verbal communication skills, see "Scorpio Relationships.")

The Pisces Woman has an instinctive connection with an ancient route to the perfect love union she seeks. This path is called Tantra. Roughly translated, Tantra means the science of ecstasy. For total fulfilment, the Pisces Woman needs a man who can go this route with her.

Tantra is a psychophysical system five thousand years old. Its goal is to create perfect harmony within. The paths to Tantra are varied. One can reach perfection, according to Tantrists, through the use of sound, visualization, or sexual intercourse.

The object of a sexual exchange within the Tantric framework is to heighten and extend rapport, to create through lovemaking a oneness between a man and a woman. To practice Tantra, the following conditions are necessary:

1 The partners need to be sexually experienced and mature.
2 They need to be a constant in each other's lives.
3 They need to be able to bounce back from failure and have the will to try again.
4 They need to devote time to this process.
5 They need to give up the Western, goal-oriented approach to sex. In Tantra, orgasm is not the goal. Pleasure is.

The Pisces Woman is a particularly good candidate for enlightened sexual methods. She crusades for spiritual growth. She has a primal need to love wholly. In order to realize herself, she needs to transcend the negative emotions that could keep her confined to depression and ultimately lead to self-destruction. Sexual energy is a potent basic energy in humans. If the Piscean harnesses it, she is using universal energy. If she misuses it, she drains herself of self-love and creativity.

Pisces anger

Anger is like snow.
It comes,
Stays,
Melts away
And is forgotten.

Loves is like a sunny day.
It shines out,
Encourages growth,
Gets covered over,
But it is remembered
For
An eternity.

Anina Bennett, age 13
"Emotions"

The sexually restricted Pisces Woman is also limited in her ability to recognize and express her anger. It takes her a long time to acknowledge her anger, to delve for the causes and situations that trigger it. Reasons for anger are often buried in the past, but the immediate provocations for anger are current. It is more productive for the Piscean to take a close look at present situations than to look far into the past.

The Pisces Woman is likely to get sick before she gets angry, to get ulcers before she yells at her children, and to protect her husband from her anger as he protects her from the violence of the world outside the home. In fact, it appears that Pisces makes an invisible bargain with her family. If they keep her unaware of the things that might make her fearful and angry, she will protect them in turn from her depressions and her anger.

The Pisces Woman dreamwalks through her early career or her childraising years. She is sweet, she is a good subordinate, and she thrives on establishing a happy atmosphere. She truly wants to believe in the American ideal of the happy home and woman. She hopes that as long as she keeps up her end of the partnership, the fairy tale will continue. She pays more attention to fantasy than to her gut feelings, the repression of which gives her headaches and stomach cramps.

When she approaches thirty, she experiences a clear-cut turning point. She becomes aware of the fact that she is very different from her mother. Though this makes her anxious, she also welcomes the change. She begins to enjoy her own independent identity for the first time. She gets in touch with strong feelings of anger and eroticism.

For the Pisces Woman, anger does not become a reality until she breaks away from her early, obedient self. At thirty, she realizes that as long as she keeps her emotions of fear, guilt, and anger checked, she cannot give space to important parts of her emerging being. At this time, in her inimitable, subtle, cautious, self-protective style, she tiptoes into great changes. Her partner and others may only notice that she seems more alive. Her body language changes. She becomes more energetic.

The Pisces Woman can always use her eyes very effectively to transmit messages (she can also receive, much like a sensitive radar device). Now, however, she lets the rest of her body express her feelings. Dissatisfaction with sex is transmitted through strong body language. She begins to express disappointment, anger at rejections, and interest in more sexual equality. If her mate has been used to an easy ride, he is in for some surprises. She gets tough about cash flow, late nights with the boys, domestic disorder—and says so.

Pisces in her thirties may turn into a self-help fanatic. She may become a personal growth cultist. If she thus sublimates her anger, she has developed a good way to cope.

In her forties, she can choose one of two directions. If she has followed the above script, she mellows. If she is just beginning to get in touch with negative feelings, she does so with a vengeance. As she discovers her anger, many separations and divorces occur.

By forty, she has had to deal with many setbacks. Life is never easy for Pisces, nor is expressing anger. At this juncture, it may seem to her that the more she feels anger and the more she expresses it, the more negativity enters her environment. This is a decidedly defeatist approach that is fueled by others' resistance to her new habits. The Piscean needs to stop worrying about whether her children need her every minute of the day; whether her husband no longer loves her because she is not perfect; or whether her employer dislikes her newfound assertiveness. She should look forward to the emotional stability and maturity the lie ahead.

In her fifties, the Pisces Woman comes to regard anger as a foible one gets used to. She develops patience with herself, chuckles more than she used to, uses laughter to relieve the pressure of her self-doubts. Her relationship to herself is better, and she enjoys other people and believes she is at her most creative. Peace has come to her.

Sexually, because of the relationship between constructively expressed anger and pleasure, she follows a similar pattern. When she is unaware of herself in her twenties, she remains emotionally restrained and sexually insecure. She neither knows what she wants nor asks for what she needs. Consequently, she is unfulfilled and frustrated; though not physically stuck at a pre-orgasmic plateau, emotionally she is arrested there.

She achieves multiple orgasms in her thirties, a prime sexual time for all women. As she accepts and expresses her anger, so can she release her sensuality. If a crisis, such as a divorce, occurs at this time, she may experience a setback to her earlier self-rejection. But as a survivor she comes back stronger than ever, and she remembers how good it felt to be able to release. Self-acceptance comes only after self-knowledge. The Pisces Woman can cast off negativity by accepting herself.

In her late thirties, Pisces comes to recognize her need for self-respect and achievement. She likes subtly applied power. She comes to see her anger as an outcome of earlier feelings of helplessness, inferiority, or powerlessness. She also begins to understand the indirect and destructive methods she had used to achieve power in relationships: through demanding attention, through sickness, through quiet suffering, and through depressions.

Pisces rarely uses anger to get what she wants, as more directly aggressive types do. For example, Aries must demilitarize her anger and express it constructively. For Pisces, the struggle begins with the acknowledgement of her anger; and then she must struggle to express it well.

The Pisces Woman can reduce frustration and avoid depression only when she accepts that *her life is defined by her own perceptions* and also that *her perceptions are her choice.* Anger is a reaction one chooses.

Coping with anger

The constructive use of anger in a partnership comes out of commitment to responsible communication about oneself and commitment to intimacy with another. The following is a guideline for the constructive use of anger, with a particular focus on the Pisces Woman.

1 The four key conditions for the constructive expression of anger are:
   a A commitment to learning new skills.
   b An environment conducive to speaking and listening.
   c Availability of time.
   d Availability of partners.
2 The rules that guide the healthy exchange of anger are:
   a The word *should* is not used.
   b The participants commit to attention, nonthreatening persuasion of point of view, specific negotiation.
   c Both partners commit to the allotted time period.
   d The anger-provoking act is separated from personality.
3 Anger is used constructively as:
   a A tension release.
   b A sign of the need for change.
   c An energizer.
   d A catalyst to overcome fear, boredom, old habits.
   e A way to gain influence.
   f A way to establish a stronger identity.
4 The constructive expression of anger for a Pisces Woman takes the following pattern:
   a Awareness of anger.
   b Conscious separation from earlier role models.
   c Development of an independent identity. Anger at mother can be very useful here to create distance from "little girl" behavior. Anger at mother can be turned into tolerance through work on self. If she sees her mother as a product of her times and as having done what she could, Pisces can accept her better.
   d Increase of adult identity. Anger at men is expected. It is useful insofar as it gives her space and time to do things on her own. She needs to explain to intimates what she is doing and set a timetable. She can consider ways to negotiate change, therapeutic methods to release anger (bioenergetics, primal scream, psychodrama, etc.).
   e Awareness of what triggers her anger and the ways to cope in each situation. Anger at men can be dealt with through constructive discussions, counseling, or women's groups. Setting professional goals and being responsible for their success or failure also lifts much of the burden of rage with

men, for this rage is competitive and comes from feelings of helpless inferiority.

f The construction of her own world with places where she feels safe in expressing her whole self.

When the Pisces Woman learns to use anger as a constructive force, when she regards it as real and universal, when she acknowledges both its positive and negative powers, when she acknowledges that as a mature woman she has choices in her emotional life, she becomes an integrated, independent woman.

Pisces lifestyles

Monogamy and nonmonogamy

Pisces is strongly committed to marital monogamy, for by nature she is conservative. However, times have changed, and she now is discovering her own unrealized desires. Her opportunities for outside sexual involvement are also more numerous.

A woman may be looking for different traits in a husband than she seeks in a lover. In addition, the Pisces Woman's needs in the first half of her life are vastly different from her needs in later years.

In early adulthood she may still be a little girl looking for a big, strong man to take care of her. Thus, she chooses a husband who is a good provider and protector, a good father, an indulgent and seemingly all-powerful male.

Later she wants a man who helps her grow up and capture a new independence. She wants him to be happy that she is developing into a responsible, self-sufficient woman. However, life is such that not all men are able or willing to assist in this transformation.

As mates, Pisces Women are loyal, sensitive, giving, creative, conservative. If convinced she has made a good choice, the Pisces Woman will suffer anything destiny brings her way. She performs miracles with small budgets and lavishes tender loving care on her mate. However, she expects rejection and easily talks herself into it. It is very hard for her to leave a man, but once she does she can easily fall head over heels in love with the next one. Pisces tends to marry more than once.

The following represent typical situations which could influence the Pisces Woman to become nonmonogamous:

1. *Fantasy love.* This may never be consummated genitally. She may carry on a platonic love affair for years. It's rooted in a yearning for something beyond the ordinary and in her fabulous imagination.
2. Personal growth. She changes radically, and so do her needs and values. If her mate does not keep up, she will try elsewhere. She may never tell him, or she may leave him with no warning. She is anything but predictable.
3. Discovering her mate's imperfections. She married when young and inexperienced. She perhaps also used bad judgment. She now discovers her mate is not who she thought, and in her disillusionment and romanticism, she gives herself to someone else; she's a version of Emma Bovary, the incurable romantic. The marriage may survive several of these episodes.
4. Repeated bad judgment. Pisces often seems to pick the wrong man. After each realization that he is not suitable, she swears off men, or her mate, altogether. Then, once again against her better judgment, she gets reinvolved. This can result in adultery or serial monogamy.
5. Low self-esteem, repressed anger. This is the "I'll show him I'm good enough for him" game, plus the "I'll show him I'm someone to reckon with" ploy. Neither is constructive, and both are bad for the marriage.
6. Lack of sensitivity or lack of emotional expressiveness in partner. This is deadly. She starts out as a flower in bloom, wilts for lack of nutrients, and searches elsewhere to survive. Many Pisces Women find themselves in this situation, for few men match their need for sensitive caring.
7. Sadism of partner. Pisces often attracts brutes. She will leave after she discovers what she has allowed to happen to her. In the meantime, she cheats in order to get support to leave. The biggest problem here is that she also tells herself she *deserves* this kind of treatment. No one does!
8. General escapism. Sometimes she just can't cope. Pisces may become a runaway wife, a suddenly compulsive career woman, or an alcoholic to get away from the relationship. The beginning of the cure is to face herself.

Alternative lifestyles

Intimate networks: The Pisces Woman would rather be queen in her own territory than share. However, friendship with both sexes appeals to her, and she may try this after turning thirty.

Communes: A prime choice for a Pisces as long as her partners' commitments are clear and her territory is not in jeopardy. She gladly undertakes shared household routines and can thrive on communal pastimes. If sex is a pastime, she prefers to have just two lovers at her side.

Group marriage or extended families: She feels the same way about this as she feels about communes, as long as here, too, there is a clearly condoned commitment by the men to her. Secure, she adores this arrangement and discovers a more lively sexuality than she has ever known. She can be tender and loving with another woman as well, *if* she has begun to work through her negative mother addiction. It is recommended that she choose another woman who is no way resembles her own mother—a good experience sensually, sexually, and intellectually, given the above conditions.

Ménage à trois: This is a good temporary arrangement in which couples may share their sex lives and/or residences with a third person. The foundation between the primary partners must be solid, and both partners must want the third. Pisces may be caught in an untenable situation in which she is used in games played by the couple.

Open marriage: The so-called revolutionary lifestyle of the 1960s, which seems to have caught on in a minor way, is not recommended for Pisces.

Gay/bisexual lifestyles: Many Pisces Women have an unrecognized sympathy for gays. After all, Pisces is a double-bodied, mutable sign. However, the Pisces conservative streak is also strong. If she can overcome the latter and the cultural taboo on gays, she can pour out compassion for their plight and be drawn into the movement even if she herself remains heterosexual. Siding with the underdog is one of her strengths.

New Age Lady Chatterley: This is distinct possibility for the evolved, sexually experienced Pisces Woman. She may remain loyal to her husband while seeking passion and sexual growth elsewhere. Only guilt stands in her way, but that is a major force. She may be able to handle it and give herself other relationships as gifts rather than as punishments.

Single woman: Pisces does not do well living alone. She needs company, support, the energy of other people. This lifestyle is definitely not recommended, especially when she is down on herself. Being a single mother is a weak possibility if she decides not to have a partner.

The common denominator of all this is change. The Piscean needs change. Her attitudes and values shift, and as a result her behavior changes. In her twenties Pisces is different from the person she will be in her fifties. She finds a new level of sexuality in each phase. New partners become available as old ones go. Her willingness to work on a primary relationship may ebb and flow.

What varies from type to type, age group to age group, phase to phase, and culture to culture is not our need to love and be loved, but the expression of our deepest needs—our courage, confidence, risk-taking ability, interest in growth, communication skills.

If the Piscean finds lasting pleasure in one relationship, she will stay with it. If she takes the affirmative route, she will love living. Monogamous or not, the Piscean is meant to pioneer ways of giving and receiving love.

Summing up Pisces

The Pisces Woman's challenge is to find positive channels for her psychic, artistic, and therapeutic powers. Many Pisceans heal by laying on of hands. Others foretell the future, paint, write poetry, or act. The can be champions of the truth and defenders of the poor and helpless.

Pisces is directed by her subconscious, her dreams. She is a vast ocean of psychic and spiritual powers. However, she must remember that she is mortal. She has a limited span on earth, at least in this physical body. Time can run short, and much needs to be accomplished. In order to discover the real meaning of physical and mental health, she must pierce the fog of her own visions, explore her repressed feelings, confront the outside world, and communicate with those around her.

She must seek out those who will embrace the talents she has—be they artistic, therapeutic, or paranormal. The energy of her group support system will prevent Pisces from slipping off into the ethers of her dreams or fears.

On the other hand, she cannot depend on others to do her work for her. She must consistently reassess, turn her self-absorption into a more detached self-investigation. Then she will recognize and affirm her own strengths while detecting her weaknesses and transforming them into strengths as well.

The Age of Pisces is about to end. The last twenty-five hundred years have been symbolized by two fish swimming in opposite directions: possessive materialism and unselfish love. The message of the next age is precisely the positive side of Pisces: the filtration and elimination of negativity and the transcendence of selfish individualism.

The Pisces Woman is, in her own way, a pioneer. It is essential that she transmit what she feels, knows, experiences, and envisions. She must build bridges, and she must act . If the Pisces Woman can share her inner visions and exteriorize the love she feels and symbolizes, if she can keep positive, focused, and active, she will be a key figure ushering in the Age of Aquarius, the age of love.

THE COSMIC WOMAN

CHECKLIST OF COSMIC WOMAN TRAITS

1. Concerned, Caring
2. Loving
3. Nonpossessive
4. Friendly
5. Patient
6. Alive, Vital
7. Aware, Conscious
8. Open
9. Tolerant
10. Visionary
11. Curious, Childlike
12. Filled with Wonder
13. Feeling
14. Tender
15. Affectionate
16. Harmonious
17. Whole
18. At Peace
19. Androgynous
20. Noncompetitive
21. Communicative
22. Joyful
23. Poetic
24. Realistic
25. Idealistic
26. Mystical, Spiritual
27. Timing Based on Cycles
28. Independent
29. Cooperative
30. Balanced
31. Fearless
32. Guiltless
33. Creative
34. Detached
35. Fulfilled Actualized

Cosmic personality

No bird soars too high, if he soars with his own wings.
William Blake
Proverbs of Hell

General traits and background

The Cosmic Woman is the archetype all women strive to be. She is the eternal feminine principle embodying all the characteristics most attractive to men. She reflects an inner strength that other women recognize and try to emulate. Her presence lights up a room. She creates a sense of excitement wherever she goes. She combines the humanitarianism of Eleanor Roosevelt with the fabled physical and mental strength of Wonder Woman, the intellect of Madame Curie, and the grace and good common sense of Shirley MacLaine. She is indeed a remarkable woman.

The Cosmic Woman represents the completed Zodiac. She is a combination of all the influences that make a fulfilled and actualized life. In her, the energies of Earth, Air, Fire, and Water are perfectly balanced, each exercising its own influence, but in perfect harmony and balance.

The Cosmic Woman is aware of all the vibrations of the different planets and has learned to use them to vitalize and energize her life. Therefore, no one planet or astrological house dominates her life. They all vibrate in perfect harmony, as she does. Every planet, every house, every correspondence is important to her, for to be wise she must know how to flow with the energies and how to focus them to do her bidding. Having learned that her finite nature is tied to an infinite source, she recognizes the limitations she must respect; but fully knowing herself, she recognizes also the myriad manifestations she can actualize within her sphere.

The Cosmic phase has the following characteristics:

1 The development of a loving, caring nature that is at perfect peace with itself and others.
2 The ability to conserve time and energy in cultivating people and things that are useful parts of life.
3 The ability to detach herself from recurring negative experiences and reorder her life patterns.
4 An ability to be in the world but not of it.
5 An ability to see herself and the results of her actions and to learn from her observations.

6 The ability to be independent but also to work with groups.
7 An ability to predict the future but to live totally in the present.
8 A tolerance and acceptance of others, wherever they happen to be in their development.
9 Joy and excitement in living.
10 The ability to draw on life's experiences in a teaching/learning process with her associates.

The Cosmic Woman is set apart by her sensitized feelings and her capacity for following them. She is intuitive and trusts her intuitions. She learned long ago that being in touch with her higher self puts her in touch with her own destiny, and that if she follows her inner voice she will never be led astray. She lives life quite successfully.

She is capable of feeling all the emotions of her twelve sisters. She can empathize with them and has learned to flow with the cycles that constitute her own makeup. Indeed, this flowing quality also sets her apart. Being so in tune with nature and her own nature, she has an assurance that most women envy but never achieve—not that it is impossible for them to do so, but few have evolved to the point where they so totally trust their feelings and intuitions.

Most women limit themselves by not even imagining what they really want. The Cosmic Woman has learned how to break down conditioned expectations concerning the boundary between the possible and the impossible. She knows that there are no limits to the mind and that anything she can *imagine* she can *do* (see *Cosmic Trigger*, by Robert Anton Wilson).

She has overcome many obstacles in her journey to becoming a Cosmic Woman. And she has welcomed each adversary as a challenge, each difficulty as a learning situation. In our age, her life reads somewhat like an updated *Pilgrim's Progress* with a cast of characters from a Fellini movie. She does not blame circumstances for determining her life; she uses them for her own growth. She does not wait for chance or fate to shape her destiny; she takes responsibility for creating her own experiences. Shakespeare put it succinctly in *Julius Caesar*. "The fault, dear Brutus, is not in our stars,/But in ourselves, that we are underlings."

She feels a special relationship to the universe. According to *Webster's*, the word *cosmic* pertains to the universe at large as an orderly system, one that is harmonious as opposed to chaotic. It relates to the material universe outside the solar system and to changes in the cosmos. It also refers to a magnitude or extent in space or time, suggesting vastness or great duration.

The Cosmic Woman prefers order to chaos. She knows that to be whole she must institute order in her existence. Her mind, her home, and her life all reflect a sense of order and arrangement that brings clarity, purpose, direction, and cohesiveness to all she undertakes.

She possesses a clear vision of the world and what makes it work. She is not surprised at the shortcomings of mankind, and she is knowledgeable about the obstacles that must be overcome to bring her dreams to fruition. She is not without dreams, but she is very realistic about how they will be realized, the amount of energy that will be required to bring them to pass, and the probability of them coming true.

The Cosmic Woman has a unique relationship to the world; she see things differently. Her perspective derives from a special viewpoint. She sees herself and her actions in relation to the whole of creation; her friends, her family, her home, her nation, her world—all are placed within an ordered universe. Living becomes a creative act for her. No thought or action is simple, for it sets in motion a new pattern or reinforces an old one.

She recognizes the cyclic nature of things—the cycles of the body (biorhythms), the cycles of the planets (astrology), the cycles of the equinoxes (Aquarian Age). All introduce changes into her life. Her awareness of these changes, some subtle, others profound, and her ability to flow with them, make life easier and more understandable for her.

The Cosmic Woman seeks to retain the nature with which she was born—simple, direct, loving, feeling, able to touch the stars. She never feels compelled to be grasping, controlling, or manipulative in order to live fully. She finds her fulfillment by following the intuitive part of her mind which leads her to her higher self and to a proper relationship with things around her.

She has come to know herself sexually and emotionally by getting in touch with her nature. She has learned how to make changes in her life without becoming their victim, as she has often been in the past. She has found the key to building her self-esteem and expressing her anger in constructive ways. She has found the source of her power to construct the lifestyles she wants. She has come to love herself and others.

The key word for the Cosmic Woman is *love*. She has found the true meaning of love, has been liberated by it, lives according to its dictates, and orders her life to reflect its joy. Hers is the love that does not try to possess. She does not use it to manipulate. It is a positive force in her life and allows her to give freely of herself and her possessions.

I believe that if we come to know and love ourselves and others, we will have the key to life. For love is the source of our power and creativity.

Concerned, caring

The Cosmic Woman's concerns are as broad as the cosmos itself, but her primary concerns are with people. In the broadest sense, and in particular cases, she expresses her concern to the people she encounters in her daily life. She is a natural teacher who by word and example helps others overcome the same obstacles she has met in her journey to liberation. Her good common sense makes her a counselor without equal.

Her concerns transcend the mundane. She is vitally interested in any institution, condition, or law that effects the lives of people. She may be found on the boards of universities, helping organize a citizens' committee on the environment, lobbying for better welfare legislation, or forming a society to study the future of mankind. Whatever the activity, she can be distinguished from others by the absence of self-interest; neither her ego nor her vested interests are served by what she does. She cares only about the job at hand and about its impact on the group.

In her personal life, she also gives expression to her concern, often in direct and simple acts that help her acquaintances. If someone needs a ride to the doctor, if there has been a death in the family or a friend needs a shoulder to cry on, the Cosmic Woman is there. She uses her time to the greatest advantage but does not let others take advantage of her. Should people start to impose on her good nature, she reminds them that her help can only go so far and that they must take responsibility for their own lives.

The Cosmic Woman truly *cares*. Starting with herself, she cares for her body as if it were a temple. She eats the proper foods; she bathes and brushes and trims. She dresses well and projects the glowing radiance of someone who loves herself. She extends this caring to everything around her: her family, her garden, her work. She hopes they will all turn out right and tends to them with a devotion that nurtures and assures that they will.

Almost everybody has a will to survive; this is the source of life. The good life of the Cosmic Woman, however, comes from what she cares about. She seeks to do something about situations. She directs her will with love and decides to take positive action.

Loving

Every action of the Cosmic Woman is an act of love. She is constantly high on life. The Cosmic Woman has discovered the difference between falling in love and being loving. When we fall in love, there is the threat of losing our own inner being, of sacrificing everything on the altar of the beloved. When we are loving, our inner core is preserved, and we are capable of giving ourselves yet returning to that center for refreshment and nurturing.

Love, for the Cosmic Woman, does not provide a path to security, power, or fame. It is an expression of a joy-filled life. She feels deeply that when she is loving, she is participating in nature as it was meant to be.

Being loving does not mean she is weak. She must be very strong to direct her energy into those areas she feels will produce the highest good. She must stand up to those who see her loving nature as weakness, who become parasitic or misuse it. She must constantly strive to bring others to the same state so that there can be a mutual exchange of loving energies.

Plato recognized the awesome power of love. The Cosmic Woman has learned how to harness that power and use it. She directs it to her relationships, to her sex life, and to the rejuvenation and actualization of her self. Hers is not a romantic love revolving around two people in a closed system; she is open to a much broader experience. She does not preclude romantic love, but she recognizes that the special circumstances that produce it are rare indeed.

Her home and her office reflect this kind of loving and regard for life—a Chinese landscape misty and lovely; a piece of stained glass in a window reflecting the sun's rays; a profusion of plants that give life and beauty—every touch is the touch of someone who cares. She makes no apologies for her concern, takes but little thought in expressing her love or calculating the results of her action. She loves because it is her nature to do so.

Nonpossessive

The Cosmic Woman has learned the lesson of possession well. She knows that all of life is in a constant ebb and flow and that applies to her possessions as well as the people in her life. She therefore looks on things and people as treasures to be cherished while they are in her care, and does not try to own them. She is aware of the transient nature of life and savors each moment that she has a lovely thing or person in her life, but she also knows when to let go. She knows that her own growth is hampered when she tries to hold onto something that wishes to fly free.

The Cosmic Woman is very giving of her worldly goods. She feels that she is the steward of these possessions to bring joy and abundance to others, and gives without hesitation. It is interesting to see that her well never seems to run dry. She attracts worldly goods and knows how to use them for the enrichment of those around her. There always seems to be room for an extra guest at dinner, a space for a lonely wanderer who has no place to stay. Her care and concern are ever present.

This same attutude is seen in all of her relationships. When she loves, she does so freely and does not try to own her beloved. She shares moments, even days and years, but when the time comes for her to let go, she is able. Being so complete in herself, she demands very little from her companions. She feels that love is a mutual response, that there has to be giving and sharing on the part of all involved, or the effort is not worth the price. She has little time in her life for the totally selfish and the totally self-centered.

The Cosmic Woman nurtures but does not possess. She cares for but does not own. She protects but does not dominate. She loves but does not manipulate. She holds and comforts, but also knows when to let go. The Cosmic Woman's only true possession is herself.

Friendly

The Cosmic Woman does not know a stranger. She looks on all creation as a whole and sees its parts as related to her in a very special way. She recognizes that the same impulse that nourishes her being nourishes all the rest of humanity, and that people are all related—different and separate—but of the same source. She seeks to know herself in studying all things, but especially in the mirror of her own kind. She looks for, and expects to find in the contacts she makes, keys to understanding her own nature.

Her friendliness knows no boundaries. She is as apt to strike up a conversation with the garbage collector as she is with a prominent banker, and she may well enjoy it more. She is interested in life's experiences no matter where they occur, and she is open to all sources of information.

She is a rare friend, for she is completely honest. She feels almost compelled to help her friends see themselves and the situations in which they are embroiled in the light of day. She is so in tune with life and has had so much experience in living that she is seldom fooled about others' motivations. And when her experience is not enough, she relies on her intuition.

Patient

The Cosmic Woman has learned the lesson of her Taurus phase very well. She has the patience of Job. Family situations that would drive others to drink do not faze her. She views them with the cool, detached knowledge that all things change. Death may be the only cure, but even this is a change and a new beginning for the Cosmic Woman. She is aware of the cycles of life and death and realizes that even death starts a new cycle in which things again have the capacity to work out.

She views life as a learning process and is patient with herself and others as they fumble through it. She may show some impatience when the going gets slow and will try to prod things along, but she is usually very respectful of the time and effort learning takes. She is a natural teacher and will use all her knowledge to speed the process. The Cosmic Woman has developed a new consciousness in which personal relationships occupy a central place. She realizes that quite a transition is necessary for everyone to discover the depths of what it means to be human.

Alive, vital

There is an expectancy about the Cosmic Woman that gives her a very alive quality. Knowing that change is the only constant, the Cosmic Woman expects and plans the changes she wants in her life. She uses her powers of imagery and fantasy to imagine what it is she really wants. She clarifies and refines the images until they match the inner feelings she has, and then she expects them to happen. She remains flexible in order to be able to change outer reality according to the impulses she receives from her inner self.

The Cosmic Woman takes good care of her body. She does not ply it with numerous drugs and harsh chemicals that upset its balance. Her vital signs are strong and pulsating, for she has both a will and a desire to live. She studies nutrition and the proper use of vitamins. She sleeps a peaceful sleep, leaving behind the cares of the day as she prepares for a learning session each night. She conserves energy, especially the energy of her own body. She has glowing good health, for she has found the proper balance for her life. She keeps not only her body in shape but also her mind. She tunes it to a positive note. She explores her negative feelings, embraces them, studies them, and works out a solution whereby she can release them. She tries never to go to sleep with unexpressed negative feelings robbing her mind and body of rest. She feels herself in the flow of life. She is conscious of the dynamic interchange of energy that is constantly taking place in an open evolution that surrounds her. This is the source of her vitality.

Aware, conscious

The Cosmic Woman is alert to the changes taking place in the world around her and the meaning of those shifts of energy. No detail is too small as she observes the world around her. It is as if she puts the environment under a microscope so as to see it more clearly. She applies the same technique to her own actions and becomes aware of what she is doing and why she is doing it. She assesses her position and the effectiveness of her use of the information she has collected.

Her aim is to be conscious of every decision she makes. She is aware to the elements and to what is going on around her. She is aware of her innermost thoughts and seeks to keep all cognizance on the conscious level. Even her bursts of intuitive insight are brought to her conscious mind so that she is acutely aware of her actions and motivations. She seeks to live as consciously as possible, for she feels that if her life is to take the direction she wishes, she must be in charge of decisions.

Once the Cosmic Woman senses that she is a combination of different energies bound together in a common body, and once she is aware that these energies can pull in different directions, she loses much of the fear and guilt that she has placed upon herself. She stops trying to punish herself for not being perfect. She gives up psychosomatic illness and relinquishes her sense of shame over her flaws. She makes no harsh judgments about her sexuality but accepts it as part of the complex energies that make up her being. She leaves guilt behind because she no longer feels it for doing what is natural and right for her body. She is not ashamed of the intuitions that come to her in the night and bring a sense of order and meaning to her life. She makes no apologies for her dreams but seeks to understand them. Having passed the self-imposed barriers of *proper* thought and *proper* action, and having entered the realm of *possible* thought and *possible* action, she is well on her way to being truly liberated. As she questions the validity of traditional mores and ethical standards, of traditional principles and codes of behavior, she is once again participating in the creative process whereby she changes herself and the world about her changes, too. She finds that the more she is totally awake and aware, the more she becomes accepting of herself and of the world in which she lives.

Open, tolerant

The Cosmic Woman recognizes very few boundaries. She is cognizant of the rather artificial world that has evolved and aware that it may not be suitable to the New Age person she is becoming. Therefore, she is open to a variety of alternatives for living. She seeks new patterns and new approaches to problems that seem to become greater with the passing of each year, and for which traditional thinking has not yet provided answers. She investigates new lifestyles that are more comfortable for the woman she is becoming. She looks for workable solutions that traditional religious, legal, and governmental systems have not found.

She is equally open in her approach to people. She pulls her friends from all age groups, from all social levels, from as many walks of life as she has the physical and mental energy to encompass. She is a pioneer on that last great frontier available to humankind, the mind. She regards people as living resources. She feels that she can learn from their experiences and enters into a teacher/pupil relationship in which open communication is of the utmost importance. Her personal progress and the progress of her friends can only happen when there is honest communication.

Having learned in her Gemini phase that communication is at the heart of successful relationships, that without it sex becomes a neurotic release rather than an experience of sharing or an encounter, the Cosmic Woman has come to tolerate the feeble attempts of those who are at least trying. She accepts people if they are trying to know and understand. Being aware of her own inner self, she is acutely aware of the struggles and self-imposed inadequacies of others. She has learned through her experiences to accept people as they are. She encourages self-discovery.

Visionary

The Cosmic Woman has a rare ability to see things as they could be. Her vision takes in the whole scope of the human personality, human relationships, and human institutions. She can spot potential in all these areas, and if she does become sad, it is because someone or something is not living up to the possibilities she discerns.

She is so aware of the cycles of nature and history that she can project into the future and catch a glimpse of what potential it holds. Being a part of this never-ending process, she realizes what a unique role she has to play in creating the future. Her past memories, both temporal and inspirational, give her a standard with which to measure progress towards the future vision she holds. She knows only too well from whence she has come what dues have to be paid to get where she wants to go.

She uses her active imagination to construct and fantasize what she really wants out of life. She has learned well in her Sagittarius phase that she possesses the key to the future, that the high ideals she learned there are indeed right for her and are attainable. She learned, too, that enlightenment is a necessary adjunct to knowledge, and she seeks to place all things in the light of her higher mind. She has learned from her Libra phase that she must bend and adjust to the river that flows around her, that she must become part of that flow if she is to be an active participant rather than a passive observer. The clarity of her vision and the depth of her perceptions provide an important identifying mark for the Cosmic Woman. Such insight has allowed her to be successful in business, in management, and in relating to other people. During the age of Pisces, which is ruled by Neptune, and where everything has been kept hidden, she has used her powers in very secret ways. Now that the age of Aquarius is at hand, she will become much more visible as she devotes her considerable skills to paving the way of the New Age.

Curious, childlike, filled with wonder

The Cosmic Woman has not lost the ability to be amazed and filled with wonder. She approaches each day with a zest for discovery. She still feels excitement for each new experience, for each new undertaking. She is able to look at a starry sky and marvel at her place within the vastness of space. She can stand at the top of the Grand Canyon and be in awe of the powerful forces of nature that carved such a wonder. She thrills to thunder and lightning and the power of a raging sea. She gets goose bumps thinking about the miracle of birth.

Her attitude toward the world and other people is very childlike. She fully realizes the vulnerability of such an approach but feels that the rewards are too great to worry much about the inherent dangers. She is really quite fearless about becoming involved because she anticipates only the positive and the good.

Her curiosity is a driving force in her explorations, whether of places, people, or the misty world of the unseen. There is no subject under the sun that she will not investigate. She may totally reject what she finds as not fitting her particular needs, but she feels confident in her ability to decide for herself the utility and validity of any system of thought. Indeed, she feels almost compelled to make the decision for herself, since she has found that many have tried to manipulate her mind during her formative years. She resists the games of other people; she wants to know what she thinks and not be bound by the projections of anyone that would try to put her in an uncomfortable stereotyped role.

Feeling, tender, affectionate

A great deal of the Cosmic Woman's time has been spent validating her feelings to herself and others. There has been a conspiracy in the male-dominated world to degrade and ignore the intuitive as too flighty, too unscientific, too irrational to be useful. The Cosmic Woman long ago dismissed these rebuffs because she *knew* that her feelings were correct and that they could be trusted more than the scientific predictions of the weather forecaster.

The Cosmic Woman possesses a settled goodwill that has regard for the feelings of others. She respects emotions, both her own and others', and can express the love and caring she has for someone. She knows that such verbalizations, even a simple "I love you," have a profound effect on the emotions. She enjoys seeing the positive reactions that her affection elicits. Her heart is very kind, and this is one of her most endearing qualities. In her Pisces phase she learned to feel, to nurture, and to heal. It is little wonder that she treats all life with such tenderness.

Harmonious, whole, at peace

The Cosmic Woman is aware that all creation is vibrating and producing sound. She has observed herself very carefully, and has found that she too vibrates differently at different times of the day and night. The rising sun causes a different emotional response that does the noonday sun. Dusk fills her with different feelings than do the stars. Each time, each season, causes her to vibrate at a varying rate. In the past, when people lived closer to the soil, it was easier to be in harmony with these natural cycles. People could more easily give expression to the feelings and urges that the hours, days, weeks, and years brought. In modern industrialized and mechanized society there is less approval given to these basic urges. However, the Cosmic Woman still feels them and preserves them wherever possible. When the Cosmic Woman learns to flow with her different feelings and to work with the energies they create, she finds herself filled with harmony. Her actions match her feelings. Just as music arises from a blending of agreeable sounds, so her life sings.

The Cosmic Woman seeks to reunite the separate parts of herself. Her memory seems to stretch back into the primordial past, when the opposing energies within her emanated from a unity in which everything functioned in harmony and accord. She has accomplished what the woman in the Gemini phase seeks but often doesn't find: the wholeness in which her male and female energies are reconciled, and her mind and body have worked out a mutually respectful truce and have agreed to cooperate. She is no longer torn between the spirit that dreams of the stars and the physical body that tends the cabbages and sweeps the floor. She knows just how aggressive to be, and just how yielding. She is totally at peace. She has learned that she does not have to give up her negative energies or suppress them and hope they will go away. She has learned how to hold them in balance by applying the positive energies that also abound within her.

Androgynous

Recognizing that she has male and female energies working in her, the Cosmic Woman seeks to understand this phenomenon and learn to utilize both in her quest for self-actualization.

Tired of the Cancer phase that has dominated our national life, where the female is expected to be submissive, bending, ultra-feminine, and a homemaker, women in the 1960s entered into the man's world with all the considerable force their male energy could muster. They sought to imitate men and thus became victims of the same trap that men have been caught in for so long. Aggressive, cutthroat, deceitful, egotistical, and a dozen other destructive adjectives became a way of life for women. They lost much of the femininity they had possessed and took on many of the negative characteristics of their male counterparts.

The Cosmic Woman is well on her way to being androgynous, that is, accepting and working with both the male and female energies she has within her. The concept is welcome, for it provides a way out of the dilemma described above. She is able to incorporate both elements into her personality and utilize whatever is appropriate for the problem at hand.

Once she is able to establish this kind of internal dialogue, the energies flow with a natural symphonic grace. She experiences *herself* as a totality and is better able to interact with others who likewise have this dual nature. The longing and searching of her Gemini phase were well spent, for she has found her other half, right inside herself. From this point on, her interactions will be much more dynamic as she relates to both the male and female energies in herself and her beloved.

Noncompetitive

The Cosmic Woman feels no need to compete with anyone. She competes only with the task at hand. To her, the challenge of doing things well is competition enough. She has no need to prove she is better than another because her satisfaction comes from doing a good job. She finds that the competitive spirit, which has been sold as the key to success, only leads to unsavory ego gratification and an unnatural need to consume goods.

In spite of her reticence to compete, she usually ends up in a favorable position, for she performs well and is thorough. Expecting only the best, she gets the best. She wins without stepping on a number of bodies to do so. Knowing that she has an inalienable right to the space she occupies, she is not threatened when people get close. She does not have to defend her turf, since she carries her sense of home with her.

Communicative

The Cosmic Woman has learned to be a master communicator. She is able to dispel any feeling of alienation when she recognizes one of her own kind. With words, gestures, or a soft touch, she instills a quality of openness, warmth, and intelligence that assures she has made real contact. Even if she should encounter an unyielding and antagonistic energy, she is able to see that person in proper perspective, without predetermined judgment, and to adjust her energy to give a suitable response.

She recognizes the important connection between love and communication. She sees that much of what is done is the name if lovemaking is so obsessive, self-indulgent, and aggressive that it amounts to little more than masturbation. Without a sense of sharing or encounter, sex becomes sex for its own sake, with no communication, no responsibility, no caring, and no love. This neurotic release of pent-up sexual energy leads nowhere in particular and leaves the participants with an empty, unfulfilled feeling.

The Cosmic Woman believes in complete honesty in communication. To one who deals in poses and stances, this is impossible. To the Cosmic Woman, it is a necessity; otherwise she wastes her valuable time and energy. In fact, one of the Cosmic Woman's greatest joys is the feeling that she has really communicated with another soul. There is a *joie de vivre* about her that is hard to miss. She enjoys living; there are not enough hours in the day or enough days in the week to accommodate her many interests and projects. Human contact is essential for her. Her joy is infectious.

Poetic

The Cosmic Woman has a very poetic soul and she expresses herself in poetic form as she communicates with those around her. She enjoys poetry because it is the best verbal means of sharing the secrets of the inner being. She also uses nonverbal means of communication and would prefer that her friends develop the same ability, for she is disquieted by the chatter that many use in their attempts to enhance their own egos.

You will find her bookshelves lined with verse, for it enhances her life and supplements her need to find the essence of things. Art, music, and literature also abound in her personal space, for she is ever in search of the deeper meaning. She loves beauty and finds close connections through her cosmic self.

Realistic, idealistic

The Cosmic Woman is realistic about her expectations. Having such a good handle on the personalities of those she meets (she has gone through all the phases and recognizes the types), she knows what she can expect and does not project her own needs, wants, and desires onto another.

She also is realistic about the way things work. Having been involved in the process of change, she has had a lot of exposure to the organized institutions of society. She recognizes the elephantine nature of most organizations and the tremendous amount of energy that is required to move them. She does not waste much time if there seems to be little chance of changing them. She realizes that the necessary changes in society will not happen until changes first take place within people. She devotes much of her time to helping people change their own inner selves.

The Cosmic Woman is realistic about time and money. She realizes that all good things take time and that there has to be some support system to provide the necessities of life. The wolf has to be kept from the door, the leaky roof has to be repaired, and the tax forms have to be filled and filed. She can do these mundane things and retain her high idealism as well.

Mystical, spiritual

In an age when it is not chic to admit that there is anything but the physical side of life, the Cosmic Woman acknowledges her soul and spirit as part of her multidimensional self. She experiences too much truth that does not have its origin on the physical plane of existence not to know and believe in a more subtle reality.

Part of her journey in becoming self-actualized took her down paths illuminated only by her intuitive powers. She learned to trust in where they were leading her. She discovered much on her journey that reinforced her intuitive knowing. She emerged much stronger, much happier, and much more sure of her place in the universe. She does not plan to lose this important side of her nature.

Timing based on cycles

Blessed with a good memory that has been refined and honed to a sharp edge, the Cosmic Woman is able to remember the patterns her life creates. She studies the warp and woof of it to find why the design emerges as it does. She is keenly aware of the cycles she undergoes and knows they have a powerful effect on her. Her life is filled with rhythms—the heartbeat, the rhythms of the breath and brain, the menstrual cycle.

She is aware of the moon's effect on her life. She can feel her emotions wax and wane with its movement. She learns to flow with these changes and to accept her nature rather than fight it. The lunar cycle is the shortest of the planetary cycles but also creates a long-range cycle that is important to the Cosmic Woman. Recognizing these subtle rhythms and the direct relationship they have to her life helps the Cosmic Woman to plan and cope with problems that many do not even realize. They would rather curse fate and die.

The Cosmic Woman is also on the lookout for patterns that recur in her life. If she has attracted three men who all have similar characteristics and have all treated her in the same negative, rotten way, she can be assured that they are there for a purpose. She has something to learn, and the pattern will be repeated until such time as she is able to deal with the problem they represent.

Independent, cooperative

The Cosmic Woman likes to be independent. She wants to take care of herself, to be responsible for her own decisions, and to have a very private space when she needs it. She is self-sufficient by nature and seldom worries about the material concerns of life. She believes that these needs will always be taken care of and is willing to exert energy to see that they are. She is much more concerned that she not waste her energy and that her precious time be respected.

When she accepts kindnesses or favors from another, she is very careful to give in return. She does not like to owe anyone anything. However, when gifts are given from the heart, with no strings attached, she can very graciously accept. Her independence is very precious to her, and she protects it with pride.

At the opposite pole, she is very cooperative. She realizes that much progress will be accomplished by groups, and she is eager to participate. She insists, however, that a clear goal be established and that egos be so submerged as to be almost indistinguishable. Otherwise there is little chance of success, and even less chance for the active participation of the Cosmic Woman. She has learned her Scorpio phase well and has left behind the power trip as being unnecessary for the job at hand. Temporal power, too, pales in comparison to the power she feels inside—she does not need anyone else to build her ego.

Balanced

The Cosmic Woman has revived her multidimensional personality and is bursting with all kinds of powerful energies. Previously she had kept many of these from seeing the light of day. Some are so negative that she scarcely recognizes them as her own. The Cosmic Woman soon learns to cope with this tornado of energies by balancing one with another. Her male energy is balanced with her female energy; her mental energy is balanced with her emotional energy; her spiritual energy is balanced with her physical energy.

She seeks to oppose one energy with another until their meeting creates a dynamic motion, much as in the Chinese concept of *yin* and *yang*. She also seeks to bring them into equilibrium as one force is applied to another. The Greek architects discovered this principle centuries ago as they created beautiful columns to interact with the downward thrust of a heavy roof. Each element exerted the same force, and a perfect balance was thus created and frozen in time for all to see.

Fearless, guiltless

The Cosmic Woman has met so many goblins on her way to becoming an actualized person that she fears very little. She does not worry about unknowns. She plunges right ahead and is prepared for things as they happen. She has passed the initiation of her Pisces phase and does not worry a great deal. She is concerned but has learned that people must take responsibility for their own lives just as she has taken responsibility for hers.

She recognizes that guilt is one of the most binding of feelings and has left little room for it in her life. She lives so clearly and purely that she never does anything she feels guilty about. Having shaken many of the guilt trips laid on her by her family, her society, her friends, and her lovers, she now recognizes that most of it was done to manipulate and control her responses. Here again she feels little need for such restraints. She is tired of being victimized by people who do not have her best interests at heart.

Creative

The Cosmic Woman can make a silk purse out of a sow's ear. Her eye for the beauty and essence of things, her knowledge of proportion and scale, her sense of balance and harmony, all support a powerful creative urge. She is able to create an environment that symbolizes her inner feelings. With a few sparse furnishings and well-selected artworks, she is able to bring any surrounding to life.

The Cosmic Woman looks on life as a creative endeavor. She seeks to soar by her own efforts. She finds herself in a dynamic process in which life and death, joy and sorrow, growth and decay, form a mosaic of ever-changing patterns. She flows with all change and is strengthened and enhanced by the process. Ever in the river of life, she grows and blossoms, receiving her sustenance from the elements around her.

She does not fear death; she knows that it is an important ingredient of change. More important, she does not fear life. She lives courageously. She learns to adjust and alter her course in light of the knowledge she accumulates. She seeks to experience as much as she can absorb, knowing that each new thing offers her the challenge of living, loving, flowing.

Detached

The Cosmic Woman lives in the world but is not part of it. This apparent contradiction is possible because she is aware of her multidimensional nature and cognizant that her true being exists on many levels. Although her physical self is firmly grounded in the earth and all the activities of that plane, she recognizes that part of her nature is related to the stars. She has evolved enough to activate both and to release other subtle forces that also exist within her.

She can do this because she detaches herself from most of the things that bind people to a one-dimensional existence. She detaches herself from her emotions and the strong energies sex creates. She knows that she is not what she feels. Her emotions are ships passing in the night. They come and they go, affecting her strongly, but not determining the totality of what she is. Nor do her thoughts determine what she is. They affect her attitude, her reactions to things, her perspectives on life, but she is more than her thoughts. There is a small, powerful center within her to which she retreats to escape from her emotions, her thoughts, her negative and positive actions which is her true self and where she really feels at home.

Fulfilled, actualized
The Cosmic Woman is happy and satisfied with her life. Her mind is liberated, for she is true to it. Her tears are genuine, her laughter comes from her heart, and her anger is bona fide. All her emotions seem to come from the depths of her soul. She is so in touch with her feelings that she expresses them with a force that approaches art. She is equally in touch with her mind. Thoughts become magic carpets that carry her to success and fulfillment. She can go wherever she imagines, and the force of her emotions propels her thoughts with lightning speed.

Peace and tranquility surround the Cosmic Woman. She has become so accepting of other people and of the world in which she operates that her presence can be felt. She projects such understanding of the world and the cosmos that she seems to know all the secrets, and she does. Though she lives life quietly and often walks softly, she nevertheless lives it to the fullest extent, with flair and style. She desires very little, for she has everything. She has been successful in joining heaven and earth. She is whole.

Cosmic relationships

Personal relationships occupy a central place in the life of the Cosmic Woman. They provide living textbooks for the study of human nature, and a walking laboratory that reflects the various phases she will undergo in her own life. She observes carefully and uses her observations to teach others about relationships. She does not feel completely fulfilled if she is unable to participate in multiple relationships. She has too much to learn for exclusivity. Many are attracted to her for help. She has a deep concern for the evolution of woman and man and works hard to be a catalyst for human advancement.

She instinctively knows that everything in life has a purpose, and she recognizes the importance of searching for the hidden meaning in her relationships. Her relationships are as wide and varied as are people themselves. Each encounter provides her with important clues to her own purpose. Each person comes into her life for a reason. Every action gives her a mirror to help her see her own actions. Even chance encounters may hold a key to her future development.

The Cosmic Woman projects instant love and acceptance, for

she truly loves herself. Reactions to her are either very positive or very negative. Those who seeks to be loved and to experience all that life has to offer will feel the warmth and glow of her love and rush to be encompassed by her caring. Those who pity themselves and seek to complicate their lives will find it difficult to be around her.

The Cosmic Woman is successful with relationships. She knows people so well that she can predict their reactions to her and to the beliefs she espouses. Even when her relationships don't work out constructively, she still learns from them. Her ability to see herself interact with others provides another key to her successful relationships. Having traveled the circle of the horoscope, she recognizes the archetypes and more often than not knows how each will react to a situation or to another type.

Freedom is a word that aptly describes a relationship with the Cosmic Woman. "Free to Be You and Me," as sung by Marlo Thomas, could be her motto. She knows that a nonpossessive relationship will grow and blossom—but a captured butterfly quickly dies.

The Cosmic Woman knows when to release a relationship. When the lessons are learned and the tasks accomplished, she lets go. Nothing lasts forever, and so it is with love. She accepts that all things are influenced by cycles. When the cycle is over, she does not try to hang on. She realizes that destruction comes from forcing things and going against the cycle. She is not bound by traditional ideas about relationships but instead goes by her own internal clock.

The Cosmic Woman surrounds herself with people who are in the process of change and growth. She has little time for those stuck in a rut. Her magnetism is such that she draws loving and caring people to her. She does not shy away from the responsibility of loving them. She thrives on adversity, for to her it is a challenge.

Childhood

The Cosmic child may spend a great deal of time with her elders. She may make friends with older people, often to the exclusion of children her own age. She wants to absorb as much of their knowledge as possible. She will ask them to teach her how to do the things she is observing. She is filled with a thousand questions that are worthy of an adult. She may have her parents shaking their heads and wishing that she would spend more time with dolls and blocks.

The Cosmic child may spend a great deal of time by herself, causing her parents to worry. It puzzles them that she does not participate in activities the way other children do. However, she simply needs to have her own space. She can become extremely quiet if forced to do things she does not wish to do. Her reactions are very often those of an adult. She is interested in her roots, where she came from, and where she is going.

The best parents for a Cosmic child are those who respect her individuality. She thinks of herself as a grown-up. Childhood is often a bothersome, awkward period for her. In her mind she harbors ideas and visions that most young women never touch upon. She needs a lot of space and understanding in which to grow. If given the respect and love she feels she rightly deserves, she is a model of decorum. If not, she can become rebellious, irritable, withdrawn. The Cosmic child is a challenge, but worth every minute of it.

She has no clear-cut idea of what she wants to be when she grows up. In fact, she thinks she is already grown up and often displays more maturity than many adults. Do not try to treat her as a pet, for she will let you know in no uncertain terms that she is a person and that she needs more than just to be fed and house-broken. She is so enthusiastic about living that she rarely idles away her time. She is highly creative.

She will start many projects that normally defy the abilities of a child. She may be designing the set for an opera, stitching up a designer dress, or painting a mural for her bedroom wall. Whatever the project, it will always show imagination, flair, and knowledge that is beyond her years. She is a hard worker who will put much energy into her endeavors and finish what she starts.

She has a rich fantasy life. Her imagination takes her to distant shores, and she has secret places in her mind that she shares with no one. She is able to visualize anything. In fact, her mind works with a variety of visual patterns. She can imagine herself in many different situations, and there is often a strong sexual basis to her daydreams.

The Cosmic child is a wonder to behold. She is an adult in a child's body. She brings with her into her life many memories of a distant past. She is very intuitive. She feels and experiences things in a different way. She expresses her innermost self. She lives a full and complete life.

How the Cosmic Woman relates: lovers and other intimates

The Cosmic Woman treats her friends and lovers with respect and courtesy. She is caring and loving and giving but realizes that she too needs to be cared for and to receive love. She never divulges all but keeps an aura of mystery about her. She wants to keep her relationships exciting.

The Cosmic Woman listens very carefully to what her intimates are saying. She does not project on them what she wants to hear but studies each response for its expressed and unexpressed meanings. Her basic honesty carries over into all her relationships. She is candid; she is discreet; she respects the rights and character of her friends. She is reliable and sure.

The Cosmic Woman keeps in touch. She jots notes, writes love letters, senses the right time to make a telephone call. She uses all her intuition to anticipate the needs of her loved ones and to communicate with them, if only to reaffirm that she is thinking of them. She really cares, and they know it.

The Cosmic Woman has a great deal of respect for sex. She does not use it as a bargaining tool. It is not a commodity to be bought and sold. She keeps herself as attractive as possible, not to titillate the senses, but to express her inner self. She takes care of her body. She purges her mind of unnecessary clutter. She fulfills her obligations. It is little wonder that people come to rely on her and love her for her caring and compassion.

The Cosmic Woman keeps love at the center of any relationship. She strives to be understanding and sensitive to the needs of her intimates. She has totally integrated her life and has created a healthy balance of all four elements: she acts with inspiration (Fire); she feels and shares (Water); she is physical (Earth); and she communicates and cooperates (Air). She draws on these energies in her relationships and employs them to bring out the best in her loved ones. That she does all this with grace and true humility is a mark of her cosmic nature.

The following list enumerates ways the Cosmic Woman has discovered to keep her love relationships alive and vital:

1 Don't push your lover to tell you he loves you.
2 Become his friend and confidante.
3 Surround him with comforts, but do not become his servant.
4 Let him know you desire him.

5 Make him proud to be with you.
6 Retain your own identity and an independent life of your own.
7 Maintain your sense of humor.
8 Build your ego by affirming his strengths and accepting his weaknesses.
9 Be honest without being destructive.
10 Trust your man, but do not become dependent on him.
11 Do not expect him to read your mind; communicate your needs and expectations clearly.
12 Get to know his needs, and try to provide for them either directly or indirectly.
13 Make pleasure a mainstay of the relationship.
14 Avoid guilt trips and games.
15 Don't be trapped into generalized sex roles.
16 Be a tower of strength as well as a soft, loving bedmate.
17 Bring him into your circle of friends and family slowly.
18 Never ask for more than you can give or are willing to give.
19 Establish an atmosphere of trust and affection.
20 Expect your relationship to change and grow; give him and yourself plenty of space.
21 Share the good times with him, and let him know you're prepared to share the bad times as well.
22 Try to anticipate swings in your moods as well as in his.
23 Never take him for granted.
24 Learn to trust and play your hunches.
25 Expect only one thing—the unexpected.

What kind of man she wants

The Cosmic Woman is most compatible with a man who is secure in himself, who loves easily, and who has a feeling nature. Her perfect partner needs to be as sensitive and giving as the Cosmic Woman.

She relishes his love, accepting it with candor and a bit of mystery. He is aware of her needs and fantasies before she verbalizes them. She has such a rapport with him that they barely need to speak; when they do, their communications are open and free. He accepts her as she is, supports her in her lifestyle, and helps provide a comfortable space in which she can flourish.

He is intuitive and receptive to her vibrations, as is she to his. It is a joy to find a man whose energy, communication patterns, and flow match hers. She prefers the man who has learned some of the same lessons she has, for she can meet him on common ground. She will not hesitate to teach a man she finds attractive, but it is a joy and a blessing when she meets one who has already learned.

She has mastered the art of resolving problems in a relationship with only those directly involved. Her man must face his own self squarely as they forge a healthy, happy, productive relationship. She is a freedom-loving creature who respects his independence. Their relationship cannot be cluttered with leftover emotional reactions and guilt from previous involvements. She trusts herself and him to form a lasting, loving bond with each other, based exclusively on nonpossessive love and the resources each brings to the partnership.

The Cosmic Woman supports her beloved's well-being and encourages his success. He will be equally supportive and encouraging, for their relationship is based on love. The Cosmic Woman provides little room in her relationships for artificial macho games and the bitchy carping they inspire. She cannot be forced to conform to any predetermined definition of femininity; likewise, she holds no stereotype of acceptable male behavior.

The Cosmic Woman can be all things sexually: aggressive and demure, womanly and childlike, patient and firm. She is keenly aware of her sexual nature and has accepted it. She prefers that her mate be of a like disposition. She expects him to love, flow, and innovate with her. She is guiltless, secure, and loving as she is being seduced. She seduces with equal skill.

The man who captures the Cosmic Woman's heart must be willing to touch, caress, cry, debate, comfort, protect, and encourage her. He is never expected to compete with her. He mirrors her androgynous nature as she mirrors his. He is flexible; he has an open mind. He returns her admiration, affection, and affirmation in full measure. He shares his growth with her and encourages her as she grows and explores. He participates directly in the inner dialogue she has with herself. He is as direct and honest with her as she is with him. He is truly a Cosmic Man.

Cosmic sexuality

It is a fact terrible to contemplate, yet it is nevertheless true, and ought to be pressed upon the world for its recognition; that fully one-half of all women seldom or never experience any pleasure whatever in the sexual act. Now this is an impeachment of nature, a disgrace to our civilization.

Victoria Claflin Woodhull
"The Elixir of Life"

The Cosmic Woman is a soul who wears a body. She accepts her own sexuality as a fact of life, one of the most natural and fundamental parts of her life. Having awakened from her spiritual amnesia, she is no longer bound to the physical. She is comfortable with sex.

She knows that sexual relations between unaware and unactualized people are never fully satisfying, for no matter how joyful and temporarily fulfilling, they are but a mere shadow of what can be found within. She has found union within herself; she is much more aware of the potentials of human relationships and of the role that sex can play in her life.

The Cosmic Woman does not have to do the Mr. Goodbar routine, for she has already found what she is looking for. Having recognized her own unity, she does not have to be frantic in her search. She can be more leisurely in locating someone with whom she can have meaningful relationships and meaningful sex.

She seeks to find other multidimensional people with whom she shares a sense of unity. She does not have to play all the one-dimensional games of cat and mouse for them. Most people exist only on the physical plane, and their lives are oriented to that realm alone. Getting and keeping power and prestige, seeking gratification and trying to process it, feeding the ego constantly—all characterize the one-dimensional person. The Cosmic Woman seeks a more evolved type.

She knows only too well the dangers of trying to find her masculine self in the world of man. She finds very few men who have developed their feminine natures and are open to the world of the psyche and of love. She has had to acquire a number of masculine traits so as not to be inundated in a world of men. She now seeks men who have also become aware of their multi-dimensional nature, who do not worship the feminine but have embraced it and know it in their own lives.

The Cosmic Woman is in touch with herself. She does not assume roles because she does not need to be other than she really is. It may be that she doesn't want to have 2.3 children. She may feel that her fate calls for her to be single and very mobile. She demands the same kind of rigorous honesty in her sex life. If it is not an expression of her inner self, she does not need it.

The sex life of the Cosmic Woman often has a karmic connection. She is attracted to men with whom she has an instant rapport; often it is as if she has known them before. It is through such contacts and the intricacies of sex that she comes to a belief in her previous lifetimes. She can see the patterns repeating themselves. The men in her life all have similar characteristics. The situations in which she became involved with them were often the same. It seemed that she was trying to work out relationships that had not been completed in a previous existence.

The Cosmic Woman has learned the lessons of her Taurus phase well and loves without being possessive. She allows her mate total freedom, expecting no more than the other can give. She is able to accept positive experiences and allow negative ones to flow right on past.

The Cosmic Woman has sought and found a wider context for the expression of her sexual energy. She has shifted to a new consciousness, holistic and integrated with the universe. With this new orientation comes a shift from a purely egocentric attitude to a more universal and connected position. She does not look at relationships and sexual liaisons solely in the light of her own needs and desires; instead she sees each action as contributing to the creation of the whole—the whole self and the whole universe.

After such a change in attitude, sex is no longer a battleground where one body seeks to control another. Sex is no longer useful for manipulation or power or supremacy. Sex becomes merely an adjunct to living. The Cosmic Woman attends to her sexual needs with as much thought as she attends to her need for pure food and pure air.

There are two key words for a better understanding of Cosmic sexuality. One is *natural*. The Cosmic Woman regards sex as one of the natural things in the physical world. Here she looks for quality. She seeks energies in a mate that are as natural as hers and as open to the universe. She has lost all the meticulousness and prudishness of her Virgo phase and accepts sex as one of nature's joys. She uses her physical energy judiciously; she does not believe in wasting natural resources.

The other key word is *guiltless*. She has escaped the guilt that is associated with sex and that traps many of her sisters. She also does not lay guilt trips on those she has sex with. Although she is very aware of the subtle energies that flow through her, she does not relegate sex to her inner life, but relates it to the physical plane. She feels no guilt for such a natural and satisfying act.

The Cosmic Woman experiences sex on a number of levels. It makes her feel good physically. She is satisfied by the closeness and the release of physical energy. She enjoys the touching and holding and caring. The close mental and physical bond also brings her happiness. She trusts in her beloved. She entrusts her most sacred temple, her body, to her mate and realizes that a close and mutual understanding is taking place. Her mind soars, and the mental images spring to life. She is confident when in the arms of her lover. She is able to express her whole being when she shares sex with a whole man.

Early sex experiences

The Cosmic Woman accepts sex as a natural part of living at a very early age and usually integrates it into her life as a child. She is usually a very evolved little woman. Having spent a good deal of time by herself, she recognizes her other worldly side early and is ready for multidimensional encounters at a much earlier age than the boys around her. She has sex early but is often disappointed that it is so onesided and flat. She knows that something is missing, but it may take her awhile to figure out exactly what it is.

After she has been able to separate her true inner feelings from her emotional responses, she is better able to cope with her sex role as a multidimensional person in a unidimensional world. She knows that there is nothing wrong with the way she is. It is just that most people expect her to react to the same single element they do. But soon she discovers that there is much more to her, and indeed that she is rather a rarity, for she expects much more from life and sex than do those around her.

It may take the Cosmic child a long time to grow up, for there are so many lessons to be learned. It is very confusing for her to realize that things are not as they should be, and it requires effort to be able to accept and deal with the seeming paradoxes that surround her on every side. It is when she learns how to truly love that things become clear.

What kind of lover she needs

The Cosmic Woman is an integrated, multidimensional woman who has crossed both the Zodiacal and cosmic planes. Hers is the understanding, the caring, the nurturing of Mother Nature; her needs, too, are basic and natural.

The honest and down-to-earth approach the Cosmic Woman embraces in her relationships is perhaps even more obvious and present in her sexual expression. She is realistic about her own needs, the needs of her lover, and the needs they share. She doesn't expect miracles; she more often creates them.

She has the wisdom to put aside her ego gratification in favor of healthy and honest expression. She is secure in her knowledge of sex, sexual needs, and sexual techniques. She needs a lover who shares her vast knowledge and who possesses the same curiosities and childlike sexual wonder. She knows the boundlessness of sex and the depths of feeling that few others are aware of. Her lover, too, must have few traditional barriers.

If her lover needs a shoulder to cry on, hers is available. In turn, his must be too. Individual sexual expression is, to her, one of the greatest basic human rights. She doesn't believe in trade-offs, in exchanges, in giving up one human right to experience satisfaction and recognition of another. Her integrated nature tells her that recognition, satisfaction, and expression of all of them at once is not only possible, but absolutely necessary.

If her lover comes to her less than liberated, she can show the way. She is a patient soul, and her tolerance is, at the very least, legendary. She can coach her lover to first be aware of self-satisfaction, self-confidence, and self-love, and then to magically expand the selves to include others. But she will not waste her time, her energies, or her feelings on a lover who cannot learn. She is not above making mistakes, and she may well find a lover who is totally incapable of feeling or, worse yet, incapable of wanting to feel. In this case she will be gone, without guilt, without remorse, and often without warning. But let that lover indicate to her that feeling and learning sexual expression is a priority, and she will tackle the sexual seminar with limitless hope and optimism.

She is the most sexually multidimensional woman in existence. She feels the heights of Mt. Everest, the depths of Neptune's parlor, and the expanse of the entire universe in her sexual enjoyment. She is capable of performing almost any sex act imaginable. She has an understanding of both the missionary position and S and M. She employs the techniques she feel will bring both her and her lover the most ultimate pleasures possible—and no matter which skill she demonstrates at any given time, you can be assured it will be with all the love she can muster.

If she cannot find the cosmic sexual experience she needs, wants, and can feel with a lover, she will be undaunted in her search. She will continue to look for the ultimate, for the best, for the lover she can truly share life with—and she will do so realistically. She learned during her Gemini phase that being realistic about sexual expectations and sexual experiences results in real satisfaction. She is not without fantasies, but isn't trapped by them or caught up in groundless expectations of finding a realistic expression for them.

Cosmic anger

When you are angry, do not be centered on the person who has aroused the anger. Let him be in the periphery. You just become angrier. Feel anger in its totality; allow it to happen within. Do not rationalize; do not say. "This man has created it." Do not condemn the man. He has just become the situation. And feel grateful toward him that he has helped something which was hidden to become open. He has hit somewhere, and a wound was there hidden. Now you know it so become the wound.

The anger will dissolve.

Shagwar Shree Rajnesh
Tantra Spirituality and Sex

The Cosmic Woman has a special appreciation for the richness and depth of her emotional being. She experiences anger, love, joy, dismay, impatience. She recognizes the various energies that flow around and through her; she does not block their flow but welcomes them as signals or feedback about her reactions to events around her. She never uses her feelings to deliberately strike at another; instead she uses them to create positive change.

Some of the things that can make the Cosmic Woman angry are injustices, infringements of others' rights, senseless physical violence, and slow-moving or unrealized potential.

She does not engage in useless competition, and she never role-plays. She is direct, honest, and nonjudgmental. In the past, she has experienced the frustration of denying her anger and also the debilitation of doing what was demanded of "good little girls." She can now transcend the circumstances that cause her anger. An unhappy childhood, failure in school, or an inattentive spouse is now seen as a challenge to overcome instead of a trigger to self-anger and frustration. She has developed the strength, sensitivity, and courage to handle her emotions in anger-producing situations. She has found the courage that is essential in self-confrontation and also in stepping out of and beyond old behavior patterns. She is no longer the victim of her own emotions.

The Cosmic Woman has learned that anger, like many other emotions, is a tool that can be used to change situations with skill and without blame or hurt. She no longer automatically assumes responsibility for failures in her life; she evaluates her role in both failure and success, and modifies her actions to be more effective in the future.

Throughout her period of growth, the Cosmic Woman has become aware of the unique significance anger plays in a healthy woman's life. She has learned the secret of true balance. Just as an increase in temperature on the body's surface often indicates a physical imbalance, so the feeling of anger signals that something is amiss in the emotional system. When this occurs, the Cosmic Woman evaluates her expectations and her role in the anger-producing situation. She identifies the belief system that provoked it and makes sure that her own response is accurate. She is thus able to deal with it constructively, effectively, and without unnecessary pain or discomfort.

Some of the things the Cosmic Woman has had to confront and overcome during her past struggles are the position of women in our society (a basically Cancerian role) and the Leo-type role men have assumed; the unhealthy and nonproductive competitiveness between women in the areas of glamour, academics, sports, child-care, and material acquisition; and worst of all, the self-destructive "I'm not as good as a man" attitude. Too often this produces an aggressive attitude as an overcompensation for the feminine side of her nature. It has created an unrealistic set of goals and a low level of self-confidence. Cosmic Woman has transcended the pettiness of life and has learned to look for significance, honesty, and love in all her endeavors.

Self-esteem

The Cosmic Woman is not a product of her environment, but a product of inner growth. She has overcome the narrow bounds of society and become universal in the process. She loves herself, and this enables her to express her emotions and her feelings freely in any situation or circumstance. Her self-love seems to generate loving energy that flows from her even in moments of anger.

The Cosmic Woman had a hard time overcoming societal attitudes toward women, but she persevered. She has now come to understand what she was deprived of, but instead of reacting bitterly and defensively toward men and male-dominated societal attitudes, she embraces each opportunity to control her life and to be truly responsible for herself. She knows that men, too, are caught in a one-dimensional world, and she works for their liberation as well.

The Cosmic Woman has "Love Yourself Day" every day; she long ago realized the importance of displaying an attitude of self-love. Her approach is indeed infectious; she feels that the more she demonstrates the advantages of self-actualization, the greater are the chances of others pursuing it as a goal. Above all the Cosmic Woman knows that she alone is responsible for her life, her happiness, her peace of mind.

The Cosmic Woman seldom second-guesses herself, and she realizes the folly of questioning every decision, of analyzing her every movement in quagmires of self-doubt. Pursuing perfection unreasonably is often the cause of self-anger. It can also preclude taking risks and being vulnerable. The Cosmic Woman gives herself permission to have fun, to take pleasure, to pursue various courses of action. She deserves to feel good about life and about herself . . . and she does.

Working with anger

All Married Couples should learn the art of battle as they should learn the art of making love. Good battle is objective and honest—never vicious or cruel. Good battle is healthy and constructive, and brings to a marriage the principle of equal partnership.

Ann Landers
Ann Landers Says Truth
Is Stranger. . .

The Cosmic Woman has learned to battle constructively, both with her mate and with the many other people she encounters in the process of living life fully. She will not hide from misunderstanding and guilt. She will instead confront it, communicate her feelings, be receptive to the communications of others, and find a solution that is equitable and honest.

The Cosmic Woman, through all life's many challenges, has learned to identify the feeling of anger, to acknowledge the feeling, to communicate the feeling without hurt or blame. In sharing her anger, she doesn't expect to change the position of the other person. By communicating more openly, she expects to better understand her perception of the things that make her angry and to avoid their beckoning in the future.

The Cosmic Woman has made a pact with herself to be healthy. She realizes that suppressed emotions, such as anger, can cause bodily functions to cease operating properly. She recognizes bodily feedback, be it sensuous or painful. The by-products of healthy expression are easily recognized; the by-products of unhealthy expression are often masked as minor irritations, aches, and pains, and they can ultimately result in extreme pathology.

The antennae that detect changes in both the physical and mental environments are turned inward by the Cosmic Woman in order to better read the messages coming through. This enables her to take the first step away from repression—being aware of change as it occurs. When defensiveness is eliminated, the Cosmic Woman opens up, receives, evaluates clearly and quickly, and communicates. She has also learned to pay careful attention to dispassionate critiques and advice.

The Cosmic Woman has learned to deploy her anger to effect creative and positive change. When she enters an argument, confronts another, or responds to anger, her performance is almost magical. Her high level of concern for the rights and opinions of others, her nonmoralizing acceptance of differing objectives, and her underlying sense of love actually get her freedom to move, to actualize her multidimensional attitudes.

The Cosmic Woman deals with displeasure, impatience, annoyance, and anger in specific ways. She recognizes her right to her opinions and feelings, and conversely, the rights of others to theirs. She involves herself with change, with helping others overcome their one-dimensional attitudes, instead of batting her head against stone walls and expecting to create cracks and fissures. She learned during her Aquarius phase that to tear down and rebuild takes a lot more energy than to renovate existing structures. Thus, she is expressive instead of defensive, creative instead of destructive, objective instead of subjective.

Life for the Cosmic Woman involves continual revaluation and growth. She combines thoughtfulness, self-love, and self-actualization to create productive scenarios for living. She is fearless in her pursuit of the New Age life she has worked for so long and so hard. She will accept criticism, she will process it, evaluate it, and salvage those parts of it that enable her to embellish her lifestyle. If need be, she will be angry. She will also be sad, happy, concerned, filled with joy. She will not, however, be filled with guilt, uncertainty, or negative, nonproductive energy.

The Cosmic Woman realizes the conflict that is inherent in life on our small planet. She sees value in it because it prevents stagnation and stimulates growth. She yields with a smile, she commands with love. She remains forever open, self-realized, and sure of who holds the key to her life.

Cosmic lifestyles

Traditional lifestyles appeal to the Cosmic Woman, as do alternatives to what we have long considered acceptable and "normal." She lives an actualized life, and if that means living communally, in an open marriage, in a group marriage, or even alone, she is capable of it. She knows how to flow with energies, and she knows also that those energies may not be found in traditional communities. She embraces them where she finds them, and when she has learned about them, she can move on to where the next energies beckon.

The concept of impossibility isn't one that she can embrace now. Impossibility often becomes possibility, given attention, love, work, and positive energies. She has the power to embrace negatives and glean from them the positive energies that she knows they must contain.

Her cyclic nature tells her that there is a learning experience to embrace each day. She may discover in a ménage à trois arrangement the key to unlocking constrictions. She may learn how to inspire commune members to deeply and honestly share all their experiences, thus making the communal setting the perfect vehicle so many seek. She knows the value of challenge and the rewards of meeting challenge. *Reward* is a key word for the Cosmic Woman; she knows that for each experience, for each challenge met, for each human embraced, a reward exists.

The often senseless chaos that exists in alternate lifestyles can become order and direction under her guiding hand. She has a seemingly uncanny ability to see through all the confusion and power struggles and to instinctively know what each person enmeshed in them is looking for, needs, reaches out for. With her cohesiveness she can help those around her actualize all the dreams they embrace. They must first be aware of their dreams, open to tailoring them to situational reality; then they need an honest approach to achieving them. Without those key ingredients, the Cosmic Woman cannot wave her "magic wand" in their direction.

The Cosmic Woman's intuition and her awareness of its value precludes her from being fooled by illusions that often attract less aware people to alternative lifestyles. She knows what she can expect to gain from exploring uncharted territories; she realizes the folly of utopian dreams. Her dreams are founded on concrete and positive indicators. She knows communes are difficult to give birth to, that they can disintegrate due to egotism, laziness, power struggles. She approaches concepts with firm beliefs and reasonable expectations.

She hold no illusions of being the savior of the masses. She knows only too well that accepting responsibility for the lives of others is not within the realm of positive human relations. She is a source of guidance, of inspiration. She delights in helping others discover inner peace, self-realization, and self-actualization. She has done it for herself; she knows others must do likewise.

One would think that upon arriving at such a fine, positive plateau, the Cosmic Woman would hunger for others to do the same, to find within themselves the answers to so many questions. She does indeed, but she is a patient woman, someone who knows that change is imminent but that it takes time. Just as she rejects the forced opinions and attitudes of others, she rejects being forceful in matters she knows can only be absorbed gradually. Though she seldom feels there are enough hours per day, days per week, weeks per month, months per year, for her to experience all she knows is awaiting her, she is not given to rushing things. Lessons are learned at different stages by different people, and until they are ready to acknowledge changes and flow with them, all the force in the cosmos isn't going to make things happen any more quickly.

She is capable of prodding and gently pushing people when she sees their potential thinly veiled by fear or clouded by the haze of uncertainty. She becomes impatient and even a tad intolerant when she sees natural resources, be they human or earthly, wasted and frivolously abused.

The Cosmic Woman has achieved a special kind of liberation—comfortable liberation. She will not try to embrace or understand something that causes extreme discomfort or that she intuitively knows is more fantasy than reality. She prefers one-on-one, intimate, sexual, emotional relationships with her life's partner, her mate, her husband. The reality of finding that one special person who satisfies her needs has come to her, and although she is capable of expanding her experiences to include sexual relations with others, her primary, overall, and most important relationship is more often than not with her one special person.

If the Cosmic Woman chooses a lifestyle that includes a mate and children, her family will be the envy of the entire community. She can bake cookies for her kids in the morning to make sure they have something to take to their clubhouse, shop for a special cut of meat for the evening meal in the early afternoon—and she will no doubt luxuriate in a scented and stimulating bath before her mate arrives home.

She has the inherent knowledge of total care for those she loves and embraces. She nurtures, soothes, inspires, and chastises; you won't hear the refrain of "Wait Until Your Father Gets Home" from her house. She is capable of providing both traditional mothering and fathering to her children, and she shares parental responsibilities with her mate realistically and constructively.

Bisexuality and homosexuality are certainly within the realm of the Cosmic Woman's experiences. She is likely to be involved at some point in her life with another woman in a sexually intimate relationship. Although homosexuality implies exclusive sexual orientation and emotional preference for someone of the same sex, the Cosmic Woman's androgyny provides a new scope for same-sex relationships. She has arrived at a perfect balance between her female and male sides. If she decides to spend her life with another woman, you can be sure that person will also have struck a distinct chord of harmony with her entire self.

The Cosmic Woman's keen sense of androgyny also precludes her from becoming entrapped in relationships and lifestyles that seek to inhibit her native awareness of women. For much of this century, women have been relegated to positions that involved *only* enhancing the Leo image, the life and spirituality of the male in our society. The Cosmic Woman will not be part and parcel of this blatant misuse of the resources of humanity; she will be in the forefront of the movement to effect attitudinal changes.

Summing up the Cosmic Woman

The Cosmic Woman has carved out a place in life for herself and for those she embraces and experiences. She calmly integrates New Age attitudes and thinking into what we commonly call "the American Way of Life." She cares, she loves, she communicates; she has feeling, ideals, independence; she has achieved a lifestyle free of guilt, free of motivation by fear. . . . Hers is the life of the fulfilled and actualized woman.

The age of Aquarius, the New Age, the new dawning of consciousness, embraces her, and she responds with demonstrative respect—respect for herself above all, and respect for humankind. She is indeed a woman in control of all her sensibilities and sensitivities; so much so that she can project them, lend them, and share them without fear of losing them.

A special note

Judith Bennett was completing SEX SIGNS only days before she died in the tragic crash at O'Hare airport, on her way to the American Booksellers Association to speak about the book. Since that time, several of her closest friends and colleagues—people dedicated to Judith's work over the years—have gathered together to finish writing SEX SIGNS in the way that she would have wanted: with dignity, devotion, and above all, love.

Joan Bowman first met Judith Bennett in a class Judy was teaching on psycho-astrology. When Joan became the Midwestern marketing manager for *Forum* their friendship was firmly cemented and their careers progressed simultaneously. Joan has helped with the sections on anger and lifestyles, and will be doing extensive promotion for the book.

Gerry Born, a former executive secretary of the American Library Association, was a close friend and associate of Judy's. He has worked on the sections dealing with personality, relationships, and sexuality, and has coordinated the rest of the group.

Kenn Calhoun, a promiment television producer in Chicago and a fantastic typist, became involved in the project after Judy appeared on a show he was producing about psychic predictions. His excitement about the book led him to help with the writing of several lifestyle and sexuality sections.

Jeannette Koszuth, a literary agent, sold Judy's manuscript to St. Martin's Press and soon fell under the spell of her charisma. Jeannette has put her literary talent to work by completing the Sagittarius chapter and offering criticism where needed.

Cheryl Storm, a registered nurse who conducts out-patient therapy groups in Chicago, worked extensively as a consultant to Judith Bennett's workshops there. She has given great input in the forms of writing, criticism, and research for the book.

Teri King
Love, Sex and Astrology £1.25

Revealing advice for would-be lovers. Spot your ideal partner; know the mating possibilities of the zodiac; find the strengths and weaknesses of your sign – through penetrating questionnaires. Teri King answers many questions on love, sex, careers and children with humour, wit and a deal of commonsense.

'All quite irresistible' MANCHESTER EVENING NEWS

Hans Wilhelm
Chinese Horoscopes £1.25

What's your Chinese sign? You'll soon find out in this entertaining guide to the thousand-year-old art of Chinese astrology. Based on a cycle of twelve 'animal' years, the Chinese horoscope is the excitingly different way of discovering the influence and personality traits that rule your life. Are you a rebellious tiger? Is your lover a wilful dragon or perhaps an amorous goat? If you're a rat and he/she is a monkey, are you compatible? All you need to consider is the year of your birth – but remember, the Chinese conception of animals is very different from our own – get ready to be surprised!

Maria Elise Crummere
Sun-Sign Revelations 80p

This is the most unusual Zodiac book you've ever read! It is a practical, revealing, unflattering, light-hearted guide to the personalities of your friends, your enemies, – and yourself.

'Not another astrological hotch-potch of kind words and vague descriptions. It is a straightforward kick in the teeth'
CAMBRIDGE EVENING NEWS

Linda Goodman
Linda Goodman's Love Signs £3.95

A new approach to the human heart and personal relationships. A compulsively readable book exploring the tensions and harmony inherent in your associations with people born under the same sun signs as yourself, or under the other eleven signs. Also features: in-depth exploration of the seventy-eight sun sign patterns for both sexes; lists of famous people under your sign; explanations of the twelve mysteries of love.

Linda Goodman's Sun Signs £1.95

Have you ever wondered about youself? What you are really like, whether you'll make a good wife, mother or lover, whether other people like you? Linda Goodman reveals the real you, your personality and character as the stars see you, in this remarkably lively and down-to-earth book.

John Astrop
Sun Child, Moon Child £1.50

Astrology is every bit as important for parents and children as it is for marriage partners. John Astrop explains the basic principles of astrology and the significant influence of the sun and moon on every aspect of childhood, and on the all-important relationship between parent and child through the growing years. *Sun Child, Moon Child* provides an invaluable guide for every parent seeking to recognize and develop their child's full potential.

Selected Bestsellers

☐	Extraterrestrial Civilizations	Isaac Asimov	£1.50p
☐	Pregnancy	Gordon Bourne	£2.75p
☐	The Thirty-nine Steps	John Buchan	80p
☐	Out of Practice	Rob Buckman	95p
☐	The Flowers of the Forest	Elizabeth Byrd	£1.50p
☐	The 35mm Photographer's Handbook	Julian Calder and John Garrett	£5.95p
☐	Secret of Blackoaks	Ashley Carter	£1.50p
☐	A Night of Gaiety	Barbara Cartland	90p
☐	The Sittaford Mystery	Agatha Christie	95p
☐	Lovers and Gamblers	Jackie Collins	£1.95p
☐	Sphinx	Robin Cook	£1.25p
☐	Soft Furnishings	Designers' Guild	£5.95p
☐	Rebecca	Daphne du Maurier	£1.50p
☐	Travellers' France	Arthur Eperon	£2.50p
☐	Travellers' Italy	Arthur Eperon	£2.50p
☐	The Complete Calorie Counter	Eileen Fowler	50p
☐	The Diary of Anne Frank	Anne Frank	85p
☐	Blitz	David Fraser	£1.95p
☐	Flashman	George MacDonald Fraser	£1.25p
☐	Linda Goodman's Sun Signs	Linda Goodman	£1.95p
☐	The 38th Pan Book of Crosswords	Mike Grimshaw	80p
☐	The Moneychangers	Arthur Hailey	£1.95p
☐	The Maltese Falcon	Dashiell Hammett	95p
☐	Vets Might Fly	James Herriot	£1.25p
☐	Simon the Coldheart	Georgette Heyer	95p
☐	The Eagle Has Landed	Jack Higgins	£1.50p
☐	Mountbatten: Hero of Our Time	Richard Hough	£1.95p
☐	The Marchand Woman	John Ives	£1.25p
☐	Smiley's People	John le Carré	£1.75p
☐	To Kill a Mockingbird	Harper Lee	£1.25p
☐	How to be a Gifted Parent	David Lewis	£1.95p
☐	The Empty Hours	Ed McBain	£1.25p
☐	Shanghai	William Marshall	£1.25p
☐	Symptoms	edited by Sigmund Stephen Miller	£2.50p